Ezzard Charles

Ezzard Charles
A Boxing Life

WILLIAM DETTLOFF

McFarland & Company, Inc., Publishers
Jefferson, North Carolina

LIBRARY OF CONGRESS CATALOGUING-IN-PUBLICATION DATA

Dettloff, William.
Ezzard Charles : a boxing life / William Dettloff.
    p. cm.
Includes bibliographical references and index.

ISBN 978-0-7864-9743-0 (softcover : acid free paper) ∞
ISBN 978-1-4766-1947-7 (ebook)

1. Charles, Ezzard, 1921–1975   2. Boxers (Sports)—
United States—Biography.   I. Title.

GV1132.A44D47 2015   796.83092—dc23   [B]   2015014215

BRITISH LIBRARY CATALOGUING DATA ARE AVAILABLE

© 2015 William Dettloff. All rights reserved

*No part of this book may be reproduced or transmitted in any form
or by any means, electronic or mechanical, including photocopying
or recording, or by any information storage and retrieval system,
without permission in writing from the publisher.*

On the cover: Ezzard Charles poses wearing heavyweight world
title belt circa 1950 (photograph courtesy of Lou Manfra)

Printed in the United States of America

*McFarland & Company, Inc., Publishers
Box 611, Jefferson, North Carolina 28640
www.mcfarlandpub.com*

To Kim

Table of Contents

Acknowledgments ix
Preface 1
Introduction 3

  1. Snooks 5
  2. No Cheap Ambition 16
  3. Jake 26
  4. The Garden 34
  5. Baroudi 48
  6. The Price 57
  7. Going Heavy 64
  8. Hey, Aren't You Ezzard Charles? 77
  9. Joe 91
  10. Unforgivable 108
  11. What They Came For 126
  12. A Good Race Horse 144
  13. Rocky 166
  14. How Much Is Enough? 185
  15. The Flood 195

Chapter Notes 205
Bibliography 214
Index 217

Acknowledgments

There are many people without whose support this work wouldn't have come to be, not the least of whom is Nigel Collins, the former longtime editor-in-chief of *Ring* magazine. Besides giving me a voice and doing his best to fashion me into a passable writer over my career at *The Ring*, Nigel gave me full access to the entire *Ring* archive for the purposes of researching this work, even as my association with the magazine was ending. His guidance and support were invaluable.

I owe a great debt to my parents, William and Priscilla Dettloff, and to my parents-in-law, Salvatore and Jean Minetta, all gone too soon. I must thank Ray and Marilyn Dowd, who opened their home to me many years ago and encouraged my writing at every turn. My gratitude also to Steve Farhood, whose crisp, fun writing style informed my earliest exposure to sports journalism and whose prose I strove to emulate when, by some wonderful accident of the universe, I started writing for him.

My sister, Mary Dettloff-Reilly, also has my deep gratitude for her steady and unyielding support over the book's long development. Whether I needed inspiration or an educated opinion on a dubious turn of phrase, she was there, always willing to inspire, to guide, and to help. I am not convinced it would have been written if not for her.

Two people who were close to Ezzard Charles took the time to speak with me and provided information I couldn't possibly have gotten anywhere else: Richard Christmas, who was Charles' boyhood friend and later his personal secretary, and Ezzard Charles II, who came along when his father was just about done fighting but who shared valuable insights nonetheless. I will always regret that the book was not done in time for Mr. Christmas to read it; he died in December 2013, about a year after our last conversation.

I am happy and thankful to have gotten the photos included within, contributed by J. Russell Peltz, Craig Hamilton and Lou Manfra, gentlemen and scholars each, as well as great friends of the fight game.

It should go without saying that it is the characters themselves and not the writers that make any story interesting; and if this one is interesting it is because of the wonderful and awful characters who inhabited Ezzard Charles' world. So it is the forgotten kings and their kind who have my profound gratitude: the great Black Murderer's Row, the journeymen pugs, the champions and the gangsters, the nameless sparring partners and bucket-carriers and late-night card-players who provided the backdrop to Charles' life. It is the Cotton Club and Toots Shor's and Dempsey's and the ladies and the cheap-seat boo-birds. They're all gone now, or will be soon, just as we will be. I can only hope that this work conveys to the reader just a hint of what it was like when they lived and breathed.

I would be remiss if I didn't use this space to thank my agent, Richard Henshaw, and my kids, Kayla, Angelina and Billy Boy, who fill my days with light and life and who I hope someday may take pity on their old man and give him a sympathy read.

Finally, this book would not have been written without the support and love of my wonderful wife Kim, who endured the long silences and lonely afternoons it required. She knows me better than I know myself, and I can only do what I do because she does what she does. She remains, in all the most important ways, my co-writer.

Preface

The idea for this project was born in 2002, when Nigel Collins, then editor of *The Ring* magazine, asked me to write a section for the magazine ranking the twenty best-ever light heavyweights. Before I started researching, I figured that the great and revered Archie Moore, who scored more knockouts than any fighter in the history of boxing, would get the top spot, followed maybe by Bob Foster or Billy Conn, then Michael Spinks, Tommy Loughran and other old pugs nobody knew or cared about anymore.

I knew that Ezzard Charles was loved by the purists and the old-heads and that he'd fought some at light-heavy, but had never won the championship at that weight and was mostly remembered for his short, fairly unremarkable tenure as heavyweight champion.

Almost for the hell of it I researched his record at light heavyweight—a kind of no-man's division between the glamor classes of middleweight and heavyweight—and found that he beat, among others, Moore three times, once by knockout, and Jimmy Bivins, Lloyd Marshall and Charley Burley, each more than once. These were the hard, great, black fighters no one else wanted to fight, especially the popular white fighters, and when he was on his game Charles went through them like they weren't there. Joey Maxim, a brilliant light heavyweight with one of the best jabs ever, was whipped five times by Charles.

Bivins, Burley, Marshall, Maxim and Moore all are in the Boxing Hall of Fame, as they should be. Charles is too, and his record against that group proved to me that Charles was the best light heavyweight ever, and not by a little. I wrote my section for *The Ring* with him at the top, and I moved on, but questions about him and his career picked at me. I looked for more information about him, but there wasn't much: a few nostalgic magazine articles; a mention here or there. There were no books about Ezzard Charles. It didn't make sense.

How was it possible that this great light heavyweight fighter had never won the light heavyweight title? Why did he have to move to heavyweight to get a title fight? How was it that he beat Moore three times and yet most rated Moore the best in the division? And why could one find several good biographies covering Moore's career and life, but none that did the same for Charles? The same went for Charles' most celebrated heavyweight opponents, Joe Louis and Rocky Marciano. There are at least a half dozen biographies covering each.

I kept an eye out for a Charles biography over the next several years. Nothing. In the meantime, two books were published about Burley, whom Charles whipped twice, fairly easily. Then one covering Bivins, whom Charles knocked so cold in their third fight that Bivins had to be revived by ring doctors. Eventually there came too a biography of heavyweight Jersey Joe Walcott, who Charles whipped twice (three times if you asked most, but that's another story). For me that sealed it. Ezzard Charles deserved to be remembered and admired. He didn't get the credit he deserved, although he was one of the best fighters ever, and even today he is overlooked. No more. I can only hope that after all this time this work does him justice. He deserves that much.

INTRODUCTION

Ezzard Charles was one of the best prizefighters who ever lived, and yet there wasn't a whole lot that even a good, experienced fight guy could do for him. Some guys had the gift of gab, or a thunderous punch, or a great back story. Some had unusual charisma or presence. As heavyweight champion Charles had none of these. He was just a poor kid from an American slum, no different, really, than other poor kids from other American slums.

But he wasn't a palooka. He didn't talk in broken or mangled English. His nose wasn't mashed, and he didn't get a big push from the mob. He'd never done any jail time. And he wasn't the first to do anything.

Charles didn't get into fistfights outside the ring, or get caught in pictures with lily-white prostitutes. Sure, he went to jazz clubs and whatnot, but who didn't? When he wasn't fighting he liked to paint in oils, read psychology textbooks, and play his bass fiddle. How was anyone supposed to sell that?

Sure, he could fight like hell. The guys who had been around for a long time could see that as soon as he got in the ring, and for decades after he died guys who knew what they were talking about looked at films of Ezzard Charles and asked: "Christ, how could they not see he was a genius?"

Plenty of guys who were fighting geniuses went to bed hungry every night because genius is always recognized too late. Charles got lucky, more or less, when a manager who saw him for what he was and knew how to work the press stole him away, like they do in the fight game, and took him to the top.

It was more complicated than that, of course, because in the 1940s and '50s the fight game was run by gangsters and mobsters who would let a good fighter like Charles starve to death if he didn't play along. That meant cutting them in on the winnings and fighting who they said, when they said. Charles wasn't a genius with the books, but he was smart enough to know when he had to play along to get along.

His big problem was that he came along right after Joe Louis, who had spoiled American fight fans by being everything they had ever wanted in a superhero—outside of being white, of course—and in comparison Charles looked like a school kid barely out of his short pants. Even after Charles whipped an aged Louis they couldn't appreciate him. In fact, they hated him not just for beating Louis but for not *being* him. Louis was everything they wanted in a heavyweight champion and Charles was everything they didn't.

They paid attention when he came closer than anyone else to beating Rocky Marciano, and they said it was the best he'd ever done; but that was because they hadn't seen him when he was young and hungry, before he was worn down by the game and its endless brutalities. They'd never seen him at his best. It was over after that, pretty much, and when he died, helpless as a baby, they named a highway after him in Cincinnati, the way they do for heroes.

Ezzard Charles was never anyone's hero. Not really. Not the way he should have been. American sports fans were looking for a hero who was as good as Louis in the same exact way Louis was. They didn't know they had someone just as good but in a different way. It never occurred to them that there was more than one way to be great. Louis had ruined it for everyone. So they looked and looked for another Louis, while Ezzard Charles was right there under their noses. How could they not see he was a genius?

1

SNOOKS

Ezzard Charles never wanted to be a killer. There were some of those in the fight business, manager types mostly, and gangsters and other miscreants who treated fighters like dogs or worse. Every once in a while you'd find a fighter like that too, one who would pound your brain stem loose just for the joy it gave him. But those guys never lasted long; they didn't appreciate the game enough. It took patience, discipline and a certain kind of smarts to be a very good prizefighter, and the psychopaths had none of those—they just enjoyed beating on another man. That wasn't Charles. To him the fight business was an honest job, a way to make a living and maybe get a closet full of gleaming dress shoes and Brooks Brothers suits.

But across the ring from him there was a twenty-year-old kid he'd just beat all hell out of, and the boy's trainers couldn't wake him up. Charles knew something was wrong with him when he saw blood coming out of both his nostrils. In all his years fighting he'd never seen that.[1] And when the kid finally went down after a long beating, he sat there on the ring canvas for a minute, one arm slung over the middle rope and the other one punching the air, like he was still fighting; but he was unconscious, his eyes half-open. And then his coffee-brown skin turned gray and he went slack like a man does when the life is running out of him. All Charles could do was watch from the other side of the ring.

That was about as bad as it could get for a God-fearing country boy like Ezzard Mack Charles, who was born in a shack on a hidden back road in the Rocky Knob section of Lawrenceville, Georgia, on July 7, 1921. Lawrenceville is roughly twenty-five miles northeast of Atlanta, and on a good day in the 1920s about two thousand souls passed their days there. Most of them were grandchildren or great-grandchildren of slaves, and no one had to tell them what it meant to be black and living in the Deep South. Lawrenceville, legend had it, was the site of one of the first Negro lynchings following the Civil War, when Mart McConnell, a former slave, supposedly assaulted a white woman and was subsequently hanged by Union soldiers, of all people, on the Gwinnett County Courthouse square.[2]

The year Charles was born, there were sixty-three documented lynchings of blacks in the United States.[3] Over the next ten years, forty-one African Americans were lynched right there in Georgia. Only Mississippi lynched more.[4] It was in this world that William Charles, a truck driver for a local cotton mill, and his wife, Alberta, conceived their second child, a boy. Their first, a girl, had died at four months of age. When Alberta got ready to deliver the second, her family got word to Webster Pierce Ezzard, the Lawrenceville doctor all the folks in those parts turned to when they had their babies and suffered their sicknesses and died hard in the wet Georgia heat.

Dr. Ezzard's office proper was at the corner drug store in town, but as often as not he could be seen navigating the dark, back roads to deliver the babies and tend to the sick and dying in and around Lawrenceville. They said he never once took a vacation and by the time he died in 1963 at eighty-three years of age, he'd delivered some three thousand babies.[5] He had a thin, lanky frame and an easy smile. After he eased the Charles boy into the dark squalor that July night, William and Alberta had no money to pay him, so they named their son "Ezzard" in his honor. They weren't the first. Several folks around Lawrenceville had done the same thing. It seemed the right thing to do. Then they made his middle name "Mack" to honor the boy's grandfather.

Charles grew up like most of the boys in Lawrenceville did, especially the ones in Rocky Knob: poor, hungry and with only the smarts they came into the world with. Lawrenceville wasn't big on schooling; the grammar school, if you could call it that, was in the auditorium of the town church. It wasn't a real school at all. Not that this bothered Ezzard much. School gave him something to do and took his mind off how empty his stomach was, but overall he didn't much care for it. It was boring, and not just in the way school is boring to most kids at one time or another.

Rather than abiding lectures and lesson plans, the boys in Ezzard's class would play a game that involved flipping through a geography book and seeing who could come closest to finding Mississippi. That's what passed for learning. One time Charles got into the kind of trouble young boys do in school, and as punishment the teacher told him to write down all the numbers from one to one hundred. As no one had taught him how to write those numbers as yet, he just drew a hundred lines on the paper. He never did learn how to read there, but when he learned how to write his name they gave him an orange.

Like all the neighborhood boys, Charles imagined himself as someday rich and famous, or at least famous, because rich was something no black man in his right mind within a hundred miles of Lawrenceville was fool enough to dream. That was the kind of thinking that could get a man killed or at least heartbroken, and if you asked the older men in Lawrenceville they couldn't tell you which was worse. In a town as small as Lawrenceville, it was better to keep your dreams to yourself or someone might accuse you of trying to be better than you were. No good could come of that.

Still, as Charles passed the long, damp days and nights in what was more accidental campground than town, he did what all the boys did: imagined himself as someday a star baseball player in the National Negro League, an Oscar Charleston or Biz Mackey. Maybe he'd make it in basketball with the "Rens" up in Harlem in New York and travel across the country, stopping in St. Louis or Atlanta or San Francisco, wherever they had basketball teams, and whipping the hometown boys before moving on to the next town. That would be fun. Or maybe he'd be a champion prizefighter. In his fantasies he'd be known as "Jack" Charles, or "Kid" Charles, something like that. "Ezzard" was no good. There had never been a hero in the history of the world named "Ezzard" anywhere. Of that he was sure. And his middle name, "Mack," was no good either. He'd given that up in school when for the life of him he couldn't get himself to write it out so that it could be read. He stopped using it altogether. His grandfather would understand.

He thought "Dynamite" Charles would be a good nickname if he became a prizefighter. He'd gotten it from the old Joe Jinks comic strip, where Joe was a fight manager and his best fighter was named Dynamite Dunn. Yeah, Dynamite would do. Or "Young" Charles, after the great little scrapper Young Stribling, who was from Bainbridge, just a couple hundred miles away. Stribling started fighting as a bantamweight, a tiny kid, just like Charles was, and wound up fighting the best heavyweights in the world, grown men. He made a good living at it, was able to help out his family, and he was famous, all right.

If Stribling could do it, why couldn't he? He'd just have to get a better name than Ezzard. Sure, Stribling was a white man, but prizefighting was about the only sport in America where a poor black boy could compete against a poor white boy, and if he was good enough and could beat him, and kept winning, he eventually could be the champion of the whole world—not just the colored world. That was the good thing about the fighting business: it was equal opportunity. Blacks couldn't play in the white baseball leagues with Babe Ruth and Lou Gehrig. There were only a couple of black pro football players. And while the Rens played a lot of white basketball teams, it was hard to get rich or famous as a black basketball player.

Not so for good prizefighters. Way back in 1902, almost 20 years before Charles was born, Joe Gans became the first black American to win a world boxing championship. He was a lightweight, a little guy, just 135 pounds, and yet they came by the thousands, black and white, to watch him fight. Then, in 1908, Jack Johnson went from being the "world colored heavyweight champion" to the heavyweight champion of the whole world, which was about the greatest thing anybody could be. Everyone knew that. Being heavyweight champion of the world was like being president of the United States.

White people hated Johnson, and he didn't help himself any by running around with white women, but he did whatever he wanted to. Imagine that—from a black man! That showed how great it was to be a prizefighter, so long as you were really good at it. Johnson was known as "the Galveston Giant" after Galveston, Texas, his hometown. If Charles became a prizefighter he'd have to have a good nickname like that one. Only thing was, as far as he knew, no one who was famous had ever come from Lawrenceville. There were other great black fighters—Sam Langford, Harry Wills, Barbados Joe Walcott. The sport was full of good black fighters and a lot of them were stars. They weren't rich, but they were stars.

There was one name Ezzard knew he wouldn't use if he got famous—his father's. When he was five, Charles' parents split up and William headed up North on his own, leaving Alberta to raise their boy alone. Father and son didn't see each other again for twenty years, until after the whole world knew who Ezzard Charles was. By then the old man was a superintendent at an apartment building in Lorain, Ohio, and it was too late for them. That was okay with Ezzard. He let the press take their pictures and he smiled along but he wasn't the first fighter in the world or the last who chose the vocation he did at least in part to show his father what a real man should be and what a real man could do. The prisons and prize rings and graveyards were full of men trying to prove this or that to their fathers, whether they loved the man or hated him or both. Usually it was both. The older men who spent their days and night in gyms and saloons and alleys knew the truth: Bad fathers created more prizefighters and criminals and alcoholics than poverty, whiskey and cheating women combined, and for as long as men failed as fathers there would be sons chasing them to their graves to show them how they had failed as men. Sometimes it made the sons better men. A lot of the time it didn't.

Either way, Charles would never be known as "William" or "Bill" Charles. But by any name he was finding a way to live, the way all kids do, no matter the state of their lives, and boxing was everywhere. In the 1920s prizefighting was the biggest sport in the world, and heroes such as Jack Dempsey, Harry Greb and Mickey Walker were treated like movie stars, or, better yet, like kings, or heads of state. And they weren't all on the other side of the world.

In 1926, Tiger Flowers, whose nickname was "the Georgia Deacon," became the first black man to win the middleweight world title. He was born in Camilla, Georgia, just under two hundred miles south of Lawrenceville. Wherever there were poor boys trying to make something of themselves, you could bet there were also boxing rings and gloves and old punching bags. And that included Lawrenceville.

Long before Ezzard Charles was born some of the older men had put together a makeshift boxing ring, and all summer long the neighborhood boys would box one another underneath the scorching Georgia sun. Adults in the neighborhood would sometimes watch from "ringside," betting, fanning themselves and sweating, and sipping tea or lemonade or whatever else a grown man or woman could get his or her hands on around town.

Sometimes it would be one boy against another. Other times there'd be a "battle royal," all the willing boys in the neighborhood in the ring at once flailing at one another—usually blindfolded—until the last one left standing, little brown chest heaving and lathered in sweat and probably some blood, too, was declared the winner. The crowd would toss their pennies and nickels into the "ring" and the winner would take home the loot. Sometimes the neighborhood boys would gather in this backyard or that and box one another in a circle formed by spectators. There wasn't much else to do in Lawrenceville.

Little Ezzard fought his first match in a roped-off section of mayor Grover Montgomery's front lawn.[6] Although he was one of the smallest kids in the neighborhood, he had little trouble running through other kids around his age—on that day and on the many that followed. This was a great and not unwelcome surprise to him, and not long after, he filled an old canvas sack with rags and sand, hung it from a tree in the backyard and stood out there for hours under that red Georgia sun, punching away at it. The more he punched at it the better he got. And the better he got the more he punched at it. Day by day Ezzard forgot about being a star baseball or basketball player and thought mostly about boxing. Not in a way that suggested to him that this is what he would do with his life—that would come later; he was too young for it now. But like all other boys, and whether or not he knew it, he'd been looking for the thing he would be good at. And at eight years old, more or less, he'd found it—right there in Lawrenceville.

It was fortunate for Charles that Lawrenceville wasn't the only place in the world where a poor boy could find makeshift boxing rings and old gloves and homemade punching bags. When he was nine, Alberta decided she couldn't make it in Lawrenceville anymore, took her son to her mother's house up in Cincinnati and asked her to raise her boy right. She'd struggled long and hard in Lawrenceville, relying on family when she could, but she was mostly alone and she wanted better for Ezzard. She didn't want her only child to be raised poor in the Deep South where a black man couldn't really be a man except in his own home, and not even then sometimes because he'd never learned how.

She knew it would be better for him up North in Cincinnati, where it wasn't heaven but at least he'd have a chance. He could be a man. She herself was headed up to Atlanta and then to New York City, where she hoped to find a job in the dressmaking business. She'd heard they had those kinds of jobs, but New York was no place to raise a young boy. So she'd go up to New York and get a job that would pay her enough to send her boy a new suit every Christmas or Easter or some kind of treat when expenses would allow. And she knew her mother would do right by her boy.

Charles' grandmother, Maude Foster, lived in Cincinnati's West End, where all the black folks lived. It wouldn't be easy for her, or for Ezzard. She made a living wage and not much more as a maid, and her little, rundown, three-room frame house, which was supported by bricks at the corners, already housed her five sons, two daughters, and her own mother, Belle Russell, a former slave. Both were slight, petite women, but the matriarchs made a formidable pair and theirs was a righteous home. Ms. Foster was firm with all her kids, and especially Ezzard, about prayer and the importance of living the right life—a good, clean Christian life. As long as a man led a clean Christian life, no harm could come to him. That's what she always said, and Ezzard believed her. Ms. Russell, his great-grandmother, made him read his Bible and preached strict adherence to its tenets and attention to the lessons it held. Between the two of them they made sure Charles would turn out to be a good boy. They made him mind his manners and kept him out of trouble. He fit in quickly with the brood, and one of his uncles gave him a nickname that stayed with him for the rest of his life: "Snooks."

Due largely to his grandmothers' influence, Charles stayed out of trouble in his new home, though there was lots of opportunity to go wrong in the West End. Cincinnati was busting at the seams. Industry had hit the town hard around the turn of the century. Like most things, that was good and bad. It brought in lots of money and created thousands of jobs for unskilled laborers. Migrants from the Deep South poured into the city, doubling its population between 1910 and 1930. Most of the newcomers settled in the downtown and West End neighborhoods along the lower Mill Creek basin. It wasn't long before the basin was choking on its new residents, with open sewers fouling the poorest neighborhoods, floods wiping out whole blocks and thick industrial smoke from the factories shadowing the entire region.

In the poorest neighborhoods you couldn't hang a shirt outside on the line to dry because one of your neighbors might need a shirt, too. The men joked that you could tell the size of a man's house by smelling his clothes; if he had a one-room place and couldn't hang his clothes outside, his shirts reeked of pork fat. If they smelled like soap rather than food, he was doing all right.

It wasn't Lawrenceville, where a young black boy couldn't look a white man in the eye without permission, or walk on the same side of the street as a white man. A man didn't have to worry about getting lynched in Cincinnati if he looked at a white girl, but if he was smart he didn't test the waters. He knew his place. It wasn't lynching country but it wasn't the Promised Land, either.

Charles' grandmother enrolled him in Harriet Beecher Stowe elementary school in the West End as soon as she could. She dressed him in his best clothes, which wasn't saying much, told him to mind his Ps and Qs and do the best he could. It was the first real school he'd ever attended; he'd never learned to read in Lawrenceville. On his first day, the school administration, not sure what to make of this shy, impeccably polite and wholly illiterate nine-year-old, put him in a class for retarded kids. There Ezzard stayed for a full three months[7] until he acquired some rudimentary reading skills and was able to join the student body at large. The teachers discovered soon enough that he was no genius with books. He plodded along but learned his lessons and once they took, he retained them. He was a determined boy and he needed to be. The West End was no place for the faint-hearted, or for boys who had little interest in mixing it up in the street.

Unfortunately, that described Charles, who, despite his many successes in battle royals and backyard boxing matches in Lawrenceville, had no inclination whatever for street fighting. Partly by nature and partly by upbringing, he was a timid boy and froze in terror at the thought of fist-fighting in the street or on the playground. And as there were always boys at school looking for fights the moment classes were dismissed, he became adept at the practice all young cowards master: charting new ways to get home. He'd take back alleys or cut through backyards or a corner grocery store, even if it took him twice as long to get home.[8]

On the occasions when a fight couldn't be avoided, his uncle Harvey, a veteran of the West End streets, fought for him. And when Uncle Harvey wasn't there, Charles took his lumps. One time when he took a new notebook to school, a bigger, older kid said he'd lost his, which happened to be the same color and size as the one Ezzard carried. He accused Charles of theft. Young Charles protested. The older boy answered with a sock on the jaw. Ezzard handed over the notebook without another word.

Charles was eleven years old and still running from fights in August 1932 when the local paper reported that the great Cuban featherweight boxer, Kid Chocolate, would be coming to Cincinnati to fight Cleveland-based journeyman Johnny Farr downtown at the Parkway Outdoor Arena. Charles and his sports-minded friends were excited. It wasn't that it would be a great match; Farr was a ham-and-egger who would never be a great fighter. But Kid Chocolate! He'd been all over the world and fought the best fighters there were—Jackie "Kid" Berg, Battling Battalino, Tony Canzoneri. These were the fighters they read about in the paper every day, fighters who were rich and famous, and now one of them was coming to Cincinnati. The week before the fight the promoter had one of his guys drive Chocolate through the West End to help build the gate. The car was huge and had the top down and Chocolate sat up high, waving to the neighborhood kids. They turned down the block Charles and his family lived on, and stopped outside a candy store.

The neighborhood kids flocked to the car and Chocolate, known not only for his ring prowess but for an immense and elegant wardrobe, shone in an expensive, impeccably tailored suit despite the summer heat. Ezzard joined the throng around the car and heard one of the kids ask, "Chocolate, how many suits ya got?" Chocolate responded: "Man, I got suits for every day in the year. I got 365."[9] And Ezzard Mack Charles, who was about as poor as any of the kids on the West End, ran from fights in the street, looked like he was half starving to death, and never spoke unless he was spoken to, thought: "I'm gonna be a fighter and have clothes like that."

After that there were no more dreams of being a famous baseball or basketball player or anything else. He knew what he would be. He'd be a fighter. He'd been one all along anyway—in the backyard, back home in Lawrenceville. He just hadn't known it yet. Someday he would be more than "Snooks" from the neighborhood, more than the kid who didn't start school until he was ten years old. He'd be more than the kid born piss-poor in a shack and more than the poor black boy whose father ran out on him and whose mother, for good reasons or bad, dropped him in Cincinnati on the way up North. He'd be the boy to make his grandmother and his great-grandmother proud, the boy who would stand out among all the other poor boys on the West End. It wouldn't matter that he wasn't white or that he still couldn't write his middle name.

Not long before the Chocolate-Farr fight the following week, the promoter, a local guy, offered free tickets to a few of the neighborhood kids, including Charles and a few of his buddies, if they set up chairs for the event at Music Hall. Charles jumped at the chance and come fight night, every chair was in place—rows and rows of them. Charles and his friends showed up to claim their free tickets, but they were nowhere to be found—nor was the promoter. Charles went home and listened on the radio like everyone else. He didn't miss much. Farr hardly laid a glove on Chocolate, but it hardly mattered. Ezzard Charles, the fighter, had been born.

Over the next four years Charles did all the things the boys in the West End did; he went to school, played ball in the park, did his chores and minded his grandmother. He started discovering girls. And just as he had back in Lawrenceville, he boxed other boys in backyards and parking lots and in ball fields, and just like in Lawrenceville, he went through them like they weren't there.

All along he remembered the day he met Kid Chocolate and what he promised himself he'd be some day, but Chocolate wasn't his inspiration anymore. Someone else had taken his place. Over the past four years a sensational black heavyweight named Joe Louis had come out of Detroit and torn through just about every fighter he'd faced. He was all anyone could talk about, even the white folks, but especially black folks, who saw him as proof that a black man could come from the slums and reach the top of the world.

In just a few years Louis had become the talk of the sports world. The newspaper guys wrote he might even be better than Jack Dempsey. Joe Louis was born into desperate poverty in Lafayette, Alabama, in 1914, the seventh of eight children born to Munroe Barrow and Lillie (Reese) Barrow, a pair of sharecroppers whose parents were former slaves. Louis' parents split after his father was committed to an insane asylum in 1916, and in 1920 his mother married Pat Brooks. After an encounter with the Ku Klux Klan, the family moved to Detroit in 1926 and Louis found his way to a youth and recreation center on Brewster Street, where he learned to box. He had his first amateur bout in 1932, the same year Charles met Kid Chocolate. He lost that fight to future Olympian Johnny Miller, but then quickly excelled, displaying mind-numbing punching power and lightning-fast hands. He won numerous tournaments over the following several years, including the 1933 Detroit Free Press Golden Gloves, the 1934 Detroit Golden Gloves, and the National Golden Gloves and National AAU light heavyweight championships in 1934. He turned pro in 1934 and was undefeated in twenty-four fights until former champion Max Schmeling upset him and stopped him in 1936 in New York. The loss to Schmeling hardly slowed Louis down.

It wasn't only his fighting skill that made him a success. His management team was well aware that much of America was still smarting over the indignities foisted on it by Jack Johnson. In order to ascend to the top of the sports world Louis had to play the game the way white America wanted him to. If he didn't, he wouldn't get the chance. He couldn't do what Johnson had done. So they mandated a code of conduct for Louis that they knew would help him avoid the deep enmity Johnson's flamboyance created among the white majority. The code consisted of seven mandates: He was never to have his picture taken with a white woman; he was never to go into a nightclub alone; there would be no soft fights; there would be no fixed fights; he was never to gloat over a fallen opponent; he was to keep a "dead pan" in front of the cameras; and he was to live and fight clean. It was a carefully cultivated and controlled public image that didn't so much sell Louis to white America as make the possibility of his winning the title more palatable. Louis' fists would take care of the rest.

To black Americans what Louis did outside the ring was of secondary importance; with every win over another heavyweight—black or white—Louis' legend grew. Every victory sent poor black folks into the streets to celebrate, to stand up and believe, to holler and cuss if they wanted and to hold their heads high, from Harlem to San Francisco and everywhere in between, including, importantly, Cincinnati. The teenage Ezzard Charles listened to Louis' fights on the radio and when Louis won, so did he. So did everyone else on the West End, and in all the other West Ends across America.

Ezzard started compiling a scrapbook of Louis' newspaper clips and photos, and before long it bulged. Louis had a chance to become an American hero, a man who would show everyone that even a poor black boy born in a shack could become the most famous man in America. So when Charles boxed his friends and other neighborhood kids he imagined himself as Louis, shuffling this way and that, landing punches and dodging counters. And after he had beaten them all, bloodied their noses, busted their lips and then sent them home bruised and dizzy, a couple of them told him he was wasting his time with them. If he loved Joe Louis so much and was so good at boxing, why didn't he go to a gym already and do it right? What was he waiting for? So he did.

In the summer of 1936 Charles went to his grandmother and asked her for fifty cents, the dues at a local boxing gym. She thought about it good and hard, prayed on it. She knew how many ways a boy could go wrong on the West End, and that no matter how much she and her mother kept after him, you never knew when a boy would go astray. It would help him stay on the straight and narrow if he had something to do to fill up his time between studies and chores.

She was no fan of fighting, and fifty cents was nothing to sneeze at; she had to wash a lot of floors to make fifty cents. But she knew Ezzard had God in his heart and with that he would be okay. The next afternoon she pressed the money into his hand and sent him on his way. There was no way she could know then what she had done for him. The best she could do was trust that God would watch over him.

Ezzard went to Danny Davis' gym on Central Avenue on the West End. The old men there laughed him out of the joint, told him there was no way he would ever be a boxer. You couldn't blame them. Danny Davis was already a local celebrity, having trained the great Cincinnati featherweight Freddie Miller, who was Cincinnati's first homegrown world champion. He'd started fighting as a teenager. By the time Ezzard wandered into Davis' Gym, Miller had already fought all over the world and won and lost the title. In four more years he'd be retired.

You didn't slink into the gym of a world champion fighter looking like Charles did and expect attention. The guys there had never seen a less likely fighter than Ezzard, what with his fine manners and spindly arms and legs. He spoke so softly they had a hard time hearing him. He looked more like a street urchin than a would-be prizefighter, and there were too many kids around who had what it took to be real fighters. Davis' gym was filled with pros and with tough kids from all over the West End who you knew could fight just as soon as you looked at them; rough kids, kids who were dirt poor, like Ezzard was, but who had used all the pain and hunger of poverty to make themselves into little men who as soon as they walked in the door seemed to know their way around a ring because they had fought on the streets every day of their lives.

Some of them had scars already—scars around the eyes or on the cheek or chin, or on their little fists. That wasn't Ezzard. He was small, soft. They told him to pick another sport; the fight game was too rough for kids like him. As he left the way he came in, they figured they'd done him a favor, saving him from a lot of beatings or worse.

They turned back to their very important work of training kids no one would ever hear of, who would toil as pugs here and there and take their lickings and then be swallowed up in the slums long before any crowd could cheer them or see their names in a newspaper. Some good fighters came out of the West End gyms in those years—Wallace "Bud" Smith,

George Costner, and a few others, but never any like Ezzard Charles. The fighting business gobbled kids up and spit them out, but the West End did it just as well.

But there were plenty of other gyms on the West End, and one of Ezzard's friends, Gene Howell, an amateur boxer himself, took Ezzard to Fred Batche's gym on Pleasant Street. Howell introduced Charles to a diminutive Welshman and World War I veteran named Bert Williams, who had been a fixture in the Cincinnati fight scene for years. If you were involved in the fight business in Cincinnati you knew Bert Williams and Bert Williams knew you. And you knew he was in the room before you could see him; he spoke in a heavy Welsh accent and with severe authority. He'd been training Howell and three other amateurs for several months when Howell introduced him to Ezzard, who told Williams simply that he wanted "to be a fighter, like Joe Louis."[10] Williams looked him up and down and frowned, the way a cattle farmer might observe a three-legged calf.

He saw a "skinny, undernourished kid who can barely stand, let alone box."[11] But the kid seemed earnest. And when Williams told Ezzard to show him how he punched and how he stood when he was going to fight, he could see the kid knew what he was doing, even though he had never been inside a real gym or gotten real instruction. So Williams worked Ezzard out. "He seemed to have plenty," he said later. "It was in his heart to be a fighter. I worked him out two or three times and saw the kid had guts."[12] On the fourth day Ezzard was there, right on time. And the next day after that, too, and the next. And after five or six days Williams decided to put the kid in the ring with one of his experienced kids, a boy named Sam Rutledge, just to see what he had, how he reacted to getting hit. He knew it was early, but he felt that Charles had something and wanted to see how much.

Like any new kid, Ezzard took a bad beating. Rutledge knocked him all over the ring, flooring him several times.[13] Most new kids disappeared after taking a beating like that. Williams would never see them again unless he passed them on the street. When Charles left that afternoon Williams wasn't sure if he'd be back. The next day, there he was, right on time. He sparred again with Rutledge and again got knocked down and beaten up, but he kept showing up, day after day.

A couple months later the building owner banned amateurs from the gym, and Williams took his small stable down to Race AC Boxing Club, which was run by Bob Bonner and Earl Butler, a couple of local fight guys. Around this time, Williams and his wife started getting closer to Charles and his family. They bought him some decent clothes to wear to school, and Mrs. Williams, who'd been a nurse in World War I, cooked dinners for Ezzard's grandmother.[14]

After a couple months at the new gym and some more beatings from Rutledge, Williams made a match for Charles against a boy named Al Jackson at an American Legion show in Newport. It was an important step: though Ezzard had been showing steady improvement in the gym, nothing mattered if he didn't show something in an actual match. Williams had to make sure Charles wasn't going to be a "gym fighter"—a guy who could fight like hell in the gym and then somehow lose it all when the lights came on in the arena and he had to do it for real, in front of paying customers. In the game they'd say a guy "froze" in the ring, just stiffened up. Williams had seen it a few times; every trainer had. In his mind it was a case of nerves. Some guys just couldn't handle the pressure of being in a real bout, and when that happened they forgot everything they had learned. You couldn't blame them. Being in the boxing ring was the closest you could come during peacetime to being in a foxhole, and Williams had seen plenty of strong men break down and cry like babies in a foxhole. Who could blame a kid for freezing up doing something so unnatural as prizefighting?

To be a good boxer you had to train yourself to ignore all of your instincts for self-preservation: to move inside of a punch rather than straight away from it; to keep your chin down instead of lifting it up for better vision; to throw short, straight punches rather than wide, looping ones; to breathe through your nose rather than with your mouth wide open, gasping for precious air. Everything that came naturally to a boy during a street fight was death to a boxer, and the best ones learned right away to control their deepest instincts. Even if he understood what made some boys gym fighters, Williams had no time to waste on them. He wasn't getting any younger. If a boy was the type to freeze up in a fight, he wanted to know early so he would not waste too much time on him. This kid Charles didn't look like the type, but he'd know soon enough. Al Jackson would show him.

At the opening bell Jackson and Charles rushed one another and started flailing, as inexperienced fighters do. Jackson's punches were a little straighter and a little harder and they landed first. Right away Charles was in trouble. He backed up to get away, and Jackson chased after him, throwing punches. A hard right hand landed on the jaw and for a second Charles went to sleep.

He woke up when his rump hit the canvas, for the first time in that strange world that all fighters come to know eventually—where you can see the ringsiders cheering but can't hear them, where you see the referee's face up close to yours but it's behind a blanket of fog and you can tell he's saying something but don't understand the language. Maybe you hear the ocean. The instincts you were born with, the ones whose job it is to keep you alive, tell you to lie down, stay where you are, you'll be fine as long as you stay where you are. Let the fight go. You don't need it.

This wasn't the way it had felt when Rutledge beat up Charles in the gym. In the gym you wore the big gloves and the headgear. There was constant noise and you could hear everything and see it and smell it and taste the blood in your mouth. When punches landed they hurt. It was real. This was different, like a dream. Ezzard neither saw nor felt the punch that floored him. All he knew was that he was down. And instinct told him: "It's okay. Let it go."

There was a place in Charles that wanted to submit to that instinct, to go back to sleep, to be safe. But he'd trained his body and mind to act like a fighter's, so he shook himself out of that world, peaceful as it was, to the real one, where he was sitting on a filthy, blood-stained canvas in a smoke-filled American Legion Hall with the referee counting over him. His left jaw ached where Jackson's right fist had landed, and over the cheers of the crowd he could hear Williams screaming instructions from outside the ropes. He felt like he might throw up but struggled up, made it to the end of the round. At the start of the second he tore into Al Jackson like no one's business and stopped him in the third.[15] Williams had his answer. The kid was all fighter.

This is what people never understood about fighters, even the very young ones: that a quiet young kid with nice manners who ran from fights in the street could, in the right circumstance, swallow all his fear and shame and stand up for himself like he mattered. The ring was the one place in the world where he could let himself be brave and where he could go bad for a while.

The kids who fought in the street and got into trouble were almost never any good with the gloves on, because they let all the bad stuff out there in the open. They burned it up. They wasted it. They didn't hold any of it in. Charles held it in. He never swore or cussed like the other boys did and he almost never got mad; even when he did, he didn't fight, even when it would have been easier to drop his books and ball his fists.

One day he saw an older kid punch one of his good friends right in the eye. The boy moaned and began to cry, helpless and defeated, cowering. As Charles walked away, he told another friend he was mad enough to fight that day.[16] If you knew him, you could see it in his face. He wanted to. But he didn't. He put his head down. He held it in. In the ring, he found a place to let it go.

2

No Cheap Ambition

Williams was hell-bent on making Charles a great prizefighter. He taught the kid everything he knew, which was a lot, and he didn't make another match for him after the Jackson fight for a good six or seven months. He wanted to give Ezzard a lot of gym time and really work with him. By the seventh month Charles had improved so much that he was knocking poor Sam Rutledge all over the ring and wreaking such havoc with other sparring partners that Bonner, one of the gym's owners, wanted Williams to turn him pro. He had the perfect style: aggressive, fast-handed, as fearless in the ring as you could want, and he could crack with both hands, especially the left. Still, Williams knew turning Charles pro with so little experience was crazy. He might have something here in this kid, and it would have to be developed and nurtured. So many kids got ruined in the ring because they were thrown into fights before they were ready. Williams wasn't going to let that happen to Charles, especially after all the time he had spent on him. He wouldn't be rushed. Bonner and Williams argued about it, and Williams, often a hothead and especially when he was right, again found himself without a gym for his budding star. Then he and Charles caught a break.

The *Cincinnati Post* announced it would sponsor the first Cincinnati Golden Gloves tournament, and set up a boxing gym at Fifth and Plum streets. Williams took Charles and his other fighters there and signed them up for the tournament. By this time it was late 1937 and Joe Louis was the world heavyweight champion, having beaten Jimmy Braddock for the title in June. Louis was all Ezzard could talk about, and Williams used Ezzard's obsession with Louis to keep him focused. He told Charles he "could be a fighter like Louis" if he "stayed away from bad influences."[1]

So that's what Charles did. He lived a fighter's life: No staying out late. Run every day. Williams couldn't have asked for a better pupil. "It was in his heart to be a fighter. He was a wonderful boy to handle. Did everything I told him. All he wanted was gym, gym, gym,"[2] he said. Indeed, as he progressed, Ezzard asked all the older men in the game what he had to do to be great fighter, and they all said the same thing: If you want to be a fighter you've got to eat it and sleep it. Square that he was, Ezzard believed every word. Most nights Williams had to kick him out of the gym.[3]

Years later when it all had gone to hell and the ride was long over, a man asked Charles what had driven him in the early years; where he had found what he needed to become what he had become. Charles, a middle-aged man then with the sad self-awareness that comes with years, told him, "It was not a cheap ambition, wanting to become the champ. To be the greatest, the best, was my dream."[4] A kid doesn't know that. He just does it.

All Ezzard's hard work paid off over the coming months. Williams fought Ezzard in smokers and small tournaments all over Ohio, and in fight after fight in American Legion halls and church basements and school auditoriums little Ezzard Charles did nothing but win. Williams had been training slum kids to be fighters for a long time, and he was good at what he did. He was careful not to overmatch Ezzard with someone who was too experienced for him, but he didn't put him in with kids he could easily bowl over, either.

There was an art and a science to bringing a kid along right and transforming him from a street fighter—or, in Ezzard's case, a backyard fighter—into a prizefighter. Rush him and a bad beating could ruin him. Match him too soft and he develops bad habits and never learns to dig deep within himself, which he surely will have to do sooner or later. Matchmaking was a tricky business, and if you weren't careful or smart you could get your kid hurt. Lucky for Charles, Williams was both. He knew all the other trainers, knew when one was lying about how many fights his kid had had and what kind of shape he was in.

There was a sense of brotherhood among the West End trainers, as there is among all men in boxing, and one of the tenets of the brotherhood is that it is understood that everyone lies all the time. That's part of the business; you get an advantage for your kid where you can. Williams understood that part of it and was good at it. With Ezzard he was like a trainer of a potentially great race horse, with just the right balance between carrot and stick.

Charles did his part by having just the right combination of tenacity and sense of self-preservation, with emphasis on the former. He was a dynamo, throwing hard, fast punches from bell to bell. And you couldn't discourage him. It was as though he were fighting for his next meal. When a kid has that kind of hunger and a good teacher and the talent and physical equipment, he is hard to beat indeed. And no one did beat Charles, not that anyone could remember, anyway. Not in forty-two straight fights over the next two years, according to Williams.

Williams soon had Charles winning every tournament he entered, including the 1937 Diamond Belt and Ohio AAU welterweight championships and the 1938 Diamond Belt, state AAU and Golden Gloves welterweight championships. The following year was even better. He claimed the Diamond Belt middleweight championship; the Golden Gloves middleweight championship, beating Pete Hantz in the finals; the Ohio AAU title; and then, finally, the National AAU middleweight championship, beating Bradley Lewis, James Toney and then Leroy Bolden in the finals.[5] Nobody could remember the last time they'd seen a kid like Charles.

Years later, when Charles abandoned Williams, like all successful fighters abandon their first trainers, and Williams was understandably bitter, he changed his mind about Ezzard's having been an undefeated amateur and claimed he'd been beaten at least six times, naming Charlie Morris and Johnny Castro as two Cincinnati boys who'd whipped him.[6] And in 1950, Artie Dorell, husband of that year's "Mrs. Texas," told a reporter at a beauty pageant in Asbury Park, New Jersey, that he had beaten Charles in the 1938 Golden Gloves.[7]

Maybe nobody licked Charles in the amateurs. Maybe a couple did. It didn't matter either way. To a kid from the slums like Charles, trophies and medals by themselves didn't mean all that much after a while. The amateurs was merely a training ground to prepare him for a professional career where his trophies and medals would be apartment buildings, suits, nice cars, beautiful women, a full stomach, and a life without struggle. That's what he thought, anyway.

When he wasn't in the gym or stockpiling trophies, Charles was living the life of a 1930s West End teenager. His closest friend in the world was a neighborhood kid named Richard Christmas, who he had met when they were on opposing baseball teams. Charles, with his broad shoulders and athletic build, hurled a wicked fastball. It was the only sport he played, outside boxing. He and Christmas, who was a year younger, forged a friendship that lasted for decades, until one of them died long before he should have. But that was later.

In 1930s Cincinnati, Charles worked when he wasn't at school or at the gym or doing chores. He washed cars. He washed windows. He got a part-time job as a porter down at Max Elkus' clothing store on Central Avenue, and on the slow days he'd run up and down the stairs to strengthen his legs. He saved his money. He passed all of his classes at Harriet Beecher Stowe—though math was a close call—and moved on to Woodward High School, having been absent just five times in his three years at Beecher.

While there he gained a reputation as a good kid, an honest one who wasn't going to set the world on fire with his brain, but who was humble, honorable, hard-working and all the other things you wanted your kid to be when you sent him off into the world. His grandmothers had done a good job with him. His teachers never saw him as dumb, but rather as one who already had his sights set and didn't have to take school seriously. Ezzard knew where he was headed and how he was going to get there, and he didn't need algebra to help him. He did what he had to do to pass his classes and please his grandmothers, and not much more.

While Charles was being a square and winning fight after fight, important people on the West End began to take an interest in his achievements. Sam Becker, a local promoter and manager who operated a clothing store at Eighth and Vine streets along with his brother Benny, promoted the smokers Ezzard fought in and knew he wanted to be around Charles when the time came to turn pro. Max Elkus was in the mix too. Owning a clothing store was good and stable, but he thought it might be fun to manage a prizefighter.

Whenever Ezzard fought, they were there. Some guys from out of town, maybe as far away as New York, would come down and hang around Charles, too, when he was in the gym or at a fight. The closer Charles came to going pro, the more attention he got. Some folks in town who cared about Ezzard didn't like it. They'd heard that the boxing business was lousy with crooks and gangsters. A nice boy like Ezzard would be better off working his whole life in Elkus' clothing store, no matter how much money he could make fighting. Boxing other boys for trophies and medals was one thing. Beating on another man for money was a whole different thing, and it was no place for a nice, church-going young man like Ezzard Mack Charles.

There was something to be said for that. The pro boxing business was nothing like the amateurs. There was money at stake—big money. Hundreds of thousands of dollars sometimes, the kind of money that can save a man and ruin him at the same time—the kind of money men will do anything for.

The crooks and gamblers always had their fingers in the game. It had always been that way. Gamblers, hustlers, drunks, whores, killers; they all felt at home in the fight business because they were among their own and because nobody was there to stop them. But their reach was limited. There had always been fixed fights, but it wasn't until the do-gooders and the religious nuts and the politicians outlawed alcohol in the 1920s that the mob in America began to move on the fight game. They'd gotten rich making and moving booze and rightly saw the fight business as the next big score, the next business ripe for a takeover.

So thugs like Arnold Rothstein and Al Capone, who wore pinstripe suits and didn't know a left hook from a right cross but had connections, started calling the shots. You couldn't touch them. If you wanted proof all you had to do was look at that big stiff from Italy, Primo Carnera. They took him all the way from circus strongman to world heavyweight champion, fixing fight after fight, and when they finally decided they were done with him, when he couldn't make them another penny, they left him broke and broken. There wasn't a more pathetic sight in the world than "Da Preem," punchy and sad, flopping around in wrestling tights to try to pay the bills.

This was the business, and by the early 1940s the guy running it from behind a curtain of extortion, violence and dirty money was Frankie Carbo, a New York City Mafia soldier in the Lucchese crime family and a hitman for the so-called Murder Incorporated, the enforcement arm of New York's organized crime racket. By the late 1930s he'd been charged with at least eight murders, but he was so well connected and protected that he kept walking. He got into the boxing racket because it was a perfect fit and because there wasn't the money in bootlegging and murder that there used to be.

If Carbo was boxing's unofficial commissioner, which is how a lot of guys referred to him, then Frank "Blinky" Palermo was his deputy. Palermo ran the biggest numbers game in Philadelphia and was a high-ranking soldier in the Philly mob. His close ties with Carbo gave him enormous power in the fight game, and between the two of them they pulled all the levers and made all the big decisions. Most of the time when you saw a guy listed as a fighter's manager he was just a front man for a mobbed-up guy that reported up to one of them. Carbo kept his name out of the papers, but Palermo got so bold that he listed his own name as the manager of record for a bunch of guys.

A fighter didn't have to get in bed with the mob if he didn't want to. He had a choice. Did he want a shot at the title? Did he want to fight in the Garden or at the big ballparks? Did he want to make money? Did he want to get decisions when he deserved them, and sometimes when he didn't? If he wanted those things, then his manager got into the Manager's Guild, which meant he'd signed a piece of the kid over to a "silent partner" or two or three, and they were always mobbed-up guys. Whenever the kid fought, the partners would get some off the top. Any time after that when a promoter or a paper said a fighter's purse would be, say, $5,000, you knew that was before all the "partners"—legitimate and otherwise—took their cuts. The fighter was lucky to go home with a quarter of that.

If the partners wanted a favor every once in a while, say when the kid was a big betting favorite, maybe they asked him to sit down in the fourth round or forget how to fight. It was only right, after all they had done for him. You scratch our back, we'll scratch yours, and everyone goes home happy. So sure they fixed some fights, but most of the time they didn't have to. Everyone had paper on somebody. You don't have to persuade a kid to lose when you own the kid in the other corner, too. You make out either way. So long as he fights who you tell him to and when you tell him to, you can't lose. It was almost too easy.

Some fighters refused to play along, wanted to do it clean and the right way. Everyone knew who they were—they were the guys getting old waiting for a title shot. They were the guys always getting ripped off by the judges and fighting in little dives in front of a couple hundred drunks when they were good enough to fight main events at the Garden. Sure, there were a few guys who were big enough stars that they could tell the mob "no thanks" and it didn't matter. Joe Louis. Ray Robinson. But most everyone else had to play the game. Sooner or later the manager had to make the call and drop off the cash. There was no other way to open the door.

It wasn't only the managers in bed with the mobsters. Most of the writers were on the take, too. Every manager who'd been around the block knew that after his kid fought at the Garden he had to take an envelope, scribble a writer's name on it, slip in some cash and drop it off at Jack Dempsey's Restaurant or across the street at the Forrest Hotel, or at the

Kit Kat Club, or Toots Shor's joint, or the Cotton Club—wherever the writers were hanging out that night, telling their lies and drinking their whiskey. That's how you got your kid a fair write-up in the papers the next day.

This was the world Ezzard Charles, high school student, entered into when he turned pro in early 1940, stopping Melody Johnson in the fourth round in Middletown. His purse was $5. Charles was just a teenager but he fought like a man, winning ten times in his first year as a pro, six of them by knockout and most of them right there in town at Music Hall Arena. He won five more the following year, 1941, when Williams got a chance to put him in with Ken Overlin at home in Cincinnati in June. It was the kind of fight a manager loved to get for his kid in those days, when you could lose a fight and it wasn't the end of the world. Just a month earlier Overlin, who *The Ring* magazine ranked second in the world at middleweight, had lost the New York version of the world middleweight title in an outrageous and almost certainly mob-influenced decision against Billy Soose—his second points loss to Soose.

Despite his age (32) and his mileage (147 fights), Overlin was far from washed up. It was true he'd been a playboy all his life and was known for partying as much as for boxing, but he had held the two together well and was still one of the best pure boxers and counterpunchers in the division. And he couldn't punch worth a lick. From Williams' perspective that was the beauty of taking the fight, and all he had to give up was a little piece of Charles' next few fights to Chris Dundee, Overlin's manager, which he gladly did.

Overlin had so much more experience than Charles did that he was expected to win. If it turned out that way, and even if he gave Charles a thorough going-over, it wouldn't ruin him because Overlin couldn't break an egg. And if Charles managed to pull out a win? Well, that would be a hell of notch in his belt, a kid barely out of his diapers, beating the former world champ. Plus, like a lot of guys, Overlin was a connected fighter and everyone knew it. If Charles could whip him it would mean a lot.

It didn't happen. Everything that Charles had going for him—his youth, his strength, his speed, his hunger—wasn't enough to overcome what Overlin had, which was experience. There would come a time when Charles was the experienced one, and he would use it to beat kids who were faster, stronger and hungrier. There was no substitute for the smarts and confidence great experience could give an old prizefighter. Overlin took his time, letting Charles make all the mistakes young fighters make, letting him burn out so that by the end he was wobbling all over the ring. And right there in Charles' hometown, the judges gave Overlin the win, just as they should have.

Williams put Charles back in at the Parkway Arena a month later and then again a couple months after that. Two more wins against nobodies got Charles ready for Teddy Yarosz, another older guy like Overlin. Born in Pittsburgh, Yarosz too had held the New York version of the middleweight title before losing it to Babe Risko seven years earlier. Yarosz was closer to the end than Overlin was, even though he was a year younger, and he had fought everyone. He'd whipped Overlin and Solly Krieger, lost a couple close ones to Billy Conn, then beat Conn, and then whipped a young phenom named Archie Moore.

Like Overlin, he wasn't a big puncher and hoped his edge in experience—he'd logged 125 fights over 11 years—would get him through against Charles. It didn't. In front of 3,500 fans at Music Hall Arena, Charles decked Yarosz in the first round with a left hook. The memory of it kept Yarosz on the defense the rest of the night, leading to a points win for Charles. Yarosz fought just once more, then retired.

Charles was just getting started. With a win in his pocket over a respected former champion, Williams took a fight against another veteran, Anton Christoforidis, who had briefly held the National Boxing Association light heavyweight title before losing it to Gus Lesnevich. (The NBA had stripped Conn of the title after Conn abandoned the light heavyweight division for stardom at heavyweight.)

Christoforidis wasn't as experienced as were Overlin and Yarosz, but with sixty-three fights on his ledger he knew what he was doing in a prize ring. Like Overlin and Yarosz he was not a big puncher, but wore down opponents with skills and a high punch output. Moreover, he had something left in the tank, even at thirty-four years old; he'd won two in a row since losing the championship against Lesnevich and saw the Charles fight as an opportunity to get another title shot.

For this fight Williams wanted to get Charles some sparring he could only find in New York, so he told Charles to go home and get his grandmother's permission to go to the big city. It took some convincing, but Maude relented, under one condition: that Charles' friend Richard Christmas, who she saw correctly as a bright, responsible neighborhood boy, go with Charles and keep him out of trouble. That was an easy sell—they were together all the time anyway.

Not much later Christmas took on the job formally as Charles' personal secretary and was ringside for about every fight Charles had, until all the fight had just about run out of him. But that was years later. In January 1942 they were young, strong and fearless and were headed to New York to give Anton Christoforidis an ass-whipping.

And that's what happened. Charles, a 6–5 underdog, jumped on poor Anton, *The Ring*'s fifth-ranked light heavyweight contender, and pounded him relentlessly. He dropped Christoforidis twice in the third round for counts of six, then knocked him through the ropes. Two more knockdowns followed before referee Pat Daley stopped it. Overlin, who was in the audience, told promoter Benny Becker that he'd be happy to come back to Cincinnati to give Charles a chance to avenge his only loss.[8]

On the surface, it looked like everything was going great. Charles was winning, he was starting to make decent money, and word about his potential was getting all the way to New York, which is where every fighter wanted to be. *The Ring* ranked him second at middleweight. And the day after stopping Christoforidis, Charles was back in Cincinnati, washing windows at Elkus' clothing store.

Bert Williams should have been thrilled. Instead he was panicking. He was about to lose the best fighter he had ever had and ever would have. When a young kid makes as much noise as Charles did in the ring, everyone wants to be a part of the show; everyone wants a piece of him and the guy who brought him there just wants to hold onto him. Williams had to know in the beginning that keeping Charles would be hard. But he and his wife had done a lot for Charles—enough, Williams, hoped, to keep the kid loyal. He'd brought the kid along from nothing, when he was 130 pounds and wearing the same rags day in and day out. Why shouldn't he make some money when Charles finally hit it big? Didn't he deserve it?

The problem was other people had done things for Charles too, and they wanted to get in on the ground floor. The first one to start making overtures was Max Elkus, who owned the clothing store Charles worked in after school. He and his son Gene had gotten close to Charles and his family. In fact, Charles felt so indebted to the Elkus family that even after he was making a lot of noise as a pro, he'd go back to the store when they were busy over the holidays and get behind the counter. Elkus' clothing store was one of the few shops on the West End where black folks could shop right next to white people. That was important to Charles. Once he turned pro and started winning, Elkus approached Williams and asked to buy a portion of Charles' contract. Williams resisted at first, but Charles pressured him. "I owe a lot to the Elkus family," Charles said. "They gave me jobs when other people would give me nothing, not even the time of day."[9] Eventually Williams relented.

Later, when Williams needed money to take Charles to New York, he sold another piece of the contract to Cincinnati restaurant owner Charlie Dyer. Dyer ended up bringing in George W. Rhein, an accountant at Proctor and Gamble. And Sam Becker, who'd been promoting Charles almost since the start, got a piece of him too (though few knew it at the time). One of them decided Charles needed an agent in New York to get connected there and hired Frank Bachman, former manager of Maxie Rosenbloom and Lew Jenkins. This is the way it starts. Before Williams knew what was happening, Charles was carved up six ways from Sunday.

Then one day not long after the win over Christoforidis, Bill Goebel, secretary of the Cincinnati boxing commission, showed up at Williams' front door with Theodore M. Berry, a local attorney who had befriended Charles and would later become the first black mayor of Cincinnati. They produced a pile of papers that said essentially that Williams' contract with Charles was void because Charles was a minor when he signed it. When Williams countered that Charles' grandmother had signed it too as the boy's guardian, they responded that she had no right to—Charles' mother was his guardian.[10]

As far as Williams knew, Charles' mother wasn't even in the picture, but suddenly she was there and they were threatening to throw Williams in jail for selling pieces of something he didn't own.[11] Not long after, Berry convinced a judge to make him Charles' legal guardian so he could protect the boy from the many sharks and predators that awaited him. He took great pride in his role as Charles' advisor on all things, frequently signing his letters to Charles, "Liaison Officer, Group Morale."[12] (In 1943 he sent Charles a letter scolding him for owning so many suits when the country was at war.)

When it was all done Williams was through as Charles' manager, though he could stay on and receive a salary as Charles' trainer, along with second Henry Lutz, who had begun working Charles' corner in 1941. But soon after, Charles stopped showing up at Williams' gym and hired Jimmy Brown, a former fighter, a neighbor, and occasionally one of his sparring partners, to be his chief trainer. Williams was out for good. Every once in a while after that, the two would run into one another at an event downtown, and Charles would avoid eye contact or look at the floor when Williams approached him. Usually Williams asked for money, but that wasn't why Charles avoided him.

Fighters are no good with conflict that occurs outside a prize ring and that cannot be resolved with a punch to the mouth. If they were they wouldn't be fighters. They never learn that skill because they're busy learning the ones they need to make a buck and stay alive. It takes a certain temperament and craft to talk to a man the way Charles should have talked to Williams, and Charles hadn't learned that skill. Plus, fighters like to please people, and Charles probably suspected on some level that he had done Williams wrong after all the old man had done for him.

It's hard to look in a man's face when you know you'll see your shame in his eyes, especially if you have a heart. Eventually you bury it along with all the other regrets and move on. That's what Charles did. Besides, Jimmy Brown was every bit the trainer Williams was, and Charles knew he could trust him in the corner. That's what he needed.

With Williams completely out of the picture Charles' new managers, Elkus, Dyer and Rhein, accepted Overlin's offer to rematch in Cincinnati. This was an important fight: a delegation of New York fight people, Mike Jacobs among them, arrived in Cincinnati a few days before the fight to scout Charles. Jacobs was the most powerful man in boxing. He got started in serious boxing promotion when he and three sportswriters founded the Twentieth Century Sporting Club in 1933. Two years later he signed an exclusive, three-year promotional agreement with Joe Louis that linked him to the fight game's biggest star and all but guaranteed his success.

Jacobs promoted every title defense Louis made. By 1938 his Twentieth Century Sporting Club had supplanted Madison Square Garden as the game's premier promoter, he'd either bought out or forced out the company's three co-owners, and he'd gotten in good with the gangsters who had almost as much power as he did. Jacobs could make or break a fighter's career with a single phone call. If he liked you and believed he could make money with you, you were in. If not, you didn't exist. You might as well go be a plumber or a roofer or a waiter, because you weren't going anywhere in the fight game.

Charles didn't set the Music Hall Arena on fire in his rematch with Overlin that night, but he didn't embarrass or disqualify himself either. Overlin was still fast, tricky and smart, and Charles, despite his wins over Yarosz and Christoforidis, was still a green, nineteen-year-old high school kid. The Cincinnati judges scored it a draw, which probably meant that Overlin had done enough to win; but you don't come into a young puncher's hometown and expect to win a decision unless you beat him up good. Jacobs went back to New York neutral on Charles, which was better than nothing, and Charles' managers put him in with journeyman Billy Pryor a month later. Charles outpointed him and then signed to fight Kid Tunero, a clever little Cuban who was coming off two decision losses to veteran Holman Williams.

Tunero, rated number six at middleweight, was slick and crafty as hell, but he was hot and cold, too. He might have beaten Charles that night even if Charles had trained right, but he hadn't and Tunero took him to school—right in Charles' hometown. It wasn't close and for anyone who might have had a sneaking suspicion that Charles was nothing special after all, that he never would get to New York and fight in the big ballparks or at the Garden, this confirmed it. That's how completely Tunero whipped him.

Charles' managers afterwards said that with his recent wins and growing purses, he had discovered the Cincinnati nightlife and hadn't taken Tunero seriously; and that later, his grandmother had taken the keys to his car as punishment and told him he wouldn't get them back until he got his head together and took his job seriously like she'd taught him to.[13]

Charles got a chance to get his car keys back twelve days later, when Overlin, who was in the navy, couldn't get a furlough for a fight he'd agreed to take against a much-avoided Pittsburgh middleweight named Charlie Burley underneath the Fritzie Zivic–Lew Jenkins main event at Forbes Field. Burley, at twenty-five years old, was something of a legend among the game's cognoscenti for his skills and grit and the anxiety he produced among the managers of other welterweights and middleweights. He was riding a twenty-six-fight winning streak and had won two out of three against longtime Pittsburgh hero Zivic, easily disposed of future NBA champ Billy Soose, and won the "colored" welterweight title against Cocoa Kid.

Old-timers who knew boxing ear-marked Burley as someone to avoid if you could. He was too damned good. If you had a kid you thought you could take somewhere, you kept him the hell away from Burley. He was the kind of guy who could ruin your kid on the right night, and as far as most were concerned he was better left fighting other good, black fighters no one else with a brain in his head would go after. But there were tickets sold already and the local matchmaker, Jake Mintz, had to find a replacement for Overlin and fast.

Mintz was talking about his dilemma with a Pittsburgh sports writer when the writer remembered a conversation he'd had with Chris Dundee, Overlin's manager. Dundee had called Charles "a boy who can't miss being a champ one day." The writer suggested to Mintz that he offer the spot against Burley to Charles. He was just a high school kid, but he could turn out to be something, the writer told him. Mintz, who had never heard of Charles, laughed. "Burley's a hell of a fighter and no high school kid should get near him outside of asking for his autograph," he said. The writer reminded him that Charles had just fought a draw with Overlin, which "even a college boy can't do."[14]

Mintz took a chance, and Charles' management accepted the fight. Burley, a 3–1 favorite and the number-three-ranked welterweight in the world, battled as hard as he could and made it a good, exciting fight, but never came close to winning it. In front of 12,134 paying customers who generated a gross gate of $31,686.50, Charles staggered Burley in the first round and then again in the fourth and the seventh. Burley did well in the third and fifth rounds but was well behind going into the tenth. He came out swinging for a knockout, and Charles tagged him with a counter right, dropping him for a three-count. He smacked Burley again for good measure while Burley was on a knee, prompting Burley's manager, Tommy O'Laughlin, to ask the commission afterward to disqualify Charles, a request they refused.[15]

The decision was unanimous and wide in Charles' favor. Mintz was flabbergasted. He'd never dreamed this kid from Cincinnati, whose name he thought was "Ezzra or something," would beat Burley. Nor did another ringside observer that night, a balding, highly respected trainer named Ray Arcel, who came away convinced that Charles already was a "legitimately great fighter."[16] Afterward some of the local writers wanted Charles to hang around for interviews. He politely declined, as he had to leave immediately to get home in time to attend his high school graduation the next day. When he arrived in Cincinnati, his grandmother handed him the keys to his car.

The win over Burley was such an upset that a lot of the folks in Pittsburgh thought their man had gone into it feeling under the weather, or at the least had had an off night. One of those people was O'Laughlin. Burley was just too good to have been manhandled by a kid like Charles. Burley hadn't complained about anything to O'Laughlin going into the fight, but that didn't mean anything; he wasn't the type to complain. Still, the way O'Laughlin figured, it had to be a fluke, so when Rooney-McGinley, the promoter, offered him a rematch a month later at Forbes Field again on the undercard of the Gus Lesnevich–Mose Brown match, O'Laughlin jumped at it. When that fight fell through they moved it to Hickey Park and made it the main event.

For his part, Burley knew what he was up against tackling Charles again; Charles was fast, very busy, aggressive, packed plenty of power and was bigger. He'd essentially outslugged Burley in the first fight. That had given the fans a good fight, and that was the reason the promoters expected a sellout or close to it for the rematch. But why should that matter to Burley? Really, he was a boxer first and a puncher second on account of his fragile hands, and really was at his best around 150. Burley had come in at 155 the first time because Charles was 160 and he thought that with the extra weight he could punch with him. He was wrong. For the second fight he would get down to 150 or 151, where he'd be faster. And he wouldn't try to outfight Charles—he'd out-think and outbox him. He'd make Charles lead and then counter him. That would do it. Yes, of course that was it: The extra weight had made him sluggish and he'd tried the wrong strategy. The rematch would be different.

It wasn't—at least in terms of who won. In front of almost 4,000 fans who paid up to $3.45 a ticket (setting new park records for total attendance and total gate), Charles asserted himself at the opening bell and never relinquished control, pounding Burley's body with short hooks and uppercuts whenever they got close. Burley discovered almost immediately and to his certain horror that not only could he not out-slug Charles, he could not outbox him, even at this lighter weight. The kid was just too good.

So the great and mysterious Charlie Burley, who had gotten used to making grown men between 147 and 160 pounds run for their lives, resorted to doing the only thing he could do to keep from getting knocked flat: he clinched. He held. He grabbed Charles behind the head. And he turned the fight into a bore. Charles broke free frequently enough and banged Burley's body with hooks, but whenever the action picked up, Burley went back to clinching.

He threatened just once—in the sixth, when he gambled early and landed a couple of hard combinations. But when his best blows failed to faze Charles, he returned to clinching at every opportunity and no one in the crowd would have blamed the exasperated referee, Red Robinson, if he'd disqualified him. But this was Pittsburgh, after all, or close to it; Burley was a local legend, and Robinson let him hang around to hear the decision go against him for the second time in two months.

The wins over Burley brought Charles national attention and Charles found Pittsburgh to be a home away from home. The fans there liked his style, the promoters liked him, and Mintz, the local matchmaker, was very fond of him. He immediately talked Charles' managers into signing an exclusive promotional contract with Rooney-McGinley promotions.

3

JAKE

Jake Mintz was in his late forties, but his balding head and stringy, unkempt hair made him appear older. He had been in Pittsburgh for about a dozen years, making matches for local draws Billy Conn, Fritzie Zivic, Teddy and Tommy Yarosz, Harry Bobo, and others. The son of a rabbi, he grew up in Charleston, West Virginia. He was a teenager working at a ten-cent store, demonstrating the many wonderful uses of certain carpet sweeper or another, when he heard of a dance that was to be held that evening in town. He attended and during the course of the festivities became embroiled in an argument that ended with his adversary stretched out cold on the floor.

"I grabbed a little girl and was dancing with her," Mintz recounted years later, "when this guy comes up. He's gonna punch me. I know damn well he's gonna punch me, so I punch him first. That kinda busted up the fight."[1] A local fight promoter saw Mintz lay the kid out and asked him if he wanted to fight in a preliminary the next day. Mintz had never been in a ring, but he said okay anyway and got flattened in the first round. He went back at it some more, fighting as a flyweight under an assumed name to keep his father from finding out.

Even then, with just a single fight on his resume, he understood how the business worked. He wanted as many fans as he could get so he fought under the name "Irish" Jack O'Boyle while at the same time wearing a Star of David on his trunks. By the time he finished fighting—a total of three fights later, all knockout losses—his nose featured more curves than Rita Hayworth. But he knew the fight game was where he had to be.

He seemed to know instinctively what the public liked and what made one fighter a champion and the next a palooka, and he knew all the angles. But before he could make a living in the fight business he hustled from one paycheck to the next, sleeping on pool tables and at bus stops. Gradually, and by the sheer force of his personality and stubbornness, he found a place in the business, but not before he was, at various turns, a carnival barker, a marathon-dance champion and a constable in Pittsburgh's Fourteenth Ward.

It was the last of these that Mintz found most lucrative, as he never saw a bribe he was too proud or too moral to accept. One time in 1933 the police sent him out to break up a crap game. He broke it up all right—he got in the game, got on a hot streak and walked out with $5,000 in his pocket. Not long after, Hickey Park, a smallish arena six miles from Pittsburgh, was put up for sale. Mintz posted the sale for 10:00 a.m. but sold the park to himself at 9:45. When would-be buyers started showing up at 10:00, he told them, "I guess my watch is fast."[2]

Mintz started promoting boxing shows there, and eventually he put on cards at the Old Moose, Northside Arena, Motor Square Garden, Duquesne Gardens and Forbes Field. A couple of his shows set attendance records.

Mintz knew what he was doing. He liked to brag that he could out-holler and out-lie anyone in the game. By the time he was making a decent living putting together matches in Pittsburgh, the fight press had more or less fallen for him on account of his weakness for malapropisms. Jake had never been much for schooling. He was emotional and talkative, and both fearless and a bundle of nervous energy; the combination produced quotes that were irresistible. Once, when a fighter on one of his shows was injured and had to pull out, Mintz said, "Fighters are like human beings. They get hurt, too!"[3] Mike Jacobs, he said, was born with "a gold tooth in his mouth."[4] A friend was out in the woods one day and contracted "poison ivory."[5] He once said about a rival matchmaker, "What's he know about the game? He's just a Johnny-Come-Quickly."[6] Mintz gave news "hot off the kettle" and spoke "expontaneously." He said the owners of the Pittsburgh Pirates baseball team must have been born with "a silver tooth in their mouth because they have so much money."[7] Mintz's "institution" told him who would win a fight before it happened, and he felt strongly that writers "shouldn't enlighten the public with the false facts."[8]

Most important, Mintz knew the first rule of doing business in boxing, which was that there were really no rules, outside of making sure you took care of those who could take care of you. If there were moral values present beyond that and in other enterprises in the world, that wasn't his business. He was a fight guy and did what he had to because in the fight game that's how you survived.

After the Burley rematch, Charles' management, who still consisted, on paper at least, of George Rhein, Charlie Dyer and Max Elkus, took Charles back to Cincinnati in July and put him against Steve Mamakos, who not long before had lasted fourteen rounds with middleweight champ Tony Zale and ten with top-rated Georgie Abrams. Charles stretched him in the first round, adding considerably to his reputation as a can't-miss prospect and fast-rising contender. Two weeks later it was back to Forbes Field against Booker Beckwith, a light heavyweight, in the semifinal of the Zivic–Norman Rubio main event. Beckwith, *The Ring*'s number-three ranked 175-pounder, had won his first sixteen fights before getting outpointed by slippery Bob Pastor. He then beat Joey Maxim, lost on points to Melio Bettina and whipped Andy Miller.

On paper this match appeared to be the most promising of a loaded card that some were calling the best ever held at Forbes Field. Besides Charles-Beckwith and Zivic-Rubio, it also featured Maxim against Curtis Sheppard, Harry Bobo against Claudio Villar and Anton Christoforidis against slugger Mose Brown. As it turned out, Charles-Beckwith turned out to be arguably the least exciting match of the night.

In front of 18,574 fans who generated a gross gate of almost $48,000, Beckwith recognized immediately that he was in over his head and fought accordingly—that is, to survive. Charles, who weighed 163 pounds to Beckwith's 171, won every round before knocking Beckwith cold at 2:19 of the ninth. The Chicago fighter, who coming in was touted almost as highly as Charles, was unconscious for three minutes, which served as proof that Charles was as deadly against light heavyweights as he was against middleweights.

Three weeks later Charles was back at Hickey Park, this time in the main event against Puerto Rican puncher Jose Basora, whose manager was Chris Dundee—the same Chris Dundee who managed Overlin. Dundee liked his kid to upset Charles: "Basora has the punch and style to beat Charles, and I'm looking forward to a big upset," he said. "I saw Charles fight twice against Overlin and while he is a pretty good boy, Jose can lick him. If I didn't think Basora had a chance to win I wouldn't have accepted the match for him."[9] Basora didn't lick Charles, but he had fun trying.

In front of a near-sellout crowd of 2,475 that produced a gross gate of $3,529.35, Basora was floored in the second round, the third round and three times in the fourth, all for nine counts, but whenever he wasn't on a knee he was in Charles' face winging punches. Time and again he appeared to be finished but he kept wading into Charles, fists churning. Nevertheless, he was painfully outclassed. As Charles moved in for the finish in the fifth, Basora, with his last bit of energy, blasted Charles with a series of right hands that sent Charles stumbling all over the ring. The crowd exploded. Charles was on the verge himself of being knocked out when Basora's tank finally, ran dry and then Charles did what he was supposed to do—he stepped forward and leveled Basora with a left hook, ending it once and for all.

By now Ezzard Charles was the hottest fighter in boxing. Pittsburgh fight writers couldn't praise him enough. One called him the "uncrowned champion in two divisions."[10] Another described him as "the brilliant, two-fisted middleweight package of dynamite."[11]

It was all in front of Charles now and this was the best it ever would be. He couldn't have known it then because he was in the middle of it and when you're in the middle of it you never know. Plus, he was a young kid, so he believed that the whole point was to get somewhere, to get past the struggle, and that when he got there the struggle would be over, he'd have won. That's what he lived for. It's what they all lived for—the part after the struggle. He was too young to know that this part, the struggle, was where the real living was done, that what came after was the lie. The struggle was brutal but it was pure.

Living in the middle of it, he was impatient and felt like he was fighting for every penny. It would have been good if someone had told him, enjoy it now, this is the best part; but no one did, because the people around him didn't get it either. When you're used to starving you don't want just to eat; you want to be full. No one guesses that it's when you're full that the dying starts. He wouldn't have believed it anyhow. He wanted just to push on. A month later they were back at Forbes Field again in the main event against hard-slugging Mose Brown, who had lost on points to Christoforidis on that big card in July. *The Ring* rated Brown number ten in the world at 160 pounds.

Brown, another Pittsburgh native, had already lost to Overlin a couple times and also to Tunero and Bettina. Those guys were all good boxers, and that type frustrated Brown, who was all puncher. When he had a guy who stood in front of him a little he was a good bet to stretch him; in his twenty wins he'd scored sixteen knockouts. Like all good punchers he believed too much in his power and too little in anything else, so a couple weeks before the fight his manager, George Engel, brought in Danny Ryan, a respected trainer, to smooth out Brown's rough edges. "Because Mose is a slugger, little attention was paid to his boxing," Ryan explained. "He just went out and banged away at the other fellow. We tried to teach him to shorten his punches and use his weight to his advantage. There were other tricks, too."[12]

Trainers had been trying to make boxers out of sluggers for as long as there had been either, but it never worked. Punchers are born, and any attempt to make them less than what they are ruins them. It didn't work for Mose either, and even if it had it wouldn't have mattered. There was no way in hell even the best Mose Brown who ever walked into a prize ring was going to whip a twenty-year-old Ezzard Charles. Old Mose gave a decent account of himself, as he always did, especially in the third round when he staggered Charles with a flurry. But it was all Charles otherwise, and when the knockout came at 0:51 of the sixth round, he was well ahead on the judges' scorecards.

Mintz wanted to match Charles next with a Toledo, Ohio, puncher named Shelton "Liberty" Bell, whose own promoters were touting him as a future champ. First Bell had to get by twenty-year-old Joey Maxim on a September 22 show at Hickey Park. The Pittsburgh crowd, and especially Mintz, remembered how easily Maxim had handled Curtis Sheppard back on that Forbes Field show in July, and they hoped against the odds for a win by Bell. He was a puncher, after all, and Mintz, for one, was excited about matching him against Charles in what would certainly be a slugfest.

It didn't happen; Maxim couldn't punch his way through a wet tissue, but he was all fighter and far too much for Bell, out-boxing him on the outside and out-fighting him on the inside on the way to a clear decision win. After the fight, Mintz did the only thing he could do: He matched up Charles and Maxim for October 27 at Duquesne Gardens. It would be, up to that point, the most important fight of their careers.

Joey Maxim was born Giuseppe Antonio Berardinelli in Cleveland in 1922. He started boxing at twelve years old when he stuck his head inside a suburban Cleveland gym that was in the basement of a dry cleaning store owned by Vic Rebersak. He told Rebersak he wanted to learn how to box, and after about a year in the gym, Rebersak turned him loose on the local amateurs.

Before long he was going by "Joey Maxim," after the Maxim machine gun, because of how fast he could jab. He won several Golden Gloves titles and an AAU championship as a middleweight and turned pro at light heavyweight in 1941, fighting exclusively in Chicago and Cleveland. Once he started winning, Rebersak became concerned that other managers would try to steal him away, so he talked Maxim's parents into letting him become Maxim's legal guardian. Barely out of the cradle yet, Maxim beat respected veterans Nate Bolden and Red Burman before losing a decision to Booker Beckwith. He lost a close decision to fellow prospect Jimmy Bivins in Cleveland and another to Altus Allen, and had won four in a row going into the fight with Charles. Charles opened as about a 10–7 favorite, but late money on Maxim pushed the odds closer—not only because of the clinics he put on against Sheppard and Bell, but because by now Maxim was a full-fledged heavyweight, expected to come in at about 185 pounds, compared to Charles' 165. Rebersak was confident. "My Joey he fought Jimmy Bivins and should have got the decision. I don't think Charles is so much tougher than Bivins and my Joey can handle him, I bet you."[13]

Rebersak was wrong. Maxim knew right away that he wasn't fast enough to outbox Charles nor strong enough to outpunch him, and ended up taking a ten-round drubbing in front of a crowd of 3,600 that produced a gross gate of $8,510.39. Despite being outweighed by sixteen pounds, Charles kept Maxim off-balance all night by pressing forward and hurling hard punches. His aggression and activity won him the first three rounds, which compelled Maxim to stand still and fight in the fourth and fifth.

They were his best rounds, but he came out of them with a mouse under his right eye. Several hard rights made Maxim's nose bleed in the sixth and seventh, and Charles pressed hard for a kayo over the last three rounds. Maxim clinched hard whenever Charles got close and made it to the end, if barely. Rebersak and Maxim begged Charles' management group for a rematch, in Cleveland this time, and they got it. On December 1 at Cleveland Arena, Maxim outboxed Charles over the first several rounds but slowed down after that from the body shots Charles landed. Charles dominated the second half of the fight, cut Maxim over the right eye again and had him reeling in the last couple of rounds. The result was the same as the first fight—a unanimous ten-round decision for Charles.

Not long after the rematch with Maxim, Charles found out his number was about to be called. He was going to be drafted into the U.S. Army. His attorney from Cincinnati, Theodore Bell, tried to get him re-classified, as Charles was the primary financial support for his grandmother and great grandmother. The request was denied. As far as Charles was concerned it wasn't the worst thing that could happen. The war was far from won, but things were turning the Allies' way. In February the Germans surrendered at Stalingrad in the first meaningful defeat of Adolf Hitler's armies. Not long after, the Allies took Tunisia, Africa. Things were looking up. So if he was going to go to war, this wasn't the worst time to go.

Besides that, Charles had begun to grow disillusioned with boxing. He was a world-class fighter, yet he was making peanuts fighting tough, hungry guys like Maxim and Basora and Mose Brown. He had a car and some nice things back home, things he'd never had before, but it seemed to him that everyone else was making real money, while he was the one taking punches. He wasn't getting anywhere. He should have been a Madison Square Garden fighter by now, making the big money, fighting in stadiums, being famous. But here he was, stuck in Pittsburgh or Cincinnati, fighting for his life against guys no one else wanted to fight in front of just a few thousand people. Wasn't he ranked high in two divisions? Hadn't he beaten a bunch of good fighters to get there? Wasn't he always exciting, always going for the knockout? So why wasn't he a star?

By this time in his own career, Joe Louis, his hero, had already fought in Yankee Stadium a couple times and was a fight or two away from winning the heavyweight title against Jimmy Braddock. That seemed like a million years away to Charles. Worst yet, things weren't going to change any time soon. The National Boxing Association and the New York State Athletic Commission had "frozen" all the titles so that the champions who were serving in

A young Ezzard Charles takes a break from training at his gym in Cincinnati, circa 1943 (courtesy Craig Hamilton of Jo Sports, Inc.).

the military didn't have to worry about losing their status while fighting for Uncle Sam. It made sense—why should they be penalized? But it made it hard for everyone else to make a living fighting.

Shortly after Charles whipped Christoforidis in 1942, Tony Zale, the middleweight champion, entered the navy and didn't fight again for four years. So getting a shot at the middleweight title was out. Gus Lesnevich, the light heavyweight champion, appeared in no rush to fight Charles, and the military was making it hard for him to fight at all. While in the coast guard he'd signed to fight Mose Brown in Pittsburgh on June 29. On June 20 the guard called and said his furlough had been cancelled, and called him back to active duty. Joe Louis himself had been in the service since '42. Not that Ezzard had any delusions that he'd be a heavyweight some day. But he pitied the guys who were.

There was no telling what was going to happen. In some divisions they were naming what they called "duration" champions—guys who were beating everyone else and were stand-ins for the real champions in service. Those guys got no more money in their pockets than they did before.

Charles still had big dreams—about closets full of suits, about nice automobiles, fine dining, a family he could take care of, and a life without struggle. Despite all he'd gotten done in the ring none of it was happening. Now he was going to war, and who knew what would happen after that? He wondered if those who'd told him to stay home in Cincinnati and get a nice, safe job and stay out the boxing business had been right. Regardless, he was still under contract, and a month after the Maxim fight his managers had him in with Jimmy Bivins, the third-ranked heavyweight in the world and the top-ranked light heavy. Bivins was probably the best fighter Charles would face, with Burley, whom Bivins had beaten on a close decision, the only possible exception.

Like Charles, Bivins was born in Georgia and later moved to Cleveland. He started boxing as a kid and in 1937 won the Cleveland Golden Gloves novice featherweight championship and, two years later, the 147-pound open division Golden Gloves title. He turned pro in 1940 and immediately established himself as a superior boxer, winning nineteen straight including victories over Burley, Mose Brown, Nate Bolden and other respected guys. By the time the Charles bout was signed, the twenty-four-year-old Bivins had already split a pair of bouts with Christoforidis, and had also beaten Yarosz, Soose, Lesnevich, Maxim, Bob Pastor and Lee Savold, a couple heavyweights. He was no joke.

The fight was the first in a tournament designed to crown the "duration champion" in the light heavyweight division. Charles, twenty-two years old now and almost mature, would have to be at his very best to handle Bivins, and he wasn't. He should have seen it as the biggest, most important fight of his career, the kind that would give him greater recognition and a chance again to get in front of important people again, people who could get him dates in New York down the road. Instead he saw it as a dangerous fight with a very good fighter—Bivins was a definite step up in class—with not a lot of benefit even if he won. But the army was right around the corner. What was the point?

He didn't want the fight, and he found an unlikely ally in Mintz, who felt Bivins was all wrong for him at this point. As a guy who was making good money matching Charles in Pittsburgh, Mintz knew a bad loss to Bivins would hurt Charles' earning power and indirectly his own, too. By this point he was going around claiming to be Charles' "unofficial advisor," so he took it upon himself to tell Charles' managers—who, let's face it, all were neophytes in the fight game—not to take the fight. Charles wasn't in shape for it and wasn't in the right state of mind for it. They took it anyway. It was a disaster.

In front of 10,335 fans at Cleveland's Arena, Bivins whipped Charles six ways from Sunday, dropping him in the third, fourth, fifth and eighth rounds. Charles started out well, pumping jabs into Bivins' face in the first two rounds and moving around the ring. After Bivins landed a hard right in the third and dropped him, Charles forgot about jabbing and moving and started standing and punching.

At his best or not, Charles was still a man and a fighter, and he'd be damned if he was going to let Jimmy Bivins whip him without a fight. The more he slugged the better it was for Bivins, who was a born counter-puncher. He ate up guys who came after him. And the better it got for Bivins the more Charles slugged—he had to make up for the knockdowns, and jabbing and moving wasn't going to cut it.

Bivins, who'd gotten a reputation as a clowner in recent fights, was all business against Charles and he never let him back into the fight. By the last couple rounds Charles was fighting just to not get knocked out. Afterward the United Press scored just one round for Charles, the second. The judges agreed. "I fought him wrong. I think I had an edge for the first couple rounds and I should have jabbed and stayed away from Jimmy from then on," Charles said later. "Instead I went in there to slug it out like I always do and—well, you know what happened. He's a whale of a fighter."[14]

Charles was at the lowest point of his career after the Bivins fight and was ready to enter the military without fighting again. He didn't care anymore. His managers had other ideas. This was a business, after all, and Charles' job was to make money. So right after a bad loss in which he was beaten all over the ring, they put him in with Lloyd Marshall, a hard-slugging middleweight and light heavyweight fighting out of San Francisco. Marshall had been born in Georgia, just like Charles and Bivins, and moved to one of Cleveland's rough East Side neighborhoods at a young age. He started boxing at 17, won the Cleveland Golden Gloves in 1934 and 1935, and compiled an amateur record of 219 wins and just 17 losses. He had trouble getting fights locally after turning pro, so he teamed up with a baseball player named Frank Doljack, who convinced Marshall to follow him out to the West Coast. In San Francisco, Marshall's fortunes improved somewhat and it became clear that he was no ordinary mauler.

In September 1938 Marshall pounded Overlin on the way to a ten-round decision win, and over the next couple years also beat Yarosz, Burley, Lou Brouillard and other tough, hard fighters no one else wanted to face. It was said that the mob took him over completely after he beat Overlin, and it was never a sure bet after that whether he was allowed to win on a given night. When they told him it wasn't his night then it wasn't his night. When they turned him loose and let him fight he was hell in short pants, which Ezzard Charles was about to discover.

In his first ring appearance back in Cleveland since his amateur days, Marshall jumped on Charles at the opening bell. The crowd of 10,537, expecting a lot from this young kid from Cincinnati, even after the Bivins fight, sat stunned when Marshall decked Charles in the first round. And then again in the third. And again in the fifth. Then again in the seventh, twice, and finally twice more in the eighth before referee Jackie Davis stopped it at 0:24 of the round.

Charles fell virtually every time he was hit solidly. If you knew the kid, had been watching him on the way up and knew the kind of fighter he was and what he was made of, you had to wonder what the hell had happened. He'd beaten Burley like Burley wasn't even there, and all those other good fighters. How could Marshall go through him like butter?

Later there were stories that Charles had hurt his back in training and had no business going into the ring like that, but because his managers knew he'd be going into the service soon and wanted that one last payday, they gave him something for the pain and sent him out to get murdered.[15] Others said Charles had gotten so discouraged and lazy he hadn't bothered training. Uncle Sam didn't care either way.

4

THE GARDEN

On May 14, 1943, Ezzard enlisted in the United States Army. He was shipped off for basic training to Fort Clark, Texas, where he was assigned to the Second Cavalry Division, a "colored" division that, after basic training, would be deactivated, with the personnel deployed to North Africa and then to Italy to work in service units, performing garrison and supply duties. During basic training Charles learned to ride horses and trained on firing 45-caliber pistols and M-1 Springfield rifles. All the officers were white save for a few warrant and non-commissioned officers; all the sergeants were black. As a private, Charles made about $50 a month, most of which he sent back to Cincinnati to his grandmother and great-grandmother.

It was a long way from the purses he'd earned fighting every month, and it was a shock to his system. He thought he'd been making peanuts fighting. But it was a hell of a lot better than fifty bucks a month. That wasn't all. Sleeping and eating quarters for the black soldiers in camp were separate and awful. The camp horses were treated better than the black soldiers; they had to be fed and cleaned before the soldiers could eat breakfast in the morning and again before they got dinner at night.

Charles had no intention of using his meager celebrity as a top-rated prizefighter to get special treatment while in the military, and by now he was so disgusted with the fight game that it almost felt good to be anonymous. That summer, however, there came a chance for him to show what he could do in a ring, and he could not pass it up. Word came through the camp one afternoon that they'd be getting a visit from the world heavyweight champ, the great Joe Louis, who was touring bases in the area, visiting the troops and doing boxing exhibitions with any of the army boys who wanted to mix it up with him.

Louis was twenty-nine years old and had had his last serious fight a year before—a knockout over the giant Abe Simon in Madison Square Garden. He was an almost mythic figure to the boys on the base, most of whom had come of age listening to him fight on the radio. Charles was reluctant at first to spar with his hero—army rations and the strict exercise regimen had reduced his weight to about 159 pounds, while Louis was around 200. Plus, it was Joe Louis!

But a couple of Charles' army buddies who knew of his civilian life goaded him into it, and before Charles knew it there he was in the ring with his boyhood idol and the greatest heavyweight champion who had ever breathed. They did three fast rounds, and although Louis never once went all out, he was not the kind of guy who let a kid take liberties. He kept you in line even when he was playing with you. Likewise, Charles held back too—out of respect and out of the certainty that if he accidentally caught Joe with something hard, Joe would strike back even harder, out of reflex if nothing else. Charles wanted no part of that.

Still, Charles did well enough in the first round that he felt comfortable enough in the second to try to get away with a little more for the benefit of his buddies at ringside. He bounced a hook off Louis' head. That was all the provocation Joe needed, and he proceeded to lay into Charles over the second half of the round—never all out, but hard enough to show Charles who was boss.[1]

That got Charles back in line, and he made it to the end of the third round on his feet. It had been a rough three rounds but not as bad as he thought it would be.[2] Besides, if he never tied on a pair of gloves again for as long as he lived he'd always be able to say he went three rounds with the great Joe Louis.

In February 1944 the Second Cavalry Division completed basic training and boarded a military troop train that took them to Newport News, Virginia, a three-day trip. From there they boarded a U.S. Navy vessel headed for Oran, North Africa. They arrived in Oran eleven days later, on March 9, 1944. If Charles was ever going to miss Cincinnati, with his grandmother's cooking and his car and the nightlife and the fresh air, it was during this trip, where thousands of army guys not used to the sea were crammed together like trapped rats and throwing up their guts every day.[3] When they finally arrived in Oran the division was inactivated and the personnel reassigned.

Charles landed in a truck battalion and over the following months he did what he was told, just like he had always done. He kept his nose clean, obeyed orders and when his sergeant told him to jump, he jumped. He was a model soldier, but it wasn't like he had much choice. He'd been raised to follow orders; it was all he'd ever done. He'd followed orders from his mother, from random white people in Lawrenceville, from his grandmothers, from his school teachers, from Bert Williams, and from his managers.

Following orders he was good at. But he didn't have to like it. He didn't have to like digging latrines and driving trucks and having white soldiers call him and the other men in his unit "niggers." He didn't have to like doing all kinds of dirty work reserved for the black troops while the white soldiers fought the Nazis and the Japs and got all the glory. But this was the army, so he did what he was told. In the military they like a man who can take orders, so before long he started getting promoted.

He'd made it to corporal when one afternoon he took a couple of buddies with him in his supply truck and drove outside limits while his unit was in area confinement. He got caught and was busted back down to private faster than he thought was possible and none too gently, which is the army's way. It woke him up.

It was okay that nobody in the army knew who he was in civilian life, so long as he wasn't getting admonished beyond what was normal in basic training, where the goal is to break every man down to his least significant self. This was different. He'd committed a military infraction and been demoted for it. He felt humiliated. Prizefighter or not, he really was no better than anyone else, no better than the lowliest grunt. Years later he would say that life in the military, and especially the demotion, made him take stock of himself. "I had tried taking the easy way out as far as fighting was concerned and saw it didn't pay off. Now, in the Army, I realized what it was like again when I wasn't making big money."[4]

The demotion was still fresh in Charles' mind one afternoon when one of the commanding officers told the unit that brass was looking for boxers to represent the army in tournaments across Europe. He still had no intention of revealing his background to any of the brass, even if it did mean he'd get an easier ride. He didn't even know if he wanted to go back to fighting when he got discharged. It turned out he didn't have to say a word. One of his buddies, the same one who had convinced him to spar with Louis, blurted out to the CO that they had right in their very own unit one of the best fighters around and pointed to Charles. That was that. His days of driving a supply truck were over.

Charles joined the Fifth Army boxing team in the special services unit, and after the allies liberated Rome in June 1944, he shipped out to Italy and spent the rest of his war days boxing in inter-allied tournaments and wooing the daughter of an Italian shipbuilder. Along the way he became fluent enough in Italian to converse freely with the locals and, just as he had back in his amateur days in Cincinnati, won every bout he had. In December 1944 he was entered in the second annual Mediterranean theater inter-allied championships at light heavyweight with other U.S., French and British soldiers.

Charles' Fifth Army team, the defending tourney champion, won nine bouts on the third day of competition, with Charles outpointing Corporal Stanley Goicz from Yonkers, New York. Reporters called him the "classiest clouter" in the competition.[5] He ended up claiming the tournament light heavyweight title with a points win over Private Adolph Barlow of Philadelphia. Even with his success boxing in the military, Charles wasn't sure he wanted to go back to pro fighting as his discharge approached in January 1946. He phoned his old friend back in Cincinnati, Richard Christmas, looking for advice.

Christmas told him that as soon as he came out he should go to some local shows, go watch some of the bums who were touted as future champs, look at the money they were making, guys Charles could whip easily, and then decide what he wanted to do. Christmas knew Charles would fight again, and he was right. After checking out some of the local talent Charles decided he'd be crazy to walk away from boxing. It was an awful, dirty, brutal business, but it was a job, it beat the hell out of being in the army, and he was damned good at it when he did it right, when he took it seriously and worked like he knew he should.

Back home, Charles started training almost immediately. Mintz, thrilled to have his meal ticket back in action, raced to Cincinnati and convinced Charles and his managers to sign a contract making him Charles' official booking agent and matchmaker in return for 10 percent of Charles' earnings. After the debacle against Bivins, how could they refuse? Mintz got to work immediately, lining up some easy fights for Charles in Cincinnati and Pittsburgh—Al Sheridan in February, Tee Hubert in March, Billy Duncan and George Parks in April, and Hubert again in May.

Charles won all but one by knockout. He was fighting himself back into shape, now as a light heavyweight, with the goal a shot at Lesnevich for the 175-pound title. His managers and Mintz had already offered Lesnevich $35,000 to fight there in Pittsburgh, but Lesnevich, who'd been discharged from the coast guard in 1945, declined. To increase the pressure on him they decided to go after the NBA's top-rated contender, the feared Archie Moore. Mintz made the fight for May 20 in the main event at Forbes Field's first outdoor show of the season.

Archie Moore, whose given name was Archibald Lee Wright, was thirty years old and one of the best fighters in the world. Born in Mississippi in 1913, he was adopted young by his aunt and uncle, Cleveland and "Willie" Moore, and moved to St. Louis. He soon fell in with a rough crowd and ran the streets stealing money and valuables wherever he could. By the time he was fifteen, he was a resident of the local reformatory for juveniles. After aging out of the juvenile system, he did twenty-two months at the state prison in Boonville, where he resolved never to get locked up again. He also had sixteen fights while incarcerated and decided that when he got out, fighting would be his bag. That was how he would make his living.

After his release from Boonville, Moore landed with trainer Monroe Harrison, who, back in his own fighting days, had fought out of a unique, cross-armed defense he subsequently taught Moore in the gym—when Moore wasn't knocking out sparring partners left and right. Moore called it the "shell" defense. That, along with his innate fighting intelligence and punching power, made him a feared middleweight. He turned pro in 1935 in Missouri and lost just two of his first thirty-seven fights before losing on points to Yarosz in 1939.

If it were up to him he would have fought more frequently than that. There were times when he had so much trouble landing fights he would offer to fight for free. "If you're not satisfied with the fight I put up, you don't have to pay me," he would tell promoters.[6] Sometimes it worked, sometimes it didn't. After the Yarosz fight he relocated to the West Coast and fought mostly out of the San Diego area, where he beat Nate Bolden several times and twice stopped Lloyd Marshall.

Several of his rivals disliked Moore intensely. When he knocked out Marshall in Cleveland, it was because Moore had seen Marshall stop a fighter named Harvey Massey in San Diego. Marshall was having his way with Massey and had him all but done; then he decided to knock him stiff. This offended Moore's humanitarian sensibilities; he thought the professional thing to do would have been to carry Massey to the end. There was no reason to knock him out that way. So after the fight he went to Marshall's dressing room and asked him why he had knocked Massey out like that when he already had him beat. Marshall said, "What's it to you?" Moore replied, "Nothing to me. We'll fight one day." Marshall said, "That's all right with me." They did; and Moore had him good and beat up and then stretched him in the tenth round the same way Marshall had stretched Massey.

But what goes around comes around. Afterward, who should come by Moore's dressing room but Bivins. "What did you knock Lloyd out for?" he asked Moore. "You had the fight won." Moore replied, "Because he knocked out Harvey Massey the same way. What's it to you?" Two months later Bivins and Moore fought in Cleveland, and Bivins clobbered him all over the ring and stopped him in the sixth round.[7] Moore ended up fighting Bivins four more times and won each time.

For Moore it was all hard fights, all the time, against good black fighters. Good white fighters wouldn't go near him. You couldn't blame them. So he fought the same good, hard-luck fighters over and over again—Shorty Hogue, Williams, Bivins, Eddie Booker, Jack Case, Curtis Sheppard, and Oakland Billy Smith. Moore had won 6 fights in a row and 79 out of 95 overall when he signed to meet Charles.

Moore and Charles weren't the only ones fighting for a shot at Lesnevich. They weren't even the only ones fighting over him that night. On the other side of the state, in Philadelphia, the mob-owned middleweight Billy Fox—whose manager of record was none other than Blinky Palermo—and journeyman Ossie Harris were doing the same thing. Reportedly the plan was that the winners of those two fights would meet and then that winner would get the shot at Lesnevich. Anyone who knew Lesnevich knew how it would turn out; neither Moore nor Charles would get the shot—the Fox-Harris winner would.

Title shot or not, you could forgive Charles if he was nervous going into the Moore fight. He hadn't had a serious bout against a real contender in almost three years. On that night, Lloyd Marshall beat him like a red-headed stepchild. And Moore had beaten Marshall twice. The bookies saw it that way too—though the fight opened at pick'em or just about pick'em, it closed at 10–8 in Moore's favor. They liked it too when Moore weighed in at 174 pounds to Charles' 171. It was Charles' first time as an underdog in Pittsburgh.

The odds were wrong. In front of a crowd of just under 7,000, Charles "belted Moore around the ring ... like he owned him,"[8] and in the eighth round dropped him for a nine-count with a left uppercut to the body. Everything that Charles had been before the Bivins fight he was again: fast, powerful, hungry and indefatigable.

The army had, indeed, improved him. Moore, as good as he was, and as cagey and strong as he was, never stood a chance. Everything that he could do—and that was a lot—Charles could do better and faster. Charles had Archie's number, he always would. If you had seen it you couldn't have helped but wonder where in the hell this Ezzard Charles was a couple years earlier. It was a rout and established Charles without question as the top challenger to Lesnevich.

Earlier that night in Philadelphia, Fox "stopped" Davis in the tenth round. There was no way Palermo would let Fox fight Charles if he could get Lesnevich first, which he knew he could—he was Blinky Palermo. He could get anyone he wanted. Rhein gave it a shot with the press anyway, saying, "We're ready for anyone in the world our weight, but I understand Fox doesn't want us and that Lesnevich refused $35,000 to box Ezzard for the title here."[9]

Mintz and the other managers knew they had to keep the pressure on Lesnevich, so they fought Charles again every month, just like they had before he entered the military. Three weeks after the Moore fight he was in Youngstown, where he knocked out Shelton Bell in five. Then it was back in Crosley Field in Cincinnati to face Lloyd Marshall again. If you were in Charles' corner you had to worry about him flashing back to the first fight with Marshall, but this fight had to be made. If Charles was going to stay at the top of the light heavyweight division, he had to show everyone that the knockout loss in 1943 had been a fluke.

Marshall had fought twenty-seven times between his first fight with Charles and the rematch, with mixed results against top fighters. He lost to Bivins, Holman Williams, Jack Chase, and Oakland Billy Smith, and twice to Moore. But he whipped Christoforidis, Curtis Sheppard, Nate Bolden, Jake LaMotta, Williams, Joey Maxim and Smith. He was still the kind of fighter who could bang you out on any given night of the week when he was allowed to. If you weren't at the top of your game he'd run you out of the ring.

It started disastrously for Charles in the first round when a crunching right hand and a pair of left uppercuts sent him to the canvas. He took a nine-count on a knee, but this wasn't the same Charles who Marshall had bounced around the canvas like a basketball four years earlier. When he got up he tore into Marshall, and a raging, back-and-forth slugfest ensued. Charles was faster and sharper, and his right hands and hooks started to break through Marshall's defense in the second and third rounds. A hard right hand in the fourth had Marshall reeling against the ropes and another in the fifth hurt him again. A hook to the body dropped him in the sixth, and he remained on all fours as the referee counted him out. Charles had his revenge.

By this time Mintz, was desperate to get Charles to New York. That's where the big time was. Fighters became stars in New York and in particular at Madison Square Garden. Charles had a following in Pittsburgh and Cincinnati, but no one got into the business to get a following; and besides that, Charles had the ability to go all the way. Also, the way Mintz figured, the farther he could get Charles away from Cincinnati and his managers, the more likely he was to get paper on Charles himself, real paper, none of this "booking agent" stuff that got him only 10 percent. That was peanuts compared to what he could take home if he could get Charles away from Elkus, Rhein and Dyer. He knew Charles had the goods, he knew he could make real money with him, and he knew it would be easier if he could get him to New York.

After Charles' win over Marshall, Mintz took the train to the city and got a meeting with Jacobs, without whose blessing and participation there would be no New York, no big fight, and no pot of gold at the end of Mintz's rainbow. They weren't necessarily chummy. In 1943 Jacobs had called Mintz to a meeting in New York ostensibly to sign papers for a

Lesnevich–Mose Brown title fight at Forbes Field under the Rooney-McGinley banner. It would be a big moneymaker for Rooney-McGinley and for Mintz. When Mintz arrived at Jacobs' office, "Uncle Mike," as he was known in the press, told Mintz that he would agree to the fight but only as a non-title affair. Mintz flipped. He wanted it only as a title fight. He had sunk money into it already and also into getting to New York for this meeting. This led to a heated blow-up in Jacobs' office during which Mintz used Jacobs' own phone, right in front of him, to call his contacts in the press and tell them what a rat Jacobs was. Afterward, Mintz bragged to the press that he could "out-holler" even Jacobs.[10] They'd also clashed over a proposed Fritzie Zivic–Lew Jenkins bout the year before, but had successfully worked together when Jacobs and Rooney-McGinley co-promoted the Billy Conn–Melio Bettina title fight in Pittsburgh in 1939, which made everyone a bunch of money.

The bottom line was that Mintz needed Jacobs to get Charles to the next level. He knew that. At the meeting he made his pitch for a Charles fight in New York in the summer. Jacobs wasn't sold. "Let him lick Jimmy Bivins, and I'll be interested in Mr. Charles," Jacobs told him.[11] It went without saying that Charles' managers had to be signed on with the Manager's Guild and further had to agree to slice Charles up this way and that, or make a hefty payment, or maybe both. If not for that Charles could beat Bivins a hundred times and never get close to the Garden.

Mintz did then what any good booking agent would do: He got Charles' managers to sign a deal to face Bivins again on July 1 at Forbes Field. On June 25, Bivins backed out, claiming a stomach ailment, and the fight was postponed indefinitely. Many doubted the legitimacy of Bivins' claim, as he was said to be out of shape and in the running to meet Louis in a heavyweight title fight in the fall. He was Louis' number-one challenger as deemed by Louis himself—this despite consecutive points losses Bivins had suffered to Jersey Joe Walcott and Lee Q. Murray, right at home in Cleveland. You couldn't blame Bivins' manager, Claude Shanes, if he'd concocted Bivins' illness; why fight Charles and run the risk of losing a fight with Louis for the title?[12]

Soon, Mintz would turn the tables on Bivins and Shanes, but first he had to get Charles back in the ring. He couldn't wait around for Bivins forever, so he put Charles back in September in Cincinnati, this time against Oakland Billy Smith, a limited light heavy from Oakland, California, with a thunderous punch. Long and lean, Smith had been in with all the good middleweights and light heavies around. If you were at a certain level, you were guaranteed to whip him; Charlie Burley and Bivins beat him outright. A lot of other good fighters did too. If you were right below that level you might beat him too, but there was always the chance that he might come over your jab with the right, and if he did, if he could reach you with it, chances were you were going to sleep. He was that kind of puncher.

Smith and Charles met at Music Hall in front of a crowd of 4,467, who saw Charles struggle early with Smith's strength and awkward style. Charles was clearly better than Smith, but it took him several rounds to find a way through his defense. Charles scored a knockdown in the sixth and they battled furiously to the final bell.

It was an off night for Charles, and he might have won even if he didn't have someone on the inside helping him out. One of the judges scoring the bout was Sam Becker—the same Sam Becker who had known Charles since he was fourteen years old. The same Sam Becker, who, unbeknownst to just about everyone in the arena that night, owned a small piece of Charles' contract.[13] Charles took the decision win and went on his way, and you couldn't blame him for that. Everyone needed a break or two along the way, even Ezzard Charles. Against Smith, he got it.

At Mintz's urging, Charles' management team kept Charles on the shelf until the Bivins fight could be rescheduled. They signed it for November at Duquesne Gardens in Pittsburgh. By the time the fight rolled around, Bivins had been idle a full five months. Was it because of his mysterious stomach ailment, or because his managers were waiting and hoping for a shot at Louis that would never come?

The odds makers didn't care. Bivins was a solid 8–5 favorite to repeat his victory over Charles, and 4,971 fans, about a thousand under capacity, showed up to see him try, generating a gross gate of $22,376.51. Charles, who was outweighed by eleven pounds, started fast, stabbing Bivins with quick, sharp punches over the first two rounds. In the third Bivins banged home a right, and just as in the Williams rematch, Charles went down and took a nine-count on one knee (Bivins' managers protested later that Charles received a slow count). Bivins rushed out in the fourth and planted a hook below the belt. Charles shook it off and later in the round staggered Bivins with a screaming right cross. Charles dominated the next three rounds but couldn't put Bivins away. "I hit him pretty good and pretty often but those big fellows—why, nothing much happens when you hit them. They don't seem to move," Charles said later.[14]

Bivins rallied hard over the last three rounds, but Charles stayed right with him and won the decision by scores of 7–3, 7–3 and 6–3–1. Bivins blamed the loss on inactivity and explained why he didn't take an easy fight to get rid of the rust before facing Charles. "I'm in boxing not because I like it any too good but because I can make money out of it," he said. "The tune-up fight wouldn't have paid peanuts and so I passed it up and went in against Charles this way."[15]

The fight was just good enough to warrant and sell a rubber match. Before the night was over Cleveland promoter Larry Atkins had come to terms with Mintz and the rest of Charles' management team to do it again. Over the next week Charles' schedule for the next several months shaped up this way: a rematch with Booker Beckwith in Chicago (Charles had stopped Beckwith in 1942); the rubber match with Bivins in Cleveland; Erv Sarlin in Pittsburgh; and then a rematch with Oakland Billy Smith in Cincinnati. All were postponed when Charles, training at his gym in Cincinnati, pulled a tendon in his right hand on January 11.[16]

Around the time that Charles whipped Bivins in Pittsburgh, Jacobs, the most powerful man in all of boxing, suffered a mild stroke at his home. Its effects, which included some minor paralysis in his face, mostly dissipated over the next eighteen hours and were forgotten. His doctors told him to take it easy, but Mike Jacobs had not gotten to where he was by taking it easy, and temperaments such as his are not easily modulated. On December 3, while preparing for a vacation trip to Miami, he was visiting a chiropractor friend in a building two blocks from Madison Square Garden when he collapsed from what was found to be a cerebral hemorrhage.

It was serious enough to render him incapable of any longer running his beloved Twentieth Century Boxing Club, and day-to-day operations were turned over to his longtime lawyer and confidante, the capable but comparatively plain-minded Sol Strauss. The occurrence of Jacobs' illness effectively ended an era in boxing when he and Joe Louis ruled the sport like no two others had, including Jack Dempsey and Tex Rickard. Fortunately for Charles and his team, Strauss had no great, secret plan of his own he'd always wished to put into effect if only given the chance, and Jacobs' promise to show Charles in Madison Square Garden if he beat Jimmy Bivins was still good as far as Strauss was concerned.

Meanwhile, Charles spent the time waiting for his hand to heal hanging around with friends in Cincinnati. They were outside Winthrow High School on the east side one afternoon when a gaggle of girls came out and piled into a car to go home. One of them caught Charles' eye. She was gorgeous: a 5'7", 130-pound, fair-skinned beauty. Lena Horne had nothing on this girl. As Charles watched the group drive off, he'd already resolved to find out who she was.

It didn't take long to get the skinny. She was eighteen-year-old Gladys Gartrell, high school senior and daughter of a white father and bi-racial mother, a pretty rare circumstance for 1940s Cincinnati. She lived in nearby Madisonville. Charles, never particularly shy around the ladies and even less so now that he was a celebrity of sorts, got right to work on asking Gladys out. She declined, gracefully and firmly, but Charles, twenty-five years old now and mature, wasn't the type to give up easily, and he kept at it.

Gladys wasn't a boxing fan and so wasn't impressed with his stature. Besides, a proper lady played hard to get, and she was a proper lady. He knew this of course, and naturally, the more she declined the more attractive she became to him, and the more resolute he became about dating her. That's the way it always worked. He could have, and did have, a lot of girls in town. He was a successful athlete and was making money, and on most nights that was all it took. It was easy. But she made him work for it, which gave him the impression, which was quite accurate, that she was worth the effort.

When she entered a contest in school that required her to sell tickets to a local event, he bought the whole lot of them. Even that didn't work. But he didn't give up. Girls as pretty and refined as "Gee-Gee," as he started calling her, didn't come around every day. She had no shortage of suitors, either, and he'd be damned if he'd let himself be outworked by some other guy.

Charles still hadn't made much progress with Gladys when he invited her to come to Music Hall to see him fight Oakland Billy Smith again in February, when his hand had finally healed. She declined, and missed seeing Charles stop Smith in seven rounds in much better form that he'd shown in their first fight. Next up was the rubber match with Bivins in Cleveland. Bivins was still rated near the top of both the light heavyweight and heavyweight divisions, as was Charles. The fight couldn't be more important, and it turned out to be the highlight of Charles' career.

In front of a near-capacity crowd of 11,519 at the Arena, Charles, weighing 170 pounds to Bivins' 184, scored an electrifying fourth-round knockout, stretching Bivins for the full ten-count at 1:14. Charles stunned him with right hands in the first two rounds, but Bivins was rapidly making his way back into the fight when a left-hook, right-cross combination put him on his back.[17] Commission doctors had to revive Bivins, who had never before been counted out.

After the fight Mintz reached out to Strauss to remind him what Jacobs had said about getting Charles a summer fight in New York if he beat Bivins. Now he'd beaten him twice. Strauss was on board. In fact, it was better than just a fight in Madison Square Garden. If things fell together right, Strauss told Mintz, Charles could get a fight with Louis for the heavyweight title in September.

This was the last thing Charles expected or wanted. He wanted the championship, but he had never dreamed he'd have to fight Joe Louis to get it. He'd have been satisfied to win the light heavyweight belt from Lesnevich and been done with it. That he was being talked about as a challenger for the great Joe Louis seemed ridiculous. He needn't have worried. A lot of things would have to happen for him to get Louis now, because a lot of things had changed.

In 1945, Louis got out of the army early after receiving the Legion of Merit. He was a greater hero to Americans than he'd been even before the war, but at thirty-one he was no longer the same fighter. He was slower, more ordinary than he'd been in the 1930s—almost mortal. It was apparent in his very first fight back, his June 1946 rematch with Billy Conn.

Their brilliant fight in 1941, won by a knockout by Louis in thirteen rounds, saw them both in their prime, two exquisite heavyweights—or, more accurately, an exquisite heavyweight and his light heavyweight equal. The 1946 rematch was desultory and lethargic in comparison, and Louis stopped Conn in eight sad rounds. The crowd even booed the lack of action. Could you imagine—a crowd booing Joe Louis? The war years had taken just about everything out of poor Billy. Louis had more left, but then, he'd started with more.

Three months later Louis dusted poor Tami Mauriello in a round. That felt like old times, but Mauriello was made for Louis like a good suit. He fit perfectly. That wasn't all. By this time Jack Blackburn, Louis' longtime trainer, was dead. A heart attack had taken him in 1942. One of his managers, John Roxborough, was in jail for running a numbers racket. The other, Julian Black, had refused to lend Louis $25,000, so Louis let their contract expire. Mannie Seamon was the new trainer. Marshall Miles was the new manager. They loved Louis and did their best for him, but it wasn't like it was before the war.

Most of all there was the debt. The federal government was after Louis to the tune of some $200,000 in taxes they said he owed. What did he know from taxes? He got paid a lot; a lot of guys, who knew how many by now, took their shares; he blew a lot of it on the golf course and gave a lot of it away, but he was rich. That's what he was supposed to do.

He went through it as fast as he made it. There were too many pretty women out there, too many parties, too many sure things, and too many folks with their hands out to keep it all to himself. What was he going to do—put it in a bank? He was Joe Louis. He could make more money any time he wanted. And sooner or later he'd make a deal with the feds to get square with the money. He didn't lose sleep over it, but it sure wasn't like the old days.

So late in 1946 they started looking around for an opponent for Louis for the summer of '47. There wasn't much out there. Bivins was a possibility, and the idea had some appeal since he'd been the "duration" champ while Louis was in the army, but then he had lost to Charles. Charles was ruled out at least initially as too small—he'd weighed only 170 for Bivins and as far as Miles was concerned the fans would see that fight as a mismatch (even though Conn weighed about that when he almost beat Louis in 1941).

But if Charles could prove he could handle a good, bigger heavyweight, maybe they could sell it. Strauss convinced Charles' management group to make his New York debut against 6'2", 200-pound veteran Elmer "Violent" Ray on June 27. (It was later rescheduled for July 25 when Ray reportedly came down with tonsillitis.) Ray had been campaigning for a shot at Louis for years. If he won and won good, maybe he'd finally get the fight. Same went for Charles.

Louis, who was calling the shots by this time as much as Strauss was—Joe had never had much say-so when Jacobs was running things—had one requirement: The winner had to win decisively and look good doing it. That was the only way to sell a fight against either of them. The only other contender they strongly considered was hulking former Pennsylvania coal miner Joe Baksi, who'd strung together a couple good wins in England against Freddie Mills and Bruce Woodcock, the top heavyweights in Great Britain. He held one big advantage over Charles and Ray in terms of getting the fight with Louis; he was white. White guys sold better, no matter who the opponent was. Against Louis they were gold. Two other opponents were considered briefly: the capable southpaw light heavyweight

Melio Bettina, and Camden, New Jersey's Jersey Joe Walcott. Bettina fell out of the running when Lesnevich knocked him out in less than a round in the Garden on May 23.

This was all great news to Mintz and the other managers, who did what they had to do to get Charles a date in the Garden. Ezzard had done his part, they had done theirs, and no one had to know any more than that. But June was three months away and there was money to be made, so in April Charles was back in Pittsburgh at Duquesne Gardens against local hero Erv Sarlin. Sarlin, who'd been born in Germany, had come up as Billy Conn's stablemate but that was all he and Conn had in common. He was mostly a clubfighter, but his rough, brawling style endeared him to Pittsburgh fight fans. They raised the roof for him when he overcame a 30-pound weight disadvantage to beat Pat Comiskey at Forbes Field in '46. He was their kind of fighter, and 5,277 came out to cheer him on against Charles, generating a gate of $20,075.45. He needed more than cheers.

Weighing 182 to Charles' 176, Sarlin jumped on Charles at the opening bell, pushing him back and trying to force an inside fight. But this was child's play to Charles by this time. He rode out the early storm and was in complete control by the end of the second. Over the next seven rounds Sarlin enjoyed momentary successes, such as when he aggravated Charles with body blows in the fourth, fifth and ninth rounds. Otherwise he absorbed a terrific beating, resulting in, as one writer put it, "his face appearing as if it had been given the once-over-lightly treatment by a buzz-saw."[18] Charles won a unanimous and lopsided decision. Sarlin had to settle for continuing his laudable streak of never having been knocked to the canvas in a professional prizefight.

The train kept rolling. Mintz inked another fight with Moore, a ten-rounder, this time in Cincinnati in May with Sam Becker promoting. It was risky considering they had already lined up a date at the Garden and a possible shot at Louis. But it was worth it. By this time the NBA had, in the press at least, grown weary of Lesnevich's refusal to face either Charles or Moore, his top two challengers, and "mandated" that he face the winner.

If the Ray fight fell through, they'd still have the light heavyweight title to shoot for. They had to keep the pressure on Lesnevich. Becker, hopeful of luring Lesnevich into facing Charles in the fall, had Gus and his wife come to Cincinnati for the fight, all expenses paid, and offered him $75,000 for a match at Crosley Field. He also tried to stir up excitement by announcing, entirely falsely, that Conn, who hadn't fought since losing the rematch to Louis, said he would face the Charles-Moore winner.

You couldn't fault Becker for trying. He sensed a less-than-capacity turnout and was proved right when 4,502 fans came out, generating a gate of $23,281.50. It wasn't a terrible showing, but the matchup warranted better: Charles hadn't lost since getting discharged from the army. Moore, since their last fight almost exactly a year before, had knocked out Buddy Walker, Jimmy O'Brien and Jack Chase, drawn with Chase and Oakland Billy Smith and outpointed Rusty Payne. His claim that he had been sick with the flu for his first bout with Charles could not be made now. He was in perfect fighting shape. Still, the oddsmakers made him the underdog. It was 2–1 that Charles would win and 5–6 that he would knock Moore stiff.

It was indeed a better Moore than the one who lost to Charles in Pittsburgh, but not better enough. Moore, weighing 172 to Charles' 173½, got some work done by staying inside all night, away from the end of Charles' long-range bombs. Whenever Charles tried to line him up for the right hand, Moore slipped inside. Charles then had to reset his feet to get back into punching position. It tied him in knots. "I just couldn't seem to find the right kind of opening," he said later.[19]

When a power puncher like Charles can't let his bombs go, the action suffers. As early as the fourth round some in the crowd were booing. That didn't stop Charles from pounding Moore's body and landing enough to get a slight edge on the scorecards. Still, Moore frustrated him, and as a result Charles landed low a half-dozen times. However, he got the benefit of the doubt from referee Tony Warndorf. In several rounds he and Moore continued punching after the bell. It was still anybody's fight in the sixth when Moore tried an overhand right that Charles saw coming. He dipped left and dug a left to Moore's body, dropping him for a nine-count, just as he had in their first fight.

Moore and his manager, Charlie Johnston, claimed the punch was low. Warndorf disagreed. Whether it was low or not, the punch slowed Moore down enough for Charles to assert himself over the last few rounds. It was a close fight and Moore was dangerous enough late to open a bad cut over Charles' left eye in the eighth round. At the end one judge called it a draw; the other two had it 6–3–1 for Charles. It was a win, but not the kind the fans and press had come to expect from Charles, especially after the way he'd laid out Bivins. He'd won, but he "didn't look like the sock-wizard of old,"[20] as one writer observed.

Some in the crowd even booed the decision. The only happy one was Moore, who apparently was delighted that even if he didn't whip Charles, on some level he'd out-smarted him. He grinned widely while telling reporters he knew Charles wanted to throw the right cross. "But Ez was smart enough to know that I wouldn't be there to receive it if he did."[21]

The win over Moore made Charles unquestionably Lesnevich's top contender, but with no offers of a title shot coming and Charles' New York debut still two months away, Mintz knew he had to get an interim fight. He didn't want to go into the Ray fight rusty. It was too important, so he made a fight against former West Virginia coal miner Hilton "Fitzie" Fitzpatrick at Crosley Field on July 14, just ten days before the Ray fight. Fitzpatrick, legend had it, had been deaf until he turned fourteen. He started reading the Bible and then started boxing and between the two, his deafness was cured. Mintz figured he'd be an easy tune-up.

Fitzpatrick was a level below Moore, Bivins and other guys Charles had been beating. He'd lost to Joe Kahut several times and to Lloyd Marshall and others, but had recently beaten past-his-prime Lee Savold and the capable Pat Valentino. He was barrel-chested and thick-armed, an exciting, two-fisted puncher, but he had little in the way of boxing skill. Charles ate those guys for lunch, and so was a considerable favorite to win by knockout. Meanwhile, on the same night in Syracuse, New York, Elmer Ray would face Scranton, Pennsylvania's Howard Chard in his own tune-up.

Ray stopped Chard in seven rounds, knocking him down five times. Charles stopped Fitzpatrick in the fifth but almost lost everything in the process. Weighing 174 to Fitzpatrick's 184½, Charles had things all his own way in the first round, as was expected. In the second, Fitzpatrick came over the top of a Charles jab with an overhand right, and down went Charles, head over heels onto his back. The crowd of 7,173 (producing a gate of $27,344) exploded and Charles, hurt worse than at any time since his loss to Bivins, barely beat the count. He grabbed and held until the round was over and many, even his own Cincinnati fans, thought he was aided by a slow count and accommodating referee.

Nevertheless, the minute of rest revived him. He came out punching in the third and late in the round put Fitzpatrick down for a nine-count. He continued battering Fitzpatrick in the fourth, and in the fifth, a left-hook, right-cross combination, just like the one that had flattened Bivins, put Fitzpatrick down for the count at 2:43. Disaster had been averted, but barely. Years later Charles recalled Fitzpatrick as one of the hardest hitters he'd ever faced. "Fitzpatrick never got anywhere but how that boy could punch. He hit me one in our fight in Cincinnati and I thought the roof caved in," he said.[22]

Three days after Charles survived Fitzpatrick, his managers made it official and hired Mintz away from Rooney-McGinley to become Ezzard's matchmaker full time. It ended some fourteen years that Mintz had spent making and putting on shows in Pittsburgh, but he knew a good thing when he saw it.

Charles was back in the gym almost immediately, getting ready for his New York debut. He had to be sharp—Elmer Ray was a deadly puncher, especially with the left hook. He'd put together some impressive knockout streaks over his long career—fifteen straight after a loss in his first pro bout, another seventeen straight from November 1945 to November '46. He'd lost just once since 1943—in some fifty-one fights—and that a close decision to Walcott. Though to be honest, most of the fifty-one were ham-and-eggers. There weren't a lot of top guys on his resume. Also, the papers said he was thirty-one, but no one really knew his age.

According to the lore, Elmer Ray was born into a family of six girls and three boys to a potato-and-cabbage farmer near Hastings, Florida. The family didn't own a Bible in which to record the birth dates of each of their kids, which was the custom in those parts, so they kept a record by making notches on the trunk of an oak tree that sat on their property. Some time after their ninth child was born, a fire burned down part of the tree and seared off the notches.[23] After that, everyone's age was more or less a guess. Ray might have been thirty-one. He might have been thirty-five. No one really knew, or if they did they weren't saying. It was enough to know that he'd come up winning battle royal tournaments and wrestling alligators in carnivals. He was a big, strong heavyweight, the biggest man Charles would face yet. He had been around the block a few times already and had been campaigning for a shot at Louis for years.

There was a minor controversy around why Ray never got a title shot during the four years that he was one of Louis' top contenders. Some believed Louis feared him. They got that idea back in 1945 while Louis was in the army and refused to face Ray in an exhibition fight in Chicago, even after his manager had booked it, and even with the bigger gloves they wore in exhibitions. Louis' exhibitions were almost real fights, and Ray was a top heavyweight, eager to make a name for himself. He'd have gone after Louis hard, and Louis knew it. Honest to a fault, Joe told reporters, "I'm in no condition for a fellow like Ray. He's a good hitter and a good fighter. I'd have to have two or three months training to go in with him."[24] Louis knew he wouldn't be able to pull his punches with Ray, that he'd have to go all out and one of them would get hurt.

Ray saw this as cowardice and never let Louis live it down while trying to get a fight with him. Louis, a humble man but a very proud fighter, took offense and decided then that he'd never fight Ray; he'd never give him that payday. Prizefighters are funny like that. You fight another man as a favor to him. You try to knock his head off so he can feed his family. The ones you really dislike you let starve. Ray had a big mouth. He disrespected Louis. That was the worst thing he could do. Besides that, Ray was black as night, and white challengers sold better against Louis. They sold better against everybody.

Finally there was the timing. When Ray was wreaking havoc in the division, mostly between 1944 and '46, Louis was in the army. By the time he got out, Ray looked like he'd lost a step, even though he'd recently split a pair of fights with Walcott. As far as he knew, the fight against Charles was his last chance at getting Louis in the ring. He had to win and win big. If that wasn't pressure enough, three weeks before the fight, the stakes increased substantially when Baksi, a 5–1 favorite, was upset in Stockholm by unknown Swedish champion Olle Tandberg. Theoretically, this narrowed down the field to the Charles-Ray winner and Walcott.

The bookies thought it would be Charles. Despite Ray's edge in experience and size, they made Charles a solid 11–5 favorite. This was due in part to Ray's age, in part to Charles' reputation, and in part to a stunning admission made a few days before the fight by Ray's manager, Tommy O'Loughlin. "I wouldn't bet a nickel on this fight. I don't know how Ray's shoulder will hold up," he told reporters after Ray finished a workout at the Catholic Youth Gym. "He hurt it in his fight with Jersey Joe Walcott in Miami last winter. He's liable to throw the shoulder out at any time."[25] The writers were shocked. O'Loughlin had been a loud and tireless supporter of Ray over the years and routinely told anyone who would listen that his man would knock Louis flat.

If you'd been around the game you had to wonder what was going on. Why would he do that to his fighter right before the most important fight of his career? It was baffling. Mintz, for his part, was doing what he always did—acting the part of Charles' manager, even though he was no such thing. Speaking from Fred Irvin's gym in Harlem where Charles was training, Mintz said, "Charles is in the best shape of his career. He will knock out Ray within four rounds."[26]

Mintz was earning his 10 percent share as Charles' matchmaker. The night before the fight he left the city and rushed back to Pittsburgh. When he arrived back in New York the next morning, a writer asked him why he'd left. It was to do a radio broadcast. "I went back to give my illusions on the fight and make my predicament," he said. "And what was your predicament?" the writer asked. "Charles in six rounds."[27] There were other predictions being made too. Based on early ticket sales, Strauss was expecting about 12,000 to show up at the Garden, producing about a $50,000 gate. Not bad for a Cincinnati kid's New York debut.

On fight night Ray's shoulder held up, at least well enough to get him a mostly unpopular split-decision win. Weighing 194½ to Charles' 174¾, Ray did what he always did: he came forward, bobbing and weaving and banging away at Charles' body and head with hooks and overhand rights. There was nothing subtle about Ray in a prize ring, and he didn't try to surprise anyone. If you could catch him on the way in enough and do damage, you could stay the whole route and maybe wear him down and get work done of your own. But his strength and work-rate could overwhelm you.

Which scenario played out against Charles depends on who you believed. This much was true: Charles did not attempt at any time to back up Ray and out-fight him. Ray was not Jimmy Bivins or Archie Moore. Charles was not going to overpower him. He was too strong. So Charles did what made sense: he used his youth and his speed and his legs to keep Ray at a distance and outbox him. He clinched whenever Ray got inside and kept his ass off the ropes. And he caught Ray a lot on the way in. He did what he was supposed to do. So did Ray. At the end, no one was sure what they had seen.

Referee Eddie Joseph and judge George Lecron saw a fairly close fight, scoring it 6–4 for Ray. The United Press saw a squeaker, giving it to Ray 5–4–1. One writer determined that anyone seated close enough to the action could see that Ray was the rightful winner. "From 10 rows back it looked like Charles all the way ... but inside 10 rows you could see the devastation wrought by Ray's jarring hooks, blasts which raised a shelf on Ezzard's cheeks."[28] This was not a universally held opinion.

Judge Marty Monroe saw Charles as the obvious winner, giving him eight rounds to

Ray's two. *The Ring* magazine reported, "Ray was the aggressor most of the way, but Charles was faster, the better boxer, and the sharper hitter."[29] Another writer was aghast at the outcome. "The decision ... was, of course, regrettably bad. The man who lost the fight was acclaimed as the winner and the tally sheets prove that two judges were so far apart in their views that it is almost inconceivable that they were looking at the same fight.... I couldn't find anyone who thought it was even reasonably close."[30] *The Ring* said Ray was "presented with a gift verdict."[31] "While ringsiders thought Ezzard won, Ray was given a split decision. The action smelled from gorgonzola," one writer reported.[32]

Ray, quite naturally, was ecstatic. His insistence over the years that Louis was ducking him had made him some enemies, because you didn't say those things about Joe Louis. It didn't matter whether Ray believed it himself or was just trying to get himself a decent paycheck to make up for all the years he'd been fighting for peanuts. When you went around saying Joe Louis was afraid of you, a lot of guys were going to call you a bum. Lousy decision or not, this was Ray's proof that they were wrong. "Yeah, I'm a bum," he said with a big grin. "Charles—huh! He's a good light heavyweight and fast but he couldn't knock my hat off."[33]

Ray's mood turned less celebratory when Strauss told him that at some point between April and July, the Louis offer went from a title fight in September to maybe a non-title match in November. O'Laughlin exploded, insisting that they'd been promised a title shot. Poor O'Laughlin. He'd been duped. Ray wasn't going to get even the non-title shot, never mind a chance at the world title. Louis still hated his guts.

When a writer asked him why he wasn't defending the title against Ray, Louis replied, "Why, he couldn't knock out a man weighing 110 pounds, let alone weighing 200 pounds." He went on to say that he had refereed one of Ray's early fights in Cleveland, didn't care much for him then, and didn't think he'd changed since. "I decided then I didn't want to meet Ray and I still don't," he said.[34]

From an economic standpoint, Strauss, Miles and Roxbourough, who had been paroled from prison and released into Louis' custody in October '46, all agreed that Charles and Ray had eliminated one another. Neither had been impressive enough to get a fight with Louis. Consensus among the New York writers who had never seen Charles before was that he should have gotten the decision, but he hadn't been exciting enough to make anyone care. He'd blown his big opportunity. But really, it was just as well. It was too soon. And among Louis' possible title challengers, only Jersey Joe Walcott remained. In August Louis made it official: he'd meet Walcott in Madison Square Garden later in the year.

5

BAROUDI

Jersey Joe Walcott was born dirt-poor Arnold Cream in Pennsauken, New Jersey, in January 1914. His father, Joseph Cream, an immigrant from St. Thomas, Virgin Islands, died when Walcott was fourteen. Like a good son, Walcott dropped out of school and worked in a soup factory to help support his mother and eleven brothers and sisters. He started boxing around the same time, taking the name Joe Walcott from the old welterweight Barbados Joe, and added "Jersey" to identify where he was from.

He turned pro in 1930 at age sixteen, stopping Eddie Wallace in the first round for a purse of $7.50. From the earliest days he showed sneaky power, especially with the right hand. He developed a busy, herky-jerky style that drove opponents crazy and often got away with dropping his hands and shuffling right and shuffling left, right in his opponent's punching range, because he was faster than most of them and smarter. He loved to walk away from an opponent and then jump in with a right hand and peck and move, peck and move, and then lay in a hard one. He was a master at feinting and at dropping in a fast right over an opponent's low left. He looked infinitely at home in the ring, and for a "cutie," boy could he punch. He did a lot of things wrong in the ring, but he did them the right way. There was no one else like him.

There was one problem with Walcott, and it was that he couldn't get a break; and he couldn't get a break because he wasn't connected. He was very good, very hungry and very poor. Early in his pro career the great Jack Blackburn trained him but before long left him high and dry to train a young kid out of Detroit named Joe Louis. That was the last Walcott worked with Blackburn until he was hired to be one of Louis' sparring partners for Louis' first fight with Max Schmeling in 1936. Even that didn't last long—Walcott was fired after a few days' work after, reportedly, decking Louis.

Walcott married young, had a boatload of kids fast—seven by the time they were done—and struggled just to stay alive. When there was work at the shipyard in Camden, he pocketed enough for crumbs and rent for the shack they all lived in. For a while he went on welfare, a misery he never got over. He took odd jobs where he could get them, and all the while he kept fighting for pennies against good, tough fighters, sometimes on just a day's notice with barely enough food in his stomach to keep a field mouse alive. On most nights he got by on sheer guts and talent in clubs in Camden, Atlantic City and Philadelphia.

He beat some good fighters—Willie Reddish, for instance, and Elmer Ray, and Curtis Sheppard. He lost to some too—Tiger Jack Fox, Roy Lazer and George Brothers beat him. Al Ettore knocked him out when they were building up Ettore as an opponent for Louis. His managers came and went—Roxie Allen, Tommy Marchisello, Billy Brooks, Sonny Banks and others—but no one could move him; no one could get him more than $25 or $50 a fight.

He retired a half-dozen times but always came back, always hoping for the one break he needed. Some years he didn't fight at all, some years just once. The low point came in 1940 when the gigantic but talentless Abe Simon stopped him in six rounds in Newark. Walcott boxed rings around him early but just didn't have enough gas in the tank to get to the end. He'd been in the game eleven years and had nothing to show for it. He didn't fight again, on the record at least, until 1944. He hardly cared anymore. He was ready to quit for good.

It was around Christmas that year that Walcott finally got his break. He was in a local grocery store looking for a cheap bird for Christmas dinner. So too was a small-time, local promoter named Felix Bocchicchio. He recognized Walcott as a fighter. When Walcott left, Bocchicchio told the clerk at the store to send the biggest bird he had over to Walcott's house. Three weeks later Walcott showed up at Bocchicchio's office. Bocchicchio gave him a few bucks to help him get by. Not long after, a few more bucks. They struck up a friendship. Bocchicchio told Walcott to come fight for him, to join his stable. Walcott said he wanted to get back to boxing but couldn't feed his family on $15 purses. Bocchicchio responded, "Try my club and you'll get every penny you're supposed to get. If you're serious, want to work and get in shape, I'll go along with you."[1]

Walcott agreed and his whole world changed, almost overnight. He still lost now and then—to Joey Maxim, to Ray—but he won twelve in a row from February 1945 to August 1946, beat Bivins, Maxim and top-rated Joe Baksi, and for the first time in his career had no trouble finding fights. He had enough to eat. He moved his family to a nice, furnished house in Camden. His children didn't wear rags to school anymore. On the record, his manager was still a local guy, Joe Webster. But that was a technicality. Bocchicchio was running things and for Walcott, that was a good thing.

It had taken him sixteen years, but Jersey Joe finally was on his way. And it was all due to Bocchicchio, who the public saw as a credible, earnest sort who once, long before he got into boxing, had had a few minor scrapes with the law. They were under-informed. Among other charges involving larceny, illegal gambling and jail-breaking, Bocchicchio had been questioned in connection with a murder in 1934 and was tried and acquitted in connection with the robbery of a tavern in 1935. Most of the guys on the beat knew more, but they didn't write or say anything because they knew better. They knew what spilling the beans would get them and what playing along would, too. This is how the world worked. They didn't have to like it.

According to the FBI, Bocchicchio was more than just a former small-time hood. He was a known criminal associate of "Blinky" Palermo[2] and he, along with Palermo, Ettore "Eddie" Coco, James "Jimmy Doyle" Plumeri, and Harry "Champ" Segal, all noted mafia soldiers, formed the group known in the underworld and to the FBI as "the Combination." The Combination was known or suspected to have fixed dozens of prizefights during the 1940s. These were Bocchicchio's people.

This was Jersey Joe's promoter, his savior. Could Walcott fight? Hell, yes. Was Bocchicchio fixing all his fights to make him look good? No. Did he make it so that Walcott and his family could live like humans instead of animals? Yes. Did he get Walcott fights against bigger names and get him paid? Yes. And were there times when Bocchicchio asked Walcott for a favor in return for everything he'd done for him and would do for him in the future? How couldn't there be?

As far as Walcott was concerned, before Bocchicchio he had gone to bed hungry every night. Every goddam night for ten years. So had his kids. After Bocchicchio joined the team everything was better. Bocchicchio knew the people he needed to know to get Walcott's career moving. So what if they weren't all boy scouts? Bocchicchio didn't create the business;

he just knew how to make it work for him. That's all a fighter could ask of a business associate. Felix Bocchicchio was the best friend a guy like Walcott could have.

Ezzard Charles didn't have a connected guy like Felix Bocchicchio moving him, but things could have been a lot worse. He could have gotten beaten up by Elmer Ray in the Garden. Instead, he'd lost a decision that the majority of writers thought probably was dirty even if he'd been so dull they didn't care much.

His New York debut was not the time to get boring, but boxing Ray instead of punching with him seemed the way to go. Mintz thought so; Jimmy Brown thought so. Charles would have punched with him, but he listened to his corner and felt he'd won the fight anyway. They all did.

Charles returned to Cincinnati fairly despondent. It didn't help when Max Elkus, one of his earliest supporters and one of his three managers, died after a lengthy illness. Max's son, Gene, inherited his father's share of Charles' contract. On the bright side, Charles had finally worn down Gladys to the point where she agreed to go out with him. Seven grueling months of courtship had finally paid off, and Charles spent much of the next five weeks with his new best girl. Then it was back to work. Mintz and the other managers brought him back against light heavyweight club fighter Joe Matisi in Buffalo on September 16. Charles was back in form, flooring Matisi four times on the way to winning a clear ten-round decision.

Next it was a rubber match with Lloyd Marshall at Crosley Field. Since losing to Charles in their rematch a year before, Marshall had fought just twice, but in one fight he had scored a significant victory. Fighting in London, he knocked out British light heavyweight champion Freddie Mills in five rounds in a non-title match, upsetting a planned rematch between Mills and Lesnevich (Lesnevich had stopped Mills in ten rounds a year before).

Marshall was thirty-four years old by this time and not the fighter he had been, the win over Mills notwithstanding. Charles knew this and tore into Marshall at the opening bell. Weighing 173 pounds to Marshall's 168, Charles had Marshall in trouble before the fight was two minutes old. Marshall barely made it out of the first round, and Charles jumped on him to begin the second. Three knockdowns later it was all over at 2:25. Charles now had twice clearly beaten Bivins and Marshall, effectively rendering their wins over him before Charles entered the army irrelevant.

Over the next couple of months, Mintz kept Charles busy against guys who had no chance against him. On October 16 it was Al Smith in Akron, Ohio. Charles stopped him in four. Eleven days later Charles knocked out Clarence Jones in the first in Huntington, West Virginia. A week later it was Teddy Randolph in Buffalo, a ten-round decision.

All this activity served several purposes: It kept Charles sharp for another showdown with Moore they were talking about for January, and also while they waited for things to shake out at heavyweight. The top of the division was in such a shambles that the possibility still existed that Charles could get a shot at Louis for the title. That was Mintz's goal all along, even though Charles was still just a light heavyweight.

Also, it kept Charles so busy he didn't have time for Gladys. Everyone knew a woman was death to a prizefighter. They made him soft and weakened his legs. The busier Charles was fighting, the less time he had to go bad. Finally, every one of those fights gave Mintz the opportunity to gain control over him. Every time they fought in a new place and registered with the local commission, Mintz had Charles sign documents naming Mintz his manager.

It was almost too easy. Mintz would come back from the commission with a pile of papers, tell Charles, "Sign here, and sign here," and that was it. What did Charles know from all this? He was smart and well-read as far as prizefighters went, but he trusted Mintz. And besides, his job was to beat guys up, not read papers all day. That's what he had managers for. Mintz was no dummy either when it came to this stuff; he knew that these documents alone wouldn't get him sole control of Charles' career, but they wouldn't hurt, either, when the time came.

In December Mintz put Charles back in with Fitzpatrick, the puncher who had almost flattened him in Cincinnati the previous July. They did it in Cleveland as the headliner of the *Cleveland News*' twenty-second annual Christmas Toy Fund Boxing Show. A sellout crowd of 13,384 saw Charles hammer Fitzpatrick from the opening bell. There would be no Hail Mary punch this time from Fitzpatrick; Charles never gave him the chance.

In the fourth a perfect right cross dropped Fitzpatrick hard. He made it up at five, all but out on his feet. Charles blasted him with another left-right, prompting referee Jackie Davis to stop it at 1:34 of the round. Fitzpatrick was so out of it that he started swinging at Charles again after the bout was stopped. Mintz told reporters afterward that Charles was "as ready as he'll ever be" for a shot at Lesnevich.[3]

Three days after Charles whipped Fitzpatrick, Louis, fighting for the first time in fifteen months, barely survived the challenge of Walcott in a sold-out Madison Square Garden. Looking older than his thirty-three years, Louis had his moments but was rendered mostly impotent by Walcott's speed, shifty style, and his own listlessness. Walcott, impossibly the same age as Louis, dropped him with counter right hands in the second and fourth rounds and hammered Louis' left eye closed.

By the end Joe's lips were so puffed up and swollen from Walcott's straight, hard punches that he could barely talk. So humiliated was Louis and so certain was he that he'd lost, that after the final bell he attempted to leave the ring, before the decision was even announced. Manny Seamon shoved him back in so he could hear the split decision announced in his favor. The Garden exploded in boos. Even mortals could tell when their god has gotten a gift decision. Louis was more disgusted than anyone. Asked afterward by a writer if he considered Walcott a second-rater, he replied, "No. I am."[4]

Louis' close call against Walcott all but guaranteed that there would be a rematch, so Charles' fight against Moore in Cleveland took on greater significance. If he wasn't going to get a Louis fight, he had to keep pressing to get the light heavyweight title. But Joe Vela, Lesnevich's manager, was always a step ahead. He had already signed up Lesnevich for a second fight against Billy Fox in March.

Lesnevich had already beaten Fox the previous February, but then Fox came through with a knockout "win" over Jake LaMotta that everyone and his brother knew was dirty—a complete snow job. LaMotta had taken a dive in return for a shot at the middleweight title. Palermo and Carbo arranged it. He'd held out as long as he could against them, but he wasn't getting any younger. You almost couldn't blame him when they said to go down against Fox and you'll get your shot. Vela, for his part, couldn't have cared less. He knew his guy wouldn't stand a chance against Moore or Charles, but he knew Fox was a sham and that even Gus, who was never a great fighter, would handle him again. He was protecting his fighter. That was his job.

There weren't a lot of people outside the camps of Charles and Moore who cared so much that they were getting screwed, but promoter Larry Atkins did. Before the fight he had posters made up advertising the fight as being for the world light heavyweight title and made it a fifteen-rounder. He appealed to the Cleveland commission to recognize the winner as the champ based on Lesnevich's refusal to agree to face the winner even after Atkins offered him a $50,000 guarantee. The commission agreed and suggested that the thirty member states do the same unless Lesnevich agreed to meet the winner within sixty days. NBA chairman Fred Saddy, however, responded that stripping Lesnevich of the title in favor of the Charles-Moore winner would be "ridiculous."[5]

You had to wonder at this point what Charles and Moore were fighting for, since it was clear Lesnevich would not be the reward. In addition to the money, it was this: they didn't particularly like one another. Moore, especially, was disliked on account of his arrogance by several of his rivals, particularly Jimmy Bivins, with whom he had an ongoing feud. And he and Charles, throughout their series, frequently fought after the bell and exchanged low blows and accusations of low blows. Plus, they were top-flight, proud, competitive athletes who had fought long, hard and well over the years to get to the top of the 175-pound division. Understandably, neither wanted to cede that status to the other.

Charles opened and closed as a 3–1 favorite despite Charlie Johnston's claims that Moore had floored none other than Elmer Ray in a recent sparring session. The betting public suspected it wasn't true, and even if it was, so what? From all appearances Charles had Moore's number the same way he'd turned out to have Marshall's number, Bivins' number, Fitzpatrick's number, and the number of most of the other guys he'd faced. Moore had fought him close the last time out, about as well as he could fight, and still Charles had whipped him.

Fighting in Cleveland Arena, Moore, weighing 173, remembered from their last fight that if he fought cautiously and stayed inside and concentrated on counterpunching, he could handcuff Charles enough to keep from getting blasted on the outside. But Charles, who weighed 173¼, had improved since last time, and when Moore tried to sneak inside he stepped to the side and threw punches. Or, he let Moore come inside and outworked him with body punches. In the third and fourth a couple of his body shots landed around the belt line or a smidge under, and the referee, Jackie Davis, penalized him in both rounds. That was okay. There wasn't a more dedicated body puncher in the business than Ezzard Charles, and he was willing to pay the penalty when he had to because his body punches broke guys in half.

Moore did business in spots because he was too good not to, but even with the penalties, Charles was way ahead on the judges' scorecards heading into the eighth. About halfway through the round, Moore, who'd been playing cautious counterpuncher all night, suddenly opened up. For a guy who mostly made his living waiting for the other guy to punch first, he could crack.

He jumped on Charles near the ropes and before you knew what was happening, Charles was bleeding from the mouth, and then Moore had him wobbly with a left hook to the ear. A right to the side of the head had Charles reeling, and just as the crowd of 8,334 was ready to let go with a collective gasp of the type that is only heard under the most shocking and brutal circumstances, Charles ended it. He turned over a left hook, and then a whipping, roundhouse right that cracked against Moore's skull with such force that some in press row winced at the noise it created.

"I was sure that something broke either in Archie's head or Ezzard's right hand, maybe in both places," one reporter wrote later.[6] Moore floundered on a knee for a moment, and Charles leveled him with a final, thunderous uppercut brought all the way from Lawrenceville, and it lifted Moore up and put him back again. He was on all fours, fumbling blindly for the bottom rope, when Davis finished the count at 2:40. Another twenty seconds passed before Moore, with the aid of his cornermen, was able to stand. And there wasn't a man in the house who could blame Lesnevich if he ducked a fight with Ezzard Charles for the rest of his natural life.

Later, Mintz was on his way back to Pittsburgh with a bunch of writer friends when some of them started busting his chops, saying that Charles was getting his ass handed to him when he landed a lucky punch. He responded in typical fashion. "Lucky! Lucky!" he hollered. "He was just playing bosom. That's what he was doing!"[7] (Mintz meant possum.)

Mintz didn't know how to make it any clearer to the NBA that he had Lesnevich's only real contender. The only thing he could do was put Charles back in the ring again. He wanted it to be in Chicago, but it had to be against the right guy—someone the fans and newspaper guys respected, but also someone Charles could beat without too much trouble. Mintz wasn't worried about Charles losing, even when they were so close to a title shot. He knew in his heart there wasn't a 175-pounder alive who could lick Charles—especially after the way he'd handled Moore. But this was a tricky business. Put Charles in now with a guy who was slippery, or awkward, or who ran all night, or a guy who was good with his thumbs or with his head, and he might throw Charles off. Charles looks bad and Lesnevich gets a way out: "See? We told you he's a bum." He couldn't have that. So he told matchmaker Jack Hurley what he wanted, and Hurley put out the word. A couple days later he came back with Sammy Crandall, a twenty-year-old kid from Akron, Ohio, son of a fifty-five-year-old rubber company employee. He fought under the name Sam Baroudi, mostly as a middleweight. One of eight children, Baroudi was thirteen years old when he won a battle royal and pocketed four dollars in the process, a pretty decent score for a little kid, and was hooked. He turned pro in '45 after winning a Golden Gloves tournament in Cleveland.

Mintz knew Baroudi. He'd considered having Charles face him a couple times before, once in Akron and once in Buffalo, but had turned down both offers because the money they would have made there wasn't worth the risk. In Chicago it was worth the risk. Baroudi was no Moore, of course; he was tough, but not overly dangerous, at least not to Charles. But he had credentials. In his previous fight, right in Chicago Stadium, he'd gotten off the canvas to twice stop fragile but deadly-punching Bob Satterfield in the second round, dropping him seven times. (In fact, that was an upset; Mintz had wanted to match Charles and Satterfield after Satterfield had disposed of Baroudi.) And at St. Nick's back in '46 he outpointed the excellent Holman Williams. Williams was a little used up by that time, but still—it was Holman Williams, a kind of living legend of the game. The win carried some weight. Williams, even an old Williams, was something else.

Though born in Pensacola, Williams had come out of the same Detroit neighborhood and gym as Joe Louis and was one of the most clever and most avoided fighters in the business. A lot of fight guys who knew what they were talking about said that everything Louis knew about the science of fighting came from watching Williams in the gym. Williams would fight anyone who would meet him. Unless you were on your game and a damned good fighter in your own right you weren't going to whip him, no matter what you did. In the early days, as a lightweight and then a welterweight, he could stand and punch with the best of them, but he kept breaking his hands. When you can't pay the bills as a puncher and prizefighting is all you know, you make adjustments or you don't eat.

So Williams became about the best stylist in the game and a defensive wizard, and he won that way, too. He went unbeaten in twenty-eight straight fights between 1932 and '35, a streak that finally ended when the great Cocoa Kid outpointed him twice in 1936. He fought Kid seven more times by the time he was done, and Charlie Burley, Archie Moore, Lloyd Marshall, Jose Besora, and Jack Chase over and over because the top fighters at 147 and then 160 wouldn't risk him. He was too good. After all that time, all those years, and all those fights he never did get a shot at the world title though he'd earned one a hundred times over. He had to settle for the "Negro" titles.

By the time he got higher-profile fights with Marcel Cerdan and Jake LaMotta he was in his early thirties already, thirteen years into the game, his best days behind him. He lost to both and a little something went out of him then. Two months after LaMotta beat him, Baroudi out-hustled him at St. Nick's, winning a split ten-rounder. One of the judges gave Williams seven rounds. He fought a couple more years after the loss to Baroudi, losing six of his last eleven fights.

It was a good move by Baroudi's manager, Mike Spinelli, to get Williams when he did. Spinelli, a doughy, middle-aged mug who owned a textile warehouse and trucking business in New York, had bought Baroudi's contract for $150 right out of the box and kept him busy—fifty-six fights in three years. Baroudi lost eleven along the way, mostly to guys who weren't in Charles' league, but the wins over Satterfield and Williams went a long way. Hurley was good at this. The only thing that bothered Mintz a little was that as far as anyone could tell him, Baroudi had never been off his feet as a pro, so he had a good set of whiskers. But that was all right. Charles needed the work to stay sharp, and the more rounds he got in the better. He'd be ready when Lesnevich and his camp finally caved and made the fight.

There was one other interesting thing about Baroudi: in 1947 he'd killed a twenty-three-year-old fighter from Philadelphia named Glenn Newton Smith in a fight in Massachusetts. After Baroudi stopped him in the ninth round, Smith collapsed in the dressing room and died a short while later at North Adams Hospital. The medical examiner said he died of a cerebral hemorrhage "caused by a blow to the base of the skull."[8] You never knew what that could do to a fighter, killing a man like that. A lot of guys were never the same again. They didn't have the same killer instinct. Other guys it didn't bother too much. They went right on fighting. Mintz made the match for February 20.

Mintz knew right away that Spinelli, the manager, was in over his head, just like his fighter was. He wasn't a boxing guy. He was a businessman with a little extra money to throw around who thought he knew boxing and probably since the time he was a kid had wanted to manage a prizefighter. So he got one in Baroudi, who was his only guy. You could tell as soon as he started talking that he was out of his element. "Baroudi is hard to hit because he has good eyesight and sees punches coming. And he has always been underrated," Spinelli said.[9]

Mintz shook his head at that but appreciated Spinelli's effort, since the fight wouldn't make a dime for anybody if no one gave Baroudi a chance. Spinelli said too that the fans shouldn't worry that Charles was a bit bigger. "We don't care if Charles comes into the ring at 176 or 178. If Sam nails him, weight doesn't mean a thing."[10] Mintz had been around long enough to know that much was true; Charles would win not because he was bigger than Baroudi, but because he was the better fighter. Laymen, forever equating prizefights to schoolyard scraps, always gave the advantage to the bigger boy, when anyone who really knew prizefighting knew this was a game of brains, skill, heart and speed. Either way, anything Spinelli said to help along the gate was okay with Mintz, no matter how asinine.

Mintz and Spinelli, working with Chicago promoters Jack Begun and Irving Schoenwald, put the fight in Chicago Stadium and did pretty well, all things considered. On a chilly, rainy Chicago night, 11,501 fans showed up, generating a $50,464 gate to watch what the newspaper boys later called "legalized slaughter."[11]

It didn't start out that way. Baroudi did well enough for himself over the first five rounds. He was a crouching-type fighter, which means he stayed low and got under a lot of Charles' punches, and pressured him. He was strong, too; he rocked Charles with a right in the fourth round. But Charles liked fighting guys who came to him, and he was as good that night as he ever was going to be, or damned close to it. He recovered quickly, hammering Baroudi with hard rights and lefts and beating on his ribcage when they got in close.

It was one of those fights that you knew was going to tip hard Charles' way sooner or later, because Baroudi just wasn't in the same league. The tip came in the sixth when Charles nailed Baroudi with a left hook that hurt the kid. From then on it was a one-way beating. He banged away at the kid however and whenever he wanted to. After that left hook it wasn't a fight anymore, it was a mugging; and watching Charles tear the kid apart and break him down, minute after minute, round after round, you had to wonder what made him do it. Out of the ring Charles was a gentleman, a polite, soft-spoken, virtuous young man, shy and sober, not a violent bone in his body, God-fearing and all the rest. But here he was all over poor Baroudi, like he was trying to kill the boy.

He could turn it off and on, the way a lot of fighters do. Most of them were gentle and thoughtful humans outside the ring, when they weren't trying to punch a hole in a man's skull. But Charles was not only raking Baroudi with legal blows, but giving him illegal ones too—punches to the back of Baroudi's head, what they called "rabbit punches"—and low blows, way below the belt. The crowd let Charles have it for that, booed him up and down. Fight crowds were funny that way—honorable, even, when you thought about it. They wanted blood spilled, but only if it was spilled fair and square. They paid good money to watch two men try to beat the life out of one another but they'd be damned if they'd let one take unfair advantage. But the booing didn't help Baroudi. Charles beat him every way a man can beat another man. There were some in the crowd who called for the referee, Tommy Thomas, to stop it. Thomas didn't do it; he couldn't. It would violate the code. No matter how bad it got for Baroudi (and it got bad), so long as he could defend himself and throw a punch back every once in a while, the referee had to let it go. That was the code. To stop it when the kid still had some fight left in him would be an injustice to him and the crowd and to Charles. What if he got lucky and Charles walked into something? There was always that possibility.

That's what kept folks watching, and you could never say a fight was over until it was actually over. Lots of guys put themselves in position to make big money by landing a Hail Mary punch when everyone thought they were done. It was unlikely; Charles had it all over Baroudi. But anything was possible, right until the final bell. Around the eighth round, Christmas, sitting at ringside, said to no one in particular: "They're gonna get this boy killed."[12]

Even with Charles taking over in the second half of the fight like he did, Mintz was worried how it would look if Charles didn't stop Baroudi, or, even worse, if he lost a decision, as unlikely as it seemed. You never knew with fight judges. Somebody owes somebody a favor, someone slips a fifty into another guy's pocket, a wise guy's got a judge on the payroll; you never knew. One crook and there goes your title shot. He couldn't risk it. Not when they were so close to finally getting Lesnevich. So after the ninth round Mintz said to Charles in the corner, "Snooks, finish him if you can."[13] Charles' other second, Henry Lutz, agreed. Charles did what he was told, just like always.

Early in the tenth he blasted away at Baroudi with both hands until Baroudi's eyes rolled back in his head and his blood was everywhere. Then Charles landed three flush, hard straight rights and then a final left hook, and Baroudi finally fell near the ropes, Charles standing over him looking like he wanted to get in another one just to make sure. He didn't have to make sure, because Baroudi was not going to get up. Not by the count of ten; not ever.

Thomas counted him out at 0:47 into the round as Baroudi's arm swung spastically, almost like he was counting himself out, the way you would expect an arm to swing when something has gone desperately wrong, when the blood is already seeping into that dark cavity between brain and bone. Baroudi's cornermen, Spinelli, Izzy Klein and Al Warner, scrambled over to him and did all the things cornermen did to bring around a fighter who'd gone boneless in the middle of a prize ring. They got in his ear and yelled his name, they slapped his face, they cracked smelling salts under his nose and thought, Christ this is bad. They were right about that.

Sam Baroudi already was slipping away, the life leaking out of him as surely and as steadily as the blood that leaked from his shattered nose. After a minute the ring doctor called for a stretcher. The crowd knew what that meant; fight crowds always know. A few shuffled toward the exits, but most stayed and watched, mostly in silence, smoking, fidgeting, as Baroudi's graying carcass, so alive just a few minutes earlier, as alive as any man has ever been because no man's more alive than he is when fighting, bobbed along on the stretcher, splitting the crowd and then disappearing into a dark hallway like a broken raft floating out to sea. Only then did the crowd start for the exits.

The ring doctor and Baroudi's cornermen carried him to the locker room in the basement and set him down to work on him some more. When they still couldn't wake him up they started to panic. One of the guys from the commission called the fire department. As a group they huddled over Baroudi, shouted his name, told him to open his goddam eyes already, but Baroudi just lay there, occasionally vomiting, turning grayer by the minute, dying little by little as they wiped the blood from his face with a white towel.

Finally the guys from the fire department showed up with an inhalator. Klein, Spinelli and Warner were happy to make room for the boys to work. They hooked Baroudi up and pumped air in and out of his lungs as his chest, still wet with sweat and blood and vomit and all the indignities of the world, rose and then fell in time with the inhalator's commands. The firemen knew as well as anyone it was a lost cause, but they kept at it for almost half an hour before loading Baroudi into the truck and speeding him over to Columbus Hospital. By the time they got there an hour had passed since Charles' final left hook had landed.

6

THE PRICE

Dr. Joseph P. Cascino, a staff neurologist at Columbus, arrived at the hospital around the same time that Baroudi did. He'd been sleeping when the call came that they were bringing in one of the guys who had fought on the card at the stadium. He rushed to the hospital, still a little groggy, but when he saw Baroudi he snapped wide awake—he reminded him of the boys he had treated in the war. He examined Baroudi and ordered an x-ray. Though the pictures didn't reveal much, he quickly diagnosed a cerebral hemorrhage, a brain bleed.

During the war he'd seen dozens of bleeds just like Baroudi's. In fact, he'd gained some distinction then because every man whose skull he'd opened after a fire fight, and there were over a hundred, had survived the surgery. Many of them had recovered. But part of that success rate lay in determining who was a good candidate for surgery and who wasn't.

Cascino ordered a spinal puncture and the results—blood mixed in with spinal fluid—confirmed a bleed. And it was severe. He briefly considered operating, recalling a case he'd heard about that had happened just a week earlier in Philadelphia. A heavyweight named Eddie Franklin had been stopped by Billy "Chicken" Thompson, and immediately afterward suffered a blood clot on the brain. Surgeons repaired the clot and Franklin survived.

But Baroudi was another case altogether; he'd been unconscious for over an hour. The sheer volume of blood in his spinal fluid suggested a very large hemorrhage. Even if he survived the operation, which was unlikely, he'd be of no use to anyone. Cascino did the only thing he could do: he waited. If Baroudi made it through the night and a couple after that, the swelling in his brain might subside. Then it was anyone's guess. Stranger things had happened. It was more likely he'd be dead before sunrise.

At around 4:30 a.m. Mintz showed up at the hospital, loudly proclaiming his intent to provide any financial support he could to help save Baroudi's life. You couldn't blame anyone for suspecting he made the decision after making sure somehow or another that Baroudi was as good as dead. He was followed by Charles, who had called the hospital several times during the night to check on Baroudi's condition. He was escorted by Chicago police, which was protocol. At 4:48 a.m. as a nurse was taking his blood pressure, Sam Baroudi died. It was the first boxing death of the year. The year before, there had been nine; the year before that, eleven. As Baroudi took his final breaths, roughly five hours after Charles' last, thudding hook had landed, Spinelli, Warner and Klein were nowhere to be found.

Dr. Cascino called the time of death and headed out to the waiting room to give the word to a small group of reporters and photographers who'd stuck around the hospital. "Baroudi had a large hemorrhage, probably caused by the knockout blow although it may have been caused by his head hitting the ring," he said, also noting the "large traces of blood" in Baroudi's spinal fluid.[1] There wasn't much else to say. The reporters, figuring Spinelli was waiting for news about his fighter, called his room at the Morrison Hotel. His son Frank answered and told them his father was already at Chicago Airport on his way back to New York "on business."

Driven primarily by their nose for a good story and secondarily by moral outrage, the press rushed out to the airport to see if they could catch Spinelli. How could a manager skip town while his fighter lay dying in a hospital? They scrambled into the terminal to find Warner napping peacefully on a bench—one of them took a snapshot—with Spinelli nearby. Klein, a local Chicago guy, was not there. The press guys told Spinelli and Warner that Baroudi was dead and gave them hell for trying to skip town. Several writers called Spinelli a bum to his face. Leonard Caplan, one of the photographers, was stunned when Spinelli replied, "The kid is dead. So what? I can't help him now."[2]

Spinelli and Warner took a cab from the airport to the Warren Avenue Police Station in Chicago, where police detained them for questioning in Baroudi's death. This was standard procedure. Charles also was detained momentarily on a technical charge of involuntary manslaughter. He was released after posting $5,000 bond (paid by Hurley, the matchmaker) and promising to stay in Chicago until the police had completed their inquest. Under questioning, Spinelli told police he wasn't trying to skip town at all. Rather, he'd planned to take the 8:00 a.m. flight to New York and had told his son to call him if Baroudi got worse.

Airline officials contradicted that, telling police that Spinelli and Warner had tried and failed to make a 3:00 a.m. flight. Responding to accusations that he didn't care that his fighter lay dying in a hospital bed, Spinelli told police that he couldn't stand it any longer and that he had cried like a kid when Baroudi was hurt. He also said he'd planned on giving Baroudi's mother her son's share of the purse—around $2,800—even though, he said, Baroudi owed him about that for money Spinelli had advanced him for clothes and what he called good times in Harlem. A writer asked Charles if he thought Baroudi had been overmatched. Charles replied, "He was a rough boy but he never had me in any trouble."[3]

In subsequent days the state attorney's office and coroner's office conducted separate investigations into Baroudi's death. Coroner A.L. Brodie found no evidence of criminal negligence on Charles' part but instructed a "blue ribbon" jury to investigate the death and "suggest improvements of the sport in Illinois."[4]

Assistant State's Attorney Dan Ryan launched an independent inquiry. During the official inquest, which began on February 22, Spinelli was the target of the most pointed questioning. Asked again to account for his attempt to flee Chicago while Baroudi was dying, he testified that he had been away from his home and family for a week or ten days already and was eager to get home.

He also said, "I understand I made a mistake. I didn't know it was going to be this serious."[5] He also amended earlier statements concerning Baroudi's purse, telling the panel that Baroudi's share of the receipts came to $5,600, of which he had advanced the fighter $1,600 and had the remaining $4,000 when he attempted to fly back to New York. He said he planned to stop in Akron on the way to give Baroudi's father the money.

Ultimately, the most serious offense with which the panel thought it might charge Spinelli was perjury: on the manager's license application he had completed on bringing Baroudi to Chicago for the fight, he had listed Baroudi's age as twenty-one, the minimum age a fighter could be to fight a scheduled ten-rounder in Illinois. Baroudi's relatives insisted he was only twenty, which later was proved true.

Spinelli found an unlikely ally in Begun, one of the fight's co-promoters. Begun, whose firm advanced Baroudi's parents $500 to cover their son's funeral expenses, told the press, "Of course Spinelli showed bad judgment in deciding to leave Chicago while his boxer was in the hospital. But I believe he has been treated a little harshly. He most certainly was not trying to 'lam' with the purse. He was like a driver leaving the scene of an accident—panicky and confused."[6]

Warner, the trainer, revealed during the inquest that Baroudi had been injured in a prior bout in Pittsfield, Massachusetts, against a fighter named Major Joe. "Baroudi was hurt bad that night," Warner testified. "His nose and mouth were bleeding in the sixth and eighth rounds."[7] Spinelli and Warner had not shared this information with the Illinois commission prior to the Charles bout because, quite simply, there was no motive for them to do so.

The commission doctor, Dr. J.J. Drammis, testified later that had he known about the injuries Baroudi had sustained in the Joe fight, he "doubted he would have"[8] approved Baroudi for the fight with Charles. But this was all after-the-fact face-saving; it wasn't uncommon for pro fighters to get knocked cold one week and be fighting again two weeks or a month later. And every man testifying knew it.

It came as no surprise when the manslaughter charge against Charles was dismissed. Assistant State's Attorney Daniel Ryan informed Judge Charles Dougherty that a coroner's jury had decided that "Baroudi's death was the result of a system and not the boxers." In clearing Charles, Dougherty observed, "Boxing will soon be singing a swan song" if fighters continued to die in the ring.[9]

The following day Governor Dwight Green called for a three-week ban on boxing in Illinois, a casualty of which was the planned Sugar Ray Robinson–Georgie Abrams fight scheduled to take place on March 31. On March 5 a coroner's jury recommended that Spinelli and Warner be banned from boxing for life. It also recommended sweeping changes, noting, "The circumstances relating to the fatal match and others are of a character so unsavory and disreputable as to warrant a wholesale revision of professional regulations and ethics in the state of Illinois."[10]

Much of this pertained to the mob's influence in the sport, especially in Chicago, but the report's authors knew better than to open that can of worms. It instead focused its language on sweeping administrative changes that were both toothless and impossible to enforce.

Among the reforms suggested by the committee were the following: weekly meetings of the state boxing commission to discuss rules infractions; attendance of all boxing matches by a member of the commission; non-political selection of commission staff; legislation permitting heavy fines and suspension of boxing personnel; renewed enforcement against rabbit and kidney punches; a requirement that all matchmakers be licensed by the commission; a requirement that any boxer whose record indicated he was incompetent to defend himself be barred from Illinois rings for life; and a requirement that all boxers be required to carry a boxing record listing each bout, opponent, date, place, and medical report on hospitalization for ring injury.

Officials demanded Spinelli's immediate resignation from the powerful Manager's Guild and accused him of deliberately misrepresenting Baroudi's age with disastrous consequences. Spinelli complied, which made sense if for no other reason than he had no fighters other than Baroudi under contract. "I'm through with managing fighters," he said. "I don't want any more of that business. No more. I'm staying away from that kind of stuff."[11]

The panel was entirely well intentioned and had undertaken their charge with the greatest seriousness. They couldn't have known that they were as powerless to significantly change the fight racket as Baroudi had been to stop the bleeding in his brain. The game had existed in more or less its current state for longer than any of them had been alive. Any pretense toward regulation was mostly a cover for well-connected managers and promoters whose best friends were in the mob or trying to get in the mob. Besides, this was how the people liked it. They kept coming out to arenas and fight clubs; they listened to the fights on their radios, rooted along for their heroes and booed the villains. Sometimes guys had to die. It was part of the deal.

The guys in their suits and ties who sat on the panel and wanted to make so many changes, and shook their heads at the waste and the deaths, they watched the fights, too, and cheered and booed right along with the rabble. What attracted them? The risks the fighters took. In the fight game the risk was always high. Any fighter could end up like Baroudi on any night, and there wasn't a better show in town than that. What the commission didn't understand was you couldn't have it both ways. You could either have boxing or you could make it safe. It was clear what was important to the public.

Joe Louis and Sugar Ray Robinson were as famous as any movie stars. Every fighter who held a world title was a household name in America. Poor boys from the worst ghettos could turn themselves into something in the fight game; it didn't matter if they were Jewish, black, Italian, Polish, Irish, Mexican or Chinese. If they could fight and knew how to play along, they could get a name, they could be someone, they could get out of the ghetto and move out to nice neighborhoods in the suburbs, maybe send their kids to good schools so they could grow up to be doctors and lawyers and politicians.

It almost certainly wouldn't happen that way. Chances were they'd end up broke, mumbly and punchy like all the rest, but what of it? What else were these slum kids going to do? Work themselves to death in a factory? Shine shoes on a box in Times Square? At least the fight game would get their filthy immigrant blood flowing for a while. If they were any good they'd hear a crowd cheer for them, they'd get a few dames that were hotter and looser than what they'd get otherwise, and maybe they'd get their name in the paper once or twice. That was better than most of the bums in the neighborhood. Plus they'd get to know the singular joy of cracking a man on the jaw with a perfect left hook, and better yet, they'd find out how it felt to dominate another man, to make him quit, to make him run. There was nothing in the world like that. It could make a poor nothing-from-the-neighborhood a god for a few minutes.

Best of all it gave them hope. It was a false hope usually, an empty hope, but it was better than nothing. Kids who went into the fight game weren't in the business of going to college someday or to Hollywood. It was the fight racket or the mob or mopping floors. Louis proved the system worked. So did Robinson and Zale, and before them, Canzoneri, Armstrong, Benny Leonard and all the rest. Naturally, some guys wouldn't make it. Not everybody could. A lot of them paid a heavy price. And of those, some, like Baroudi, would pay the heaviest price. It was unavoidable.

So the papers made a big deal out of the commission's findings and recommendations, and a month later they were on to their next big story, and the American sports fans were rooting for this or that ballplayer and looking forward to the next big fight, the next big game, the next big thing. And the guys who made up the "blue ribbon" panel puffed out their chests and hugged their wives and felt like they'd made a difference in the lives of the poor, uneducated brutes who made up the fight racket. They hadn't. They were a paper tiger. They could recommend anything they wanted.

The fight game, in Illinois and everywhere else, played by its own rules. A week after Baroudi died, a featherweight named Leroy Decatur was stopped in the fourth round by Frederico Herrera in Hollywood, California, and died later that night. Two weeks later, welterweight Francesco Loi died after Fernando Jannilli knocked him out in Rome. The game went on, just like it always had. You could have it be safe, or you could have boxing. You couldn't have both.

The night Sam Baroudi died, Charles fell asleep only from sheer exhaustion. It hit him hardest the next day. He walked the streets in a daze, replaying it in his mind, as any thinking man would.[12] He couldn't stop the images. He decided then that he would fight one more time, donate his entire purse to Baroudi's family, and then retire from the ring, maybe go back to being a mechanic or truck driver like he'd done in the army.

Mintz and Begun jumped on the first part of the idea, announcing they would hold a benefit card from whose proceeds they would donate $10,000 to the Baroudi family; $5,000 from Charles' share of the purse and $5,000 from the promoter. Mintz sought to assure the press that Charles would not retire.

"Naturally, the boy is affected by Baroudi's death. He took it very hard and said he would quit fighting but I'm sure that after it is pointed out to him that he wasn't directly responsible for the fatality, he'll change his mind. Meanwhile, we're going to do everything we can for Baroudi's family."[13] Mintz was right. Charles was convinced to keep fighting, and the advice came from an unlikely source: Baroudi's father. Mintz had gone to him and asked him to talk Charles out of retiring. "This is a terrible accident, but my fighter's got a great future," Mintz told him. "He's taking this bad. Brace him up."[14]

"Go on and win the championship. This was a terrible accident. Our family bears no bitterness at all towards you," Crandall told Ezzard. "Don't give up your career. The same thing happened to my boy last year. One of his opponents died after a bout with him. We know how you feel and we understand. Please dismiss it from your mind and go on fighting."[15]

Charles came around, just as Mintz knew he would. He'd already started working with Begun and Schoenwald to arrange a benefit bout with the proceeds to go to Baroudi's family. They scheduled it for April 7 in the same ring where Charles had killed Baroudi. The intent was to match Charles soft—it was supposed to be a benefit show, not a real card. That plan was scrapped when the guys who made the decisions and pulled the levers decided that benefit matches, no matter the cause and unless they involved Joe Louis, drew poorly. There was money to be made.

They wouldn't make peanuts for an exhibition. Mintz and Begun changed gears and told Hurley to get Charles a real opponent. In the meantime, Mintz put the screws to Lesnevich's camp by offering him a fight with Charles in Chicago Stadium with Charles' entire purse being donated to the Baroudi family. It was purely a publicity stunt; Mintz knew Lesnevich was already committed to facing Billy Fox in March. But if he got lucky, maybe he could get a commitment for the summer. Lesnevich's manager of record, Joe Vela, refused to bite.

"We were very sorry to read about Baroudi's death and would like to help the family, but as far as boxing Charles goes, we'll have to wait until after the Fox fight to make up our minds," Vela said. "As it stands now Charles would do well to box another opponent if he really wants to give the family some money. Lesnevich would have to be well paid."[16]

Elmer Ray got the call, and that was okay with Charles. He'd never forgotten the lousy decision he'd lost to Ray in New York and had always wanted to avenge it. He'd avenged every other loss of his career. Plus, Ray was older now and more worn down than he'd been in their first fight. He hadn't improved, while Charles certainly had—so long as he could put the Baroudi fight behind him, where it belonged. Charles would give up seventeen pounds to Ray, a little less than last time, but was still a heavy favorite going in.

Charles-Ray would be the first fight in Illinois since Baroudi's death, and it remained so even after Charles twice postponed it, complaining of a sore back. When it finally came off on May 8, a full 9,319 paying customers, generating a gate of $42,703, saw Charles withstand Ray's early attack, lay off the gas in the third, fourth and fifth rounds, and then wear Ray down through the middle rounds with movement and sharp counterpunching—just like in the first fight.

In the ninth Charles drove a hard right hand to Ray's belly while they were near the ropes. Ray dropped his hands and looked pleadingly at referee Tom Kenneally, apparently waiting for Kenneally to call it low. Instead, the ref said, "Fight." Charles promptly stepped forward and leveled Ray with a left and a right, as was his obligation. Kenneally counted him out at 2:46.

Years later Charles described what it was like fighting again for the first time after the Baroudi fight. "When I entered the arena I just stopped and remembered that awful night. The crowd was applauding, some fans were booing, but I paid no heed. I just stood there for some time. I finally walked into the ring, sort of in a daze. Once the bell sounded and we began fighting I forgot about everything."[17]

As promised, Charles donated $5,000 from his purse, and Begun and Schoenwald kicked in another $5,000 for Baroudi's family. Afterward Charles said, "No one will ever know how difficult it was for me to go back in that same ring with Ray, how tough it was for me to knock him out."[18] To make matters worse, between the $5,000 for Baroudi's family and the cuts everyone took, Charles didn't make a cent on the fight.[19]

Mintz was already on to more pressing matters. "We wouldn't take an offer to fight Joe Louis now if it was offered to us," he lied. "Before we go for the heavyweight crown we want to establish ourselves as the absolute tops in our own class—and that means Lesnevich has got to fight Charles."[20]

And for the rest of his life—indeed, for as long as people remembered Ezzard Charles—they would say the Baroudi fight ruined him, made him a pacifist, as fighters go. A fighter who didn't have it in him to hurt another man was no good to anyone, and even the people closest to Ezzard Charles, who knew him for decades, used the Baroudi fight to explain away his later failures, as though Baroudi's ghost was there tugging at Charles in the ring, keeping him from fulfilling his greatest dreams. Like many obvious truths it was hogwash.

Charles did become a more hesitant, cautious fighter after the Baroudi fight, but it was because he switched almost entirely to fighting heavyweights—guys who were much bigger and who could punch and could take his punch. When he didn't fear his opponent's punch, he was as aggressive as ever.

In 1951 a writer he'd known for years, who had watched him on his way up, knocking stiff one guy after another, suggested to him that the Baroudi fight "had something to do with his current hesitancy" to go in for the kill. Charles responded: "I can't quite agree with you. It did bother me for a while, but I believe the real answer for my not knocking out opponents ... as I used to do is that I am meeting bigger men now. Heavyweights can absorb more punishment."[21] A couple years later, after Charles had won and lost the heavyweight title, one of his managers offered another explanation for his frequent passivity, and it had nothing to do with Baroudi. "Ezzard's trouble as a champion was that he was too cautious," said Tom Tannas. "He didn't want to take any chances of losing the title. He was willing to fight everybody, and he did, but the title made him cautious."[22]

After the initial horror of the Baroudi fight, Ezzard Charles came to understand what every mature prizefighter understands: terrible things can happen when grown men hit one another over and over on the head. The next time it could just as easily be him. But fighters don't think about that, any more than tightrope walkers imagine their insides splayed all over the ground one hundred feet below. Prizefighting is a job. It was a job to Charles more than to most. "Fight night is a man going to work," he said. "Accidents can happen, but you push that out of your mind because it's just a job."[23] Two weeks later he was at work again in a rematch against Erv Sarlin, this time in Buffalo, New York. After another ten-round decision win, Mintz patted Charles on the back in the dressing room and told him, "When you become a champion you should follow in the two-steps of the great Joe Louis."[24]

Fifteen months after Baroudi died, his father hired attorney Russell Alexander to sue Charles for $15,000 on the grounds that Baroudi's death was caused by "innumerable rabbit punches and low blows." Citing the Illinois rulebook, the suit stated that Charles took "unfair advantage" of Baroudi by "repeatedly hitting below the belt, by holding decedent with one hand and hitting with the other, by deliberately striking decedent with innumerable rabbit punches and committing other and various acts."[25]

7

Going Heavy

While Charles was trying to get over killing Sam Baroudi, American sports fans were still trying to recover from Louis getting the nod over Walcott two months prior. Outrage over the decision was universal and loud. Several days after the fight, the powerful New York Commission, headed by Colonel Eddie Egan, still had not ruled out reversing it, though such a move was unlikely; they'd never reversed a decision before. Walcott's supporters made the case that Louis won more rounds, but Walcott was awarded more points. Under the New York scoring system, the points system was used only when the referee and two judges failed to agree on a round-winner. Walcott had indeed gotten more points. In fact, referee Ruby Goldstein had Walcott up both ways—on points and in rounds.

It didn't help Louis that twenty-four of forty writers polled at ringside reported seeing Walcott as the winner. Nor was it a comfort to learn that x-rays taken of his right hand, which he believed he'd broken in the fifth round, turned out to be merely bruised. For the first time in his career, Joe Louis was not the hero; he was the villain. Governor Dewey's office in Albany was flooded with complaints. All the papers blasted the decision. Even the *Police Gazette*, the oldest boxing magazine in the world, recognized Walcott as the new heavyweight champion. "The decision favoring Louis was one of the most raw I've ever seen," said Gazette publisher H.H. Roswell. "We are wiring Governor Thomas E. Dewey and boxing commission chairman Egan demanding action."[1]

The upside to all this, of course, was that the rematch would make everybody rich. It was why the fight game loved a rotten decision so long as it was a clean one, as was the case here. No one could say it was fixed in the conventional way; Walcott was the one with the connected manager, and it was he who was robbed. Louis' contract was carved up so many times and so many ways by this time that no one—probably not even Miles, his manager of record—knew who really owned him. The point was that the rematch would be huge. Before Louis' eyes had even healed, it was set for some time in June.

For several months, Walcott and Bocchicchio refused to sign the contract for the return. The original agreement stated that if Walcott won, he and Louis would split the money for the rematch 30/30. He hadn't won, at least not officially. But in their eyes, and in the eyes of just about everyone except the judges, he had. "Walcott beat Louis Friday but didn't get the title so that return contract is out," Bocchicchio said. "But they can't have a return fight without Walcott and they can't draw a million dollars with Louis doing a solo or in fighting someone else. So we're in a spot to get what we think we're entitled to, and we're not taking less than 30 percent."[2]

Sol Strauss refused to budge. "If Walcott wants to fight for the championship again he will have to come to me and accept my terms," he said. "He will not only have to take 20 percent, but he will have to sign a contract to defend the title for the 20th Century Club in the event he wins."[3]

Louis, who went on a lucrative exhibition tour in Europe after the fight, didn't care what Walcott was getting as long as he, Louis, was getting his 40 percent. He preferred Walcott because he wanted to get back at him, but he helped out Strauss by claiming he was just as willing to face Lesnevich, who he called a harder puncher than Jersey Joe. This was hilarious to those who knew Lesnevich wanted no part of Louis and was happy to stay at light heavyweight and continue to duck Ezzard Charles.[4] Eventually Walcott and Bocchicchio capitulated and signed the return-fight contract in late February 1948. Louis and Walcott met on June 25 after the fight was delayed because of rain.

Meanwhile, Mintz did not get Charles any fights after the Sarlin rematch in May. He'd been hearing lots of rumors about what might happen after the Louis-Walcott rematch, and he wanted Charles free to take the best available fight. It was true Charles still wasn't a heavyweight, or anything close. That didn't matter to Mintz. He knew there was a changing of the guard coming soon, and he wanted Charles to be there for it. He'd worry about the details later.

It turned out to be a smart move indeed, after Louis stopped Walcott in the eleventh round and immediately announced his plans to retire from boxing and enter politics. It was a mostly dull bout, with Walcott working his full repertoire of feints, shuffles, three-step jigs and head-bobs while Louis, at thirty-four years old, statue-like compared to his younger self, stalked him, looking for the bomb. Walcott floored him with a right in the third but couldn't or wouldn't follow up. Just as in their first fight, Louis couldn't quite time Walcott's hokey-pokey rhythm, but he assured his corner after almost every round that he was getting closer. The action was such that the crowd frequently booed, and referee Frank Fullam admonished the boys several times to pick up the pace. Walcott later cited this as the reason he stood still and punched with Louis in the eleventh, creating the opportunity Joe needed to finally land home some bombs. Good thing for Louis he did; Walcott was leading on the scorecards of two of the three judges at the time of the knockout and had hammered Louis' left eye almost closed.

Louis' retirement talk was greeted by many with skepticism; according to Twentieth Century, there already was an agreement in place for him to face Lesnevich provided he beat Walcott in their rematch—and whether Lesnevich liked it or not. Also, there was a lot of haggling in the days before Louis-Walcott II was signed about a rematch clause—if Louis was going to retire, why did he need that?

Lastly, Louis had threatened to retire several times before. Way back in 1937, before his rematch with Max Schmeling, he had said that after he beat Schmeling he would leave the business for good. He was sick of it already, even then.[5] The next time was when he entered the army in '42. "By the time the war is over I'll be in my 30s and that's too old for fighting," he said. "I'm too old *now*."[6] He was 28.

So you could forgive the newspaper boys for doubting him. But this wasn't 1937 and it wasn't 1942. It was 1948, and he'd been a pro for fourteen years. At thirty-four he really was an old man as far as fighting went, and he was tired. And it wasn't like he hadn't warned anybody. In August 1947 he said, "Just three more fights and then I quit in 1948."[7] The way Louis saw it, the win over Walcott was a good one to go out on. Everyone knew that. Usually, prizefighters have to be beaten within an inch of their lives to know it's the end. It takes a good beating, long and sustained and with exquisite humiliation and indignity, to get a grown man who's made a good living punching other guys in the mouth to admit to himself that he's had it.

And if the retirement is going to last past the first time a check bounces, that last fight has to hurt. It has to hurt so much that later, when he looks in the mirror at his soft gut and disappearing hair and gets up on the balls of his feet anyway and starts shuffling around thinking maybe he's still got some left, the memory of it grabs him by the collar and shakes him out of it. Louis didn't feel that kind of hurt against Walcott, not even close; but it was okay. He had a different kind of pain—the dull, constant ache that came from being an old man in a young man's sport, the pain of a coming divorce from his wife, Marva, and the pain of the government hounding him. It was enough, already.

So it didn't matter to him that the last fight wasn't a bad knockout loss. He didn't need it. He'd quit and it would take. He was Joe Louis, after all. He wasn't like all those other bums. He could go out on a win, walk away from the ring forever and still be the Brown Bomber and know that against Schmeling, the only man who had ever whipped him, he had gotten revenge and then some. That would be enough. Sure, some of the newspaper guys would say he'd be back. You couldn't blame them.

In August a writer ambushed Louis at a golf tournament and tried to get him to say he would fight again. "No more. Just won't—that's all," he said. Not only that, he already had a good idea as to who would succeed him. "[Ezzard] Charles is the best puncher of anyone today," he said. "Nobody is going to beat Charles."[8]

Louis was certain he'd never fight again and besides, it wasn't like he had no way to make money. He was still Joe Louis, and that was enough to make plenty of cash—maybe not enough to pay the government everything they said he owed, but still, he'd get all the pretty women he wanted, and he could still gamble and play golf and enjoy the good life. He'd gotten a bit lucky against Walcott. Walcott got a little too comfortable, the same way Conn had; he'd stood still a little long, right in Joe's range, and Joe caught him. He could still do that if a guy stood still a little too long. But it was enough already.

Jacobs, who had recovered enough from his stroke at this point to regain part-time control of his beloved Twentieth Century club, had other ideas. Louis was money in the bank, and Jacobs had lent and advanced him so much cash over the years that he, Jacobs, held considerable sway over Louis. He wanted Louis to continue fighting and was negotiating a fight for him for the summer. Louis, however, wanted out so badly that if he was going to fight he needed more than just his usual 40 percent cut. A lot more. He told Strauss he wanted 40 percent plus $100,000—tax free. The way it was working now, every time he got paid he went deeper into the tax hole. The only way he could get out was to get some that no one knew about. Strauss told him he was crazy.

Louis responded by going down to Jacobs' mansion in Miami and trying to negotiate with Jacobs directly. That went nowhere. Louis went back to Strauss, telling him that he feared that if he fought again he'd be beaten, and what would Twentieth Century do for him then? Strauss said they would put him on the Twentieth Century payroll and give him $25,000 a year to assist in making matches, doing publicity at training camps, that type of thing.

"You mean I will have to work?" Louis asked.

Strauss answered, "Yes."

"Then I will work one day a year," Louis replied.

"That wouldn't suffice," Strauss said.

"Well, I want to play golf. I don't want to work," Louis said.[9]

The meeting ended, but Louis didn't have to fight again if he didn't want to, and Jacobs couldn't force him. For the last year his people had been working on a way he could make money—real money—and he'd never have to get punched in the face again.

In mid-1948, Louis, along with his press agent, Harry Mendel, and lawyer, Truman Gibson, started talking over a plan to gain a monopoly on the heavyweight division after Louis' retirement. It went roughly like this: Louis would retire, "sell" his title to a wealthy entrepreneur, and sign the division's top four contenders to exclusive promotional contracts. Louis would join the resultant promotional company and be its face to the sporting public. The new company would run old Jacobs right out of business and pick up Madison Square Garden and all of boxing along with it.

Louis, Mendel and Gibson went through a couple of suitors before getting a meeting with Jim Norris—fight fan, playboy, degenerate gambler, lover of sharp suits, owner of several hockey franchises and inheritor of considerable family wealth. The story went that as a kid Norris had gone with his father to see the Dempsey-Willard title fight in Toledo in 1919 and fallen hard for the fight game—not only the fighters and the fights, but the danger, the gambling, the gangsters, the filthy glamor, the booze, the money. All of it. When he grew up and inherited the family businesses and had more money and time than he knew what to do with, he plotted to get into the fight racket. When he heard Louis was retiring he put out the word that he was ready to go all-in.

Gibson and Louis met with Norris in Chicago at the Belmont Hotel. Norris brought in his friend and business partner Arthur Wirtz, a shrewd Chicago real estate millionaire and co-owner of Sonja Henie's Hollywood Ice Revue. It was nice and easy. They chatted. They smiled. Wirtz promised to put Louis in touch with the comely Henie, with whom Joe was smitten. Louis grinned. Norris drank and thought how happy his buddies Blinky Palermo and Frankie Carbo would be when he told them he'd just sewn up Madison Square Garden and with it all of the fight game. Wirtz had the papers drawn up.

A couple weeks later they met again at Norris' home in Coral Gables, Florida, and made it official. They would form the International Boxing Club (IBC), a promotional company. Louis got a check up front for $350,000 along with an annual salary of $20,000. The $350,000 represented payment for Louis' heavyweight title and for the contracts he would "negotiate" with the top contenders. Those contenders would be Charles, Walcott, Lesnevich and Lee Savold, and the "negotiation" would consist essentially of Louis telling each of the four parties to sign on the dotted line lest they be excluded from the tournament. Easy work. It would go into effect as soon as Louis "officially" announced his retirement. If he wanted to fight one more time or two, that was fine. Up to him. But when he was done he was done.

Not long after this, Mintz was at a function with Charles in Pittsburgh when he was told he had an important call from Miami. He figured it was Jacobs. It wasn't. It was Mendel, who asked Mintz what matches he had coming up for Charles. Mintz told him he had Jimmy Bivins in Washington, D.C., after that big Joe Baksi in the Garden, and then maybe Joey Maxim again at Cincinnati Gardens. Mendel told him to "sit tight and not make any more." Then Louis got on the phone with Mintz and told him the same thing. Mendel got back on the phone and told Mintz to come out to Chicago for an important meeting.

Two days later Mintz met with Mendel, Louis, and Wirtz in Chicago. "It was all very hush-mush," Mintz said later.[10] Mintz thought Mendel and the rest wanted in on Charles' contract. They didn't. They told him it looked like Louis was going to retire, and in the event he went through with it, they wanted Charles to face Walcott for the vacant title. Mintz was thrilled but didn't sign the agreement they showed him that day because he "wanted time to think and look the situation over from both barrels."[11] He left Chicago and then, for a while, nothing happened.

On July 26, Charles' pursuit of Lesnevich came finally to an end when Lesnevich was beaten up, decisioned and dethroned by the wholly ordinary Freddie Mills in London. The next day Mintz announced that Charles would henceforth fight only as a heavyweight. Lesnevich's loss to a second-rater like Mills "proves that Charles is the best boxer in the world," he said.[12]

That marked the end of an era for Charles. No more was he a member of what would eventually become known as the Black Murderer's Row, that special, cursed group of brilliant middleweights and light heavyweights of the 1940s and '50s who never got what they were due. By moving to heavyweight and onto a path that would lead to a title fight—even though he remained, in truth, a light heavyweight—he had graduated from the rarefied ranks that included Burley, Lloyd Marshall, Holman Williams, Herbert Lewis Hardwick, Jack Chase, Eddie Booker, Elmer Ray, Aaron Wade and Bert Lytell, all wonderful, gifted prizefighters who were his inferiors but not by much. You could argue that their only sin was not being big enough, lucky enough, connected enough, or ordinary enough to get the title shots they deserved. If not for that one sin they would be remembered as kings, too.

No one knew it then, but Charles had also left behind Archie Moore, who would have his success against the big men but would eventually be best remembered as one of the great light heavyweights, and owner by the time he was done of more knockouts than any fighter ever. But Archie could never do a thing with Ezzard Charles. It was during that period that Charles now left behind, dating from 1942 until his official ascension to heavyweight, that he became one of the great fighters not only of his era but of any era. He'd beaten Burley twice and Marshall twice, Moore three times, Joey Maxim twice, Ray at least once, twice if you asked enough people, and Bivins, the patron saint of Murderer's Row, three times by this point.

The success rate Charles realized against a group of fighters this good was unparalleled. It is the kind of achievement and genius that only can be seen and admired in retrospect, when time has worn away all the prejudice and bias. And he wasn't done yet. The heavyweight version of Charles would get a lot of good work done, but on the best day of his life he was no more a heavyweight than was Ray Robinson, and he never would be as good there as he was at light heavy and below. And now that was behind him.

With everything that had happened with Louis' people, Mintz was terrified of having Charles face Bivins in Washington, D.C., on August 2. Sure, Charles had beaten Jimmy twice already, but Bivins was still a hell of a fighter. Why risk everything? He had to try to get out of it. Bivins could ruin everything. So on July 31, Mintz asked for a postponement from August 2 to August 9, claiming Charles had a "glandular disorder" that gave him a sore back. That was a short-term solution, but it was better than nothing and gave Mintz time to think and maybe call in a favor or two. Unfortunately for him, news about the "hush-mush" plan had already leaked out; matchmaker Gabe Menendez, working on behalf of Bivins, went public with it and demanded that Charles be examined by commission doctors.

Menendez revealed that he knew all about the proposed Charles-Walcott fight. "Shortly before the fight, Joe Louis will officially announce his retirement and the New York State Athletic Commission is expected to recognize the Charles-Walcott winner as the new heavyweight king," he told a writer. "If Charles is examined here Monday and found physically fit to go through with the bout on August 9 and he refuses to do so, then watch the fireworks. A defeat for Charles at the hands of Bivins would put a crimp in the proposed Charles-Walcott title bout."[13]

On August 2, three commission doctors examined Charles and found him fit to fight on August 9. Mintz disagreed, making his case as only he could: "The diagnostic of the whole thing proves that the diagnoses is all there."[14] That failed to sway the commission, but Mintz didn't give up easily. Calling upon all his powers of persuasion and who knew what else, he somehow got everyone to agree that Charles and Bivins would meet on September 13. If he couldn't think of anything to get Charles out of the fight by then, at least he gave him some time to get into top shape. He had to be for Bivins.

The Washington, D.C., boxing commissioner suspended Charles from fighting in D.C. until he fought Bivins there and urged all other NBA states to honor the suspension. Eventually, George Rhein, who made a point to the press of identifying himself as Charles' "manager of record," deposited a $5,000 check with the District Boxing Commission as a guarantee that Charles would finally meet Bivins on September 13.

"I'm so nervous about the Charles-Bivins fight I believe I'm getting romantic heart fever," Mintz said a week before the fight.[15] Mintz had never liked Bivins against Charles. He was testy at even hypothetical questions suggesting a Charles loss. When a writer said to Mintz, "If Bivins should win..." Mintz cut him off. "He should live so long! He shouldn't build his bridge before he crosses over."[16]

On fight night Mintz told Charles to be careful with Bivins, not to take any chances. There was too much on the line. Charles listened. Fighting much more cautiously than he had in their previous fights, he boxed and moved his way to a unanimous but mostly uninspired decision win in front of 11,631 fans at Griffith Stadium. He controlled Bivins for the most part with his left, stabbing him from outside with the jab and drilling him with uppercuts up close.

Bivins, aware of how well Moore had done against Charles by staying on the inside, tried the same strategy, but Charles generally outfought him there, too. Neither fighter appeared hurt at any time, and the crowd mostly sat on their hands until the tenth, when both fighters suddenly opened up and went for the knockout. Charles didn't have to; he was ahead on points. At the end referee Ray Bowen scored it for Charles 6–3–1. The judges liked Charles 5–3–2.

Mintz, almost beside himself with relief, hollered to the press afterward, "Charles is the next world champion. Bring on whoever you got!"[17] He didn't specify the division over which Charles would reign, but it was clear that Charles' future would be at heavyweight— even if the fighter himself didn't like it. Charles weighed just 176 for Bivins, two and a half pounds less than Jimmy and just a pound over the light heavyweight limit. "I feel strong at this weight but I got no fire, no pep," he complained afterward.[18]

The press was generally unenthusiastic over Charles' showing, even though he'd decisively whipped one of the best heavyweights in the world. "Ezzard Charles Unimpressive in Beating Bivins," headlined one piece that read, in part, "Against an established puncher Charles is not the two-fisted destroyer he is against foes who are not so dangerous. Ezzard was cautious to the extent of occasionally being dull."[19] The writer lamented that, in terms of punching power, Charles was no Joe Louis. This was possibly the first time but certainly not the last that Charles would be compared unfavorably with Louis in the press.

Four days after Charles beat Bivins, Louis shocked everyone by saying he wasn't retired after all. "If Baksi and Charles put up a good fight and the winner comes through good, I'll fight him," he said.[20] This was complete hogwash; Louis no more wanted to fight again than he wanted to fly a spaceship to the moon. The truth was that Norris and Wirtz were concerned about a fight that was supposed to go off in Jersey City between Walcott and

Lesnevich that was being put together by rival promoter Tournament of Champions. The main event was Tony Zale's defense against Marcel Cerdan. If the Walcott-Lesnevich bout came off, the IBC's proposed Charles-Walcott-Lesnevich-Savold tournament would fall apart. They knew that if Louis rescinded his retirement, the Walcott-Lesnevich bout would never go through because Lesnevich, especially, would figure he would get a Louis bout and the payday that went with it. Louis was, if nothing else, a good soldier and did as he was asked. Sure enough, on the very same day that Louis announced he would face the Charles-Baksi winner, Lesnevich pulled out of his fight with Walcott. Before it hit the press, Tournament of Champions matchmaker Andy Niederreiter called Mintz in a panic. He said Lesnevich was out and asked if Mintz would consider having Charles replace him.

"How much?" Mintz asked.

"$25,000," Niederreiter replied.

$25,000!?" roared Mintz. Charles was getting just $9,000 from Twentieth Century for the Baksi fight, so twenty-five grand was great, except for one thing: He knew that both Lesnevich and Walcott were guaranteed $50,000. He couldn't let Charles get underpaid like that. "Are you saying you don't think my boy is worth the same as Lesnevich?"[21]

Mintz got Niederreiter up to $40,000 but no higher. The conversation ended with Mintz asking for time to think it over. He could use the money. He was dead broke. He was always dead broke. Nothing was official with Louis' group yet, and he could take the fight if he really wanted it. $40,000 was a hell of a lot better than the $9,000 Charles was getting from Twentieth Century. But he'd made a deal with Jacobs and Strauss and was trying to think about the long term. He decided to stick with the Baksi fight. He just about wept as he called Niederreiter and turned down the offer.

A little while later the news came in that Lesnevich claimed to have broken his toe tripping on the stairs at his local post office in Cliffside Park, New Jersey. Niederreiter never did get a replacement for Lesnevich, and in the main event Cerdan stopped Zale in the eleventh round.

Meanwhile, Charles was in the midst of training for Baksi when, on October 8, the fight was postponed after Baksi reportedly injured a finger that then became infected and prevented him from sparring. The fight was rescheduled for December 10. Mintz didn't want Charles going against Baksi after a long layoff, so he put him in Music Hall Arena in Cincinnati on November 15 against two hundred-pounder Walter Hafer, an unranked clubber from Kentucky.

You wouldn't have thought Charles against a no-hoper at this point in his career would do much business, but Sam Becker knew how to promote a fight. It didn't hurt that a month before, right there at Music Hall, Hafer had knocked out the Austrian Joe Weidin, who Jack Dempsey was telling everyone was going to be the next champ. Charles-Hafer did a $20,577.40 gate, and 4,843 fans saw Charles drop Hafer four times and stop him in the seventh round.

With his finger healed, Baksi was ready to go against Charles. He had fought only once since his embarrassing and bizarre upset loss in Sweden to Ollie Tandberg, stopping clubfighter Willie Brown in four rounds in Massachusetts. The Tandberg fight had cost him the payday of a lifetime—Twentieth Century had guaranteed him $125,000 for the Louis fight, and even if he did need Louis like he needed a hole in the head, how do you walk away from that payday?

Still, everyone and his mother thought he'd beaten Tandberg—even the Swedish press, and even Tandberg, who said afterward that he hadn't fought well and deserved, at best, a draw. It would have gone down as the worst decision of the year if the judges in the Garden hadn't screwed Walcott the way they did against Louis. It was that bad. Baksi had really pissed off someone.

Baksi didn't have it in him much to be a fighter anymore, and he'd ballooned up to 257 pounds after the Tandberg fight. But it was no good to go out on a loss like that, especially for a guy as big and white as he was. So when they asked him if he wanted to face Charles at the Garden for $9,000, he figured why the hell not? Charles was a light heavyweight; Big Joe could get down to fighting weight, or close to it, and still have 30 pounds on him. If they were going to throw that kind of cash at him to push around little guys like Charles, he'd be crazy not to take it.

At the same time Baksi was getting ready for Charles, another guy, more Charles' size, was doing the same thing. Billy Conn, the great light heavyweight who fought out of Pittsburgh and for a while under Mintz, had retired after his postwar loss to Louis in their rematch in 1946. He'd talked on and off since then about coming back. Strauss, running Twentieth Century, was especially keen on making a Conn-Charles match if Conn could get in shape. If he could beat Charles, Louis-Conn III would be a monster.

Conn's motivation for coming back wasn't just the money or getting another shot at the heavyweight title. It was also to make everyone, especially himself, forget the terrible showing he had put on against Louis in their rematch. It kept him up at night. He also figured the division was mostly bums. "I figure I have a chance to win the championship. You know why?" he asked a writer. "There's only one good prospect in the bunch: Ezzard Charles."[22]

Conn, who was now thirty-one years old, sold the idea of an exhibition bout between himself and Louis in Chicago on December 10—the same night Charles and Baksi would meet at the Garden. It was an easy sell. Louis loved Billy and would do whatever he could to give him a chance to make a payday so long as everyone knew that he, Louis, was and always would be the better fighter. If he was being honest, Louis would admit he had disdain for most fighters. They weren't in his league. Bums and cowards, mostly. But Billy.... Billy could fight and had big balls and Louis loved him for it.

They'd wear the big gloves, and a crew of writers would serve as "judges" and decide who had won. Conn trained hard and in November stopped clubfighters Mike O'Dowd and Jackie Lyons, each in the ninth round. If he could manage to get the newspaper decision over Louis in Chicago or maybe if he just didn't embarrass himself, he'd get a fight with Charles and then maybe Louis for the title, if Louis decided not to retire after all.

While Conn was preparing for his last shot at Louis, Charles was back in New York winding down training for Baksi. He was a solid 3–1 favorite and so naturally, all anyone wanted to talk to him about was how he felt about the prospect of fighting Louis after he whipped Baksi. He was wrapping his hands in a gym in Harlem before a workout, Mintz at his side, when he answered the question the best way he could. "I don't like to think about fighting him," he said. "I wouldn't want to be the one to knock out Louis. Somebody might but it would make me sad to do it. Joe will always be the champion to us folks."[23] He told Jimmy Brown that fighting Louis would be like a man fighting his own father.[24]

On fight night, Charles weighed 178, the heaviest of his career, and still Baksi held a 32½ pound weight advantage. It didn't matter. Charles spent the first few rounds stabbing and pounding Baksi's big body. He was far too fast and slick, and he out-maneuvered and out-fought his lumbering opponent at every turn, even if he couldn't really hurt him. "Ezzard buzzed around Baksi like a bumblebee around a bull,"[25] one writer said later.

Baksi made the odd decision to give up his height advantage and fight out of a crouch so he could get close to Charles and lean on him and pound his body, and in spots this strategy worked. For the great majority of every round, however, Charles speared him over and over. After a while it took on the look of a hyena taking apart a gigantic wildebeest piece by piece. By the fifth round Baksi was in a terrible way, and Charles could have ended it any time he wanted to. The big guy bled from a cut over his left eye and from his nose and from his mouth, his right eye was swollen shut, and he was exhausted. Charles was unmarked and fresh. In the sixth some in the crowd of 11,194 started calling on him to end it. They figured he was carrying Baksi. As the rounds passed more and more hollered, "Knock him out Charles!" and before long the entire arena echoed with boos.[26]

Charles went on his way though, taking no chances, jabbing, jabbing, stepping over, because this was a big man in front of him. Why get careless and walk into something? He didn't realize yet that he was a heavyweight now, no matter what the scale said, and if he expected to be liked and cheered, he'd better start knocking guys the hell out—especially if he had it in his mind that he was going to replace Joe Louis. Louis would have blasted Baksi out in a round or two and sent everyone home early and happy. That's what they were used to and that's what they wanted. This was the price Charles paid for moving to heavyweight.

Charles cut Baksi to pieces in the tenth, but referee Ruby Goldstein took the round from him for hitting on the break. Finally at 2:33 of the eleventh poor Baksi, who had never been stopped in sixty-three fights, couldn't take it anymore and begged Goldstein to call it off. "Stop it. I can't see. I can't see," he cried.[27]

In the late editions the papers described the job Charles did on Baksi as "thorough, workmanlike,"[28] "calculating and deliberate."[29] There wasn't a "sensational" or "exciting" to be found anywhere, which again was a reflection of the higher standards against which Charles the heavyweight was now being measured. "The Cincinnati Ebony man was hardly a tiger ... he is still a light heavyweight trying to campaign among the big boys," one writer observed.[30] Another wrote, "Charles can box and he can cut you. But he must have nailed Baksi with a hundred or more full rights to the chin without jarring him. The public, expected to put out good money to see a heavyweight championship [fight], needs further proof that Charles is the right challenger."[31]

Afterward the writers asked Charles again what he thought about meeting Louis in his next fight. He couldn't have given them a more honest answer or a worse one. "I don't know about Louis. I'd have to be in better shape for the champ than I was for this thing," he said. "Then, too, you know how I feel about Louis. I'd rather not meet him. 'Cause, after all ... well, he's the champ, that's all."[32]

The writers saw this as an admission of fear rather than respect and in their columns the next day they all played up the angle that Charles was afraid of Louis, because anyone with a brain in his head, especially a little guy like Charles, would have to be crazy to want to face him. It didn't occur to them that Charles was still a humble kid from the slums of Cincinnati who had been idolizing Louis almost since he was in diapers, and this wasn't fear in the way they knew it. It involved something else that all men feel about their heroes but that only some unlucky prizefighters have to someday reconcile. Still, it didn't put Charles in the best light among fans, and Mintz knew it. He did his best to spin it to Charles' advantage. "Charles still thinks the champion is a great guy. But like he told me, 'I'm a man and that hero worship stuff will have to be sidetracked. I want the title and I'd like to fight Louis in June.'"[33]

Later that night Louis and Conn met in their exhibition in Chicago in front of 6,517 hopeful romantics. It was a disaster for Conn. Louis toyed with him, hurting him when he wanted to and backing off when he didn't have to. He won the newspaper decision easily, 6 rounds to 2. It was the easiest $7,000 he ever made. Conn had nothing. Afterward the writers told Louis of the mess Charles had made of Baksi in New York. Louis acknowledged Charles was his top challenger if he was going to fight again. Then, looking at Conn across the room, he said, "Billy is a pretty good fighter and now he can go for Ezzard Charles. Conn should keep up his comeback."[34] "I hope to," Conn responded. "I know I can beat all the heavyweights around. They're all a bunch of bums, but Louis … he is great."[35] Conn knew better than anyone that he was talking out of his ass. He wouldn't stand a chance in hell against Charles. He went home to Pittsburgh and never fought again.

Mintz knew he had to keep Charles busy and in front of the fans, so after a short layoff following the Baksi fight he signed him up for two fights in February; one against former two-time victim Joey Maxim at the new arena in Cincinnati, late in the month, and the other against another giant like Baksi. The press and fans believed Charles was too small to be the heavyweight champion. Mintz had to change that so he matched Charles with big Johnny Haynes. Haynes was mostly a ham-and-egger but he was also 6'4" and 214 pounds of sculpted muscle.

Mintz put the fight in Philadelphia. It would be Charles' first time fighting there, and Haynes' first since September 1948, when he had killed a local heavyweight named Billy "Chicken" Thompson. Like Baksi, Haynes made Charles look like a welterweight. Charles ate as much as he could leading up to the fight and cut down on roadwork, but still came in at just 179, the heaviest of his career but still 35 pounds lighter than Haynes.

Since the Baksi fight Charles had learned, with some help from Mintz, how to talk to the press about Louis. He told the Philadelphia writers that he hoped Louis "would stay retired so I don't have to fight him," but if he got the chance to face him "it will be my job to flatten him."[36]

A crowd 4,731 producing $11,247 came out to the arena and watched Charles box cautiously from the outside for the first two rounds before hurting Haynes with a left hook in the third. Charles stepped in to press, and Haynes suddenly started winging heavy shots. Charles backed the hell off like anyone with a brain would and when the crowd saw that, they let him have it. He said to hell with them and kept boxing, eventually opening up a cut over Haynes' right eye in the fifth. Still boxing from a distance, he dropped Haynes for a nine-count with a right uppercut in the seventh.

It looked for all the world like it was over, but Haynes stormed out of his corner at the start of the eighth and chased Charles around the ring with a series of roundhouses. The crowd and much of the press, too, sadly, thought he had Charles on the run, that he'd hurt him, but Charles knew it was the big man's last gasp so he let him take it.

Charles let him burn it up, and then he stepped in with another right uppercut that put Haynes on his back. He made it to a knee by the time the referee's count reach "ten" at 2:38 of the round. The crowd, apparently incensed that Charles refused to stand and fight with Haynes, booed him mercilessly. The press didn't treat him much better, despite the fact he'd knocked a man flat who outweighed him by thirty-five pounds. If he wanted people to take him seriously as a heavyweight and especially as a possible heir to Louis' throne, he would have to do better.

"Charles did not add to his prestige in the victory. The fans just couldn't visualize him in the same ring with Louis," reported one writer, who summed up the reports of most of his colleagues when he added that Charles "appears to be resolutely carrying out a campaign of self-elimination."[37]

A couple days after the Haynes fight, Mintz took Charles to New York. They went to Louis' home, where they met with Joe and Gibson. Louis reiterated that he was thinking of retiring and wanted Charles to fight for his vacant title. All he had to do was sign a contract naming Louis his promoter—the contract they had given Mintz several months earlier—and it would be done. If he didn't? No fight. Walcott had been presented with the same deal. He signed. So too did Charles. It would have been crazy not to. Mintz was beside himself. "I'm walking on eggs," he told Charles.[38] Charles was relieved. If Louis was going to be his promoter, it meant he'd never have to face him in the ring.

Charles and Mintz hoped up to make up for the bad press after the Haynes fight with a solid showing against Maxim three weeks later. A lot had changed since their last fight seven years earlier. The rascal Jack Kearns, who had managed Jack Dempsey to stardom and Mickey Walker to something close, was running the show now for Maxim. It was the best thing that could happen to a guy like Joey. Everyone knew Kearns, and Kearns knew everyone. He had connections nobody else did. He was the best there was at ballyhoo, better even than Mintz, and nobody could schmooze the press like he could.

Maxim had also been busy. He'd lost his share—to Curtis Sheppard, to Lloyd Marshall, and a couple of squeakers to Walcott—but he'd won a lot more. He'd whipped Sheppard in their rematch, and Bivins and Bob Satterfield. He'd beaten Nate Bolden and Walcott right in Camden, and in the Garden he had outpointed Tandberg, the Swede who'd beaten Baksi. Going into the fight with Charles he'd won fifteen of his last eighteen including two draws against tough Pat Valentino and was boxing as well as he ever had. At twenty-six years old, he was at his physical peak, as was Charles.

The fight was a big deal for Cincinnati. They'd just opened the Cincinnati Garden, a shiny new arena that was the city's pride and joy. The Charles-Maxim card was a big step up from the arena's first events—a hockey game and a couple of college basketball games. Charles was acutely aware that he had to make a good impression after the shafting the press had given him over the Baksi and Haynes fights, and he trained as hard as he ever had. Every morning he was up at 5:30 a.m. for roadwork, either in the hills at Eden Park, or from his house in the 900 block of Lincoln Park Drive to Music Hall and then to Union Terminal—ten times before he was done. Jimmy Brown, who lived next door, would watch him go by and count the laps.

Despite Charles' two prior wins over Maxim, the odds were close—6–5 Charles or pick 'em. Partly through Kearns' charm, partly through Maxim's recent hot streak, and partly through how good he was said to look in drills at the Becker Gym, you could find a lot of action on Maxim if you were looking for it. It also helped that he was white, and fight fans are susceptible to betting with their hearts.

If it wasn't enough that Charles was fighting in his hometown in a big, brand new arena against a skilled, troublesome guy like Maxim, rumor had it that the winner would get a fight with Louis if Louis rescinded his retirement. Charles had to be sick of hearing it by this time—he knew that Louis wasn't coming back; that he, Charles, would be fighting someone for the vacant title, and it wouldn't be Louis. But, it could all change. For all he knew Louis could change his mind tomorrow.

All the talk about a possible date with Louis added to the excitement of the event. On fight night, anyone who was anyone in Cincinnati or in the fight game was at Cincinnati Garden, among the 14,062 fans who paid $72,818, the largest gate in Cincinnati boxing history. Important boxing people were everywhere. Louis had people there. There were Madison Square Garden reps everywhere, and important gangsters and other business types. Lee Savold was there to "scout" Charles, which gave Mintz a big laugh. He'd been trying for two years at least to get Savold. He wouldn't go near Charles.

Charles wasn't facing a giant this time—Maxim weighed in at 184—but he still came in at 182 pounds, the heaviest of his career, and the extra weight slowed him down. He took the early rounds the same way he had in his first two fights with Joey—by backing him up and throwing hard punches. One of those punches, an overhand right, busted open Maxim's right eye in the third. But a strategy that simple was only going to work so long on a seasoned pro like Maxim, whose bread and butter was handling guys who came hard after him.

In the fifth Joey finally got his jab working, and that meant trouble for Charles. Time after time over the middle rounds, Maxim's jab landed square on Charles' face, knocking him off rhythm and bloodying his nose. When Charles got close and tried to work inside, Maxim smacked him with a left hook, tied him up and smothered him before Charles could get his punches off.

With his jab humming, Maxim took the fifth, six, seventh and eighth rounds, but began to slow down just a step in the ninth. Charles' pressure was wearing on him. If you kept after a guy long and hard enough, even a great cutie like Maxim, sooner or later he had to slow down. It helped Charles that he had fifteen rounds to work with rather than ten. They'd made it a fifteen-rounder to emphasize its proximity to a title shot. It was lucky for Charles that they did. Little by little he closed the gap over the final five rounds while Maxim faded. A hard right hand in the thirteenth took anything Maxim had left.

"I shouldn't have coasted the last three rounds," Maxim said later. "It was on the advice of my handlers."[39] Whether he was coasting or just running out of gas, Maxim lost the fight then, but no one knew that when the last bell rang. There were plenty in the audience who thought Charles had blown it, and those same observers booed heartily when the decision came back in Charles' favor, though not unanimously. While two judges scored it for Charles, the third had it a draw. Smiling widely in his dressing room later, Charles called Maxim a "real clever boy" and suspected that maybe he'd gotten away with one.[40]

The fight press, mostly in agreement that Charles had won, or at the least noncommittal on it, were nevertheless unenthusiastic about him—again. A typical headline read, "Ezzard Charles Unimpressive in Maxim Bout." The subtitle read, "Cincinnati Negro Gets Decision but Adds Little to Challenger Prestige."[41] Charles had to wonder then what the hell he had to do at this weight to please people. He never did figure it out.

On March 1, 1949, the day after Charles' close win over Maxim, Louis made it official, formally retiring and relinquishing the heavyweight title in a letter to NBA commissioner Abe J. Green. At a press conference in Miami Beach, Harry Mendel confirmed what many in the business already knew: Louis had formed a promotional company with Jim Norris and Arthur Wirtz and already had contracts signed with Charles and Walcott to fight for the vacant title in June. Within ninety days the winner had to face either Lesnevich or Savold.

"I am certain you know how sorry I must be to let the championship go this way," the letter read. "I have held it for a long time and I won it in the ring. I expected to lose it in the same way I won it. However, things have developed so that I ought to stick to the decision to retire that I announced some time ago."[42] And with that, it appeared, the Joe Louis era was over.

It also marked the end of Twentieth Century Sporting Club and Mike Jacobs, whom Louis, Norris and Wirtz had effectively frozen out of the heavyweight title picture. Jacobs, aged and never fully the same after his stroke, saw it coming. For selfish reasons he had tried to talk Louis out of promoting, but Louis was his own man, and he didn't have to take orders from Jacobs anymore. Though Louis said publicly that he wasn't deliberately setting out to ruin him, Jacobs knew what it all meant, and he vented in the press. "I never thought he would do this to me.... We ain't conceding nothing," he raged.[43] He didn't have to concede. It didn't matter. He was over. The IBC was about to do to him what he'd done to the Garden, because what goes around comes around—especially in the fight game.

8

Hey, Aren't You Ezzard Charles?

In April, Mintz sent Charles on a small exhibition tour. It was easy money and helped keep him sharp. Over the next month they hit Detroit, Indianapolis, Omaha, South Bend, and Gary, Indiana. Back in the cities in offices and meeting rooms, there was a lot of bickering.

It seemed not everyone was happy about how Joe Louis' successor was being chosen. Who did Joe and these new guys think they were, anyway? Why, Wirtz and Norris were babes in the business. Why did they get to decide? And the NBA? Everyone knew they were as crooked as they came. They'd call Mickey Rooney the heavyweight champ if they could make a buck out of it. So right off the bat there was resistance. Louis or not, the IBC was a promotional outfit, and no promoter should be in the business of naming a champ, especially when all four of the guys fighting for the title belonged to that promoter. It reeked.

Sure, the game was as rigged as could be, but that was all behind the scenes. No one was supposed to know about that, and that made it okay. But this? This was an outrage. Forget that the guys who'd challenged Louis all those years all had to sign exclusive deals with Twentieth Century in order to get a shot at him. Forget that in the fight business you always had to be connected to get somewhere. This was business as usual and the ones crying about it were mostly the ones who didn't think of it first or were getting frozen out somehow.

Jacobs hated it, of course, but no one cared what he thought anymore. The British Boxing Board of Control wasn't having it either. They said straight away that they wouldn't recognize the Charles-Walcott winner as the new champion. What about their guy, Bruce Woodcock? He'd just stopped Freddie Mills, who'd beaten Lesnevich, who was in the tournament. Why wasn't he invited?

The New York State Commission, headed by Chairman Eddie Eagan, passed, too, if only to distinguish itself from the NBA, with whom it was at constant odds, not that that made it any less rotten. *The Ring* magazine, the second-most influential fight magazine around after the *Police Gazette*, said it too wouldn't back the Charles-Walcott winner as the new champ. All of them said they would withhold recognition until the winner of Charles-Walcott faced the winner of the Woodcock-Savold bout, which was scheduled for September.

As far as Mintz was concerned, Eagan and the Brits were irrelevant. He was thrilled. He'd taken a skinny little middleweight from the Cincinnati slums all the way to the world heavyweight championship, or close to it. And he'd done it while still making fights for his Pittsburgh bosses, and he'd done it for a measly 10 percent of Charles' purses. Did Dyer, Rhein and Elkus know how much work that was? Did they have any idea how many scumbags he'd had to kiss up to, how many deals he'd had to make, how many enemies he'd made?

Not that he minded doing any of it. It was what he was born to do, what he was good at. Those three from Cincinnati didn't know their asses from a hole in the ground when it came to the fight game. Sure, they had some history or something with Charles, and maybe deeper pockets, but without Mintz, Charles would still be going life and death against Bivins, Burley and Marshall for pennies back in Cleveland, Cincinnati and Pittsburgh. It was Mintz who was always pushing him to go bigger. It was Mintz who was making connections, getting Charles' name in the paper, working the writers, getting publicity. It was him. And it was time he got a raise.

After Louis made his retirement official, Mintz called a meeting with the managers and made his case for a raise to 15 percent. It wasn't unreasonable, considering everything he'd done. And there, at the meeting, the managers agreed. They weren't crazy about this little weasel, Mintz—he was too wild for their taste, too uncouth and bawdy. He was everything that was wrong with the fight game. If any one of them knew the game and the business as well as he did, they wouldn't have needed his services. But they didn't. They had to admit that.

As crazy and annoying as Mintz was, he had done everything he said he would with Charles and more. They weren't dopes; they knew he wanted to take over Charles completely, but they were businessmen and figured they were smarter than he was when it came to dollars and cents and contracts and such. So they threw him a bone and cut him in for 15 percent, figuring it would keep him quiet for a while. And they hoped for the best.

Charles' managers weren't the only Cincinnati natives getting worked over. A couple hours after Charles squeaked by Maxim, Charles' old friend and promoter Sam Becker bought dinner for Charles' managers and Bocchicchio and told them he wanted to hold a Charles-Walcott fight there in Cincinnati. The group stayed up until 2:00 a.m. talking about it in a Cincinnati hotel and agreed to finish negotiations the next morning. When Becker came down for breakfast, he found out that Mendel had come in and whisked Walcott and Charles out of town.

Becker got ahold of Mendel on the phone and told him he wanted to hold Charles-Walcott in Cincinnati. Mendel told him he had to speak to Norris in person. Becker flew to Miami and met with Norris, who told him that if he wanted to promote the fight he had to hand over $150,000.

"Why all that money?" Becker asked. "After all, I promoted Charles ever since he was 14 years old. What changed?"

"Well, Charles belongs to me now," Norris said. "Walcott belongs to me."[1] Becker said to hell with it and the fight ended up at Comiskey Park in Chicago and promoted fully by the IBC.

Even Charles wasn't crazy about the whole setup. He'd make more money and have a bigger profile, but this wasn't the way he was supposed to become champ. Back when he was fighting middleweights in Cincinnati, he never thought in a million years he'd one day be big enough to be the heavyweight champ of the world. He knew deep down that he really wasn't, but Mintz kept telling him he could make it happen and damned if he hadn't gotten him this far.

Still, if he was going to be the heavyweight champ, he wanted to be the real heavyweight champ. He never did want to fight Louis, but he didn't want to get it this way either. It just didn't feel right. It didn't make a lot of sense to him, and as far as he was concerned this would just be another fight. They could call it anything they wanted to, the writers and the NBA, but to him it was another day at work. All he had to remember was to get in shape, fight hard and stay the hell out of the way of Walcott's right hand.

To help Charles do that, Mintz hired George Nicholson to assist Jimmy Brown in camp. Nicholson had been one of Louis' main sparring partners through much of his championship tenure. During the war years he and Louis had fought hundreds of exhibitions at military camps all over the world. For the last three years of Louis' reign he had been Joe's assistant trainer, and when Joe more or less retired after the Walcott rematch, he put Nicholson out of work.

Louis loved his old army buddy and more than that, he trusted him, so when he "suggested" to Charles that he take Nicholson on as assistant trainer, Charles and Mintz complied. What did they have to lose? If he was good enough for Louis, he was good enough for them. Plus, he had the experience of twice going against Walcott.

Hiring Nicholson was proof that Mintz and the rest of Charles' managers were taking no chances getting Ezzard ready for the fight. This was the big one, whether Charles thought so or not. It meant everything, and when you're fighting for everything you don't train in your own little hometown gym. That's what the nobodies did, the bums, the losers. Charles was a big-time fighter now; he was fighting for the world title. When you do that you don't train where your buddies are and your best girl. They're distractions, so you go out to the country, you go out and run in the hills in the fresh air, and when you're not in the gym you play cards or read or talk to the writers hanging around camp looking for a story, because Lord knows there isn't anything else to do.

So in late May they set up Charles and his sparring partners, Lloyd Gibson, Gene Jones and Charley Banks, on the grounds of Sunset Hills Golf Club in Momence, Illinois, about an hour from Comiskey Park. Everywhere you looked there were trees, grass and sky. It was easy to get close to nature. Walcott set up camp about twelve miles away at Peaceful Valley, also in the Kankakee River Valley. When the writers came out from New York to write their stories they called it God's country.

Even the peaceful setting couldn't stop Mintz from making a scene. On June 7 he drove over to Walcott's camp and heckled him while he sparred. Bocchicchio climbed down from the ring apron and tackled him. The two had to be separated. Mintz stormed out, saying, "I'm going back to see a *good* workout!"[2]

The fight didn't need Mintz and Bocchicchio to generate publicity. Despite the suspicion among the press and fans that Walcott was too old and Charles too timid, the bout was doing business. By June 14 Mendel was telling everyone they had $150,000 in advance sales. A lot of it was about Louis and his new role.

The old bomber was more or less stationed at the fighter's camps where he greeted writers, tended to their questions about the fight, that sort of thing. He liked to say that he picked the date of the match, which was the twelfth anniversary of his title-winning knockout of Jimmy Braddock in the very same arena where Charles and Walcott would meet for his old title. Maybe it was his idea. It didn't really matter.

The week before the fight Jack Dempsey, boxing royalty, showed up to help drum up publicity like he always did at the important fights. In return the promoter would kiss his ass. That's the way it worked with Twentieth Century. He'd get set up at the nicest hotel, put his meals and booze on Jacobs' tab, take pictures with the fighters, and schmooze with the writers and fans. All he had to do was hang around.

On his first day at Charles' camp Dempsey made the mistake of telling a reporter the heavyweight title shouldn't be awarded "by commission." The next day everybody read it in the papers, and the day after that Dempsey was spotted carrying his bags out of his hotel on his way back to New York. He said he'd gotten the cold shoulder from the promoter and wasn't interested in sticking around anymore. That's how the IBC did things. You were either with them or against them. No one much missed him anyway.

Charles opened at about a 13–5 favorite. Considering how the press had turned on him in recent fights, it was a surprise he was favored at all. A lot of that had to do with how long Walcott had been off. As far as anyone could tell he hadn't stepped a foot inside a prize ring in almost a year, or since his rematch with Louis. For a man his age—reportedly thirty-five, but who knew?—a layoff that long couldn't be good, especially against a young, fast kid like Charles.

But Walcott wasn't worried. "Charles is a good fighter but I know too much for him," he said a week before the fight. "Youth is a wonderful thing, I admit. But I don't think Charles will benefit by it. I have too many advantages over him. I am heavier and stronger. I think I hit harder and have a lot more experience."

When someone brought up Walcott's fights against Louis, Jersey Joe brushed aside the comparison. "I don't want anyone to think I have too much mouth when I say not only will I beat Charles but I will knock him out. I did knock down Louis three times, which ought to prove that I can hit. And Charles is no Joe Louis. Not by a long shot. Oh, no."[3]

Maybe it was Walcott's confidence, maybe it was something else, but late money came pouring in on Jersey Joe the week before the fight, lowering the odds to 8–5 Charles. By fight night they were down to 6–5. Louis, Wirtz and Norris were satisfied enough when the crowd at Comiskey Park numbered 25,392, putting $246,546 in their pockets plus the $35,000 for TV rights, minus 25 percent for each of the fighters. It wasn't the 45,000 that came out to see Louis knock out Braddock 12 years earlier, but it wasn't bad for their first outing as a promotional company. If only it had turned out to be a better fight.

It started out well enough, all things considered. Walcott, weighing 195½ to Charles' 181¾, fought aggressively, eschewing his usual shuffling and feinting and taking the fight to Charles. He got some decent work done, but Charles stayed with him. He was faster and more energetic, and whenever Jersey Joe got close and attacked, Charles stung him with counter-punches. It was true Charles wasn't doing the leading, but he pounded Walcott downstairs. It was nip and tuck over the first six rounds. Midway through the seventh round the fighters became entangled in a clinch and Walcott, desperate to gain some advantage, threw Charles to the canvas. The result produced the best moments of the fight.

Apparently enraged by Walcott's manhandling, Charles attacked and landed a pair of head-rattling right hands that left Walcott teetering like a drunk on a surfboard. He was all but ready to go, and at that moment Charles had the chance to start his reign as heavyweight champion of the world with a convincing, exciting knockout. It would have shut the mouths of all of those who had doubted his authenticity as a heavyweight over the last year, had he stopped Walcott right then and there, a full four rounds quicker than had Louis. But he didn't.

Instead of finishing Walcott, Charles backed off. He said later that he fought as his handlers had told him to,[4] and it was true that they told him not to take chances. This was admirable from a tactical standpoint, but no one likes a heavyweight champion who won't take chances. The fans couldn't know what his seconds had told him. How could they? All anyone knew was he had his man ready to go and he took his foot off the gas. Later in the round Walcott rewarded Charles for his caution with a right cross that rattled Charles to his bones. "I gave him plenty of leather in the seventh round and thought I had him," Charles said later. "But he wouldn't go down. He can take it, I'll say that."[5]

After the bell, Louis, who was sitting in the fourth row, looked like he'd gotten a whiff of some rotten fish. Charles' blown opportunity had offended him both as the fight's promoter and as the greatest knockout puncher who'd ever breathed. "He should have followed him. Sure could have knocked him out if he had done that. Should have chased him. That's what I would do. I wouldn't have let him get away," he told a writer seated close by.[6]

Nevertheless, Charles' seventh-round wallop took about everything out of Walcott. Had Charles pressed, he might have gotten rid of Walcott any time over the next few rounds. Walcott looked exhausted. Instead, Charles continued to lay back and counter, and the fight became a slow waltz. The crowd booed long and hard, as was their right. Charles hurt Walcott badly again in the tenth but even that didn't stop the boos. "The eighth, ninth, 10th, 11th, and 12th rounds were horrible to watch. Walcott couldn't fight and Charles wouldn't," was the way one writer described it.[7]

Another was even harsher: "The Charles-Walcott bout was billed as a championship affair and as it turned out it was an insult to the No.1 division in boxing."[8]

It got so bad that between the twelfth and thirteenth rounds Joseph Triner, chairman of the Illinois state Athletic Commission, ordered referee Davey Miller to tell Walcott's handlers to make him fight.[9] Charles could have used the same advice. It didn't help. Old Joe was out of gas. Charles stepped forward enough over the last couple rounds to seal the victory by scores of 77–73 and 78–72 (twice). And that included a sixth-round penalty he incurred for hitting Walcott on the break.

Walcott complained afterward that he thought he won nine rounds, but he was all alone in that opinion. *The Ring* scored it for Charles 8–5–2 in rounds. The United Press had Charles winning 76–74. Even the writers who were disappointed in Charles' performance had him clearly winning. "[Charles] whipped Walcott by a wider margin than the officials gave him, controlling the bout from the sixth round on, but when he had his turkey ready to serve, he laid the knife aside," one complained.[10]

The announcement of the judges' scores should have been the highlight of Jake Mintz' career, if not his miserable little life. He finally had the heavyweight champ of the world—sort of. But he wasn't thinking about that. In the moments before the decision was announced, he was plotting a way to take attention away from Dyer, Elkus and Rhein, who were in the ring waiting for the decision so they could immediately get their pictures in the paper with the new champ.

Mintz couldn't have that, so as soon as the scores came in, in the middle of all the hoopla, just as the three Cincinnati managers were getting ready for the moment in the sun, he clutched the top rope in a neutral corner and keeled over. Right there in the ring, ol' Jake took a swan dive and for all the world looked like he'd fainted dead away. And that did it. The management trio didn't get in a single picture the next day. But Mintz sure did—even if he was "unconscious" at the time.

When they "brought him to," Mintz mumbled that it must have been all the excitement over Charles winning that did him in. If you knew Mintz you knew it was malarkey. There was only one reason Jake Mintz did anything, even if it looked involuntary, and that was to get some publicity for him or his fighter. That's what made him good.

When they finally got Mintz up and cleared the ring, Louis headed over to Charles' dressing room to congratulate the new champ and talk to the writers. He got angry when he saw reporters and even some of Charles' relatives huddled around his dressing room door, unable to get in. The door was locked and the tiny room was packed with "glad-handers" and other hangers-on.

Louis elbowed his way through the throng, demanded to be let in, and when he entered the room, barked, "Why's all the newspaper men on the outside—they've got to talk with the new champ. Get the champ cooled off and take him to the Bard's room [the White Sox private press room]."[11] Charles' seconds did as they were told—you didn't back-sass Joe Louis, even if you were the heavyweight champ, more or less. Charles got to the press room and gave the boys what they wanted.

"What are you going to do next, champ?"

"I want as many fights as I can get, but now I just want to go home and play some golf for a while. Although I trained at a golf course they wouldn't let me play. I want to be a champion like Louis and I want to play golf as good as him, too."

"Who would you like to fight next?"

"I'll tackle anyone the champ says." (Charles still called Louis "the champ.")[12]

A couple of hours later Charles and his entourage were at a party at one of the big hotels, celebrating the win. The usual suspects were there—the managers, assorted gangsters, IBC suits, and writers. Charles and Christmas grew bored and snuck out to a local Chicago nightclub. They weren't looking for attention. In fact, at Charles' insistence, they did everything they could to avoid being recognized, including donning dark glasses and pulling down their hats. It didn't help. Visitors kept coming over to the table.

"Hey, aren't you Ezzard Charles?"

"Nope," Charles would say.

"You sure do look like him. Didn't you just beat Walcott tonight?"

Here Christmas would jump in.

"No. People are always mistaking him for Charles. He's Bob Harris, a bass fiddle player from Springfield, Ohio, and I'm a drummer." That got them by for a couple hours until a friend barged in and yelled "Hi Ez!" They left not long after, because Ezzard Charles didn't fight for the attention.[13]

The next day Mintz got with the managers to get his cut from the Walcott fight. The way he figured, he had about three grand coming his way—a pretty nice payday. They handed him a check for about $2,300. Ol' Jake was never too good at arithmetic but he knew when he was getting the bum's rush, so he reminded them, none too gently, that they'd agreed before the fight to up his share to 15 percent.

The problem was the trio had grown suspicious of Mintz and his designs on their fighter, and also tired of his antics. The swan dive in the ring at the end of the Walcott fight didn't help. They decided as a group—led in the main by Dyer—that they didn't really want Mintz around anymore. They figured now that Charles was the champ, they didn't need him. They didn't have to go out and look for fights anymore—the title belonged to Charles. The fighters had to come to him. And they had the IBC for everything else. Shortchanging Mintz was their way of firing him without actually firing him. They figured the little hothead would be so furious he'd quit on the spot. They didn't know Jake Mintz as well as they thought they did.

A couple days later Charles and Mintz attended a function with the fight press at the Palmer House in Chicago, where Charles would be officially awarded the heavyweight championship belt. Charles wore a small bandage at the corner of his left eye and a large lump under it, remnants of his fight with Walcott. He was shy, as always. Mintz did most of the talking. In light of his recent troubles with Charles' managers, he relished more than ever the perception that he was Charles' spokesperson and the guy in charge.

"Gentlemen, I'm gonna make a statement and it's gonna be positively official and backed on up 100 percent by my three co-partners Charlie Dyer, Gene Elkus and George

Rhein—and there is not gonna be no other statement," Mintz began. He lived for moments like this. It was what he'd always dreamed of.

"We are not gonna fight no Lesneviches, we are not gonna fight no Maxims at the present time. We are gonna accept a challenge from the Savold-Woodcock winner," Mintz said. "We have the champion but we will be happy to accept the challenges with the approval of the Joe Louis outfit and [IBC rep] Harry Markson of New York, who we are going along 100 percent."

This was a surprise to most everyone in the room, press and IBC representatives alike. They all understood that Charles' original deal with the IBC was that the winner of Charles-Walcott would meet Lee Savold or Gus Lesnevich within ninety days. Mintz and the other managers had decided, apparently, that gaining universal recognition as the heavyweight champion was more important, for the moment, than fulfilling the requirements of the contract with the IBC, even if Mintz was making sure to pay respect to Louis.

"We are also going along with Abe Greene who helped make this bout and should be commented for being successful," Mintz continued. "Charles is gonna have a little pleasure of himself personal to which he is entitled to."[14]

When Mintz finished his speech, a writer asked Charles how it felt to be heavyweight champion. "I don't know. I got more satisfaction out of winning the Golden Gloves," he said. "I don't feel like the champion because too many other people are talking about other fighters. When I beat the rest of them I'll probably feel different. I said it before and I'll say it again. It was just another fight as far as I was concerned."[15] This wasn't just for the press. The morning after he beat Walcott, Charles and Christmas were having breakfast at a hotel. Christmas asked him, "Well, you feel like heavyweight champion of the world?"

"Nope," Charles replied. "Do you?"

"Nope," Christmas replied back.[16]

That made Charles a minority in Cincinnati. Two days after the fight the city government, working with Mintz, Dyer, Rhein, Elkus, Becker and a few others, threw a big parade in Charles' honor, beginning at the train station and ending at the courthouse, where mayor Albert Cash gave Charles the official city greeting. Charles said a few words, mostly about wanting to play golf and defending the title in his hometown—all the things he was supposed to say. Becker came on and announced he wanted to make a fight between Charles and the winner of the upcoming Lesnevich-Maxim fight.

By that time some of the zing had gone out of the celebration. The car Charles rode in while waving to the crowd struck and injured three people on the parade route: Dan Tehan, the city sheriff and a well-known local sports official; Carl Wellinger, a photographer for the *Cincinnati Enquirer*, and city resident Percy Hill. Miss Lulu Belle Henderson, who was driving the car, said later that her foot had slipped off the brake. Two years later Tehan sued Charles for $24,050 for injuries he said he sustained in the crash.

It wasn't long after Charles' homecoming parade that Norris and Wirtz reminded Mintz and the rest of Charles' managers of the details concerning Charles' first title defense. They didn't give a rat's ass if certain parties didn't recognize Charles as the heavyweight champion. Lesnevich had signed on with the IBC and had long had friends in the right places. How did anyone think he'd gotten away with avoiding Charles for so long?

And before you knew it Mintz, Norris and Lesnevich's manager of record, Joe Vella, were at the IBC offices hammering out an agreement for the two to fight on August 10 at Yankee Stadium—just forty-nine days after Charles won the title against Walcott. By meeting Lesnevich, Charles would break the record for quickest first defense of the heavyweight title set by Louis when he defended against Tommy Farr sixty-nine days after dethroning Braddock.

The news broke on July 6 and Christmas, for one, was furious. All those years Lesnevich had ducked Charles and now, after Charles moved to heavyweight and won the title, Lesnevich was getting the first shot. It was absurd. It was even worse than that. Even though he was champion, Charles would get the same 25 percent cut of the gate that Lesnevich would—that's the way the contract with the IBC was written. The champion was supposed to get the lion's share, but Wirtz and Norris had slipped that one past Mintz. Even if he'd seen it, what was he going to do—turn down the deal?

Lesnevich, who had no business even being in the tournament, didn't like the idea to begin with. Before Charles beat Walcott, Lesnevich told the press he and Walcott should fight for Louis' vacant title, since he had beaten Tami Mauriello and Melio Bettina, and Walcott had twice done well against Louis. "All right, who else is there? Ezzard Charles?" he asked. "I personally feel Charles hasn't yet proved he can whip heavyweights. Elmer Ray was the only one he ever beat who amounted to anything."[17]

Anyway, Christmas could be as mad at Charles as he wanted to be. Charles never was in the business of turning down fights, but although he didn't like having to give Lesnevich the first shot either, it was out of his hands. The guys in the suits made the fights; he fought the fights. It wasn't his job to pick the opponents; it was his job to win. Besides, when he got Lesnevich in the ring he'd make him pay for ducking him all those years.

It was ironic, of course, that it was a fifteen-round title fight being held in New York, where Eagan didn't recognize Charles as the champion. So how could it be a title fight? It was, and it didn't have to make sense, because the guys making the deals said it didn't. And truth be told, it didn't make much of a difference. "Our boxing commission has refused to certify the show as a championship affair," wrote one reporter. "I doubt that anyone cares very much."[18]

He was right about that, mainly because Charles had lowered expectations so far with his performance against Walcott that nobody expected anything special from him. Also, Lesnevich was thirty-four years old, a confirmed bleeder, and in his last fight had been outpointed by Joey Maxim. Two fights earlier Freddie Mills beat him over fifteen rounds. He was the sixth-rated heavyweight in the world, but it was the end of the road for him, or close to it, and everyone knew it.

Charles was a 4–1 favorite right off the bat, and the odds never budged. The most the press could reasonably hope for was an interesting fight. They got that, not so much from Charles and Lesnevich, but from the guys running Charles' career. A few days before the bout Dyer ramped up his efforts to get rid of Mintz when he petitioned Eagan to bar him from working the corner during the fight. Dyer said Mintz's fainting spell at the end of the Walcott fight had resulted in "bad press" and he was fearful Mintz would engage in a "similar goofy performance" at the end of the Lesnevich fight.[19]

This was nonsense. The reason the trio wanted Mintz nowhere near Charles was that they found out that a week earlier, he had gotten Charles to sign an official New York State Commission contract naming Mintz his manager for the next two years, reportedly guaranteeing Charles $50,000 a year. "How much a week is that?" Charles asked when Mintz gave him the news. "Boy that really puts me in the bucks."[20]

The commission had an old contract on file showing Rhein as the manager, but it had expired. Rather than getting the managers together to sign a new contract, Mintz had one drawn up with his name on it, and Charles signed it. It could not have been easier. So in

New York at least, inarguably the center of the boxing universe, where all the important fights took place, Mintz was Charles' official manager. Technically, Dyer and Elkus were too, but not in New York and not for much longer. Whether they knew it or not, their association with Ezzard Charles was about to end, mostly because they had underestimated Mintz.

The only other angle the fight press could come up with in the days before the bout involved Charles' alleged lack of punching power, which was code for "he's no Joe Louis." Asked point-blank if he thought the writers were correct that he couldn't punch, Charles was terse. "Maybe they're right. And I'm not going to argue with them. I'm going to let my record speak for me," he said.[21]

As the fight approached, he became testier when questioned about his legitimacy as the heavyweight king. "I may not be any Louis, but name me anyone else who is. Just because I was unlucky enough to not look sensational the few times the New York writers saw me fight doesn't mean I have no right to be the champ."[22]

Really, you couldn't blame the New York writers for not falling in love with Charles. He made them work too hard. One reported that an interview with Charles "is not a rewarding experience," and included in his story a transcript of a chat they had had as Charles wound down training at his camp at Pompton Lakes, New Jersey.

"What do you weigh, Ezzard?"

"About 180."

"What will you come in at?"

"About that. Maybe a little lighter."

"How many times have you seen Lesnevich fight?"

"I saw him fight Billy Fox in the Garden."

"How did he look to you?"

"When you're a fighter you're interested in your own weight class. I was a middleweight then, and Gus was light heavyweight champ."

"Do you expect to knock him out?"

"Oh, I don't know, if he walks into it sure he'll get knocked out."[23]

Luckily for both Charles and the writers, Mintz did enough talking for the both of them. Feeling good about his recent coup, he beseeched the writers to give Charles a break. "What do they want from my boy? He win the title didn't he? He's the champeen, isn't he? He's the best man around today, isn't he? Can't punch? What are they talking about? He knocked out Jimmy Bivins with one punch. He stopped Lloyd Marshall. He cut up Joe Baksi from ribbons, didn't he? What more do they want from my tiger?"[24]

A lot more, apparently. On the night of the fight, which happened to be the hottest day of the year—it was 98.7 degrees outside Yankee Stadium and 102 at ringside—only 16,630 fans showed up, generating a gate of $75,832 (plus $17,500 for the radio rights). If it had been sanctioned as a championship fight, it would have been the poorest-performing heavyweight title fight in history.

Charles, who weighed in at 180 pounds to Lesnevich's 182, tore into Lesnevich from the opening bell, showing none of the reluctance that had hampered him against Walcott. Maybe it was because he didn't fear Lesnevich. Maybe he was tired of hearing how he couldn't punch. Maybe he wanted to pay Gus back for all the years he had spent chasing him. Either way, Lesnevich took a pounding.

It was all Charles, and any question about who the winner would be was answered early. "It became evident as early as the third round that a gradual battering would bring

Gus down," *The Ring* reported.²⁵ Charles could hardly miss. By the fifth both of Lesnevich's eyes had been hammered almost shut and a gaping cut beneath the right bled freely. If anyone wondered why Lesnevich had avoided Charles all those years, here was their answer.

Lesnevich knew as well as anyone that he wouldn't last much longer, so in the sixth he said to hell with it and opened up with both hands, briefly wobbling Charles. But in the seventh Charles went back to torturing him, and after the round Lesnevich took a deep breath, sat back on his stool and told Vella he'd had it. Vella called over referee Ruby Goldstein and told him, "He can't do this anymore." Goldstein said to Lesnevich, "What do you say, Gus?" Gus replied, "What my manager said," and that was that.²⁶

The judges had Charles up six rounds to one at the time of the stoppage, as did everyone else, and afterward Vella and Lesnevich's wife, Georgiana, announced that Lesnevich was retiring. No one was heartbroken.

"Make no mistake about that Charles," Lesnevich mumbled through puffed lips afterward. "The guy can fight. He's young and fast and clever and he knows what he's doing all the time. He can hurt you with a right hand but he's not what you'd call a knockout hitter."²⁷

"I'm ready to go back to training as soon as they can get me another fight," Charles said. "I feel that I am champion and if anyone wants to fight for the title they should fight me. I'll take on any of them." Naturally someone had to ask if that included Louis, if he was in the frame of mind to make a comeback. Charles grinned. "I guess I have to fight anybody now, don't I?"²⁸

Though no one could rightly fault anything Charles did, few in the press overtly praised him. Even those who did couldn't help but remind everyone who he wasn't. "The doubting Thomases who still hold out are looking for another Joe Louis," one writer noted. "Brother, there just ain't another Joe Louis around. You might as well get used to Ezzy, for he may be with you for a long, long time."²⁹

"Ezzard Charles sold himself to New York as the best of a poor lot of heavyweights," wrote another.³⁰ One was even more insulting, writing, "Lesnevich made even Charles appear good," and that Lesnevich did Charles "more good by not being able to dodge his punches the other night than he ever did Charles harm by deliberately dodging him when he wore the light heavy crown."³¹

Mintz didn't fare much better with the remaining managers than Charles did with the press. When it came time to split up the purse, they balked again at giving him the 15 percent they'd agreed on. This time Mintz said to hell with it. He cut all communication with them and on September 9, without their knowledge, he met with the IBC and a California promoter. Four days later he signed up Charles for a title defense in San Francisco against brawler Pat Valentino on October 14. What were they going to do—sue him? Let 'em. He had as much right to Charles legally as they did, more even. He had paper on Charles in New York, the only place that really mattered in boxing, and he had his name on plenty of other contracts, too. Besides, he'd been doing all the work anyway.

The way Mintz saw it, Charles had been his fighter all along—from day one. Those clowns from Cincinnati just didn't know it yet. Well, they'd know it now. They would sue, of course. So what? He had the heavyweight champ of the world. What did they have? He'd cross that bridge when it had water under it, or something, so he waited to get the lawyer's papers and went about getting Charles ready for Valentino, who was no slouch.

The twenty-nine-year-old Valentino took over Lesnevich's slot as the number-six rated heavyweight in the world after Lesnevich retired. He had a head of thick, bushy black hair that became a mess a round into every fight, no matter how much he'd tamed it beforehand. He was all puncher, a street fighter in the ring, and not much on defense. Truth be told he didn't care for fighting, never much saw the use of it; but he was good enough at it to make a few bucks here and there. When you're dirt poor and your old man—a second cousin of 1930s Hollywood legend Rudolph Valentino—gets his rocks off beating the daylights out of you and your seven siblings every day, you take what you can get. Besides, the crowds in San Francisco loved him to death. Where else is a poor Italian kid going to get that kind of attention?

He got lots of attention on the way up, fighting exclusively on the West Coast. A 1947 knockout loss to bomb-throwing Fitzie Fitzpatrick slowed him down a bit, but a year later he'd gotten good enough to twice draw with Maxim, no small feat, and last the whole route with Bivins. By September 1949 Valentino hadn't fought in almost a year on account of having surgery on his right eye. He had just gotten the okay to start training again when his manager, a used car dealer and skunk named Jack Andrade, showed up at the gym and told him, "You're fighting Charles in four weeks." Valentino told him, "I can't be in shape to fight the champ in that time—push it back a bit." Andrade blew him off and told him to get in the best shape he could.[32] Valentino was guaranteed $8,500 before everyone took their cuts, so what was he going to do, turn it down? He got in the best shape he could.

It wouldn't have mattered if Valentino had a year to train, and this was reflected in the 5–1 odds in Charles' favor (it was even money that Charles would stop him), but you had to give the kid credit. He had balls and figured to take it to Charles like nobody's business. It was the first heavyweight title fight in the Bay Area since Jack Johnson had flattened Stanley Ketchel down the road in Colma in 1909, and the fans came out in big numbers—19,951 to be exact—to root for the hometown boy, producing a record California gate of $158,188.50.

Andrade, the manager, did his part by insisting that Charles shave his mustache, and the California commission, which only enforced its prohibition against facial hair when someone complained, had to go along. It was okay with Charles—he was guaranteed $40,000 whether he had a mustache or not.

The indignities didn't stop there. Charles was booed passionately on entering the ring, and then was the first to be introduced—the heavyweight king in forty-eight states introduced before his challenger! It was the champion's privilege to be announced second, always, and anything else was a blasphemy. But unless you were one of the screaming 20,000 rooting with your heart, you had to figure Charles would set things straight sooner or later, and eventually he did.

Charles, weighing 182 to Valentino's 188½, started by boxing neatly and jabbing and hooking on the outside. Valentino, all ropy muscle and nervous energy, charged in again and again, banging Charles with thudding rights to the body. That was his strategy and as far as the crowd seemed to know, that was all he had to do to win; every time one of his swinging rights crashed against Charles' flank over the next several rounds, the roof of the Cow Palace arena shook off its moorings.

It was quiet most of the rest of the time, when Charles was shaking Valentino with right uppercuts and left hooks. To his credit, Valentino never gave up, charging headlong into Charles' piercing counter-punches even when it was clear he didn't have the punch to hurt Charles or the skills to outbox him. His willingness to keep launching himself into combinations that sent his hair flopping this way and that delighted the 20,000, hoarse by the fifth round. You could see why they loved the kid.

By the eighth Valentino was slowing down. Nervous energy takes you only so far, and after that, if you're still rushing in you'd better be throwing punches while you do it. Valentino was taking a blow right in Charles' punching range, and you don't do that with a guy who can fight like Ezzard Charles could, even if you did get introduced to the crowd last. Charles cracked him with a perfect left hook and then turned all his 182 pounds into a right hand that dumped Valentino on his ass. The arena was so quiet that even in the cheap seats you could hear referee Jack Downey count all the way to ten.

Charles was happy enough to get the knockout, given all the talk about his lack of power before the Lesnevich fight, but he didn't need it. The Associated Press and all the ringside writers had him way ahead, so the official scorers did too, right? Wrong. Downey, the referee, and judge Frank Carter, both from San Francisco, had Valentino up on points. Frank Manfredo of Fresno had Charles leading by two points.

"Charles is a foxy fighter with a clean punch," Valentino said afterward. He was bruised over both eyes and cut on the nose and lip. Charles left the ring unmarked. "He's smarter than any other boy I've ever met."[33]

Charles praised Valentino, saying, "He's a good fighter. I'll fight him again anywhere, anytime." One of the local writers, as in love with Valentino as the fans, asked Charles how he'd managed to stand up under the pounding Valentino had given his body when they got in close. Charles shrugged, honest as always. "Maybe tomorrow or the next day my inside will be sore but I don't hurt there now."[34]

Mintz announced he was taking a page from Louis' book; he'd scheduled Charles for a six-week exhibition tour, during which he figured Charles would fight a couple dozen times all over the country against amateurs, sparring partners, local pros, and firemen and the like. This was how heavyweight champions made money. It was a lucrative gig; Louis was making a fortune doing it.

Also, a tour would keep Charles sharp and in the ring, and away from his Cincinnati managers. Mintz knew he'd have to deal with them sooner or later, but in the meantime he wanted to make a few bucks himself and keep Charles close. He'd work on getting another real fight done some time before January, and by that time maybe the thing would work itself out.

In fact, he already had a guy picked out: a clubber named Freddie Beshore, from Harrisburg, who had sparred with Charles some for the Valentino fight. It was in the works before the Valentino fight even came off, maybe for November 30 in Cincinnati. Mintz and Sam Becker had met in New York about it.[35]

Back in Cincinnati, it didn't take long for the lawyers to come. On October 25 Rhein, Elkus and Dyer sued Charles for $43,518.51, the amount Charles received for the Valentino fight. Of course, Mintz and Charles expected this, but Charles felt personally attacked. He'd known these men a long time. He'd more or less grown up with Elkus at the store. They were from his hometown.

At Mintz's urging, Charles gave some thought to moving out to Pittsburgh, leaving Cincinnati altogether. A couple months earlier he'd been asked to leave the River Downs clubhouse because only whites were allowed. What kind of way was that to treat the heavyweight champ of the world—in his own hometown?[36]

The news kept getting worse. Charles made it only three weeks into his exhibition tour, hitting Salt Lake City, Los Angeles, Oakland, and San Diego before injuring his left hand, which forced him to cancel a show he had scheduled in Spokane against Al Hoosman. A doctor diagnosed the injury as a rupture of one of the collateral ligaments involving his

Charles slips a left from Joe Modzelle during a four-round exhibition in Chicago in September 1949, a few weeks after defending the heavyweight world title against former light heavyweight champion Gus Lesnevich (courtesy Craig Hamilton of Jo Sports, Inc.).

thumb and ordered no boxing, sparring or bag-hitting for at least three weeks. So much for the tour—and the easy money Charles and his guys were counting on.

That put Charles out of commission entirely until some time in December. He went back to Cincinnati and sulked. He didn't like this; not just the injury, but all the squabbling and arguing between his managers. He wasn't a dramatic person. Some guys thrived on the chaos and the anger. Not Charles. He wanted it to be nice and peaceful, for everyone to get along. He couldn't concentrate on fighting with all this other nonsense going on. He didn't care much how it got resolved so long as it did and he could get on with things.

He didn't have to wait long. In early December Mintz convinced Tom Tannas, a real-estate broker and city clerk for Arnold, a suburb of Pittsburgh, to buy out the other managers' interest. Tannas had been working with Mintz and Charles in an unnamed capacity for about a year. In fight circles and the press he was sometimes referred to as "the power behind the throne."[37] He was the polar opposite of Mintz: polite, soft-spoken, business-first. He did not chase publicity or fame. He had a tragic history. He was fourteen years old when his parents died in the flu epidemic of 1918, leaving him to take over the household and raise his two younger brothers, Dolphie and Alex, and sister, Louise.[38]

Although the precise amount Tannas paid the other managers was not reported in the press, reliable rumors placed it between $50,000 and $60,000. Details concerning the new arrangement were never made public, but it was believed that Mintz got his 15 percent off the top whenever Charles fought and Tannas got the manager's standard 30 percent.

You could be excused for wondering how a city clerk had the money to buy the contract of the heavyweight champ. In 1938 and 1939 Tannas had pleaded guilty to two charges of operating a gambling house. (This didn't come to light in any serious way until 1959, when Tannas was charged with lying about his criminal record when applying for a $60,000 loan from the Small Business Administration.)

You did not get into the gambling business in the 1930s and then the fight business at a very high level in the 1940s and '50s without a few well-placed escorts. It was not an open club. You didn't get to those places by accident. To get where Tannas was you had to have friends with access to ready cash and the willingness to do you a favor so long as you were willing to pay them back in some way or another down the road. Maybe you'd give your friend's fighter a shot at the title when there's really no good reason to. But that's the way things worked. Sooner or later you had to pay back. It was just a matter of time.

It wasn't all that important to Ezzard Charles. He was just the fighter. He knew that. He had no more control over who and when he fought than he did over the weather. But it had always been like that. With Tannas and Mintz running things at least he could get back to business and go about trying as best as he could to make everyone understand he was the heavyweight champ whether they liked it or not, even though he wasn't Joe Louis. If he could make some money along the way that sure would help.

9

JOE

A couple weeks after Tannas bought out the other managers, on December 30, Ezzard and Gladys were married at a friend's home in New Kensington, Pennsylvania. It was small and private, and everyone present was sworn to secrecy. Charles had made the decision to keep the story out of the papers, mainly at the urging of Christmas, who despised the media for the way they treated his friend and employer. He figured it was none of their business.

Charles agreed. Besides, it would make it easier to be with other women when he was away from home. Not that he'd have any trouble even if everyone knew he was married; it would just make it easier. He loved Gladys and wanted a family with her, but a man is only as faithful as his options, and Ezzard Charles had lots of options. He continued living in Cincinnati with his grandmother while Gladys stayed at her home in Madisonville. It was an odd arrangement for a married couple, but he convinced Gladys it was for the best, as he was away from home so much.

Later the same month, Mintz entered Mercy Hospital in Pittsburgh for surgery to repair a hernia. He later recounted the story for the local press: "They thought I had some golf stones there so they took an autograph of my heart and said, 'One of your ulsters is worn out.' Then they had to do something so they cut out my herndon over here."[1]

By late January 1950 Mintz had recovered enough to hammer out a deal to have Charles defend the title against Beshore in Buffalo on February 28. As champ, Charles would get 37½ percent plus training expenses and a guarantee of at least $20,000. Beshore, the ninth-ranked heavyweight, would get 17½ percent with the rest to go to the local promoter and an unnamed percentage to the IBC.

Charles' career seemed to be going well again: He was aligned with the most powerful promoter in the business. His management squabbles were over, and his left hand was healed. And now that he was a family man, it was time to go to work and get some money in the bank. And then everything went to hell.

On February 23, just six days before the Beshore fight, Charles was in a Buffalo gym sparring with local heavyweight Jeff Clanton. In the first round of a six-round session, Clanton landed a blow high on one of Charles' ribs on the left side. Charles thought little of it. He was sore later but dismissed it as a bruise. He said nothing about it until the 24th, when he felt pain while hitting the speedbag. It had gotten so that he could barely lift his left arm.

Mintz had Charles examined by Dr. Louis A. Kaiser, who noted a lump on Charles' rib in the area of the pain and said there might be a cartilage separation or a crack at the base of the eighth rib. He ordered x-rays. Before the results were even known, Mintz pulled

Charles out of the fight. Beshore's manager of record, Ralph Gold, accused Mintz and Charles of faking the injury.

"They had spies in our gym every day watching Beshore work," Gold said. "I think they found out Charles was in for a tough fight and wanted more time to get ready. He weighed almost 190 pounds Thursday and they know what Beshore would have done to him with his body punches." Mintz seemed genuinely offended. "We'll go through with this fight before we fight anyone else," he assured the writers. "But I can't send in my boy with one hand."[2] The bout was rescheduled for April 5. Charles returned to Cincinnati to rest.

Training started up again a couple weeks later and proceeded without incident. A week before the bout both Charles and Beshore were examined by Dr. Kaiser, who found no issues and in fact noted that x-rays of Charles' rib indicated that if it had indeed been broken (copies of the actual x-rays were never released), it had healed.

Under normal circumstances everything might have ended there and the fight would have gone on as planned, but these weren't ordinary circumstances. On February 22, a popular middleweight named Lavern Roach died after getting knocked out by Georgie Small at St. Nick's Arena in Manhattan. Worse yet, he was white. Worst, it was seen on television. When fighters died in the ring it spooked the suits that sat on commissions.

All that considered, the commission had to appear, for a while at least, to be seriously interested in the safety of fighters. After a while things could go back to normal, but it had to be a little while. No fight commission, especially one as vital as New York's, could have good, clean, wholesome white kids dropping dead on its watch, especially on TV. It was bad publicity. So Charles was sent for more tests.

At Columbia Presbyterian Medical Center in New York, Charles was examined by a trio of physicians who reported that the injury he had sustained to his rib had also "bruised a heart muscle."[3] He would not be permitted to fight again for at least two months. Immediately, the Beshore fight was cancelled. Gold again accused the Charles camp of misdeeds, saying Charles appeared perfectly fit during his last workout. Gold abruptly left Buffalo to go to New York.

You couldn't blame Gold for thinking something smelled rotten—and not because Charles was afraid of Beshore. He had to know his boy was no match for Charles. The whole thing stank. Either way his fighter was not getting a shot at the title.

The fight was re-scheduled again, tentatively, for June 7, pending a re-examination by the New York commission doctors. On May 3, Charles underwent a three-hour examination ordered by the NBA and administered by the Illinois State Athletic Association. At the end Drs. J.M. Houston and Earnest Nora found that Charles suffered from a "vascular condition of the heart" and was found "not fit for strenuous exercise at the present time."[4]

Later, Dr. Frank R. Ferlaino, chief of the New York Commission's Medical Advisory Board, told media that use of the word "vascular" to describe the nature of Charles' injury was not only incorrect, it was unnecessarily alarming. There was nothing "vascular" about it. If there was, Charles would never fight again. Rather, when Charles suffered a fracture through the tip of the eighth rib, the injury touched the exterior surface of Ezzard's heart, producing a bruise. That area wasn't getting enough blood to heal as quickly as it should. Once it had fully healed he could fight again.[5]

The NBA said it would give Charles' heart another ninety days to mend. If he failed a physical at that time he would forfeit the title. Mintz was crushed. "It's a shock to me," he said. "I don't know what to say. Charles was given a clean bill of health by the Cincinnati doctors and we expected him to pass the NBA examination in Chicago."[6] In the moment it seemed entirely possible, likely even, that Charles would never fight again.

Charles was flummoxed. Back in Cincinnati, he told writers he had no intention of retiring and felt fine. "I've just begun to fight," he said. He insisted that the injury had been exaggerated by the doctors and with a couple months rest he would be back and as "good as new."[7]

He spent the next several weeks setting up the Ezzard Charles Health and Athletic Club downtown (complete with "slenderizing salon"). It kept him busy during the day, but the nights were hard. For the first few weeks he'd wake up in the middle of the night wondering if he'd be able to fight again. What if the doctors wouldn't let him? What would he do? Boxing was all he knew how to do. It wasn't like he could go back to the Elkus' store. He'd never let on, especially not in front of Gladys, but it scared the hell out of him. But there was nothing he could do. He just had to wait.

While Charles was wondering if his career was over, another career that was presumed over appeared to be starting up again. The IBC, and Norris in particular, was unhappy with the way Charles' championship reign had been proceeding, even before the latest delay. With the exception of the Valentino fight, Charles was a bust at the box office. The fighting public was just not buying him as the heavyweight champion, and that was reflected in the gate receipts.

Moreover, England's refusal to recognize Charles as champion threatened to screw up the IBC's monopoly on the heavyweight title. Jack Solomons, the biggest promoter in England, was lobbying to have the winner of the upcoming Bruce Woodcock–Lee Savold fight recognized as the world champion. Neither Woodcock nor Savold was bound to fight for the IBC. If Solomons succeeded, the IBC would be frozen out of the heavyweight title picture. Also, the Tournament of Champions group, despite losing the proposed Walcott-Lesnevich fight in 1948, was still trying to make big fights at its arena in Jersey City, and they had deep pockets. Norris did not like competition.

The solution was clear: Joe Louis would have to come back and fight whoever it was the world saw as heavyweight champ, whether it was Charles or the Savold-Woodcock winner (Savold eventually stopped Woodcock in four rounds in June 1950). Later, after it was all over, a lot of guys said that had been the plan all along, to "retire" Louis, wait for his successor to be found, then put together a huge fight between that successor and Louis.

Maybe that was the case. If it was, Louis gave a credible impression of a man ready to retire. Sure, he missed the game—he said later he felt dead watching Charles and Walcott up in the ring fighting for his old title, like a sort of ghost. It didn't feel right, but he kept telling himself, "What the hell, I'm tired, but I did my job and I did it better than anyone else had in Lord knows how many years."[8]

And yet, for a guy who was so tired, Louis sure stayed busy in prize rings. He had been fighting exhibitions almost nonstop since his "retirement" and in 1949 alone made almost $300,000 from exhibition tours.[9] Two of those exhibitions were against Elmer Ray, who Louis once swore he'd never fight because he disliked him so much.

They met in January 1949 in Miami, and though Ray "pressed" Louis and "maddened" him, a majority of observers found Louis the clear winner.[10] Ray wasn't satisfied with that; he wasn't the kind of fighter to be satisfied; and so he did the worst thing a guy could do who had escaped a Louis fight with all his faculties—he fought him again. Louis was the greatest fighter who ever lived when it came to rematches, and when they got together again in February, Ray was easy pickings.

As one writer reported, Ray "didn't give Louis anywhere near the trouble [he] had in January ... and [Louis] sent Ray staggering into the ropes in the third round."[11] It was the worst beating anyone ever gave Ray, even though it was an "exhibition" with big gloves. You can bet he was glad Louis had "ducked" him for all those years. Ray fought just twice more after that night, and after losing both bouts he retired. Citing the concussion Louis had given him in their second meeting, he told reporters he was getting out "while I still got my health."[12]

The effort Louis expended to completely demoralize Ray became typical as the months passed. Even as champion Louis had treated exhibitions more seriously than may have been necessary or in good taste, because he was proud and vain in the way all men of great accomplishment are. He wouldn't be shown up.

But his exhibitions took on a different look entirely as rumors circulated that he was coming back and would face Charles for the title, even as he strung the press along, one day saying he would fight again and then next day denying he had ever said such a thing. He still didn't train much, and he played around and ate what he wanted. As a result he weighed between 215 and 230 pounds, well over his fighting weight. It didn't matter.

In one exhibition in late March in Orlando, Florida, Louis floored Dixie Lee Oliver for a nine-count in the first round and then knocked him out cold in the fourth with a long left hook. Oliver was hospitalized. (Louis later visited him in the hospital and offered to pay his medical bills.) In November Louis floored Boston contender Johnny Shkor three times for nine-counts over the course of ten rounds. A couple weeks later he dropped Johnny Flynn for an eight-count with a left hook.

Finally, in December '49 in Detroit, and in the most obvious indication yet that he was using his exhibition bouts to get ready for a comeback, Louis met the very same Pat Valentino who'd given Charles an interesting night in San Francisco just eight weeks earlier. Louis toyed with Valentino before calmly cornering him in the eighth round and knocking him out. The newspaper guys said Louis could have stopped him any time after the fourth round but seemed to enjoy beating on him.

Valentino, his face a mish-mash of swelling and cuts, was so dazed after the seventh that he went to the wrong corner when the bell rang. And this was with the bigger ten-ounce gloves they wore for exhibitions. In the eighth Louis bludgeoned Valentino with a four-punch combination that put him out cold right in front of Charles, who was sitting ringside. The timing seemed no coincidence; Louis wanted to stop Valentino—who was beaten up so badly that he never fought again—in the same round that Charles had.

Charles didn't buy it. "I don't think Louis had any idea of planning it that way," he said afterward. "He was shooting for a kayo as early as the first round." A writer asked what Charles thought about reports that Valentino did a lot better against him than against Louis.

"Valentino was scared to death," Charles replied. "He wasn't afraid of me but he was afraid of Joe. He showed it from the very first round."

"So Valentino feared Louis but didn't fear you?" the writer asked.

"That's right," Charles said. "In fact, no one fears me. That's the way I want it."[13]

The job Louis did on Valentino was so thorough that Tex Sullivan, manager of Lee Oma, a world-rated top-ten heavyweight who was scheduled to face Louis in an exhibition the following week, abruptly pulled his fighter out, accusing Louis of taking his exhibition fights too seriously and using them as tune-ups for a comeback. If his boy was going to fight Louis it would be in a real fight with a real payday.

"Exhibitions, nuts!" Sullivan shrieked. "They're not exhibitions, they're real wars. That guy [Louis] is in there throwing bombs. Look at what happened to Pat Valentino in Chicago last night. Look at what he did to Johnny Shkor in Boston and Johnny Flynn in Kansas City. They were fights, not exhibitions. People are wondering if Louis will make a comeback. Take it from me he's already come back."[14]

Louis denied it one day, confirmed it the next then denied it again. He was having fun. The press hung on his every word. He liked jerking them around. In reality it was a done deal and everyone on the inside knew it. Sullivan was right: Louis wasn't coming back. He was already back. Norris was making sure of that. He and Louis had met to confirm it and Louis' only requirement was that the big fight, against Charles for the world title, happen in December at Madison Square Garden. That would give him plenty of time to get back in fighting trim, and he liked fighting at the Garden. It was his home.

Norris wouldn't hear of it. December would be too late, he told Louis. Solomons would have everyone thinking Lee Savold was the goddam heavyweight champion if they waited until December. No, it had to be September. And the Garden was out. Norris wanted it at Yankee Stadium, outside, a big ballpark fight, like the old days. They could do a better gate there, he reasoned. Then he played to Louis' ego. Why, he could climb off the couch tomorrow and whip Ezzard Charles. He was Joe Louis!

Louis resisted as best as he could, but he never was a match for a wealthy old suit who held all the money and the cards and called the shots. Jacobs had dictated to Louis for years and gotten away with it because Joe was easy-going on most things and because Jacobs advanced him money whenever he needed it. Norris was the same way, even if he was more of a snob about it than Jacobs was. Jacobs was self-made, had come from nothing. Norris was old money, his daddy's money, and he knew how to use it to get what he wanted.

Eventually Louis relented. Just one more fight, he said, and maybe the revenue people would accept his cut of the gate in total settlement of his back dues. They never said yes. He went along anyway. And it was the worst-kept secret in boxing. All that was left was the formal announcement. Louis would continue to fight himself back into shape while Charles' heart mended, assuming it did. If Charles won he'd would be universally recognized as champion, and the IBC owned him. Same deal if Louis won.

In July 1950 Charles returned to the ninth floor of the Columbia-Presbyterian Medical Center in New York for what he hoped would be his last examination. Mintz, Tannas and Markson, the IBC director, and a couple writers were there with him. Dr. Robert Levy, the cardiologist who had examined Charles before, retrieved him and disappeared into an exam room. Two hours passed before the two returned to the waiting room.

"Let's go into this office," Levy commanded the group. As they rose he said, "Shall I speak in front of this man?" pointing to Charles. Mintz's heart sank. Why would he ask that if he had good news? He almost burst into tears. All his work for nothing. All the wasted years. He'd have to go back to sleeping on pool tables. Tannas spoke up: "Why not? He's the one most concerned with this."

They sat down in Levy's office. Levy announced: "He's okay. He's okay with me. This lad can fight again." Mintz leapt up and whooped. He grabbed Levy's hand and shook it for all he was worth. He grabbed Tannas' hand too and almost tore his arm off, he shook it so hard. No more pool tables after all. Back in business.

The calmest one in the room was Charles. If you didn't know the man you'd have thought he was drugged up or slow or something. It was his career after all, and he hardly reacted. But that was his way. "I'm sure glad I didn't lose my championship to them machines," he said, before Levy took him downstairs to make it official with the New York Commission, who had members waiting on the outcome.

In the hallway the newspaper guys took pictures and one of the writers asked Charles, "How's it feel?"

"Great," Charles replied.

"Is that all?" the writer asked.

"Remember when I got the title in Chicago beating Walcott and somebody asked me how I felt and I said no different being champ than before?"

The writer said he remembered.

"Well, it's a little different now a year later. I appreciate being champion now. I guess I got to feel now that it's good being the best in whatever you do. I feel that way now."[15]

Mintz was beaming, slapping backs and shaking hands. He was back in business. It felt wonderful. "This guy's got a heart," he yelled at everyone and no one. "What a heart this guy's got. He'll fight anybody, ain't ducking nobody like they say a duck takes to water. We ain't afraid." Mintz was just warming up. He knew what the writers wanted and he gave it to them. "Charles will start lumbering up exercises tomorrow. He is in a perfect physical spectacle, the best I ever seen him in. My tiger will be ready for anyone in six weeks and that includes Joe Louis."[16]

When he found an opportunity to interrupt Mintz, Charles expounded on how the hiatus had changed him. "I never gave it a thought about being the best fighter or the best anything in the world. It never even entered my mind. But after the doctors said I might have some heart trouble, I thought plenty about it. I thought how it felt to be champ. How much it would hurt if I'd lose it. Then I found out it's the greatest feeling in the world. Not just knowing you're the best boxer—but that you're champion of anything. Best in the whole world. And here I might have lost the title without losing a fight. If any guy ever asks me again how it feels to be champ you'll never hear me say again that I don't feel any different," Charles said. "Everything looks like one big green field now."[17]

Charles started earnest training for his long-delayed fight with Beshore. But, things being what they were and Beshore being who he was, all the writers wanted to talk about was Joe Louis. Beshore was an afterthought. It was okay with Charles. He was used to it by now. It had been that way as long as he'd been a heavyweight. He had just finished a workout when a writer asked him what he thought about Louis' comeback.

"I think Louis' return is a great thing for the boxing game. Did you notice all the stories in the newspapers the last week or so? You hardly read anything about fights before Joe announced he'd fight again," Charles said.

"How do you feel about fighting him?" the writer asked.

"It'll not only mean a good payday but the opportunity to prove myself a worthy champion. I forgot all that business about Joe being my idol a long time ago. This is a tough game. I want to fight him and I'm going to try to beat him."

The writer turned to Mintz, who was at Charles' side, naturally. Seizing on a theme many writers had been exploiting, that Charles would be facing a used-up, old has-been, the writer smiled and asked Mintz, "Why do you want to pick on a fat old man?" This was right up Mintz's alley.

"Fat old man! That Louis ain't a fat old man. He has been playing bozom [possum] all the time. While everybody thinks he's in the retirement business he was going around the world fighting exhibitions to keep in shape. All the writers are offering sympoly [sympathy] for what's going to happen to Louis. They should have sympoly for us. My tiger isn't going to be fooled by that 'fat old man' talk. He knows Louis will be ready. So will he. We'll be in good shape."[18]

On July 27, before any contracts were even signed, Louis headed to West Baden, Indiana, for light training—chopping wood, roadwork. After three or four weeks in West Baden he, Mannie Seamon, George Nicholson and the sparring partners would meet up at the camp at Pompton Lakes, just like in the old days, and start the real work. He was about 230 pounds, give or take, which wasn't bad for a guy who'd spent the summer golfing. He could drop 15 pounds in a few weeks and be right at fighting weight. Even heavy, he didn't look all that bad for the average Joe, or even for a retired heavyweight champion—a little puffy around the face and the midsection was all. But he'd earned the right to get a little soft. All those years, all those training camps. It was never the fighting itself that wore Louis down. It was the training camps, the isolation, the day-in, day-out drudgery of it all. Any fighter will tell you fighting is the easy part. You get in the ring, you do your job, you get paid and go home. You take it easy until the phone rings. What wears you down, what fills you with dread, is the training. That's where the pain is: two or three sparring partners taking their shots at you every day, your trainer up your goddam ass all the time looking over your shoulder, no women, no golf. It's like a goddam prison.

That's what it felt like to Louis toward the end, and that was why he had to get out. These exhibitions he fought, why, he didn't even have to train for those. He showed up where they told him to, put on the gloves and headgear and fought, and still there wasn't a man out there who could lick him.

Half of these guys he had to carry. But pro fighting, real fighting, was different. This fight with Charles was different. It wasn't that he was afraid of Charles. There wasn't a man alive that Joe Louis didn't think he could lick, no matter how old he was. He just knew that this was a real fight. He'd seen Charles plenty, knew what he was about, what he could do and what he couldn't do. He told the press, "Charles is a good man, but I figure with my experience I should take him."[19] This was the humble Louis everyone loved. That would change later.

But this was before anything was even official. While Louis was dodging beavers and raccoons in backwoods Indiana, Charles was wrapping up training for his fight with Beshore at Buffalo's Memorial Stadium. Mintz, Tannas and the rest of Charles' camp knew what was at stake. It wouldn't hurt if Charles looked spectacular taking out Beshore, which shouldn't have been difficult—he wasn't anywhere near Charles' league. To remove a little ring rust, they had Charles do a four-round exhibition against clubfighter Joe Modzelle in Pittsburgh on August 3. He looked fine.

Beshore, *The Ring*'s number-nine rated heavyweight, was a busy pressure fighter, game and always in shape, but he had no real punch. It would be a walk in the park for Charles, and potentially a lucrative one. An impressive knockout of Beshore might get Mintz and Tannas some extra leverage at the bargaining table with Louis' team and the IBC. Mintz even told the press to be on the lookout for the "new" Ezzard Charles, a more aggressive, combative Charles: a "tiger," he said. Anything else and Mintz and Tannas would lose any bargaining strength they had. They hoped for the best.

If they didn't get the opposite, they got something like it. Charles stopped Beshore on cuts at 2:53 of the fourteenth round and was mostly dreadful, pecking away at the challenger before a crowd of only 6,298, which paid an abysmal $28,666—a record low in both attendance and receipts for a modern heavyweight title fight. (The previous record had been set by Louis and challenger Johnny Paycheck, who drew only 10,609 to Madison Square Garden in March 1940.)

The 5–1 odds in Charles' favor didn't help the promotion, nor did the two postponements. Still, Charles had the chance to make a statement against a guy who couldn't hurt him, and he failed. It was only in the fourth, tenth and fourteenth rounds that he attacked with any vigor, opening cuts on Beshore's right ear and under his right eye, and drawing blood from his mouth and nose. (Charles also suffered a small cut over one eye.) It was entirely one-sided; when referee Barney Felix stopped it, the judges had Charles ahead 12–2, 12–1–1, and 9–3–2 (the AP scored it 10–2–2). But it was also devoid of any action or drama. Charles didn't even score a knockdown. He never really came close.

The crowd booed the stoppage and they booed Charles. When it was over, promoter Dewey Michaels' reward for bringing Buffalo its first heavyweight title fight was to have presided over a financial disaster. The papers had a field day with it, and just as Mintz and Tannas had feared, support among the press swung heavily in Louis' favor.

"Poor Showing Makes Louis Favorite"[20] read one headline. "Ezzard Wasn't Any Tiger Winning over Beshore," read another, with the subtitle, "Joe Louis' stock rose sharply today following Ezzard Charles' one-sided but lackluster conquest of Freddie Beshore."[21] One more: "Charles Win Boost to Louis" over the sub-title, "Ez' TKO in 14th Not Impressive."[22]

Mintz entertained reporters afterward, saying the referee was "absotively right" to stop the fight and calling Beshore "a soaking-up sponge" who was "human to punishment" (i.e., immune to punishment).[23] He then went into damage control. "[Charles] needed the workout. It was his first fight in 10 months and he wasn't as sharp as he should be. His timing was off. But he'll be ready for the next one, whoever it is."[24]

Of course, Mintz knew who the next one would be, as did Charles and everyone else. So at least Charles got in fourteen rounds of work. And the news wasn't all bad: There was no sign of the rib and chest pain that had twice resulted in postponements of the Beshore fight. Charles would take a week or two off, let his cut heal and then go into training for Louis while Tannas and Mintz negotiated the contract with the IBC's Al Weill, Harry Markson and Truman Gibson.

On August 17, the two sides reached an agreement to meet at Yankee Stadium on September 27. The winner would be recognized as the heavyweight champion by all American boxing authorities, including the New York Commission and *The Ring* magazine. Louis would get a full 35 percent of the net receipts, while Charles, the reigning heavyweight champion in 47 states, settled for 20 percent.

It was the first time in history that a heavyweight title challenger would make more than the champion, but Louis was an exception to all the rules. There had never been a challenger as beloved as he. Besides, after the stinker Charles had put on against Beshore, he had no right to complain; he had effectively tied his managers' hands. Some other details about the contract: the fight would be aired live on CBS television and be sponsored by Pabst as one of their regular Wednesday night "Blue Ribbon" fights.

There would be no local blackout, meaning many New York fans could watch on television. The fight would be available to a staggering twenty-five million customers on TV, and the radio and television rights combined would bring in $140,000. Mintz started selling immediately. "It's the greatest collosical in the history of heavyweights.... Two champions fighting at the same time. It will be the greatest fight in the history of boxing that happened in the last 10 years," he said at an interview at IBC's office in New York.[25]

A few days after the fight became official, Mintz and Tannas started looking around for a good location for a training camp. After considering several sites they arrived on the Nemerson Hotel in South Fallsburg, New York, a summer resort tucked high in the Catskill

Mountains. Typically the resort closed around Labor Day, but Mintz and Tannas convinced the general manager, Abe Markus, to keep it open for Charles and his team. It would be good for business. The entire team—Charles, Mintz, Tannas, Brown, sparring partners Lloyd Gibson, Levi Bryant, Al Smith and Joe Lindsay, Christmas, and Charles' personal chef, Fred Huldock, convened at the Nemerson on September 1 to begin serious training.

Tannas and Mintz wanted someone to assist Brown in the corner. George Nicholson, who they'd hired on Louis' advice for the Walcott fight, was now back with his old army buddy and employer. So they arrived at veteran Ray Arcel, who had been knocking around the fight game for years. He'd handled sixteen world champions over his career, more than any other man, and was best known for working the corners of many of the challengers Louis had turned away during his long reign as champion. Johnny Paycheck, Al McCoy, Paulino Uzcudun, Nathan Mann, Abe Simon, Buddy Baer, Lou Nova and others all had had Arcel in their corner when Louis flattened them. As a result, Arcel had acquired the nickname "Meat Wagon."

Legend had it that before the start of the Mann fight, when the fighters met in the center of the ring for the referee's final pre-fight instructions, Louis looked at Arcel and asked, "You here again?" Despite his fighters' failures against Louis, Arcel was widely respected in the fight business. When the great lightweight Benny Leonard made his comeback in 1931, any trainer in the game would have been happy to sign on as his chief second. Leonard picked Arcel. But it wasn't only Arcel's technical acumen that made him attractive to Mintz and Tannas. It was also that the press liked him, he was white, and he'd seen Louis up close more times than any trainer in the world other than Seamon.

Arcel didn't need much convincing to join the team. He felt Charles had the right equipment to beat Louis—that is, he was fast and mobile and those guys (like Billy Conn and Walcott) gave Louis trouble, whereas most of Louis' easiest fights came against slow, face-first punchers.

As far as Charles was concerned, Jimmy Brown was still the boss in his corner and the man he listened to the most. Arcel was there in an assistant's role. If Charles didn't need him at the moment, Arcel would work with the sparring partners. Still, it was good to have him around. He joined the camp on September 10 and soon discovered that Ezzard Charles was not your typical prizefighter.

"I've never known a fighter like him," Arcel said. "I wake him up in camp and we go out on the road. It's six o'clock in the morning and I say to him, 'How did you sleep last night?' He says 'All right.' Maybe he didn't sleep all right, but he won't complain to anyone and that's the extent of our conversation."[26]

Brown established Charles' daily routine right away but first laid the ground rules: no swimming in the hotel pool and no riding the horses; too risky. Also, no milk for Charles in camp, and no coffee. Beyond that, all of them were up at 5:30 a.m. and, weather permitting, were on the road putting in five miles of roadwork.

When they returned to camp Charles would drink a large glass of orange juice, and then Brown would give him a rubdown. Charles would go back to bed until 10:30. When he rose, Huldock would serve a breakfast of prunes, a dry cereal, lamb chops and tea. Charles had the next couple hours to himself to play cards—gin rummy was the camp favorite—or to catch up with his mail, read the morning papers, or whatever he liked.

At about 2:00 p.m. Charles would get ready to head over to the gym and by 2:30 his hands were wrapped. He'd shadowbox six straight minutes in the ring, then on most days spar between four and six rounds. After sparring he'd go several rounds on the heavy bag and then the speed bag. If he'd happened to miss running that morning, he'd put in several rounds skipping rope. If he'd put in his five miles the rope went unused. The workout would end with calisthenics and then the showers.

For dinner, which was served at 6:30, Huldock would make Charles steak, roast beef or broiled chicken along with fresh vegetables and tea. After dinner the entire team would get together and discuss strategies, ideas, rumors and whatever else came up about the fight. After that Charles would play cards again or catch a movie at the hotel, or go into Liberty, the local town, to a theater there. Sometimes he watched films of Louis' fights against Tony Galento, Buddy Baer, and others. Bedtime was 9:30 sharp.

After a month in West Baden, Louis and his camp set up in Pompton Falls. Louis was already down to 218 pounds—way ahead of schedule. Sparring started on August 31. Louis had brought along his three favorite guys: Baby "Dutch" Culbertson, a short, barrel-chested heavyweight from Brooklyn; Shamus O'Brien, who had been one of Joe's main sparring partners for years; and Gene Felton from Detroit, who was there to emulate Charles' style in the ring.

A fourth boxer, Young Harry Wills from Los Angeles, rounded out the group. Louis did a round apiece that first day with Culbertson, O'Brien and Felton and looked good enough that his manager, Marshall Miles, said to a reporter on-hand, "Looks good doesn't he?" The reporter replied that Louis appeared surprisingly well conditioned. "Surprised me too," Miles said. "I didn't think he could do it, but he has. He's not going to have an alibi if he don't win. He's almost in shape right now."[27]

Later, after the workout, Louis, Seamon, a visiting writer and Nicholson shot the breeze in the locker room. The writer offered that Charles had told him he didn't think Louis was confident going into the fight.

"That's his opinion," Louis said. "He's entitled to his opinion even if he's wrong," and then went on about how Charles didn't hit hard enough to hurt him. It was this, more than most things, that comforted Louis on the rare occasions when he doubted himself. At heavyweight, he believed, Charles was no puncher.

Nicholson, one of Louis' oldest and most trusted friends in boxing, piped up. He'd worked with Charles and Jimmy Brown for three fights and rightly considered himself the most knowledgeable man in the room about Ezzard Charles. "Listen—you say Charles don't punch hard," he said to Louis. "I disagree. He bangs pretty good with two hands."[28]

Nicholson then dazzled the room with an uncanny impression of Charles boxing—the footwork, the feints, the overhand right, the defensive moves, all the while explaining what Charles did well and how he generated power. He'd absorbed a lot working with Charles. After a couple of minutes he stopped to catch his breath and surveyed the room. Louis shrugged. How could he be impressed with anyone's punch? He was the greatest puncher the game had ever known.

Later the writer caught up with Nicholson and asked him for his straight opinion on Charles and the fight. "He's a good fighter, that fellow, real good. Only thing, he hasn't been hit yet by Joe Louis," Nicholson said. "That's the difference. That's what will make the fight different for Charles."[29]

It was Louis' punch more than anything that he and his supporters were counting on to restore his glory. The old heads liked to say the punch was the last thing to go on an old fighter; that first he loses his legs, then his reflexes, maybe his chin too, if he isn't careful. But an old puncher could punch until they put him in the dirt. That's why so many of them fell in love with their punch and then forgot to quit when they should have. They believed that no matter what, their punch wouldn't abandon them, and as long as they had that they had a shot. It appeared to be the case with Louis, even if his sparring partners took liberties, especially with the right hand. Wills, especially, scored rights against Louis like no one's business. There was no doubt; Louis was slow. He had trouble getting out of the way and his counters were still a little off, even deep into training. Some in the press sounded the alarm, noting that Louis was "taking more punishment than he was dishing out."[30]

At the same time, however, Louis seemed to be hitting as hard as ever. Poor Culbertson was getting knocked all over the ring. More than once O'Brien had to take a knee or walk away from the action to regain his wind or his senses, depending on where he'd been tagged. Felton, the Charles impersonator, was floored several times. This moved one writer to report, after watching both fighters spar in camp, that Louis appeared "slower but more powerful than this writer has ever seen him."[31]

Indeed, it seemed that Louis was banking everything on his ability to knock out Charles. He no longer ran six miles during morning roadwork, as he had in his prime. Now he ran three miles and walked three. A concession to his thirty-six years, he said. Instead he loaded up on sparring, logging ninety-eight rounds by September 25. "I'm training for a fight, not a race," he told camp members.[32]

This was smart strategy. Charles was the younger, fresher fighter. Louis had to get to him early or not at all. He knew he still had the punch to rock Charles if he could nail him. The exhibitions had shown him that. They'd shown Charles, too. "Joe may have retired officially, but he has always kept in pretty good shape," Charles said in early September. "His last real fight was with Jersey Joe Walcott two years ago, but since then he has had 55 exhibition bouts, and has shown that he still can punch."[33]

The power Louis showed in those exhibitions and then against his sparring partners was all most "experts" needed to pick him outright. Former champions couldn't pick him fast enough. The great old lightweight and welterweight world champion, Barney Ross, who retired in 1938, said after watching Louis spar that Joe "looked the Louis of old."[34] Former world heavyweight champion Primo Carnera, whom Louis had obliterated in 1935, watched Louis floor O'Brien and then Felton, and told the press, "[Louis] will need two rounds to warm up with Charles and two more to knock him out."[35]

Only the great welterweight champion Sugar Ray Robinson, in training for an early-October fight in Boston against Joe Rindone, at first would not pick Louis outright. "Ezzard Charles is the most underrated fighter I know," Robinson said after watching Charles spar six rounds. "Charles is in superb fighting condition. I refuse to go out on a limb in predicting what the outcome of his fight with Louis will be. But I'll say this much, Ezzard looks very good to me."[36] However, pressed for a pick, he conceded: "It would be treason to pick any other than Joe."[37]

Others were not as diplomatic. Gene Tunney, who ended the championship reign and ultimately the career of the legendary Jack Dempsey, predicted a fifth-round knockout win for Louis and added, "If Jack Dempsey is not the greatest fighter who ever lived, then Joe Louis is. There is no reason to think, because Louis is 36, that he has not retained the skill and power that he had when he retired."[38]

One influential writer, long a Louis fan and a consistent Charles detractor, said plainly that all Louis needed was his punch. "Charles has it on Louis in every respect but one—the punch," he wrote. "The Brown Bomber has to hit him only once to win and the firm belief here is that Louis will get in that one good punch. So the pick is Louis by the only way he can win—a knockout."[39]

On September 11 Charles and Louis drove from their training camps to the state commission office to sign the official contracts and undergo physical examinations. Chairman Eagen made sure everyone knew the winner would be recognized in New York as the heavyweight champion, and that the title had been held "in abeyance" since Louis retired. Seamon took the opportunity to gloat over Louis' condition. "He's in better shape right now than he was for the second fight with Joe Walcott," he beamed. "And he still has two weeks of training to go."[40]

Charles, meanwhile, was being Charles: going about the quiet, steady business of getting sharp and ready for the biggest fight of his career. He was quiet and reserved, especially with the press, as he always was, but toward the end of camp he asserted himself more during interviews. He bristled when reporters told him Louis said Conn was a better boxer than Charles, though Charles hit harder.

"He can't know how I fight or how I can hit because the only time we fought was in a three or four-round exhibition in Fort Clark, Texas, in 1943 when I weighed 159 pounds," he snapped, recalling their long-ago meeting.[41]

Charles then shocked reporters when he said he wouldn't move and box against Louis. This seemed crazy. Everyone knew that if he was to have any chance he had to use his speed and legs and box Louis like Conn had in their first fight. Look at what had happened to poor Billy when he got too cocky for his own good and tried to knock Louis out. He ended up in a heap. Charles was adamant.

"I intend to mix with Joe. I'm not afraid of him. I'm faster and younger and I know my reflexes are sharper. Perhaps I could outbox him if that's what I made up my mind to do, but frankly I haven't decided that this would be the best thing to do."[42]

Charles didn't spar like he intended to box and move. He was far more aggressive with his sparmates than usual and like Louis, he was taking more punishment than was typical. Those who knew him knew he was capable of blocking or slipping many of the blows his sparring partners—all bigger and heavier than he—were landing. The scribes were confused. Those with trained eyes were not. Former middleweight champ Billy Soose knew what Charles was up to.

"Charles knows what he is doing, make no mistake about that," Soose said after watching Charles spar. "He is training for a 15-round fight by crowding as near as possible 15 rounds of fighting into each day's training session whether it's four rounds or six rounds he's doing." Soose noted, too, how much time Charles spent tying up and smothering his sparring partners' attacks inside, something he knew he'd have to do against Louis.[43]

The week before the fight, Arcel told reporters that Charles had been on edge and why. "Ezzard feels like the IBC wants Louis to win because Louis has always been worth such big money at the box office. Ezzard feels that he's being used, that they lent the title to him and tried to build him up as the champion and now they want to take the title away from him. And he keeps saying to me, 'They're not going to do it.'"[44]

Charles' last prefight statement corroborated Arcel's story. "I'll knock out Louis to prove that a man can't lend me his title and hope to take it back," he said.[45] Charles' strong words left most observers unmoved. A United Press poll taken the day of the fight found that thirty of forty-eight writers picked Louis to win.[46] The betting odds favored Louis 2–1.

At noon on September 27, the fighters weighed in. Louis, at 218, was two pounds heavier than he'd planned and the heaviest he'd ever been for a title bout; and Charles, at 184½, was two and a half pounds heavier than he'd predicted. The judges, appointed by the New York Commission, were familiar names: Mark Conn, who also would referee, Joe Agnello and Frank Forbes.

The training was done. Camp was over. All the organizers and assistants and cooks and gophers and hangers-on collected all their things, packed them up, headed over to the stadium. Everyone was quiet. This is how it was on the day of a fight, all the time. No one ever knew what to say. The writers filed their last prefight columns, made their predictions. Everyone looked forward to going home. A couple of the sparring partners had fights on the undercard. Whatever happened next would be up to Louis and Charles.

Later, a crowd of 22,357, producing a live gate of $205,370, filed into Yankee Stadium to root for the old man to get his title back. It wasn't the crowd Norris and the rest of the IBC were hoping for. Three weeks before, Willie Pep and Sandy Saddler, a pair of featherweights, had done a live gate of $262,000 at the same venue. There was no live television or radio broadcast of that fight, but still. The way the numbers came in it looked like when all was said and done Louis would walk away with $100,458, not nearly enough to pay off his debt to the government. And that was before all the mangers, unnamed and otherwise, took their cuts. Charles would clear just $57,405 before expenses. Chump change for a champion.

There was a Cincinnati contingent on hand—busloads, if you believed the newspaper boys. Good luck finding them. The night could not have been less about Ezzard Charles if he'd been holding the spit bucket for one of the prelim boys, or, better yet, handing out wash towels in the men's room.

This was all about Joe Louis. They were there to see him. Charles was the understudy, of no more relevance than the judges or the referee. Sure, he'd be involved, in some way or another, but in a bit part. What none of the 23,000 stargazers knew then was that during the long wait in the locker room before the main event, some time probably during Dutch Culbertson's third-round knockout loss to Elkins Brothers in the main prelim, the unthinkable happened: Joe Louis started to doubt himself.

It happened to all fighters—or almost all of them. The dressing room before the fight is a dungeon of doubt and anxiety for prizefighters, the place in which a man about to walk into another world has to assess his readiness: Did he do all his roadwork? Did he do enough pushups? Did he cheat in training? Even if all the answers came back good, the dressing room had a way of playing tricks on you, making you doubt yourself. And if they came back bad, heaven help you.

A man could go crazy in the locker room waiting to go on. There was no calling things off, no turning back, and no more time to get ready. It was the last stop before the big show. Some guys left their fight in there, talked themselves out of things in the last minutes before going on, and then fell apart under the lights. You could forgive even a strong man for seeing the dressing room before the fight as a kind of exquisite torture.

Louis used to love that last hour before a fight. When he was champ, the challenger's dressing room seemed almost to work in concert with him. He relaxed in his room, mindful that his reputation was across the hall wreaking havoc on his challenger's mind, feeding on his fears and insecurities, filling him with dread. There had never been a fighter better than Joe Louis at using the dressing room before the fight to reduce his opponent to a harmless ball of anxiety.

Kingfish Levinsky, a competent heavyweight contender who'd beaten Jack Sharkey, was so frozen with terror before his fight with Louis in 1935 that the promoters had to move up the time of the fight by an hour to keep him from fleeing the building. Former heavyweight king Max Baer was so anxious before his fight with Louis that when his friend and mentor Jack Dempsey stopped by the locker room to wish him luck, Baer pleaded with him to get the fight called off. Dempsey had to threaten to lay him out right there to get him to the ring.

Even light heavyweight king John Henry Lewis, who was a personal friend of Louis, appeared terrified before Louis stopped him in the first round in their fight in 1939. And top heavyweight contender Lou Nova resorted to kicking everyone out of the dressing room and doing yoga in an attempt to calm his nerves before he faced Louis in 1941. It didn't work. Observers reported that he appeared petrified before being stopped in the sixth. Arcel, who was in Nova's corner, later said, "Lou knew how to fight. But he lost all control of his whole system. He didn't know who he was."[47]

And here, after all those years of scaring other fighters silly, the great Joe Louis, the epitome of a stone cold killer in the ring, a man who never went into a fight thinking he could lose, was doubting himself against Ezzard Charles, a man whose punching ability he did not respect. He was as surprised by it as anybody.

It was not in Louis' nature to doubt himself the way other fighters did. He'd always known, as every fighter knows, that if he stayed long enough sooner or later there would come a fighter who would beat him up, and it would be terrible. And whenever he had the choice to get out or to fight one more time he'd ask himself if this might be the one fight too many, the one he'd always regret. Is this the one he would lose? And the answer always came back: not to this guy and not tonight.

But sitting in his locker room with Seamon, Nicholson and Gibson, it was all Louis could do to keep from telling Seamon to call the whole thing off.[48] He wasn't ready—not for Ezzard Charles, anyway. Seven weeks was not enough. Even with all the exhibitions and with almost a hundred rounds of sparring, he was no match for Charles and he knew it. He had suspected it all along in camp, even on his good days, but then he'd knock one of his sparring partners sideways and think, if I get Charles with that punch he'll go, too. That's what carrying that kind of punch does to a man. It fools him.

But now, when there was nothing else to think about and no more time to do anything but fight, he knew what he was in for. He cursed himself for letting Norris bully him into this date. If only he'd had more time. He still believed Charles couldn't hurt him. Still—seven weeks; for Charles?

Maybe he could pull it off. If he got lucky and could land something heavy early on, just maybe he could pull it off. And wouldn't that be something? No heavyweight champ in history had won back the title. If he could do it, boy that would be something. That alone would make it all worthwhile. After a while Mannie gave him the word that it was time to start warming up. As best he could he pushed the fear and doubt to the back of his mind and reminded himself who the hell he was.

And across the hall, Ezzard Charles, scrawny, undersized product of the West End slums, paper champion, who no real heavyweight feared, not even the bummy ones, relaxed and hummed along contentedly to Billie Holiday, Sarah Vaughan, and Billy Eckstine. He'd brought their records from Cincinnati, had Jimmy Brown play them on his portable phonograph. You'd have thought he was on a picnic, or at a jazz club, with not a care in the world.

Outside the locker rooms, the crowd at Yankee Stadium was disappointing in its size but not its makeup. As Charles and Louis and their corners weaved their way through the crowd to ring, they passed New York governor Thomas E. Dewey and his lieutenant, Joe. R. Handley, at ringside. Acting New York mayor Vincent Impellitteri had a ringside seat too, as did Supreme Court justice Ferdinand Pecora, famous army general Lucius D. Clay, and one-time heavyweight contender Luis Angel Firpo. The ringside seats, priced at $30, had gone quickly and were occupied by the usual suspects from Hollywood and the sports and music worlds who attended all of Louis' fights in the old days.

The ball players were there, and the crooners and the actors. In the old days the Rat Pack and the gangsters and all the rest showed up to be seen as much as to see. They weren't all there for this fight, but a lot of them were. Frank Sinatra was there with girlfriend Ava Gardner. He idolized Louis and despised Charles for everything Charles wasn't—namely, Louis. Whenever he was out with some new dame and the newspaper boys came nosing around asking who she was, he'd reply, "Ezzard Charles." It became Sinatra's special, running gag. It was a brush-off to the writers of course, but it was an insult to Charles, too.

The beautiful people at ringside all remembered how it had been in the old days. As Louis made his way to the ring they smiled at him and waved while he stared ahead, stoic as always. They wanted it to be the old days but knew it wasn't. It didn't have the same feel. So they shook their heads after he passed and pursed their lips and hoped the old man would make it through okay.

The writers in the press section, the guys whose job it was to not root for anyone, all rooted in their hearts for the old Bomber, and most of them didn't care if you knew it. Not tonight. Half of them were on the take every other night of the week—there wasn't a scruple among them—but they wanted it to be the good old days for Louis. But even the ones who publicly picked Louis had to know in their hearts, as Louis did himself, that it was not his night. It was nothing against Charles; he seemed a decent fellow, if a bit boring. But anyone who was someone in America, and even the nobodies, wanted Joe Louis to be the heavyweight champion again.

It had long been the custom in world title fights to introduce the challenger to the crowd first, and then the champion. But in another concession to Louis' stature—and probably also to the fact that he never lost the title in the ring, but rather relinquished it—Charles, recognized as heavyweight champion in forty-seven states, was introduced first, to polite applause. The crowd's response to Louis' introduction was passionate and long and, if you listened closely, pleading and hopeful. The fighters met in ring center for the referee Conn's final instructions. Louis looked like the heavyweight champion. Charles looked like a middleweight.

At the opening bell Charles charged forward and dug a right hand to Louis' body, because that's what you do when your opponent has thirty-three pounds on you and doesn't respect your power. He stayed right on Louis and threw some more shots to the old man's ribcage, then came up to the head and then spun away. Louis hadn't even gotten on track yet and there was Charles, in and out, jabbing, throwing lead left hooks and getting away with it while Louis' punches sailed over his head.

It was more of the same in the second, though Louis got his jab going and late in the round scored his first hard blow, a right hand that landed high on Charles' head. Charles dominated again in the third, bloodying Louis' nose and stunning him with a four-punch combination late in the round. By then Charles' strategy was clear: When there was distance between them he would jab and keep moving to his left, and when the moment was right he'd jump in with a left hook and then stay there, ripping uppercuts and hooks to Louis' body and head. When they got too close to punch anymore he'd get his head up under Louis' chin and then stand straight up, which had the effect of knocking Louis off balance. All of it together kept the old Bomber guessing and without the time and leverage he needed to line up and deliver his power punches. Charles, Brown and Arcel had done their homework—and Louis knew it. "I knew after the third or fourth round I was washed up," he said later.[49]

Louis got some good work done in the fourth, and that gave the crowd some hope, but Charles hammered him again in the fifth. After the round Ray Robinson made his way from ringside up to Louis' corner and told them, "Joe's got to keep sticking with that left hand. He's got to take the play away from Charles and keep him off balance."[50] If only it were that easy.

By the sixth Charles was ripping Louis apart inside. Hard, stinging blows to the head and body puffed up Louis' face, especially around his eyes, and left red welts on his torso. His lips were bruised and swollen. He shuffled forward, as he always had, right into Charles' slashing punches.

To be sure, Louis landed his clubs on occasion. Charles' left eye was swelling closed too by the seventh, and a hard left hook had his nose pouring blood in the ninth. Still, Charles had it all over Louis, and by this time Louis' mother, watching on her television at home in Detroit, had snapped off the TV in horror. "I couldn't watch it all the way," she said later. "I just couldn't stand it."[51] She should have waited a little longer. Early in the tenth round Charles got a little careless inside, just for a second, and Louis saw the opening just in time to land the kind of left hook he'd been trying for all night. It didn't land perfectly, and in the old days it wouldn't have had to in order to do the job. On this night and against this man it came close.

The blood rushed from Charles' nose anew, and his legs sagged under him. Brown, Arcel, Mintz and Tannas gasped at ringside. Arcel had seen that hook land time and again back when Louis was young and lithe, and he knew that Joe, even this version, would now open up and try to get Charles out of there. He had to—it was his only chance. If Charles could get through it the fight would be his. If he couldn't, well, you had to give the old Bomber credit.

It was the very moment everyone had been hoping would arrive, and a big cheer came up not only from the fans in the stadium but from the press section too, which held some four hundred-odd writers who had come from all over the world to witness and report on this very moment. What a glorious headline it would spawn, they all imagined, the old Brown Bomber back from the dead to score a late-round knockout against this impostor of a heavyweight champion.

There was a Pulitzer in it for them, there was no doubt, if Joe could just finish the job. Louis pounced as best as he could manage and clubbed away at Charles, who looked for all the world like the lone sailor on the deck of a teetering ship, floundering this way and that.

Looking at Charles then, left eye swollen shut, blood pouring from his nose, his legs barely under him, you could be forgiven for thinking he'd been the one getting the beating all night. Louis tried everything he knew to get rid of him there; he knew as well as anyone it would be his only chance. He threw bomb after bomb but just couldn't land the second or third shot he needed to further the cause. Charles was too slippery. He twisted and turned and squirmed. None of it looked very manly or how you wanted your heavyweight champion to look, but it bought him time and when his head was clear enough he fought back. The moment was lost and a great breath left the building.

Later the writers asked Charles if Louis had ever hurt him. "Sure, he hurt me—especially in the 10th round. But he didn't panic me, and I never had any idea that he was going to punch me out," he said.[52] When Louis trudged back to his corner at the end of the round, out of breath and no closer to victory, you could almost see him thinking: "Oh, if I could have gotten to you five years ago."

Charles had survived, and Louis certainly had spent whatever he had left trying to end it, but Brown and Arcel weren't taking any chances. All night they'd been pushing Charles out for the next round with the reminder, "Move around; hands up!" But at the beginning of the eleventh they shouted a different message with a new urgency: "Get close and hold!"[53] They needn't have bothered. Exhausted and discouraged, Louis had no more big moments left in him. Charles battered him in the eleventh, twelfth, and thirteenth rounds.

The last piece of drama came in the fourteenth when Charles tortured poor Louis the way a matador tortures a blinded bull nearing a drawn-out death. He strafed Louis with an uppercut and then a pair of right crosses near the ropes, stinging Louis so badly that the great one stumbled back and grabbed the top ring rope with his right hand, his face twisted in pain and exhaustion. It was a pitiable sight and, before it happened, an unthinkable one. As it played out, the most curious thing happened: The crowd let out a roar. Not a moan of anguish and sorrow for its dying hero, but the roar a fight crowd lets go when one fighter is about to finish another.

Among the masses the lust for a knockout supersedes alliances to a particular fighter. Just as in nature wild animals turn on the pack leader when it is ill or injured, fight crowds turn on their heroes. *Individuals* covered their mouths in horror and turned away as Louis groped blindly for some kind of help that wasn't coming. But the *crowd* wanted a knockout.

They didn't get it. Charles didn't press for it, saying later he had the idea Louis was playing possum.[54] He was not, and maybe just to remind Charles who he used to be, Louis threw a right after the bell ending the round. It landed. And as if to remind Louis of the sad truth about who he was now, Charles responded with a left of his own. It landed better.

The decision was a surprise to no one, least of all to the grown men, seen and unseen, rubbing tears from their eyes. Agnello and Forbes gave Louis just three and two rounds, respectively. Conn, the referee and apparently the sentimentalist of the bunch, found five rounds to give Louis. The consensus around the ringside press was that Louis had won maybe three rounds—the second, the fourth and the agonizing tenth.

"Joe was always dangerous and I did not want to take any unnecessary chances," Charles said afterward. "Why, when I felt his left jab in the early rounds I could understand why he became heavyweight champion of the world."[55] He was still praising his boyhood idol. You couldn't blame him; he owed Louis a great debt. But now it was his turn. He had turned in the performance of a lifetime. Years later, when Charles was still a decent fighter but one who couldn't get out of his own way, Arcel remembered his performance against Louis this way: "The night Charles defeated Louis, Ezzard was good enough to stop Louis at any time in his career."[56]

Later that night at the Edison Hotel, Charles' headquarters, Mintz and Tannas threw a victory party commensurate with the significance of the night's events: free booze and broads for everyone; family, friends, the newspaper boys and other assorted hangers-on and gangsters all celebrating the moment and toasting the man of the hour. Mintz, delirious with glee, booze and who knew what else, bellowed, "I always knew that Louis was a bum. I tell you, Ez is going to be one of the greatest heavyweight champions of all time."[57]

In an upstairs bedroom, Ezzard Charles, his face bruised, lumpy and cut up from Louis' jabs, lay in bed, flat on his back. Arcel gently worked him over with wet washcloths and ice packs, because the heavyweight champion of the world should at least look like himself when the writers and photographers came calling.

10

Unforgivable

Mintz and Tannas wanted to get as much out of the Louis win as they could, so they arranged another big homecoming parade in Cincinnati, just like the one they had had when Charles beat Walcott for the NBA title. Truth be told it was a little silly to have another one, especially since they had been saying all along Charles already was champ and didn't have to beat Louis to prove it; but he had done it, and the folks back in Cincinnati were open to it. Plus, it would be good for Charles to go home now, knowing there was no way anyone could say he wasn't the heavyweight champion of the world.

You couldn't blame Charles for feeling on top of the world. Here he was, a poor black boy from the slums of Cincinnati, now the heavyweight champion, and there was nothing anyone could do or say about it. He wasn't the "NBA" champ. He wasn't a "paper" champ. They didn't recognize him as the world champ in Great Britain, but so what? *The Ring* magazine said it and the New York commission said it, so it was done.

But it was even better than that. They'd told him he couldn't whip Joe Louis in a hundred years, no matter how old the Bomber was. And he'd done it anyway. He remembered how after the Baksi fight they'd asked him about fighting Louis. No wanting to sound boastful, he'd replied, "My goodness no," and later one of the writers who'd heard him wrote that he, Charles, would sooner jump out a window than face Louis.[1] What should he have said? "Bring him on?" It wasn't him. It would have sounded swollen-headed. But none of that mattered now. He'd whipped Louis, he'd proved them wrong, and now he could sit back a little and savor the victory. He'd be respected now. Wherever he went they would call him "Champ" and they'd mean it.

"Now I am the champion. What a relief to be the undisputed title holder," he said when he got back home to Cincinnati. "Not to read aspersions on your title, not to hear folks refer to you as a 'dime store' champion."[2] *The Ring* magazine even put him on its cover on the December 1950 issue. Underneath his picture it read: "Ezzard Charles, the Heavyweight Champion of the World."

You had to admire Charles' optimism, his naiveté, to think everything had changed for the better, that he'd now be accepted. How could he not know that as Louis was half-carried back to his dressing room that night, exhausted and bloody, they were crying their eyes out in Harlem and Chicago and Detroit? And that they were doing the same thing in Atlanta and in Jackson, and in Baltimore and Montgomery? Wherever black folks had grown up and grown strong listening to Louis on the radio in the early days, when every victory of his in the ring was a victory for them outside of it, they were crying for Joe Louis. How could Charles not know that they would never forgive him? And it wasn't only black folks.

If there was ever a black man who was a hero to white America, it was Joe Louis. Sure, all things being equal a white guy would have been preferable, but when they needed someone to show the Nazis how strong America was, Joe was there, blasting apart Max Schmeling. When the boys out on the front lines needed to know America was behind them, Louis was there, in uniform, touring all the bases, fighting exhibitions, signing autographs. He had saved the fight game and given it dignity, humility and class, no small feat.

Grown men who'd been at war cried like little boys when Louis said through shredded lips that he was through with fighting, that Charles had shown him he was washed up. People don't forget. Charles had to know this. At first it may have been good enough to be appreciated for what he was in his small circle in the bright afterglow of victory. But when a man has proven himself he wants the world to know it and to acknowledge it. But that wasn't going to happen. Not for him. Beating Joe Louis was unforgivable.

Some writers saw it only in hindsight. Years later one confessed, "From the moment they raised Ezzard Charles' hand as the victor you would have thought they had just put him on the FBI's 10-most-wanted list."[3]

Ezzard didn't know it yet, so he and his guys took the train back home to Cincinnati and they held the parade on October 5. Charles sent a few requests ahead of time to Walter Houston, chairman of the reception committee. He was the heavyweight champion of the world now, conqueror of the great Joe Louis, and he had some requests.

First, he wanted a one-minute moment of silence to honor those killed in the Korean War, which had begun two months before. He wanted places in the parade reserved for members of his church, Calvary Methodist, and also for members of Stowe Grade School and Woodward High School. Houston made it happen. When Charles got off the train they put a giant wreath of yellow flowers on his head and sat him high in a convertible so he could wave to the few thousand people who lined the mile and a half parade route from Union Station to the Hamilton County Courthouse. Four separate marching bands led the way and some ladies clubs had put together some floats, too.

The parade was delayed when a group of kids broke through police barriers when Charles came out of Union Terminal, but after that it hummed right along. No one was run over or otherwise injured, like last time. Charles recited a short speech in front of the courthouse at the end, saying, "It does me proud to know that you are happy over my victory. There is no other land where a Negro could get the reception I have had from you."[4]

After the parade they held a press conference at the Hotel Manse, where Charles told the local press that while New York was where the money was, Cincinnati was his home. It was all too much—exactly as he'd always imagined it. Even Mom Charles got into the act, telling a bunch of newspapers reporters how proud she was of her boy and that it was all like a dream.

A couple days later Ezzard drove through his old slum neighborhood and saw the poor kids in their alleyways and on their stoops and in the dirt playing their games, the same games he once had played, wearing the same kind of rags he once had worn, bony and too thin, like he always had been. They had the same angry, starving look in their eyes that he remembered from his own youth and that he still saw in the mirror on the bad days. He wanted to go to them and tell them not to worry, that if they worked hard and believed, they could get out of those slums like he had; it wasn't impossible, even for poor black boys like themselves. They could someday have enough to eat, live in a nice house, own a car and have a nice life.

It wasn't in his nature to go right to them unless he was called, so he waited for them to signal somehow that they would believe him if he said it, that they had been waiting all their lives for the moment when someone like him would come and give them a reason to think maybe they mattered. He looked at them and waited for that signal, but nothing came back. They paused from their games, yes, and stood tall, glaring at him. They knew who he was. That he knew for sure. They knew where he had come from—from these very slums.

But they did not signal him. They did not clap or cheer him. They didn't even ask him for a dime or some penny candy. They stared at him with resentment, and then some of them started to hoot and boo at him. Soon they all joined in, booing and catcalling the heavyweight champion of the whole world, right in his own neighborhood, right where he stood, right where he had once stood with them. He could do nothing but put his head down and drive away and try to approximate dignity, if it were possible.

Those poor black boys had not been waiting all their lives for him, it turned out. The man they had been waiting all their lives for he had beaten up and sent back into retirement. To these kids and these families Joe Louis was everything. It didn't matter that he, Ezzard Charles, was not only a black man too, but had skin blacker than Louis. It didn't matter even that he had grown up here, played on the same ball fields, sat on the same stoops, felt all the same pains, and dreamed the same dreams. It was Louis who had changed their world, who had given them hope. He, Ezzard Charles, was just another fighter. Just another kid from the West End. He was nothing. Worse than nothing.

A writer who was close to Charles and pitied him tried to figure it out in his column. "The sense of independence was stirring and Louis was proof that a Negro could escape the slums. They yearned from him to last forever. It made them ache because he could be defeated. It didn't matter that Charles was black. He had beaten Louis, and they would not forgive him. He had stolen something from their lives. They refused to claim him as one of their own."[5]

Nevertheless, it made sense for Charles' next (or first, depending on your point of view) title defense to be in Cincinnati, so Mintz and Tannas signed a deal with Sam Becker for a defense against Nick Barone, *The Ring*'s number-six-rated light heavyweight, for November 28 at the Cincinnati Gardens Arena.

Charles would get 42½ percent of the gate to Barone's 17½ percent with Becker promoting and kicking up five figures to Norris and the IBC. Capacity at the Gardens was 15,000; Mintz figured Charles would do 12,000 fans there easily, giving them at least a $60,000 gate, with tickets ranging from $2.50 up to $15 for ringside.

Barone would be a soft touch for Charles and everybody knew it, but if anyone deserved it Charles did. Barone, a twenty-four-year-old from Syracuse, New York, had never been off his feet in fifty-two pro fights. "The Fighting Marine" had just one stoppage loss on his record, that against Jim Rousse, who stopped him on cuts in six rounds back in 1947. Compact and powerful, he planned to get low and go to Charles' body to wear him down. Charles was several inches taller, weighed in five pounds heavier (the first time Charles would outweigh an opponent since moving to heavyweight) and also had a five-inch reach advantage.

Charles was quickly made a 5–1 betting favorite, but that didn't bother Barone, whose real first name was Carmine. He had an older brother named Nick. When the war came, he was too young, at sixteen, to enlist. So he took his brother's birth certificate, enlisted in the Marines and eventually saw action at Iwo Jima. He was tough through and through, and in the days leading up to the fight his manager of record, Henny Andrews, tried to goad Charles into slugging with him. "We dare Charles to mix with Nick. If he does, I know he won't be there at the end of the fifteenth round. Barone will rip him to pieces if he doesn't run."[6]

The local press knew better, saying Charles was more likely to lose his mustache than his title belt, as the Cincinnati commission had a strict rule against fighters wearing facial hair into the ring, even when they were hometown kids made good. The press were right. They made Charles shave off the mustache. A few days before the fight a massive snowstorm hit Cincinnati, forcing a one-week postponement. Conditions still weren't ideal on December 5 when the fight went off—the Ohio River was on the verge of flooding in several areas. Still, 10,085 fans generating $53,334 braved the snow drifts and icy sidewalks to see Charles stop Barone at 2:06 of the eleventh round.

It went as expected. Barone spent the early round whacking away at Charles' midsection, hoping to slow him down for the later rounds. Charles fought smartly and conservatively, taking his time. "I had 15 rounds to do the job and I was just going along—hook, jab, feint, you know, trying to pick my spots for the right punches," he said later.[7]

A left uppercut took most of the fight out of Barone in the fifth, and another uppercut followed by a barrage of right hands dropped him with a minute left in the eleventh. He turned on his side at the count of six and stayed there until he was counted out by referee H. Warendorf.

"He's deceiving," Barone said afterward. "You're doing a pretty good job chasing him and banging him on the inside, you think. All of a sudden you're tired. He hits you some sharp raps. You're on the floor so fogged up you can't get up."[8]

"[Charles] isn't given proper credit for his fighting qualities," Barone was quoted. "His straight punches carry a sting. They jar your head. They set you back. In several rounds, especially the second, I thought I had him. But just when things look bad for him he cuts loose with a variety of punches that turn the tide. He is a far better fighter than you writers credit him with being."[9]

Almost unanimously, the press praised Charles' performance. One magazine writer reported that if it had been Louis in the ring with Charles instead of Barone that night, "Joe would have been halted 'ere the seventh, so accurate, sharp and effective was Charles."[10]

It wouldn't have been an Ezzard Charles fight without Mintz unintentionally cracking up reporters in the locker room. Referring to some gossip or another he'd come upon, he told the assembled press he'd "heard a rumor through the grape-wire."[11]

Mintz, Tannas and Norris wanted Charles right back in the ring. That was okay with Charles. This business was about striking while the iron was hot, making your mark and making your money and then getting the hell out before you got ruined. Plus, the way the IBC figured, Charles was never going to make them a lot of money all at once. But if they kept him fighting frequently enough he could make them a lot of money a little at a time.

Norris told Mintz and Tannas to defend against thirty-four-year-old longtime contender Lee Oma, from Buffalo, New York, via Detroit. In September he'd beaten the dangerous Bob Satterfield to avenge a knockout win Satterfield had scored four months earlier—Oma's only loss in his last sixteen fights. (One of the fighters Oma beat during that stretch, Italy's Enrico Bertola, died of head injuries the day after Oma outpointed him over ten rounds.)

Oma also had recently whipped Charles victims Freddie Beshore (twice) and Barone. All of Oma's important wins were by decision. He wasn't a big puncher. He won with an awkward, hit-and-run style that crudely approximated Joe Walcott's, if Walcott had been 80 percent less talented. He'd harangue an opponent with a ten-punch combination, then drop his hands, walk away and nod to friends at ringside. He'd switch to a lefty stance, throw a punch, switch back and then switch back again. He'd sidestep; stick out his chin, the whole thing, throw a punch and shuffle away. It drove his opponents nuts and the writers, too. In one fight he'd look like a world-beater, in the next like a bum. You never knew which Oma was going to show up. Truth be told, he probably didn't either. He'd been through a lot.

His given name was Frank Csajewski. He'd quit school in the fifth grade. Not long after, a priest at St. Lawrence Parrish taught him how to box. Out of respect he went under the fighting name of "Lawrence Parrish." Then he shortened "Lawrence" to "Lee." Later he was almost run over by a van belonging to the Omaha Trucking Corporation. So he traded "Parrish" for "Omaha," then shortened it to "Oma." At one point in his career when fights were harder to come by he went by the name Levi Omanski, "the Jewish Jolter."

During one stretch from 1943 to '44, Oma won thirteen bouts in a row, including one over Lou Nova. In another run in 1947, he dropped five straight. His dedication to training was as inconsistent as everything else about him; as a mature fighter he had fought as low as 183 pounds and as high as 235 and lived the life of a playboy whether he had a fight coming up or not.

Consequently the book on him was that he certainly would run out of gas at some point during a fifteen-round title fight, a distance he had never navigated. It was for this reason and many others that he was made a 6–1 underdog to Charles not long after the bout was booked for Madison Square Garden on January 12, 1951. Odds were 9–5 that Charles would score a knockout.

Oma wasn't put off by the odds against him. "Well, if Jimmy Braddock could do it (against Max Baer) and if Joe Walcott could come close (against Louis) then maybe I can do it," he said.[12] Alas, he could not. He did make Charles look ungainly at times, but this was his specialty.

Scrapping in a more orthodox manner than usual but mostly clowning and fighting to keep from getting knocked out, Oma made Charles miss dozens of punches over the first few rounds by rolling with Charles' blows, slipping them, or twisting and turning in ways that were heretofore unseen in a prize ring. This frustrated Charles to no end. He wanted to prove (again) that he could punch, so he went after Oma with one wild swing after another. Oma was the worst possible guy to do that against. He couldn't do much, but he knew how to make a guy look bad, and at points he made Charles look like anything but the heavyweight champion of the world.

This was not at all pleasing to the crowd of 11,504 who paid $54,185 and was made up mostly of Oma supporters. They booed and hissed Charles at every opportunity and especially when referee Ruby Goldstein docked Charles the fifth and eighth rounds for hitting low.

The crowd saw many more low blows than did Goldstein, but the veteran referee knew why it looked like Charles was constantly going low: Oma's corner had hiked up his trunks: the oldest trick in the book. Midway through the fight one of Oma's cornermen admonished Goldstein for not penalizing Charles more. Goldstein replied: "Pull his trunks down before they choke him."[13]

As bad as Charles looked, Oma was worse. In the tenth Charles finally caught him with a series of left hooks. Oma's hands fell to his sides and Charles smashed home five more clean punches. The challenger stepped back toward the ropes, staggered and limped toward his corner, clearly out on his feet. Referee Goldstein immediately waved the fight off at 1:19 of the round.

"I just ran out of steam," Oma said later. "I couldn't get my hands up. Charles caught me a good one just after the start of the round and I felt myself go dead. I tried to move but nothing seemed to happen. I kept seeing [the punches] coming but couldn't get out of the way. And don't let anyone tell you he can't hit."[14] Oma retired after the fight and never fought again. Charles left the ring to a resounding chorus of boos. He couldn't figure out why.

"I'm sorry the crowd didn't like the fight," he said. "I thought I was very sharp. I felt good. Felt eager. I think I fought a good fight. Oma was tricky and tough and hard to hit. But the crowd wasn't satisfied."[15]

It finally hit Charles then, too late, because we realize all the big things too late, that there was nothing he would ever do in a prize ring that would make them forget Joe Louis. He could beat all the Lee Omas of the world and all the Freddie Beshores, Nick Barones, Joe Walcotts and whoever else they threw at him, and he could beat them for a hundred years, but he could only do it the way he did it. He couldn't do it the way Louis did it. Even after that day they'd hooted and booed at him he thought that if he kept winning, kept stopping guys, then at least they would have to respect what he did in the ring, even if they didn't respect him as a man. But that was a lie, too. It didn't matter what he did—in the ring or out of it. "They want a big man. They want a killer," Charles continued in the dressing room, the writers gathered around him. "I'm a little disappointed I guess. I thought that after I whipped Joe Louis the fans would accept me as a true heavyweight champion. But now I know they want a bigger, different type champ. Joe made those quick knockouts popular. It's a bit tough on the guy that follows him. But I am satisfied with what I have done."[16]

A writer put it succinctly. "[The crowd's] trouble, and it probably extended to most of the radio and television audience, was that they couldn't forget Joe Louis—the Louis of several years ago," he wrote, under a headline that read "Charles Can't Please Fans." "The Brown Bomber might never have caught up with the side-stepping, hard-to-hit Oma, but if once he had the range it would have been boom, boom and out. Charles takes more than two booms but the net result is about the same."[17]

Later, when Charles was back home in Cincinnati, a writer suggested that to the fans there was still some confusion over who was at the top of the heavyweight division. Charles let loose. "There is no confusion in the heavyweight division," he snapped. "It is the same old story year after year. All you hear and read is, 'There are no real boxers. There is a dearth of talent. The game is going to pot. There is no young talent and the veterans are going to pot.' As I see it, I am the champion, and rating myself, a good one.

"Do you remember what they said before I came along? They insisted that Joe Louis would have to quit and turn in the title because no one would be able to dispute his supremacy," Charles continued. "Away back when Max Baer was champion, I read that there were no worthwhile contenders. Then Louis came along to beat Jimmy Braddock and gain the title. He was a fighting champion just as I intend to be a fighting champion. He took on everybody and anybody who had a right to enter the ring with him. What was the result? The papers said, 'Louis is following a bum of the month program.'" It was rare that Charles was so open with the press, but he was frustrated. A man wants to be respected.

"I do not expect the fight fans to accept me as the Louis counterpart. Maybe I am, maybe I am not. But I deserve the chance to prove myself," he said. "I read about Stephen

Charles weighs in for his title defense against tough Nick Barone in Cincinnati on December 5, 1950, as Barone looks on. The Cincinnati Commission made Charles shave off his mustache. Charles stopped Barone in the eleventh round (courtesy Peltz Boxing Promotions, Inc.).

Foster, the song writer. When he was alive, they said, 'This bum can't compose any music. He's a joke.' During his lifetime, Foster had a tough time keeping the wolf from his door. Times when he didn't, either. Now I read that Foster was a genius. So where does that leave the heavyweight situation? Confusion?" Charles chuckled the way a man does when he knows he is right and it doesn't matter. "Yes, sometimes there is real confusion."[18]

Charles fought a couple of exhibitions in early February in Louisiana, then returned home to be with Gladys for the birth of their daughter, Deborah. He was officially a family man. He didn't know much about taking care of babies and wasn't much interested in learning, but he had fun with her and felt the deeper responsibility most men report on becoming fathers for the first time.

Fighting came first. Before the Oma fight was even done Tannas and Mintz had met with Norris about facing Walcott again, this time in Detroit, in March. The day after the Oma fight they signed the contract and made it official. Charles would receive 40 percent of the gate to Walcott's 17 percent. This was a surprise when it was announced, since Walcott had lost miserably—and somewhat curiously—on points to Utah's young Rex Layne in November at the Garden. Layne had been fighting professionally a mere eighteen months and was a solid 5–1 underdog. Walcott "never showed anything like the form he displayed in two fights with Joe Louis"[19] and if you didn't know better you might think old Jersey Joe had gone into the tank.

After all, a fellow and a few close friends could clean up betting the underdog at 5–1. The loss was especially troubling when you considered that Walcott had put together a nice streak since his loss to Charles in June 1949, winning five in a row, four by knockout, including one over promising young Harold Johnson in Philadelphia. Then he lost to Layne. He blamed it on being out of shape, but it looked fishy to get a title shot right after losing to a green kid like Layne; almost like he was being rewarded.

Either way Walcott was getting another title shot—his fourth—and he predicted he would knock out Charles within seven rounds.[20] Whatever the case, to Mintz and Tannas, fighting Walcott again in what would be Charles' seventh title defense made some economic sense. He was still one of the better heavyweights out there and had the name and credibility to bring a big gate. People liked Walcott. Plus, Mintz didn't see him as a huge threat. Charles had taken him fairly readily the first time around, and Jersey Joe had only gotten older since then. Charles, it could be argued, had improved, especially since his win over Louis. Why Detroit? That was easy: It was Louis' hometown. The Bomber's fans would come out by the thousands to root for Charles to get his head knocked off.

Louis, meanwhile, had announced his re-retirement in the dressing room after the Charles fight. In the immediate and terrible aftermath of such a loss it was the only thing he could do, the only thing that made sense. Quickly enough, however, he changed his mind. It didn't take much, especially once the cuts and bruises started to heal. He merely had to convince himself that he'd have whipped Charles if he'd just had the time to prepare for him that he'd asked for. The loss didn't prove Charles was a better fighter or that Joe was past it. It proved only that on that night Charles was better prepared.

"I did not have it against Charles," Louis said while training. "I know I hurt that boy several times, but when I tried to follow up those advantages, I could not do it. I got awful sore at myself and said, 'Joe, you're through. You're just through.' The next day I said, 'Joe, you can do better. Try some more. You can't be washed up at 36. The field is made for you.' So I started to come back."[21]

Old prizefighters are wonderfully skilled at lying to themselves, and in this regard Louis was the same as any of them, or better. He had been so superior to his competition for so long that he had nearly a full lifetime of evidence to which to point to quell any fears he retained over his ability to knock a man unconscious. Intellectually, he had to know he couldn't go on forever. But deep down in his bones he felt that he wasn't done yet—not tonight, not against this man—and at the least, he could knock Charles cold if he got back into fighting shape and got him in the ring again. To do that he'd have to fight every month, or close to it—just like when he was first coming up—and he'd have to fight all the contenders out there so eventually Charles would have no choice but to fight him. So that's what he did.

Two months almost to the day after the loss to Charles, Louis beat tough Argentine Cesar Brion on points in Chicago Stadium. Five weeks later he bludgeoned and stopped Beshore in Detroit ("The way Louis looked against me he would have beaten Charles," Beyshore said afterward, somewhat unhelpfully.[22]) A month later Louis decisioned Omelio Agramonte in Miami and then stopped Andy Walker in California. That was four wins in four months, which for most guys was nothing. But it qualified Joe Louis for a rematch as soon as Charles took care of Walcott in March.

Louis didn't look especially impressive in any of these outings. He was described almost universally, even by the sportswriters who worshipped him, as slow, plodding and easy to hit. But he still had that great left jab, and when a guy stood with him he still had the punch to wreck him. The other stuff didn't matter to Louis. He just had to keep grinding out the wins, fighting his way back into shape, and sooner or later the IBC would get him Charles again. They had to. The gate would be huge. And a win would make Louis bigger than ever. That, as much as anything, drove him out of his bed every morning to do his roadwork, to put his thirty-six-year-old bones through the mill in the gym.

To help matters along, over the next month or so Louis insulted Charles whenever he had the opportunity. Asked to rate Charles among all of his career opponents, he placed him sixth, behind Billy Conn, Max Baer, James J. Braddock, Max Schmeling and Tommy Farr, each of whom he had knocked out, with the exception of Farr, whom he outpointed in his first title defense.[23] By contrast, when Charles was asked to rate his toughest opponents, he placed Louis at the top, followed by Walcott, Joey Maxim, Archie Moore, Pat Valentino, Jimmy Bivins, Gus Lesnevich, Lloyd Marshall, Elmer Ray, and Nick Barone.[24]

Louis claimed he was too heavy for the first match with Charles, that he had a cold during training camp, and that he had a better chance at regaining the title than did all the heavyweights who had tried before him and failed. Why? "I don't think Charles is as good a fighter as the champs the others had to meet."[25]

Charles, weary of Louis' insults, told a reporter that he could have finished Louis in the fourteenth round of their first fight but didn't, a compassionate gesture he wouldn't repeat if they met again.

"You know, even in the middle of a fight you say things to yourself and, when I saw him grab the top rope and blink I said, 'There's the great Joe Louis ready to go. It isn't supposed to happen,'" Charles said. "My hands were pretty sore by then, and I didn't want to hurt them. I suppose I could have thrown everything, but funny things go through your mind. Well, it won't ever be that way again. It might be different next time we fight."[26]

Norris was after Tannas and Mintz about the rematch before Charles had even faced Walcott in Detroit again, and they agreed to it in principle. Only the details had to be worked out, the biggest one involving how the money would be split up. Miles, Louis' manager, insisted on each fighter getting 30 percent rather than the customary champion/challenger split of 40–20, a concession Charles had to make again, he insisted, to Louis' enduring popularity. Mintz refused on the grounds that Charles was the heavyweight champion, had already beaten Louis and therefore deserved a bigger slice of the pie. But this was not a deal-breaker. An agreement would be reached eventually.

As long as Charles kept winning and Louis kept winning it would happen—probably in Chicago in April, according to both sides. So although it would be a stretch to say that Charles was looking past Walcott, there can be little doubt that fighting Louis again, and retiring him for good this time, was on his mind.

On the day of the Walcott fight, Charles worried the few supporters he had when he weighed in at a career-high 186 pounds. Some pointed out that he'd stopped sparring a week before the fight, a very strange thing for a champion, and wondered if he was hiding an injury. They needn't have worried. Charles wanted to come in bigger for Walcott and had to drop some routines from training to keep on the weight.

"I went home after sparring the other night and I weighed 177 pounds," Charles confided to Eddie Futch, a forty-year-old trainer who'd grown up sparring with Louis at Brewster's Gym there in Detroit. "If I continue sparring I'll be below the light heavyweight limit."[27] People were always forgetting: Ezzard Charles was a light heavyweight who happened to be the heavyweight champ of the world.

Walcott weighed in at 193, the lightest he'd been for a fight in four years. And, as it turned out, putting the fight in Detroit turned out to be a smart move, indeed. New attendance records were set at the Sportsman's Gymnasium, where both champion and challenger trained, and on fight night an enthusiastic crowd of 13,852 paid $75,502 at Olympia Stadium even though the bout was being aired on both radio and television. Charles was a 4–1 favorite.

You could not overstate how deeply the Louis fans in Detroit wanted to see Ezzard Charles lose, as was evidenced in part by the thunderous applause Louis received when introduced to the crowd, and in part how passionately they booed the champion. Walcott received a generous ovation.

The throng very nearly got their wish in the fourth round when Walcott crashed home a right hand that sent Charles reeling, as badly hurt as he had ever been in a title fight, maybe as badly as he had ever been hurt in a prize ring. He wrapped his arms around Walcott and hung on for a full sixty seconds before referee Clarence Rosen pried him off. By that time his head had cleared. He made it to the bell and after that, Charles boxed more cautiously, which didn't thrill the crowd any, as if they needed any more reasons to boo him.

Charles had to be careful. Walcott was far more willing than last time they'd met to charge in and throw hard punches. And the old man could punch. Sure, he still shuffled around and feinted and did all that herky-jerky stuff he always did, and a couple times he did that walk-away bit, trying to lure Charles into the kind of short right hands that had dropped Louis. Charles expected that. Walcott was a cutie by nature, and no fighter as old as Walcott was going to change his style wholesale.

But he was more aggressive than Charles had ever seen him. So Charles boxed over the next several rounds. Even if the crowd didn't like it, he did it better than any heavyweight in the world. He took a commanding lead, and late in the ninth he sidestepped one of Walcott's bull-rushes and banged home a counter left hook that Walcott walked straight into. It dropped the old guy for a nine-count and many in the crowd—and probably Walcott too—expected Charles to come charging out for the knockout in the tenth. He did not, and the crowd let him have it for that, too. Charles had good reason to take his time.

When Walcott hurt Charles in the fourth, he aggravated a bruised left ear Charles had suffered the prior week during sparring. After the fourth round it started swelling and by the ninth it looked ready to burst. Arcel told Charles after the round to play it safe. "My words to him after the ninth round were, 'Take it easy the rest of the way. You're out front. If you take any chances and try for a knockout he may nail you on the ear and it's all over,'" Arcel said afterward.[28]

Arcel had been around long enough to know that a swollen, bloody ear isn't a serious injury and Charles could fight through it. He also knew that if the swelling burst there would be blood everywhere and the referee probably would stop the fight. Charles caught a break when Walcott, who was throwing mostly right hands early in the fight, switched to left hooks later on. "When I saw him using those left hooks, I just prayed Walcott would do nothing else the rest of the way," Arcel said later.[29]

Charles still fought hard enough to hurt Walcott again in the fourteenth, and Walcott returned the favor in a wild fifteenth round. At the bell Charles raised his arms in victory, as did Walcott. Both thought they had won. Among the press at ringside, there was little doubt: thirteen writers seated along press row scored the bout for Charles.[30] The Associated Press had Charles winning, 80–70. This mirrored the official verdict, as the referee and judges voted for Charles by scores of 80–70, 83–67 and 84–66. But when the decision was announced the crowd erupted in boos and catcalls.

Manny Seamon, sitting at ringside for the sole purpose of scouting Charles for the rematch with Louis, gave Charles ten of the fifteen rounds. "What are the fans complaining about?" he asked. "Charles won easy in my book. Walcott put up a better fight than in Chicago but he only fought in spurts."[31]

Predictably, Walcott and his team claimed he was cheated. "It's the third time he's been robbed," screamed Bocchicchio, Walcott's manager. "They didn't give him the decision against Louis the first time, and they hooked him again against Charles in Chicago."[32]

"The last time I fought Charles the decision could have gone either way," Walcott complained. "But this time there was no doubt that I won." He added that he thought he'd won at least eight rounds and that two or three more were even.[33]

Across the hall, Charles and Mintz didn't understand what all the hubbub was about. "I didn't think Joe had me in trouble at any time," Charles said. "Some of his right hands to the head stung me, but I never felt dazed. Jersey Joe was tougher this time, but I didn't ever think he was going to get me." Eventually one of the writers asked Charles the question it seemed he was asked after every fight: Did the boos bother him? "No, I'm used to that kind of reaction when I fight."[34]

After the newspaper boys got their quotes, Charles went to the hospital and had his swollen ear drained. Dr. Ray Clark confirmed a ruptured blood vessel and ear drum. The treatment? No boxing for two months. And there went the rematch with Louis, at least for April. Tannas broke the news to the press. "The champ is okay but he'll have to give the ear a chance to heal before he does anything else," he said. "However, Charles is willing to fight anyone the International Boxing Club offers. And that includes Louis, as soon as Ez is ready."[35]

Charles went home to Cincinnati while Mintz continued negotiating with the IBC and Miles over the purse split for the Louis fight. A couple weeks after the Walcott fight, the papers finally broke the story about Charles being married. A weekly had started running rumors about it just before the fight and Charles would have gotten it all over with by then, but he didn't want all the distractions so close to the match.

He came clean on the 21st. He had been denying it long enough and now, with Deborah a little over a month old, Gladys insisted he tell the truth. It didn't look right if he didn't. He knew she was right and he confirmed that the rumors were true. The papers went wild—more than they did for his fights. The reporters were aghast that Charles still lived at home with his grandmothers in Cincinnati, while his wife lived with her parents in suburban Madisonville. What kind of marriage was that?

"We just think it's best to live this way while I'm boxing," Charles told them. "I'm away from home so much. Being an athlete, I don't think I should set up a house at this time. We want to wait until things level off. I hope to buy a house here."[36]

"I just thought it was best if we live apart, me being an athlete and everything. But when the baby came, my wife insisted that people should know we were married. I tried to tell her it didn't make any difference what people knew—that she knew she was married—but it's better now and I sense the responsibility more," said Charles.[37] By this time Charles certainly had the money to buy a house for his family if he wanted to, even though he was probably the poorest heavyweight champion since the Dempsey era. He lived in a brick, three-story house at 929 Lincoln Park Drive, a short drive from the Cincinnati ball park, with his grandmothers, two aunts, four cocker spaniels, several bass fiddles and a few dozen suits, hats, caps and pairs of shoes that he wore to the Cotton Club downtown when he wasn't in training. (Not quite Kid Chocolate numbers, but still pretty good.)

He owned a powder blue Cadillac, a tenement on Blair Street, and the gym at Clark and Central streets, which he'd bought for $10,000. Before going into the army, he'd been a part owner in a small sports arena in Pittsburgh. While he was stationed overseas, the place ran up $8,000 in "amusement" taxes, on which Charles still owed $3,000 after the Louis fight. He'd hardly made a living at middleweight and light heavy. So while he certainly had come a long, long way from the slums of his youth, as far as heavyweight champions went, he had a long way to go. Plus, being heavyweight champion came with a price.

"Being a champion is expensive. You have to do things you didn't have to do before," he said after beating Louis. "Tips here, tips there. Folks expect you to live up to the title."[38]

It was even worse than when he'd been fighting at middleweight and light heavy, before he won the title. He'd be dieting to make weight, all but living on cups of tea, and his buddies were drinking Scotch and eating steak—on him. When he became very successful and went to the Cincinnati Cotton Club there were guys who would hit him up for eight, nine dollars every single day. Some guys would borrow as much a $30 a day from him. He didn't realize then that they probably were junkies.[39]

Gladys, meanwhile, though relieved the truth was finally out, had no interest in making herself available to the press. She let them have a couple photos of her and Deborah that Ezzard had taken, but politely declined when the reporters came knocking on her parents' door in Madisonville, a suburb of greater Cincinnati. She'd spoken to the press a little after Ezzard had beaten Louis and all she said then was the truth: that she and Ezzard were not engaged, but "had an understanding."[40] That understanding was that they would be married when he felt the time was right, and about that he had kept his word.

By early March, and despite the win over Walcott, negotiations for the rematch with Louis were collapsing. Norris told the press Louis wanted more money for a June outdoor fight than he had been willing to take for the proposed fight in April. Miles' argument was that Louis was losing money every day the fight was pushed back.

After trying for two hours to hammer out an agreement with both sides over the phone, Norris said to hell with it and told the press, "We're too far apart to reach any agreement by June. If Charles hadn't suffered that injury to his left ear ... the fight very likely would have come off in Chicago in April."[41] Mintz was furious, saying, "We don't care if we ever meet Joe Louis again but if we do it will be on our terms."[42]

Louis then tried a different tactic, telling the press he would retire if the fight wasn't signed soon. When that didn't work, he and Miles relented on their demand for a 30–30 purse split and in late April agreed to the customary 40–20. "Now that we're willing to accept their terms of the purse, Charles doesn't have any excuse for not fighting Joe," said Miles. "He will be shamed into giving Joe another crack at the title—the public will demand it."[43] But that wasn't all that Mintz wanted. He wanted some kind of assurance that if Louis won, there would be a third bout. The problem was no one could say for certain what Louis would do if he won. And you couldn't write a contract that prohibited a fighter from retiring if he wanted to. "Jake Mintz wants something of a substantial nature. What it is I don't know," said the IBC's Markson. "If Louis beats Charles, Mintz doesn't want Joe to retire. If that happens Charles would have to start another tournament."[44]

With that, Mintz and Tannas went ahead with their Plan B: another title defense,

Charles' eighth, against light heavyweight champion Maxim on May 30 at Chicago Stadium; and then Walcott *again*, and then Louis if they could come to terms. They'd get a nice $100,000 for the TV rights, plus radio, and maybe they'd get 12,000 fans if they got lucky. Charles would get his 40 percent to Maxim's 20.

The last fight between Charles and Maxim, the one in Cincinnati, had been close enough to warrant a rematch, and Kearns, that old bastard, had been crying ever since about how Maxim had been robbed. Mintz was fine with the fight. It was a good time to get Maxim in the ring. Since stopping Freddie Mills in ten rounds to win the title some sixteen months earlier, he had fought seven times, but they were all non-title bouts, exhibitions really, against bums and no-hopers—Joe Dawson, Bill Petersen, Big Boy Brown, and Hubert Hood. Most of these guys didn't belong in the ring with a top-*twenty* guy, forget about the world champion.

The NBA was threatening to strip Maxim of the title until he signed a contract promising to fight Bob Satterfield on June 27 regardless of the outcome of his fight with Charles. So to Mintz the timing was perfect. Maxim couldn't be as sharp fighting these bums as he would be had he been fighting top guys over and over the way Charles had been. Not only that, there were rumors that before he started training, Maxim had ballooned up to over 220 pounds. This was the perfect time to get him.

None of this really worried Kearns or Maxim. If it did, they didn't show it. They planned to compensate for the time off from serious fighting by having Maxim spar a full 250 rounds in camp, roughly twice the number of rounds he normally put in. (Charles sparred 104 rounds, about his usual.) To get the press drums beating, Kearns told everyone who would listen, and a few who wouldn't, that he had Maxim bobbing and weaving more in training—like Jack Dempsey—rather than standing straight up in his usual posture.

This was nonsense, of course. Maxim was no more a bob-and-weave fighter than was Charles. He was a born cutie and a damned good one at that. Kearns plowed ahead regardless, using Maxim's kayo of Mills to assert that Maxim would be a big puncher on fight night. One of Kearns' many specialties was creating drama and doubt among the press and fans when a fight looked, if not like a mismatch, then like there was a very clear favorite. Charles opened as an 8–5 favorite, but Kearns worked his magic and as the fight got closer, so too did the odds. Even Maxim got into the act, playing up the angle that he was more of a puncher now than a cutie.

"The public thinks I'm a powder-puff puncher but I'm going to surprise everyone on Wednesday night. I hit just as hard as Charles. I found that out in our last fight in Cincinnati in 1949. I staggered him in the sixth and 12th rounds," Maxim allegedly said after a workout at the Catholic Youth Organization gym.[45]

None of this concerned Charles, who saw it for what it was—showbiz. He played along. "Maxim is apparently trying to get more leverage on his punches. If he is in a crouch maybe I can get a crack at him with my right. When I fought him last time he was a side-wheeler and I only had his left shoulder as a target." Either way, Charles wanted no controversy this time around. "[The last fight] was a close fight and it has to be more decisive this time. I'll either score a kayo or get knocked out this time."[46]

Kearns also worked up a rumor that Mintz was worried that Charles wasn't working hard enough in the gym, which sent the writers scrambling over to the Midwest Athletic Club, where Charles was training, to get his reaction. "I can be as good or bad as I want to be," Charles told them before tearing through a trio of sparring partners over six rounds. "If Jake Mintz wants to worry about my workouts, far be it from me to discourage him."[47]

Charles tries a right to the body against Jersey Joe Walcott in their rematch in Detroit on March 7, 1951. Charles scored a knockdown in the ninth round and won a unanimous fifteen-round decision in defense of the world heavyweight title (courtesy Peltz Boxing Promotions, Inc.).

Kearns worked every angle he knew to even out the odds, even getting Dempsey to go on record picking Maxim to win. "Joey Maxim is a clever boxer. He knows how to hit his opponent and get away and often leaves the other fellow missing and looking bad. I have watched Maxim in many of his fights and pick him to win over Ezzard Charles," the old mauler allegedly said, presumably with a straight face.[48]

The fight got more publicity when the weigh-in was televised, a first for a title fight at any weight. Forget that for heavyweights there is no weight to "make," so the entire ceremony is a sham except as a selling maneuver and maybe an indicator of a fighter's readiness. Fight crowds love a weigh-in, and that this one was filmed live in a place called Goldblatt's Department store, where the usual fight mob mingled with startled and confused-looking afternoon shoppers, was either genius or stupidity.

In any event, Charles weighed in at 182, the lightest he'd been for any bout since the Valentino fight in San Francisco. Maxim was just a half-pound lighter at 181½, but you could tell he'd lost a lot of weight quickly. There was a softness around Joey's middle that his fans weren't used to seeing, and it made them nervous. If made Kearns nervous too, even if he wouldn't admit it.

Maxim couldn't get out of his own way but one time in all of fifteen rounds and took the licking of a lifetime. Afterward Kearns would say his guy just didn't have it tonight,

Ezzard and the former Gladys Gartrell share a laugh while talking with the press in 1951, not long after revealing that they'd been married for almost fifteen months and had a five-week-old daughter named Deborah (courtesy Craig Hamilton of Jo Sports, Inc.).

that he'd had too much time off from a real fight. He even floated the idea later that his fighter had maybe been "doped" the week before the fight.[49] What he should have said was that he was glad only 7,226 fans (paying $77,319.22) had shown up at the stadium. On any other night that was almost a disaster. The way his fighter looked this night? The fewer witnesses there were, the better.

Sometimes a guy gets cracked hard right after the opening bell and doesn't recover until a week or two down the road. That's what happened to Maxim. "He hit me a hard one in the first round and after that it was an awful tough one," he said later, when the doctors finally let him talk to the newspaper boys.[50] Charles teed off on Maxim from the opening bell and pounded him with hooks, right hands, jabs, uppercuts, everything. He teed off on him after the bell ending the first round, too, and that should have told everyone something about the kind of night it was going to be.

In Chicago Stadium against this man he knew he could whip any way he wanted, Charles was the tiger everyone wanted him to be, the slashing, bloodthirsty whirlwind he'd been at light heavyweight. He was a punching machine, belaboring poor Maxim at every turn, a step ahead of him every time. When Maxim tried to escape left, there was Charles, cutting him off and pounding away. When he tried to pivot right for an angle, it was like Charles knew it in advance and was there waiting for him, and he gave him a left hook or two or three for his troubles. Whatever Maxim tried, Charles had an answer. And everything Charles tried worked. "He was the same old Maxim—only this time he was trying to fight like Walcott and couldn't," Charles said later.[51]

Because it was the only thing he could do to survive, Maxim clinched over and over, and so to the fans in the stadium and especially to those watching on television, it was a bore: one man throwing punches, the other man taking them and then grabbing. But to Maxim it was a fight to survive. To Charles it was a race to stop a guy who had been stopped just once, way back in '43 when Curtis Sheppard got lucky and caught him cold in the first round. Maxim came back three weeks later and pinned Sheppard's ears back for him, because that's the kind of guy Maxim was.

He was a cutie, yes, but he was a tough son-of-a-bitch, and that Charles was trying his damndest to get him out and couldn't, proved it. He came close in the fifth and sixth rounds, but Joey was as stubborn as he was smart and he wouldn't go. He knew he wasn't going to win tonight, but he'd be damned if Charles was going to stop him.

Maxim's big moment came in the ninth when Charles charged headlong into a straight right that Joey had all his 180 pounds behind. It stopped Charles in his tracks, froze him there for a second, and Maxim, even for all the shots he'd taken, had enough wits left to see the damage it did. His eyes got wide at the chance and he got off two more crackling right hands, right on Charles' chin. It was Charles staggering and holding then, and the crowd, mostly silent through the terrible beating except when they were booing Charles, exploded for Maxim, but Charles hung on. When the bell rang Maxim had lost his chance. When he got back to his corner he told Kearns, "Jeez, I wish I had something in there, I could have killed that guy then."[52]

But he didn't have anything. He knew it and Kearns knew it. In fact, Kearns knew it early on. "That wasn't my boy in there tonight. He didn't have a thing. Joey looked good in the gym but the first three rounds proved to me he didn't have it tonight," he said later.[53] But that's the thing. A fighter never "has it" when he's in with a guy who's just too good for him. Maxim didn't have it against Charles in Chicago because he would never have it against Charles.

The only one who did any damage besides Charles was referee Frank Gilmer, who harassed Charles endlessly over fouls only he saw occur, broke apart the fighters inside far too quickly—preventing a knockout by Charles in the process, some complained afterward[54]—and then turning in an indefensible score of 78–72 for Charles, giving Maxim four rounds and calling four more even. Judges Tommy Thomas and Ed Hintz had it 85–65, which was about the only way anyone could have it who didn't have something going on that nobody knew about.

Even Kearns didn't bitch about the decision. How could he? Maxim's right eye was swollen all but shut and he bled above it and below. His torso was one bright red welt. His nose bled from the thirteenth on and he passed out in the dressing room afterward. For the next forty-five minutes the doctors put an oxygen mask on him to make sure he didn't forget to breathe.

None of that mattered to the crowd, of course. They booed Charles when he was introduced. They booed him during the fight. They booed him between rounds. They booed him while he was giving Maxim, a hell of a good prizefighter, the shellacking of his life. They booed him when Gilmer raised his hand in victory. It was hard to figure. Even the writers couldn't make sense of it. "They razzed, booed, and hissed the world heavyweight king! Was it his fault that his opponent wasn't good enough to make a fight of it? Was Ezzard to blame for being the aggressor, for tossing punches in every round without getting hit much in return? He did everything one could possibly ask except tear in and finish his man," one wrote. "If anyone ever needed proof that Ezzard Charles is a far underrated heavyweight king, Maxim's appearance was it. There is no champion in any division who

The heavyweight world champion engages in one of his favorite pastimes, listening to jazz records, at his home in Cincinnati, circa 1951 (courtesy Craig Hamilton of Jo Sports, Inc.).

cuts his opponents into submission as does Ezzard yet he is booed and harassed by the fans every time he fights no matter how good he appears."[55]

Another reporter defended Charles too. "Someday, maybe, the public is going to abandon comparisons with Joe Louis and accept Ezzard for what he is, the best fist fighter of his particular time."[56] Charles repeated an old refrain: "No matter who's picked to fight me, the public says he's a bum. So I can't look good no matter how well I do. I'm in no contest of comparison with Joe Louis. I'm only in a contest when I get in that ring."[57]

But that was later. Across the hall from where Maxim was clinging to sweet life through an oxygen mask, the reporters were giddy for Charles. This was the Charles they'd wanted all along, even if he wasn't able to get rid of Maxim. One of them asked how he planned to celebrate the victory. Angry about the boos, Charles got snippy. "This is just another payday to me," he said. "You don't celebrate every payday do you? I don't either."[58]

It was a damned good payday too, he might have added—a $70,927.68 payday, his biggest to date thanks to the hundred grand they got for the TV rights. And there was more good news. Negotiations for the rematch with Louis were just about done. All Charles had to do was get past Walcott one more time. Maybe then, after he whipped Louis again, the fans would start to come around.

Outside in the hall, someone asked Walcott, who'd had a ringside seat, what he thought of Charles' victory. "I hope he fights me the way he did Maxim tonight," he said.[59]

11

What They Came For

"Walcott again? What do we need him for?" Tannas had just told Arcel they had signed a contract for Charles to fight Jersey Joe again after the Maxim fight. Tannas fidgeted in his chair. He knew Arcel would give him trouble about this. But Arcel was just the trainer—and not even the head trainer at that. Tannas was in charge of these decisions, and he had his reasons. If he wanted Charles to fight Walcott again, Charles would fight Walcott again.

"We've had enough of him already," Arcel said. "The last time, he was coming on at the end. We got nothing to gain." Arcel knew what he was talking about. The rematch with Walcott was closer and harder for Charles than their first fight was. He'd hurt Charles badly in the fourth round, had him out on his feet almost, and then hurt him again in the fifteenth. It was his style. It didn't favor Charles. It was all wrong for him.

Really, it was about the damndest thing Arcel had ever seen—this guy was going on thirty-eight years old, as far as anyone knew, and he was hitting harder and fighting better than ever. Why take chances? Nobody except Walcott and his manager had had any problem with the decision in their last fight. Why keep pushing it? Especially with the Louis fight a done deal, provided Charles beat Maxim (which he would) and Louis got by Lee Savold (which he would). The Louis fight would do a $500,000 gate. Why risk that kind of payday? It made no sense.

"Look," Tannas said. "Walcott can't beat Charles and I want to do Felix [Bocchicchio, Walcott's manager] a favor. He's a friend of mine. This may be the last one for Walcott and they need the money. Felix is broke. I want to give him a chance to make some [money] before he loses his fighter."[1] Tannas got up and walked away. Arcel shrugged his shoulders.

Arcel had to know what was going on. He knew how these things worked. Bocchicchio needed money like J. Paul Getty needed money. Sure, Tannas wanted to do his old buddy Felix a favor. A lot of guys did Felix favors. That was the business Bocchicchio was in—collecting favors.

There were only two reasons anyone did a favor for Felix Bocchicchio: Because one was "asked" for a favor or because one was repaying a favor. Arcel didn't know which one it was, but he knew it was risky. Walcott was a tough old nut, and dangerous. But he, Arcel, was only the assistant trainer. Tannas was the boss. What he said went. All Arcel could do was help Brown get Charles ready for Maxim and then for Walcott and hope Tannas was right about Walcott not being able to beat Charles. It would be nice for Charles to get Louis in the ring again and settle things once and for all, for anyone who didn't think things were already settled. The kid deserved that much.

Two weeks after Charles beat Maxim, Louis fought the Cuban, Agramonte, again, this time in Detroit. Louis had outpointed him three months earlier in Miami and he gave Louis ten good rounds that night, so why not try him again? Joe needed the work. Then it would be on to Savold, who was a top guy. It was already a signed deal. But Savold, he was made for Louis. He knew it, Louis knew it. After he beat Savold he'd get Charles again, and that would be that.

Louis dropped Agramonte for a nine-count in the second round and came close to doing the same in the ninth. That was good enough for a unanimous decision. With the Savold fight six weeks away at the Polo Grounds, Louis didn't have a care in the world. Savold was thirty-five years old and hadn't fought in over a year since beating Woodcock for the world heavyweight title of England.

Savold was easy to hit, probably ten years removed from his prime, and had been stopped at least eight times already. And, he was a straight-ahead guy, the kind of guy Louis loved. Louis could beat guys like Savold for as long as he was above the ground. The 3–1 odds in Louis' favor were a reflection of that. As far as Louis was concerned, this was his time to send everyone a message—including Charles.

"This is the fight. The others were just experimental fights," he said. "They criticized me because I didn't knock them dead. I wasn't trying to. I was happy most of them went the limit. I never alibied the fact that I didn't knock them out. You can't do things overnight.

"I've been training to bring my body back to top form slowly and surely," Louis continued. "My left hand has been working as good as it ever was. My right, there's nothing wrong with that either. I just didn't want to overdo it when I didn't need to. I may need it against Savold and don't worry I'll use it and prove I can hit as hard as I ever could."[2]

Despite the significance—the winner reportedly would get Charles—there was relatively little excitement for the Louis-Savold bout. Not only because it was viewed as a mismatch, but also because many felt that Louis had appeared on television so much and looked so ordinary that some had lost enthusiasm for him and his comeback.[3] The papers had a ball with the advanced age of the combatants, calling the fight "The Battle of the Aged."[4]

To the promoters, all this meant it was time for an experiment. With radio and especially television causing a drop in fan attendance across the sport, for this fight there would be no TV and no radio. Instead the fight would be shown on closed-circuit television in nine theaters in Baltimore, Chicago, Pittsburgh, Cleveland, Washington and Albany. Most of the theaters would charge 40 cents a head, which was less than anyone would pay to see it live. Would it work? They'd find out, but not until the bout was moved to Madison Square Garden after two rain-outs at the Polo Grounds. And then all hell broke loose, proving the old Brown Bomber had some juice left—with the fans and in the ring.

A last-minute rush to buy tickets at the Garden caught the promoters completely by surprise and was so violent that the commission had to delay the start of the fight by ten minutes. A raucous sellout crowd of 18,179 stuffed the Garden to the rafters, paying almost $100,000. The theaters running the fight in Baltimore, Chicago, Pittsburgh, Cleveland, Washington and Albany reported sellouts across the board, and several had to turn away hundreds of fans. It was as though everyone thought that this might be the night Joe Louis would look young again. They were right.

Louis battered Savold from the opening bell, knocking him all over the ring. He wasn't fast, but he was faster than Savold. He wasn't young again, but he was young enough. And he didn't have his old power, but what he had was enough to turns Savold's face into hamburger meat over the first five rounds. In the sixth he hammered Savold savagely and then blasted him with a hook that spun Savold around and put him on his back. The time was 2:29 and you'd have thought it was 1938 again and that Savold was Max Schmeling.

It wasn't, of course. It was 1951, Joe Louis had a bald spot, and Savold was tired, old and never that good in the first place; he probably would have been hard-pressed to beat any top-fifteen heavyweight in the world that night. But nostalgia is a tricky and powerful thing. When it came to Louis, people wanted badly to believe he was young again, because if he was maybe they could be, too. So the Garden exploded.

It was a big party in Louis' dressing room afterward. The newspaper boys were all over Joe, just like in the old days, and everyone was smiling. Milton Berle came back and congratulated Joe. Other stars too. People hadn't seen Louis look so happy in years. "I felt better than since the first Billy Conn fight," he said. "I knew what I was doing all the time. This is the one I went out for. In my other fights I was just trying to work myself into shape. This time I knew I was ready."[5]

Mintz, never one to miss a party or an opportunity to get in the papers, elbowed his way through the crowd, laughing and joking along with everyone else, and when he got to Louis he put a hand on his shoulder and grinned and told him, "We don't want any part of you now. You can wait a year," and they all laughed, even Louis. Mintz turned to the reporters. "I'm only kidding. First we have Walcott. Then we'll take Louis. It ought to be big, real big."[6]

The reporters jumped all over that one, asking Louis how he thought he'd do against Charles this time. "I won't press my luck in the predicting league," he said, still smiling. "If I feel like I did against Savold I'll beat him." Across the hall, Savold agreed. "I'll go along with Louis over Charles," he said. "He was sharp, real sharp. I just couldn't get off."[7]

So it was all but done. Everyone was ready for it. Louis was ready. Charles was ready. America was ready. The mob was ready. The September 1951 issue of *The Ring* ran an artist's rendering of Charles and Louis on the cover with the caption: "Ready to Repeat in World Title Bout." Everyone would clean up. All Charles had to do was get past Walcott in Pittsburgh. Just one more time.

The fight press was so used to Charles beating Walcott by now that they spent more time trying to guess what the attendance and gate would be than they did the outcome of the fight. Most set attendance at around 20,000 to 30,000 and a gate from $150,000 to $200,000. Asked for his prediction, Mintz replied, "I do not like to be conservatively. My predicament is 35,000 fans and a quarter of a million dollars."[8]

The commission chose popular local veteran Ernie Sesto to referee the fight. Sesto had worked hundreds of fights over the years, big ones too, including some for Louis, Charles, Ray Robinson, Jake LaMotta, Billy Conn, Fritzie Zivic, and Bob Montgomery. All the big names. Bocchicchio immediately objected, claiming Sesto had shown favoritism to local heavyweight contender Bob Baker in Baker's win over Agramonte in July.

In a testament to Bocchicchio's many and important connections, the local Pittsburgh commission—namely the recently appointed John Holahan—advised Sesto that he'd been replaced by Buck McTeirnan. Sesto, outraged that his integrity had been questioned, wrote a dramatic resignation letter to the Pennsylvania State Commission. He later recanted and worked more fights over the next decade, though never a big one again, proving that everyone in boxing has long memories. The thing was, it wasn't Holahan who bumped him.

It was the *state* commissioner, John "Ox" DaGrosa, from Philadelphia, and Chairman George Jones, from Williamsport, who overruled Holahan in his own district. They'd come to Pittsburgh ostensibly to help him in his first very big fight, to make sure things went smoothly. In reality they were there to make sure things went the way their friends wanted them to go. Poor Holahan never stood a chance. They ran the show from the moment they arrived in Pittsburgh, taking over the weigh-in ceremony and press conferences, and made every important regulatory decision there was to be made—including one that almost prevented the fight from happening.

In the days just before the fight, Mintz made it clear he wanted only local judges right in Pittsburgh to score the fight; if any outside guys were going to be brought in he wanted to know in advance who they were. It was standard procedure. That's how Bocchicchio knew about Sesto—from the commission. Mintz didn't want any funny business going on. He knew Pittsburgh, he knew the guys there, and he knew his man would get a fair shake on the cards so long as the commission didn't bring in anyone he didn't know—especially anyone from around Walcott's hometown of Camden.

He knew the people Bocchicchio knew and he didn't want to take any chances. He was told up front by DaGrosa and Jones not to worry, that everything would be taken care of. And then they sent word down to Philadelphia to bring up Charlie Daggert, a former fighter and well-known Philadelphia judge. Screw Mintz. Who the hell was he to tell them who could judge and who couldn't? Daggert was going to be a judge in that fight, and if Mintz didn't like it, too bad. Holahan, worried about how it would look to have a judge from what was essentially Walcott's hometown, and not one from Cincinnati to balance things out, begged DaGrosa and Jones to keep their word to Mintz and use a local guy. They refused.[9]

Nobody outside the commissioners, the judges and maybe Walcott's team knew Daggert would be one of the judges until the ring announcer, Joe Tucker, introduced him to the crowd along with McTiernan and Stewart "Red" Robinson, a former fighter and well-known Pittsburgh-area official. They'd never told Mintz about Daggert even though they had the chance, and thus never gave him the chance to object to him the way Bocchicchio had objected to Sesto.

When Daggert was introduced to the crowd, Mintz exploded. He climbed from the ring down to the front row of the working press section and screamed at Holahan that Daggert had no right to work the fight. DaGrosa, huge, portly and formidable, saw what was going on and lumbered out of his seat, went over to where Mintz and Holahan were arguing, and began berating Mintz. Mintz laced into him with every curse word he'd learned over a lifetime spent in the close vicinity of dice games, whore houses and fight gyms and shook his little, veiny fist in DaGrosa's face.

When he got nowhere with DaGrosa, Mintz climbed back into the ring and worked one section of the press after another, leaning over the ropes to yell that there wasn't going to be any fight tonight. "It's a black market on Pittsburgh, bringing in this stranger!"[10] Jake screamed, helpless as ever against his inclination toward malapropism. It took on the look of a circus.

"It means the boxing commission is as much as saying it has no confidence in Western Pennsylvania officials!" Mintz found no allies in press row, whose numbers wanted merely for the fight to begin and couldn't have cared less for the origin of the respective officials. They'd been dealing with Mintz's histrionics for the better part of two years now and had grown tired of him. It was announced later that night that he'd been suspended and fined $500, and most of them applauded it in their columns the next day.

But this was not trivial; Philadelphia was the base of Walcott's manager's criminal operations and was right over the river from Camden, Walcott's hometown. The way

DaGrosa had hid Daggert until the last possible moment stunk to high heaven and everyone knew it, even if most of them didn't care. Mintz cared, and he and DaGrosa went back and forth. In all the history of organized prizefighting there never was a manager who fought harder for his guy in ten minutes than Jake Mintz did at Forbes Field in Pittsburgh for Ezzard Charles.

It ended, finally, when DaGrosa told Mintz that if his guy didn't fight he'd lose the title by forfeit. Even then DaGrosa had the police come over to help Holahan pull Mintz away so the fight could start. Poor Jake was relegated to the cheap seats, but he'd put everyone on notice. If it went the full route everyone would have their eyes on Daggert's scorecard. That was something, at least.

While all this was going on Charles sat on a stool in his corner looking alternately bored and embarrassed. You couldn't blame him. All this stuff wasn't his to worry about. All he had to do was the fighting. He couldn't care less who the judges were or where they were from. That was Jake's job if he wanted it, and Ezzard knew that deep down Mintz loved this kind of stuff, even when he looked enraged. He loved the attention. He loved managing the heavyweight champion of the world and everything that went with it.

That didn't mean Ezzard had to be happy about it all the time. Sometimes Jake went a little too far, like when had he "fainted" at the end of the first Walcott fight. It wasn't in Ezzard's nature to scream and holler the way Jake did, and to call attention to himself. But he figured if someone had to do that job it might as well be Jake, since he was good at it and liked it so much.

The downside for Jake was that when something went wrong the loudmouth got the blame. A couple days after the fight, when everyone who cared about Charles was looking for someone to blame, some of his relatives arrived on Mintz. "It was that fellow Mintz' fault," Mrs. Emma Russell, Ezzard's aunt, declared from Cincinnati. "He had Ezzard so nervous before the fight he just couldn't do his best."[11]

Sitting in his corner waiting to be gloved up, Charles felt like Mintz was the least of his worries. He hadn't felt like himself the past couple days. He was nervous, on edge. That wasn't like him. He felt restless. The only other time he'd felt like that was before his third fight with Bivins back in Cleveland in 1947. Not because he was afraid of Bivins per se, but because the local press had made such a big deal of it, and they'd been building up Bivins for a shot at Louis. He felt a lot of pressure to perform. The night before the fight in his hotel room his teeth wouldn't stop chattering, and it wasn't because he was cold. He couldn't sleep so he prayed, and pretty soon he fell asleep. He did just fine in the fight, stopping Bivins in the fourth round.[12]

This felt something like that, but not exactly. There was this, too: Whenever he had a fight coming up he'd go over the fight plan in his head—right before the fight while his hands were being taped up, the day before the fight in the gym, the nights before the fight as he went to sleep. He'd at least have a plan for the first few rounds, how he'd start out. It wouldn't be for the whole fifteen rounds, but surely for the first few. But for this fight there wasn't any. He'd envision the first round, see himself there, but he wouldn't be doing anything. It was blank. There was no plan. Nothing. And he couldn't force one.

It was probably the anticipation of finally getting Louis again, he thought. But why should he worry? He'd beaten Walcott already—twice. He knew what he was about. All he had to do was make sure he wasn't taking the old man lightly, and he knew he wasn't. He'd had a good camp. He hadn't taken any shortcuts.

He'd learned his lesson against Kid Tunero back in 1942. Jimmy loved to remind Ezzard of that night, to razz him about it, whenever he thought Ezzard was slacking off a bit in the gym. He almost never had to, because the sting of it never left. So he never took another opponent cheap, and that included Walcott. Maybe subconsciously he didn't respect Walcott the way he should, but the point was he had done everything he was supposed to do—run all his miles, put in all his rounds at the gym. Camp had gone smoothly.[13]

For this, his ninth title defense, Charles had set up training in Ligonier, right outside Pittsburgh. Walcott trained in McKeesport's Rainbow Gardens. The fight was a big deal for Pittsburgh. Even though it had always been a reliable fight town and some great fighters had come from there—Harry Greb, Billy Conn, and Fritzie Zivic—this was Pittsburgh's first heavyweight title fight. The whole city would be watching, and when it was all over 28,000 fans would pack Forbes Field to the tune of $245,000, breaking all gate receipt and attendance records in the city.

A local radio and TV blackout helped the gate, and for those outside Western Pennsylvania, Pabst Blue Ribbon kicked in $100,000 for the TV rights. Ringside seats went for $25 and every one was sold. Walcott, always a confident guy and still certain he deserved the decision in both of his previous fights with Charles, promised a knockout victory. Really, he guaranteed it. But that was Walcott being Walcott. Nobody had to work that hard to sell the fight. Everything went smoothly. But something wasn't right, and Charles, sitting in his corner watching Mintz get chased out of the ring, knew it. It was too late to do anything about it now.

When the cops finally got Mintz out of the way the show got started with the usual roll call of attending fighters. Primo Carnera, the big goon, got a big ovation from the crowd. Only Louis himself would have gotten a bigger ovation, but he wasn't there. He was in training in Belle River, Ontario, for his fight in San Francisco on August 1 with Cesar Brion.

Louis didn't have to fight Brion. He would get his shot at Charles based on the win over Savold, but people had to get paid and he wanted to stay sharp. So he'd watch this fight on television. Why break training for Charles-Walcott III? He'd been ringside for the first two between these guys, and neither was anything to write home about. He didn't care what happened so long as Charles won and came out uninjured so they could fight in September and Joe could get his title back and be done already. Miles knew to call him as soon as it was over. He was certain he wasn't missing anything.

Finally it started. Charles still couldn't shake the sense something was wrong. He won the first round anyway because Walcott, oddly, hardly threw a punch, but even with that Charles couldn't get started, couldn't do anything right. He couldn't get loose. Over the next couple of rounds Charles' malaise continued, and he realized it wasn't anything Walcott was doing, necessarily. By the third round he could see the old man was fighting harder than he had in their other fights, and was throwing everything from left field, as hard as he could, and mostly left hooks—just like he did late in their last fight. But so what? Fighting for the heavyweight title brought out the best in everybody.

Every pug out there fought the best fight he would ever fight when the title was on the line. Walcott was no different than any other guy, fighting hard to win the championship. So Walcott wasn't any different than he'd ever been. But he, Charles, was. And he couldn't do anything about it. He just had to fight through it and hope things would come together. He was making $98,000 plus some change, before everyone took their cuts anyway, his biggest payday yet—it had better come together.

It never did. Afterward the writers tried to describe what it was like, watching him fumble around like he was in a dream. "I kept thinking you'd get started the next round," one writer told Charles.[14] Another wrote, "Charles was not himself that night, and he took a beating from the cool, wise old campaigner from Camden, New Jersey."[15]

"It looked like he left his fight in training camp.... It was not the Charles of the past, for among the assets that were missing was the spark that had carried him through eight successful title defenses," wrote another.[16] Still another opined, "Charles boxed as if he had never seen Walcott before, and as if Jersey Joe were Jack Dempsey and Joe Louis in their atomic primes."[17]

Days later Charles tried to put into words what it felt like. "I just couldn't get off. I don't know why. I just couldn't get together with myself. I never opened up. Dreaming and dozing, that's me. Thinking to myself, don't do this. Do this and do that. I just couldn't get together with myself. I have only myself to blame."[18]

Most frustrating was that he couldn't take advantage of Walcott's over-eagerness. "He was taking chances with haymaker punches and leaving himself wide open but I couldn't seem to do anything about it," he said.[19] If you didn't know better, by the fight's halfway point you might have thought someone had gotten to Charles beforehand and told him it wasn't his night. That's how bad he was.

The fight was half over and Charles trailed on points, the first time he'd trailed Walcott at the midway point in any of their fights. In the seventh round he backed across the ring. He could see Walcott trying to get into position to throw the hook. He could see it coming. Anyone could. He got ready to counter. He watched Walcott dip his shoulder and he knew it was aimed at the body. That was fine. He'd catch it on the elbow and counter.

And just as he bent at the waist to catch the blow on his elbow, Walcott brought it up just the smallest bit, changed its trajectory and it exploded on Charles' chin. *Damn. Not a hook. An uppercut.* He'd miscalculated. And just like that, Ezzard Charles' world went black and everything he had fought for over the last eleven years, hell, all his life, vanished in the time it took for him to collapse face-first. All of it. And in that shattering darkness, it wasn't all about the money after all. It never had been.

It was about all the years in prize rings and all the punches counting for something, not just a thing that passed the time until the gravedigger called. It was about the poor black boy who got out of Lawrenceville and then out of the West End slums and made something of himself. It was about mattering and about being a man.

If it was just about the money, Charles wouldn't have been trying like hell to beat the count. He was getting paid the same amount whether he got up or not. The money would still be green. But with everything he had and with everything he was, Ezzard Charles tried to get up. And not because he wanted more goddam suits and caps in his closet or a new pair of shoes. Like all men, Ezzard Charles wanted to matter.

But in the spinning chaos that was his mind as McTiernan counted over him, Ezzard Charles wasn't Ezzard Charles the heavyweight world champion defending his title outside at a big ballpark, he was "Snooks" back on the West End, and Al Jackson had just put him on his ass at an American Legion Hall in the neighborhood. The room spun. He felt sick. Bert Williams was screaming at him to get up in that thick Scottish accent of his. He heard the ocean.

Charles snapped awake in time to hear McTiernan yell "six!" and he lifted his head off the canvas. By "eight!" he'd worked his arms free; they'd been pinned beneath him. Somehow he'd gotten to his knees when McTiernan yelled "Ten!" and then he toppled over backwards and it was over.

The crowd in Pittsburgh was happier than it ever dreamed it could be, almost as happy as if Louis had won, and not just because that fraud Ezzard Charles had finally got his head handed to him, though that too was great in itself. Sure, Charles had a following there, he'd fought a lot in Pittsburgh on the way up and Mintz was known there, but they were happy for the old man Walcott, with all those kids he had to feed, and the great story he had, the perseverance and determination he showed. He was the American dream. So what if they said his manager was a gangster and that's why he kept getting so many title shots?

He proved he was worthy of every single one of them. Remember, too, that he'd been robbed in the first Louis fight. So he had every right in the world to fight for the title over and over. He'd finally won it. Good for him. They'd go home and tell their kids they could be anything they wanted to be if they tried hard enough and never gave up and read their

Charles weighs in for his title defense against Jersey Joe Walcott on July 18, 1951, in Pittsburgh. As Walcott (left of center) looks on, his manager, Felix Bocchicchio, stands behind him (far left). State commission chairman George Jones operates the scale, while Pennsylvania Commissioner George "Ox" DeGrosa is at right. Walcott won the heavyweight world title with a knockout in the seventh round (courtesy Lou Manfra).

Bible every day. They wouldn't be lying this time, because tonight they had seen a black man who was once on relief and didn't know how he was going to feed his family become the heavyweight champion of the whole world. This crowd got what they came for. This certainly was a great country.

"I knew I could do it and nobody believed me but my friends," Walcott said after getting a police escort back to his locker room. Such was the frenzy his win created among the crowd. "I knew it all the time. From the last fight I knew he was vulnerable to a left hook and my strategy was built on that. And it worked." He smiled a big smile and then gave everyone what they'd come for. "I prayed before the fight and during each round. I prayed all the time. I really wanted that title. And now that I got it, I'll fight anywhere they want me to fight. I want to be a credit to the game like the two champions before me."[20] Beside him, Felix Bocchicchio beamed.

Afterward Charles sat in the dressing room in the horrible vacuum of silence that pervades the locker rooms of all shocked favorites. It was the second time he'd been stopped in his long career and his first loss in four years, ending a twenty-four-fight win streak. He was disconsolate—not that he'd lost a fight. He'd lost before. But he'd lost the *title*. He'd lost *the heavyweight championship of the world*. That wasn't just a fight. Years later he might recognize that somewhere, way down inside where men hide their most awful secrets so they can never be accidentally spoken, a tiny part of him was relieved. Being the heavyweight champion of the world was an awful lot of trouble for a man of his sensibilities and maybe, just maybe, not worth it.

But he was years away from knowing that, if he ever did, and on this night in the evening's cruel aftermath and in the sweltering regret of the loser's dressing room, he shook his head and said over and over, "I just can't believe it. I just can't believe it."[21] What else could he say? Arcel and Brown and Mintz told him how it happened. He'd ducked right into the punch. It didn't matter. He told the newspaper boys, "How I got in the way of it I'll never know." What else could he say? He didn't feel like talking. They wouldn't leave. He gave them what they wanted.

"What happened, Ezzard?"

"Let's face it, he's a big, rough, tough guy and he can punch. What can you say after you've been knocked out? The guy just hit me."

"Do you think you got careless?"

"I couldn't have been careless. If anything I was too cautious. I just got hit."

"Would you call it a lucky punch?"

"It couldn't have been lucky, the guy was trying too hard to hit me."

Then he asked a question of them:

"Did they count me out? I know I was up before 10."

"Well, you fell back, Ezzard."

"Well, I don't remember that part."

There wasn't anything else to say. A sad, awkward silence filled the room. Jimmy Brown broke it. "Don't you worry none," he told Charles. "You just loaned him the title for 90 days." He looked at the reporters still in the room. "And you newspaper guys can quote me."[22]

Mintz had made sure the contract included a rematch clause that would force Walcott to fight Charles again within ninety days. Thank goodness for that. It was little consolation to Ezzard right then, but it would be later. Most of the reporters shuffled out of the room then, and Marshall Miles walked slowly in and made his way to Charles. Charles gave him a sad smile. "I sure messed up our plans," he said. "You sure did," Miles replied.[23]

Later Miles told the press Louis was "disgusted" by the outcome. It pushed back his title shot by probably six months. But that wasn't Charles' problem. What did he care about Louis now? Someone came into the dressing room with the judges' scores. McTiernan, the ref, had Walcott ahead 5-1 at the end. Robinson had it even at 3-3. Daggert, the Philly judge, had it 4-1-1 for Walcott. None of it mattered anyway. As Charles said later about the judging controversy, all they'd needed was a guy who could count to ten.

At the hotel later that night, the photographers wanted to get pictures of the new and former champions together. Someone went to retrieve Charles from his room. Etiquette dictated that he, as the loser, should come to Walcott's room. Walcott disagreed, saying they all should go up to Charles' room. When the party arrived and the two fighters were face to face, Walcott extended his hand. "I'm sorry you had to lose, champ." Charles smiled, stretching the two stitches in his lower lip. "That's all right. I would have been rooting for you if you were fighting someone else."

The two chatted, respectfully, amiably, the way two men do who have fought one another hard and well and taken one another's measure. There can be no greater human understanding in the world than the kind that exists between prizefighters. They have their own language, much of it unspoken. And so the photographers got their pictures and when they were done and readied to leave, Jersey Joe put his arm around Charles' shoulders and told him, "Take it easy, Ezzard." And then he added: "See you in September."[24]

If the conclusiveness of Walcott's knockout of Charles helped clarify the picture of heavyweight boxing in America, it had the opposite effect in Great Britain, which found itself with a new champion as same as the old champion. His name was Joe Louis. The British Board of Boxing control had never recognized Charles as heavyweight champion, so Walcott couldn't claim the title by beating him.

"Joe Louis is the champion of the world. He became champion when he knocked out Lee Savold, who had taken the title by stopping Bruce Woodcock," the board said in a press release, shortly after Walcott stopped Charles. "We must be consistent. We cannot change our decision simply because Walcott stopped Charles and Louis stopped Savold. Let Walcott fight Louis and we will recognize the winner as the champion. In the meantime Louis holds the title."[25]

Mintz and Tannas and the IBC couldn't have cared less about who Great Britain saw as the heavyweight champion. Their priority was to get Charles the rematch with Walcott as soon as possible. At first it appeared they would be successful. When the IBC drew up the contract for the fight they had lawyer Michael Strauss, one-time attorney for promoter Mike Jacobs, insert a clause that required Walcott to face Charles within ninety days and before any other challenger in the event the title changed hands. This was standard.

Mintz knew this, of course; he had been around the block; and so he suspected that Bocchicchio might try to put Charles off so he could make his man some money before probably losing the title back to Charles. That's what he'd do if he were Bocchicchio. Whatever happened in Pittsburgh, Charles would be favored in the return and everyone knew it—especially Bocchicchio. So why not try to make some money before handing the title back over? That's why the clause was there.

At first it appeared all would go according to the plan. At the press conference right after the fight, Walcott told the reporters, "Ezzard Charles deserves to get a return chance at the title and he's going to get it first." Bocchicchio agreed. "Walcott is the greatest fighter in the world and he's going to be a great champion and defend his title as often as possible—just like the last two champions, Louis and Charles. We're contracted to give Charles the return within 90 days and it will be held in September."[26]

But the summer of 1951 hurried toward autumn without a peep about the return, and what everyone expected to happen happened: nothing. Some papers were predicting as early as August that Walcott wouldn't defend until the following year.[27] So there went September. In the meantime Jersey Joe went on television, toured the country, and told his Cinderella story. Mintz harassed Norris about the return clause. Norris in turn harassed Bocchicchio.

And so over the next several months there developed a rift that was surprising, all things considered, between Bocchicchio and Norris. Norris wanted the fourth Charles-Walcott fight to take place as soon as possible and in accordance with what he and the Charles camp believed to be an unimpeachable contract. Bocchicchio wanted to put off the fight for as long as he could so that Walcott could cash in on the title and make some money on personal appearances, television spots and the like, and also have a big-money fight or two against guys he thought he could whip—namely Harry Matthews or a young, crude puncher out of Massachusetts named Rocky Marciano.

Born Rocco Francis Marchegiano in 1923, Marciano was raised poor on the northern edge of working-class Brockton, the son of a pair of Italian immigrants. One of six kids, he grew up playing ball and had dreams of being a catcher in the big leagues. He played some football too in school, lifted weights, and banged around an old, homemade heavy bag in his backyard. He dropped out of school in the tenth grade and after failing to make the final cut in a tryout for a minor league baseball team, he settled for good on boxing.

After a short amateur career and a stint in the service, Marciano turned pro in 1948 and quickly developed a reputation as both a clumsy novice and a terrifying hitter. At just 5'11" and about 188 pounds, he was smaller than many of his opponents but regardless knocked out one after another. Marciano possessed an unheard-of combination of strengths that wasn't immediately apparent but would become so down the road: He was virtually impossible to hurt; he was indefatigable, due in the main to a near-pathological dedication to training; his punching power, while clumsier and more clubbing in its delivery than Louis', was nevertheless positively authentic; and he had an inordinate volume of will and self-belief. He could not be discouraged in a prize ring.

If all that wasn't enough, he was managed by Al Weill, head matchmaker at the IBC. Not that he needed any help; Marciano was special, even if his clumsiness and connections to the IBC blinded many to it. His stature as an IBC "house fighter" elicited scorn from many writers who resented what they saw as preferential treatment that took the form of undeserved headline events at the Garden. Bocchicchio was among those who guessed that Marciano's clumsy, wide-open style would make him easy pickings for Walcott, and certainly an easier task for his man than Charles, who, it must be remembered, had beaten Jersey Joe two out of three times.

With virtually no movement on Walcott's part by mid-January, things began to heat up politically. Louisiana, for what it was worth, withdrew its recognition of Walcott as the champion because he failed to defend the title within six months of beating Charles. (Interestingly, Massachusetts never recognized Walcott as champion, as the state commission forbade any boxer older than thirty-six to hold a world title.)[28]

Norris started calling in favors, and on January 22, the powerful and well-intentioned but hopelessly mob-entangled new New York State commissioner, Bob Christenberry, designated Charles Walcott's "legitimate" challenger and gave Walcott fifteen days to sign an agreement to defend the title. He said the fight should come off no later than March or April.

Norris also appealed to the Pennsylvania State Commission to withdraw its recognition of Walcott as champion for failing to fulfill the rematch clause in the contract. They declined, saying that the contract had never been filed officially with the commission prior to the fight in Pittsburgh, nor with Abe Green, the NBA commissioner. Had the contract been filed officially, they said, there would be no controversy, though they did "not deny that there is a moral obligation on the part of all."[29]

To Bocchicchio this was all child's play. He fully expected that Christenberry was bluffing and that he knew good and goddam well he wasn't taking Walcott's title. In addition, Bocchicchio reportedly had the leverage he needed against Norris: an offer from Harry Hunt of Los Angeles, who wanted to give him $250,000 to have Walcott face Matthews in Las Vegas, Nevada. All Norris had to do, Bocchicchio told him during a conference between the two in Miami, was match that offer with a fight against Marciano. The winner would get Charles.

There was a reason Bocchicchio was being so stubborn, and it didn't involve solely his worry over Charles beating Walcott. On several occasions when he was moving Walcott up the ratings, Bocchicchio reportedly had lost money because he paid Walcott's opponents more than their market value just to get them into the ring.

One such opponent was Lee Oma, whom Bocchicchio allegedly had paid a guarantee of $35,000 to face Walcott in 1946 at the Garden. Walcott won a decision, but Bocchicchio allegedly lost $4,500 on the deal. Bocchicchio wanted very badly to make back the money that he had put out to move Walcott up the ratings.

Making Walcott-Marciano first wasn't Norris' ideal choice, but it was something. He would just have to get the Charles camp to agree to step aside. "We are trying to work out a Walcott-Marciano fight and still satisfy the Charles people," he said on February 5. "Walcott wants to make some money on his next fight and a Marciano fight will be his best bet. I'm going to call Charles' managers and maybe get them down here and see if we can work out something."[30] It helped when Weill, Marciano's manager and a loyal IBC soldier, said he would not pursue a fight with Walcott unless Charles stepped aside.

Norris never stood a chance. The reporters got Mintz on the phone first and told him what was going on. This was right up Jake's alley. "I'm laughin'. Laughin' hard," Mintz said. "If they want to save time and double-talk let's have the Walcott-Charles fight first. Speaking for myself and Tannas, we are not interested in no kind of meetin'—except one in which Walcott will fulfill his contractual obligations."[31]

Walcott, for his part, and in direct contrast to his statements after the fight in Pittsburgh, seemed surprised that he was expected to defend the title at all, never mind against Charles. Reportedly choking back tears, he said in late January that he hadn't made $15 since winning the title because he'd been making charity appearances all over the country. When done with that, he wanted to embark on a lucrative exhibition tour leading up to a big fight outdoors in June.

"I promised God that if he saw fit to make me champion I would do some good with the title," he said. "That's what I've been doing with charity appearances. I've been defending my title every day for the youth of this country. I wanted a full year before defending the title."[32]

None of the writers present asked him why he thought he should get a free ride for a year when his two predecessors had been the busiest heavyweight champions in history. Walcott clearly believed he was owed something for all the years it had taken him to get the title. A less subjective observer might have suggested that, having been the recipient of a record five tries at the heavyweight crown, it was he who owed something at the least to the man who had given him the last two—Ezzard Charles. This is not how Walcott saw it. "I think boxing owes me the year for which I asked. I worked 21 years to win the title—and I've done a lot of good with it. They don't remember that though," he said.[33]

Bocchicchio also offered a rather bizarre and no more convincing rationale for keeping Walcott out of the ring. "We intend to fight only once a year. The heavyweight title has been cheapened by being kicked around so often," he said. "There should not be a battle for the heavyweight crown any more often than there is a world series in baseball," he continued. "Suppose we had a world series in June, and again in August and for a third time in October? What would be the significance of the championship? How strongly would the fans be attracted to the frequent competition? It would ruin baseball. That situation holds true in heavyweight fighting. Once a year is enough."[34] Nobody bought Bocchicchio's subterfuge, instead seeing it for what it was: an attempt to justify putting off the return with Charles and making some money off the championship by less violent and dangerous means.

Charles wasn't shedding any tears for Walcott. After the loss in Pittsburgh, Arcel and Brown agreed that he needed a good rest. After all, he'd been fighting at a hell of a clip for a heavyweight champion—in the two years since he beat Walcott for the NBA title, he'd fought ten times, making him the busiest heavyweight champion ever, and that included Louis. He'd made a lot of people a lot of money, especially the folks at the IBC and their many influential and suspect friends, and got himself a few new suits and hats in the process, too.

Not long after Walcott stopped him, Charles' wardrobe consisted of seventy-five suits, which cost from $135 to $195 each, and a couple dozen pairs of shoes, some of which cost $100. He owned nearly a hundred hats and had no compunction over getting rid of one if it became dirty. He wore silk pajamas and silk underwear (the latter of which cost at least $45 a pair) and owned ten topcoats and overcoats, some of which cost $225, and hundreds of ties. Everything was top of the line, and when he tired of an article of clothing he simply gave it away. Usually he'd charge a guy $10 for a suit, however, so as to preserve the recipient's dignity. "I think it's better for the guy that way," he once said.[35]

All that earning is what Arcel and Brown believed caused Charles' malaise against Walcott. That and being trained "too fine" for the fight. A man needs a break, especially one who makes a living with his fists. It was a fine line fighters and their handlers had to balance; sit a guy too much and he loses his edge in the ring, gets rusty, and loses his timing. He can't find it in the gym, though; he has to fight. Fight him too much and sooner or later he just gets stale, the way they figured Charles had. So they sent him home to Cincinnati with his wife and his family. There was no parade this time, no near-riot at the train station, nobody getting run over in all the hubbub. And no giant entourage. It was just Ezzard Charles, Jimmy Brown and Richard Christmas playing cards on the train.

Back in Cincinnati, Ezzard relaxed and did the things he enjoyed. He played the bass fiddle in Christmas' jazz band and listened to his favorite jazz records. He bought more suits and hats, worked on his oil paintings, and played with "Splooper," his pet name for Deborah. On July 1, another daughter, Leith, was born. When he wasn't with Gladys and the babies he read poetry by himself, golfed and went to the track with his buddies to put a few dollars on the horses.

With his earnings from the Walcott fight, he bought his mother a house in Manhattan's Upper West Side. He waited for the phone to ring. At home, Gladys made him all the candied sweet potatoes and fried chicken he wanted—it was his favorite dinner and he wasn't

Ezzard Charles sinks to the canvas after absorbing a left uppercut from Jersey Joe Walcott in the seventh round of their bout in Forbes Field on July 18, 1951. Charles was counted out by referee Buck McTiernan at 0:51 of the round. The loss ended a twenty-four-fight winning streak that lasted four years (courtesy Lou Manfra).

in training, so he ate what he wanted. Same thing at lunch. He'd go to Sky's up on Fifth and John on the West End and order his favorite: ham-and-egg-and-cheese double-deckers and a vanilla malt with a raw egg mixed in. Dessert was sweet potato pie.

On Friday and Saturday nights he went out with friends to the Cincinnati Cotton Club or the Sportsman's Club in Newport. The Cotton Club was his home away from home when he wasn't in training. It was the place to be. Cincinnati's only integrated night club was situated in the Hotel Sterling at Sixth and Mound. Charles loved the place, and he wasn't its only famous patron. Louis went too when he was in town, and Mae West, and Pearl Bailey and others. All the best black musicians played the Cotton Club in Cincinnati—Duke Ellington, Count Basie, Lonnie Johnson, Tiny Bradshaw, and Hank Ballard. Local talent, too.[36]

Charles never was a drinker but when he wasn't in training he wouldn't leave the place until dawn. Gladys wasn't crazy about him spending so much time there, especially since they had a family now, but he'd done it before they were married and he wasn't going to stop now. She knew what went on in places like that and knew too that the kind of women who went there loved Ezzard. He was a professional athlete after all, and famous and handsome with broad shoulders, nice suits and all the rest. She was a smart woman who knew how the world worked, so she knew that a man like Ezzard was going to be a man. She knew that he loved her and she was right about that; of all the women in Cincinnati he could have married, he chose her.

But women were going to throw themselves at him and there was only so much temptation a man could resist. And over the years, during their marriage, Charles was linked in the papers to many beautiful women, among them Carol Drake, a model and actress and future wife of jazz crooner Billy Eckstein[37]; Norma Washington, a dancer at Las Vegas' Moulin Rouge[38]; and Lula Belle Ferguson, proprietor at the Cincinnati Cotton Club.[39]

While Charles was relaxing in Cincinnati, Louis was hard at work. Charles' loss to Walcott didn't ruin their big-fight plans as much as they delayed them, provided Charles won the return fight. Walcott's stalling, of course, didn't help any. It was as though the two of them, Charles and Walcott, were conspiring to keep Joe in the game but out of the title picture for as long as they could. If that was their plan it was working.

Louis outpointed the journeyman Cesar Brion on August 1 at the Cow Palace in California, then signed to face Charles' nemesis from the old days, Jimmy Bivins, two weeks later in Maryland. Old Jimmy had done all right for himself over the years. He'd won some big fights, lost some and kept his name out there. By this time, at thirty-two years old, his best years were behind him. He knew the Louis fight was his last chance, and he'd waited a long time to get it. He'd beaten so many guys who were future or former champions—though he never got a title fight—that he'd lost track of the exact number.

Bivins and Louis had met once before, in an exhibition bout in 1948, and Bivins did well, surprising some folks. Not that it mattered to Louis. Bivins still had a name and Louis had to stay busy. Louis' situation with the government hadn't gotten any better, and the people calling the shots had to get paid. Plus, he wanted to stay sharp for when he finally got the title fight.

He might have been a little too sharp. Weighing just 203½, his lightest in ten years, Louis, thirty-seven years old now, jabbed a slippery and dreadfully reluctant Bivins almost to tears on the way to a ten-round points win but could accomplish little else. He later blamed his halfhearted performance on coming in too light.

"I was just too light to get that right hand over," he said. "No question about it, I was five pounds too light."[40] All the momentum, good will, hope and excitement he'd built in the Savold fight was entirely dissipated. He was seen now, universally, for what he was: an old, washed-up fighter with neither the reflexes nor the speed nor the punch he'd need to ever win the title again, almost no matter who held it. His jab, once a thing of beauty, but only as a first act in a two-act play, was now the only act. Nevertheless, right after the Bivins bout, Miles and the IBC signed a contract for him to meet Marciano October 26 in New York at the Garden.

Jersey Joe Walcott (left) consoles Ezzard Charles in his hotel room after knocking him out to win the heavyweight title at Forbes Field. Photographers wanted Walcott to pose with his fist against Charles jaw where the knockout punch had landed, but Walcott declined, saying it would be disrespectful to the former champ (courtesy Lou Manfra).

In early September Charles' phone finally rang. He would face Utah's young puncher Rex Layne on October 8 at Forbes Field in Pittsburgh, in the same ring where everything had gone wrong against Walcott. (Later it was moved to October 10 to accommodate the World Series and because the IBC was offered $25,000 for the television rights if they moved the date.) Charles would get 35 percent of the gate to Layne's 25 percent. That was all right with Charles. He was eager to set things straight, and the old saying was true—it was easier to win the title than it was to defend it. Although there would be less money, it felt good in a sense to be chasing the title again rather than trying to live up to it. That was a lot of pressure. And he was fine facing Layne—they'd boxed a four-round exhibition in October of '49 at the Fairgrounds Coliseum in Utah when Charles did an exhibition tour after beating Walcott for the NBA title.[41]

Layne was just a kid then, twenty-one years old and a pro for only five months, but he had some amateur credentials. He'd never laced on a pair of gloves until he was in the army as a staff sergeant with an airborne division in 1946. He took to the sport quickly and won the troop's heavyweight championship. After his discharge in '47, he continued boxing while tending to crops on his beet farm, and narrowly missed making the U.S. Olympic team. He turned pro after winning the 1949 National AAU Heavyweight Championship, and there he was, eighteen months later, beating Walcott in a huge upset. He'd also whipped Bob Satterfield and Cesar Brion.

Layne was just the kind of opponent Charles liked—he came forward throwing punches, he didn't worry about defense, and he was easy to hit. He was no cutie like Oma; just a strong, rough-and-tumble guy who could punch pretty good with the right hand. That had been enough to get by Walcott, but Charles was sure he could outbox Layne all night, maybe even stop him.

He and Layne also had something in common: They'd both been knocked out in their previous fight. A few days before Walcott landed his left hook in Pittsburgh, Layne was knocked stiff by Marciano in a big upset at the Garden. It was only the second loss of Layne's career and the first time he'd been stopped. He'd gone toe-to-toe with Rocky for five rounds, taken a lot of good wallops along the way and stood in there and kept trying. In the sixth, Rocky's overhand right sheared off Layne's front top teeth at the gum line and sent his mouthpiece, with the teeth still in it, flying into the first row. The ref counted to ten. If Charles had beaten Walcott and Layne had beaten Marciano, they'd probably have been meeting now for Charles' title. Despite his big edge in skills and experience, this was a risk for Charles; if he lost to Layne he lost his return date with Walcott. He could not mess this one up.

Layne, *The Ring*'s seventh-ranked heavyweight, arrived in Pittsburgh on October 1 to wind down training. Charles did all of his work at his gym in Cincinnati, went out to Pittsburgh the last week in September to box an exhibition to help build the gate, then returned to Cincinnati to finish up.[42] Mintz claimed to be thrilled with Charles' condition. "Charles is stronger and is punching sharper than in his last three bouts," he told the press. "He isn't worried about the fight. Don't be surprised if he scores a knockout."[43] More importantly, Mintz said, "I think the layoff has done Ezzard a great deal of good. Psychologically, he's up for the fight. Physically, he's sharp."[44]

Mintz was right about that. Charles, though at 188 pounds the heaviest of his career (too much sweet potato pie!), was too fast and too skilled for Layne, who weighed 195. He took the early rounds with sharp left hooks and left uppercuts to Layne's head and body, and handled Layne's thudding right crosses, headbutts and elbows without consternation. By the middle rounds he was beating Layne around the ring. After their feet became tangled in the tenth, he belabored Layne on the ropes with hooks and right hands. Layne went down hard. The bell saved him midway through referee Buck McTiernan's count, and Layne's cornermen dragged him to the temporary safety of his corner.

Early in the eleventh Charles landed a crashing right hand and down went Layne again. He beat McTiernan's count, barely, but McTiernan stopped it, giving Charles the knockout win at 2:32 of the round. At the time of the stoppage Charles led 9–1, 6–3–1 and 7–3. The Associated Press had Charles ahead 5–3–2.

It wasn't a masterpiece; few fights involving Layne were. He was just too rough and awkward. The papers, unsurprisingly, were harsh. "Charles Far from Ready for Return with Walcott," one headline scolded.[45] Others, including *The Ring*, were impressed with Charles' tenacity. "In all of his previous fights, [Charles] never displayed the killer instinct he did against Layne in the last two frames. He appeared unlike the former world champion who so often has been referred to as a listless, ordinary fighter who can't get support of the fans because he is a colorless battler." Still, *The Ring* lamented, the fans pummeled Charles with boos as he left the ring. "No matter how the fight ends, Ezzard Charles leaves the arena with the boos of the crowd. Even a knockout, which usually brings cheers, doesn't help Charles' position with the fight fans."[46]

More important, the fight was a financial flop, grossing just $59,673 including the $25,000 for television rights. A meager 6,257 rattled around Forbes Field in their overcoats and top hats as temperatures hovered around the low 50s, which local promoters, working with the IBC, said kept down the gate. They probably were right—at the end of every round Arcel ran from the corner and wrapped a big blanket around Charles to keep him warm between rounds.

Two weeks after Charles whipped Layne to assure his return with Walcott, Louis' comeback and his hope to become the first heavyweight ever to regain the title came to a painful and crashing end when Marciano stopped him in the eighth round in Madison Square Garden. Louis, a 7–5 favorite, used the only weapon he had left, that once-magnificent jab, to keep Marciano outside for most of the first seven rounds. Marciano cooperated by lunging at Louis with haymakers that Louis, even at his age, had little trouble avoiding. But when he got inside, Marciano chopped away, and the pressure he put on Louis, just by constantly moving forward and making Louis use those old legs, tired out the old man. Late in the eighth, a sweeping left hook dropped Louis. Moments later two lefts and a right put him through the ropes and on his back, and referee Ruby Goldstein stopped it without a count.

And just like that, the long soap opera starring Louis and Ezzard Charles was over. Louis never got the chance to prove he'd have beaten Charles if given more time to train. Charles never got the chance to prove his victory over Louis was no accident. "I saw the right coming but I couldn't do anything about it. I was awfully tired. I'm too old, I guess," Louis said.[47] When he quit this time it was for good. It was the kind of loss that stuck. If a little piece of Louis died in the dressing room that night, then so too did a little piece of America.

12

A Good Race Horse

Marciano's convincing upset of Louis did little to motivate Bocchicchio and Walcott to defend against Charles. In fact, it had the opposite effect. Marciano was suddenly the hottest thing going and was thus a more attractive opponent for Walcott than ever. So the stalemate continued. Charles couldn't wait around forever—there was business to be done and there were TV dates to be filled—so the IBC put together yet another meeting with Maxim, Charles' fifth, this time at Cow Palace in San Francisco.

The promoter of record was Oakland's Jimmy Murray, who wildly overstated the business the fight would do, predicting a sellout. But both the fight press and the fans had seen quite enough of Charles-Maxim, and just 9,000 came out to the 16,000-seat arena to see Charles punch Maxim around the ring on the way to a unanimous decision win. If there was any doubt beforehand that Charles still was superior to the light heavyweight champion, this fight removed it once and for all. Everyone knew beforehand how it would go, but Kearns was in so deep with the IBC that he could have told them he wanted to match Maxim against the ghost of John L. Sullivan and they'd have found a way to make it happen. Not that Kearns was friendly with Carbo and the gangsters. On the contrary, they were bitter enemies.

But Kearns was at the helm of the powerful Manager's Guild, whose members were complaining to Gibson and Norris that they weren't getting a big enough cut on the IBC's telecasts and had started a strike in 1950. Kearns smoothed things over with the guild members to the extent that he could, helped the IBC make matches and was paid handsomely for his efforts.

Either way, Maxim was such an easy win for Charles that just nine days later he found himself in Portland against Oregon journeyman Joe Kahut. Once an interesting prospect who went unbeaten in his first twenty-three fights, Kahut floundered when the level of his competition improved. Losses to Lesnevich, Maxim, Layne, Pat Comiskey and other, less notable names placed him decidedly outside the division's upper tier. Still, the fight was a big deal to the locals, 6,724 of whom contributed $31,310 to produce the largest gate in Portland boxing history. Alas, Charles spoiled the party by pummeling poor Kahut from one end of the ring to the other on the way to stopping him in the eighth round.

In mid–February, Bocchicchio and Norris finally reached an agreement for Walcott to defend the heavyweight title against Charles in June. As it turned out, the agreement was reached just two days before the deadline Christenberry had imposed and was announced via telegram to Christenberry's office.[1] Bocchicchio had decided after all, apparently, not to call Christenberry's bluff.

His bargaining power irreparably compromised, Walcott was forced to accept a deal where he would receive just 30 percent of the net receipts instead of the standard champion's 40 percent. Charles also would get 30 percent but a lower share of the TV money. When all was said and done, Walcott's reported purse was $103,123 compared to Charles' $92,483, an insult to a heavyweight champion and one that deepened the growing acrimony between Norris and Bocchicchio.

With the big fight four months away, Charles had another vacation back home in Cincinnati. Mintz and Tannas decided to keep him out of the ring until training started, so he had more of Gladys' candied sweet potatoes, more vanilla malts, more fun nights at the Cotton Club and a lot of time to think. Give a fighter a lot of time to think and he'll sooner or later come up with an excuse for every fight he's ever lost. It wasn't long before Charles landed on the reason he had felt so out of it against Walcott in Pittsburgh.

"I was dull at Pittsburgh because I didn't get the right amount of sleep at my training camp," he said. "We were near a resort on a highway. The trucks and hotrod cars and the noise at the resort kept me awake."[2] This sort of thing made Charles no friends.

Meanwhile, the IBC worked on landing the fight somewhere. Pittsburgh wanted it. So did Detroit and Chicago. It ended up in Philadelphia at the mammoth Municipal Stadium—not only because all the locals would come out to see their hero in his grand homecoming, but also because in Philadelphia Bocchicchio could feel at home and call in all kinds of favors if the need arose. Clearly it was hostile to Charles—he was the villain in any locale, but in addition, Mintz's history with the commission was obviously not good after his display in Pittsburgh. He was acutely aware of this and a result remained on his best behavior, even after his suggestion that Joe Louis referee the bout was met with an embarrassing silence.

Six weeks out from the fight, Charles and his crew set up camp in Pleasantville, New Jersey, a good distance away from any highways, just to be safe. Sparring partners Al Smith, Julian Keene and Walter Parker put Charles through his paces in the gym, and Charles pasted them on a daily basis, beating them up more harshly than usual, the press noted. Along the way Charles got the idea in his head that he should be bigger and heavier for this fight than he'd been against Walcott in the past. He'd be able to bull Walcott around more and maybe handle his left hook better, too. He started camp at 204 and did the same amount of work—the same number of miles every morning, the same number of rounds in the gym—but he ate more and didn't feel the worse for it. He felt just as fast, but stronger. He planned to come in around 190 or so, the heaviest of his career. Arcel agreed with the weight increase, saying Charles had been too light at 182 for his last fight with Walcott.

Despite the 12–5 odds in Charles' favor, Walcott couldn't have been more confident in the press, and it wasn't about building the gate or acting brash. He just felt he was better than Charles. He always had. The last fight had introduced the possibility to the masses, and this fight would confirm it. "I'll knock him out again. I've got his number and he knows it," Walcott said.[3] Mintz, on the other hand, was so confident Charles would win that he reserved a big room at the Essex Hotel in Pleasantville for a banquet of five hundred along with rooms for one hundred guests. "We'll start icing the win for the celebration before Charles steps into the ring," he said.[4] Walcott trained close to home at Bader Field in Atlantic City and from all reports wasn't especially impressive against sparring partners Oakland Billy Smith and Pete Nelson. Still, by fight night, late money on Walcott had moved the odds to almost 2–1. Local promoter Herman Taylor, working with the IBC, instituted a radio and TV blackout in a seventy-five-mile radius around Philadelphia to boost the gate, and it worked.

A full 21,599 paying customers shelled out $210,313 to watch Walcott and Charles go at it one more time in the same arena where Gene Tunney had dethroned Dempsey 26 years earlier in front of a massive crowd of 120,757. Both were at ringside—Tunney was booed lustily when introduced to the crowd—along with the usual luminaries and derelicts from the mob and the fight crowd. Charles weighed in at 191½, on target. Walcott was five pounds heavier.

At 10:00 a.m. on the day of the fight, Buck McTiernan, Pete Tomasco and Zach Clayton, three local officials, were informed by the commission that they'd be working the fights that night and were to be at the stadium at 7:00 p.m.[5] Clayton worked the first prelim on the card and then took his seat at ringside for the rest of the show. At 9:45 p.m. he said later, he was informed he would be working the main event. It was a big deal. He would be the first black man to referee a world heavyweight title bout.

Clayton, a city fireman and former professional basketball player, had been refereeing around Philadelphia for years and was well known to local fight fans and to the fight mob. He was a busy man in boxing. You didn't get to be as busy as he was in the Philadelphia fight business without knowing how things worked in the business and who ran it. In all of boxing and especially in Philadelphia, favors were everything. You do someone a favor and he does one for you in return. You both make a buck. So when the fight turned out the way it did a lot of guys wondered if there was a reason they had chosen Clayton, that maybe he was a guy you could count on to return a favor when one was called for.

Not long after this fight, Clayton became the darling of the Philadelphia boxing commission, receiving far more assignments than did his peers, leading one, a respected veteran official and 1920 Olympian named Willie Clark, to resign from officiating. In his resignation letter Clark suggested his boss look into the Gil Turner–Johnny Saxton fight in which Clayton voted for Saxton—whose whole career was handled from beginning to end by the mob—while the judges had voted for Turner. One writer noted, "In addition to being involved in a number of disputed decisions, Clayton has been openly jeered by fans for constantly interfering. His close range circling tactics in the ring have spoiled a number of fights for hometown and television viewers."[6]

It was a lousy fight no matter who the referee was. Walcott backpedaled and clinched and looked for the big knockout blow. Charles feinted and retreated and hesitated. They jabbed. They clinched some more. They jabbed again. They walked around. They each threw a power punch and then clinched. Charles was more cautious than ever and moved his hands only when they were inside. Walcott was slower than ever, if always clearly dangerous. Every now and again one of them would rock the other with a power punch and then not follow up.

In the fifth a right hand by Walcott staggered Charles. Another right did almost as much damage a round later. After six rounds McTiernan and Tomasco had Walcott ahead 4–1–1 and 5–1. Clayton had it 6–0 for Walcott, and you got the sense he'd have taken points away from Charles if he could have gotten away with it.

Clayton repeatedly broke the fighters whenever they met on the inside, where Charles was getting his best (and only) good work done. In the third, fifth, sixth and thirteenth rounds, he warned Charles against low blows that to everyone else looked legal. He berated Charles' corner over the amount of grease they put on Charles' face and late in the fight wiped it off the fighter. When Mintz started to object from the corner, Clayton threatened to disqualify him.

It wasn't only to Charles sympathizers that the officiating looked askew. Later, *The*

Ring reported, "It was fairly obvious that Clayton's sympathies were with Walcott, and this cropped up time after time. He fairly badgered Charles. Once he took Walcott by the arm and, with touching solicitude and caressing sympathy, said to him, "Come on, baby."[7] Another writer agreed: "Referee Clayton, a negro, ordinarily is an excellent arbiter. Last night he harassed, nagged and warned Charles unjustly at times for fouls the 30-year-old did not commit."[8] Still another reported, "Practically every newspaperman present at the fight, including reporters for the *Pittsburgh Courier*, most prominent of Negro papers, charged Clayton with incompetency."[9]

Even with Clayton's incessant haranguing, Charles took over the fight, more or less, in the second half. Two rights buckled Walcott's legs in the tenth, the most clearly either man had been hurt, and Charles hammered away at his body to good effect. He took the eleventh and twelfth rounds too, as Walcott, clearly exhausted, staggered from a right near the end of the twelfth. In the thirteenth Charles made Walcott clinch repeatedly from a hook to the body and a right to the chin. Still, these were single outbursts sandwiched between clinches and feints, as opposed to the abandon with which Charles had attacked Maxim, for example, and that's what Charles' corner wanted from him and believed they needed. They knew they wouldn't win a close decision in Philadelphia. Everyone knew it.

In the corner, Tannas told Charles, "You've got to fight this fellow every minute. You can't afford to let him steal any rounds."[10] Charles, convinced he was winning, dismissed him. After the twelfth, Tannas told him again that it was close and he'd have to go all out in the last three. "But he thought he was ahead and taking chances just didn't seem smart to him,"[11] Tannas said later. Walcott clinched through the fourteenth, another Charles round, then did just enough to make the fifteenth questionable.

At the end Charles was cut over the right eye and under the left eye. The area around his left eye also was swollen. Walcott was mostly unmarked. Charles waited stone-faced for the decision. Mintz and Arcel and Brown looked anxious. Then it came: McTiernan, 8–7 for Walcott. Tomasco 7–6–2 for Walcott. Clayton 9–6 for Walcott.

The crowd at the stadium loved the verdict, as did Walcott. The majority of the press did not, and the next day many columns expressed a tone similar to one another. "Ringside observers were aghast when the scoring was announced. Maybe Walcott appeared the winner from the referee's roving position inside the ring, and the two judges' seats on the outer edges. Elsewhere though, it seemed all Charles," observed one.[12] "Pappy Joe seemed to have been helped immeasurably to his triumph by three Prince Charmings in the persons of the referee and two judges who rendered the rather freely predicted unanimous verdict," wrote another.[13] Still another cut right to the chase: "There is no defending Jersey Joe's title gift."[14]

Even if this view was ubiquitous, it was not unanimous. Of the forty-one writers polled after the fight, twenty-four had Charles winning, compared to seventeen for Walcott. The minority too all had a similar bent. "A crown, especially a heavyweight crown, should not be brushed off a man's shoulders as though it were a fly; it should be forcibly taken from him. And this Charles did not do to Walcott even though his more rabid partisans may say he did," is how one put it.[15] Another wrote, "Charles was too timid to take the title away."[16] Another, who had always favored Charles, blasted his performance. "It was a sorry performance by Charles, who boxed with even more than his customary caution and with considerably less than the skill he has demonstrated in the past."[17]

All of them essentially echoed the sentiments of McTiernan, who said after the fight, "You can't take the fight away from a champion in a close fight like that."[18] And really, that was the rub. Charles had fought without passion and as a consequence permitted room for argument. As one writer put it who scored the fight for Charles, "Almost to a man, those who voted for Charles were agreed that he didn't deserve to win back the title on his lackluster display."[19]

Even Tannas said later, "Ezzard could have regained the title if he had fought a little the last two rounds instead of coasting."[20] None of this had anything to do with Walcott, who reportedly was too out of breath to talk with reporters for fifteen minutes after the bout, yet when he could talk expressed no doubt that he'd won at least eight or nine rounds. "I had no intention of gambling. After all I am the champion and Charles had to come to me. I think he expected me to shoot the works in five or six rounds, but I fooled him," he said.[21]

In the loser's dressing room again, Charles was grim like a man is who knows he has lost something dear and has accepted the terrible reality that he is wholly to blame. He would bear the brunt. He had to. It was in his makeup. It would have been easier to blame everyone else and everything else. Many men, many lesser men, had little trouble doing that when they, like Charles, had failed at the most critical moments, through cowardice or some other sin. If Ezzard wanted the easy lies and excuses there would be no shortage of supporters. Mintz, Arcel, Tannas and Brown all were good soldiers and would argue to the grave, rightly so, that Clayton was up Charles' ass the whole night and was almost certainly in the bag for Walcott. And the decision in any event was obvious home cooking. Even most of the writers said that—the same ones who hadn't seen fit to give Charles one break over the last five years agreed that he deserved the decision.

"The referee annoyed him all the way!" Arcel barked as soon as the reporters filed into the locker room. "When Ezzard got his eye cut the referee wiped off the stuff we put on it. He kept telling Ezzard to keep his punches up and that he wouldn't warn him again." Seated on a table with his back against the wall, Charles mumbled that he was sorry he'd lost. Arcel cut him off. "You didn't lose. You didn't lose. You won!"[22]

But all of them knew in their hearts what Charles knew in his: that he had all the physical advantages going in; that he'd allowed Walcott to rest and fight on his terms; that he had hurt Walcott a couple times but hadn't followed up; and that he never went after it the way he should have, the way a fighter does when a win means everything to him, the way a win on this night should have meant everything to Charles.

It shouldn't have been close. Charles allowed it to be. And that wasn't Clayton's fault or the judges' fault or the fault of the ghost of Sam Baroudi. Charles was grim. "I have no alibis," he said, softly and with considerable effort. "They gave it to him and that's the way it has to be. I'm just another fighter now. I'll never get another chance. I guess I've had it."[23]

He'd have been happy to send them home with that, but that sort of thing was never enough for them, and they prodded him for his reaction to the decision. "I thought it was close, but I thought I won it."[24]

In a corner of the dressing room but within earshot of Charles, Arcel fumed. And not because he'd gone on record saying there was "no chance" Charles would lose, and not because of Clayton, either. It was because they'd been so close to winning. It was right in Charles' hands if only he'd reached out and taken it.

A writer picked up on Arcel's body language and walked over and asked him if Charles had disappointed him. Arcel let out a heavy sigh. "Well, yes," he said. "How so?" the writer asked. Arcel shrugged and sighed again. "You work out a plan but who knows what a fighter is going to do when the bell rings and he walks out there?" Charles heard Arcel and then said to a writer, "I guess that I just can't work on orders from the corner."[25] If only it were that simple. Years later another writer asked Arcel what it had been like to train Ezzard Charles. Arcel replied honestly; that Charles was "like a good racehorse that won't run for you."[26]

Charles was eager to get back in the ring after the Walcott fight. It helped that a majority of writers thought he'd won and had been vocal about it. So long as his cuts healed up, which they did, he'd be ready to fight before the end of the summer. On June 28 Mintz and Tannas nailed down a deal with Ogden, Utah, promoter Kenny Mayne for a rematch with Layne, this time in Layne's hometown in early August. Both Charles and Layne would get a straight 35 percent of the gate with no TV or radio money. It was risky facing Layne in his home town, but Charles was certain he'd beat him again and even quicker than last time. He started training in Cincinnati in July with a plan to head out to Utah a couple weeks before the fight.

Arcel was in charge of making arrangements for Charles' accommodations on the road. He went ahead of Charles and the rest of the camp members—Brown, Christmas, the sparring partners and a few of Ezzard's buddies from Cincinnati who went everywhere with him—and reserved hotel rooms, found suitable training quarters, etc. This wasn't easy work outside big cities like Detroit, New York and Chicago. The more remote the area, and also the further south it was, the harder it was for Arcel to find places that were willing to accommodate a group of black men. He'd been relieved when he was told before leaving for Utah that the mayor of Ogden had made all the arrangements for Charles and his crew; all Arcel had to do was go to the main hotel in town and tell the owner he was there to reserve Ezzard Charles' room.

Arcel arrived in Utah two days ahead of Charles, who was traveling by train. He found the hotel and then the owner, who wore a gun on his hip. Arcel said to him, "My name is Ray Arcel. I'm from New York. The mayor told me to see you, and that you would give us some rooms."

"Give who rooms?" the hotel owner asked.

"Ezzard Charles and his entourage," Arcel said.

"Is he a nigger?" the hotel owner wanted to know.

"Well, he's a black man."

"I don't allow any niggers at my hotel."

"But the mayor told me he had spoken to you and made arrangements."

"The mayor doesn't own this hotel, I do."[27]

After some discussion, the hotel owner gave Arcel the name of a place that had recently opened and told him to try his luck there. Arcel did that and paid the husband and wife that ran it cash, in advance, for six double rooms. Because he had run into situations like this before, he always carried five or six thousand dollars on him. It came in handy. When Charles and his entourage arrived at the hotel two days later, the owners froze in horror at the site of ten black men piling into the lobby. Arcel hadn't told them who the rooms were for.

He had to assure the owners that as a prizefighter, Charles was there to take care of business and there would be no music, no girls and no hanging around the hotel during the day. That did the trick. He also went back to the first hotel owner, arranged for Charles and his entourage to eat their meals there in two private rooms, and paid for everything in advance. He thought that was the end of his troubles. He was wrong.

Mayne, the promoter, hadn't even arranged for a proper gym where Charles could train. He set him up at a roller skating rink and sent over a removable ring and punching bag that Charles' guys had to take down and re-assemble every time they used it. Arcel was incensed. A few days later he was in town and ran into an old friend who was in uniform. It turned out there was an air base nearby with a fully equipped gym. Arcel went over and met the master sergeant, who ran the gym and was black. Charles was training there by the end of the day. When they were in the gym it was as good as if they were back home in Cincinnati.

While Charles was training for Layne, Marciano and Harry Matthews met at Yankee Stadium for the right to face Walcott for the title. Marciano had stayed busy after retiring Louis, stopping Lee Savold, Gino Buonvino and Bernie Reynolds. Matthews, a pro since 1937, was a stylish, prodigiously gifted mover and counterpuncher out of Seattle who could feint the best, most experienced guy out of position and then jab him silly without breaking a sweat.

Two months before meeting Marciano, Matthews had outpointed Layne in Oregon. Despite Matthews' vast edge in experience and skills—and a seventy-bout winning streak—Marciano was an 11–5 favorite, mostly because Matthews had always done better against light heavyweights, and Marciano, despite his smallish stature, was no light heavyweight in terms of punching power.

Matthews boxed the hell out of Rocky the first round, busting open his left eye and drawing blood from his nose, but this was the way Marciano liked it. In the second he caught Matthews with exactly two left hooks and knocked him flat. Not long after, they made a deal for Rocky to face Walcott in Philadelphia in September for the title. Walcott finally had the big money fight he wanted, and everyone would find out once and for all if Marciano was for real.

Back in Utah, Mayne, the promoter, came up with a gimmick to help promote Layne and Charles. Since Layne, whom *The Ring* ranked eighth in the world, held a victory over Walcott, and Charles had, to the eyes of many, beaten Walcott in their last fight, Mayne had a title belt made up that he would present to the fight's winner as the "people's champion." The locals loved it. They loved this, too: Jack Dempsey would referee the fight and, in accordance with the Utah rules, would also be the only judge. If the fight went the distance, he would decide the winner. Dempsey, as everyone knew, had spent a good chunk of his youth in Utah and was very friendly with members of the Layne camp. What could go wrong?

The day before the fight so much late local money came in on Layne that he was a 6–5 betting favorite. The boxing press flown in to cover the fight found this laughable, but what did they know? On fight night 25,000 fans packed Ogden Stadium, piling into a makeshift arena converted from rodeo grounds and producing a gate of $131,501, the largest in Utah sports history.

Charles, having decided he liked the extra weight he had carried into the last fight with Walcott, came in at 190 to Layne's 195. He started slowly, content enough to work Layne's body over the first half of the fight to wear him down, even after a hard left ripped open a cut over Layne's left eye in the opening round.

Layne took the opportunity to crash home some right crosses on Charles' jaw over the fight's first half, but Charles was unconcerned. He had taken Layne's best shots in their first fight and knew he could handle them. Layne was no Jersey Joe in the power department, but he was better and more active in this fight than in their first meeting. He roughed up Charles continually and hammered his own blows to Charles' body.

You could make the case that Layne took the majority of the early rounds with his higher work rate, but Charles took over from the sixth round on and never gave an inch after that. He wasn't as active as was Layne, but his blows did far more damage; at the end

Layne was cut on the lip and over the left eye, bruised under the left eye and also on the left cheekbone. Layne, exhausted and battered, held throughout the ninth and tenth and barely made it to the final bell. It had been a rough, hard fight and a good one for the crowd, but anyone could see Charles had won it. A poll conducted afterward revealed that ten of eleven writers at ringside felt Charles earned the decision win.

At the final bell Dempsey—again, the referee and sole judge—raised Layne's hand. His scorecard was puzzling, to say the least: he scored two rounds for Layne, one for Charles and seven even. A moment after he raised Layne's hand, the clouds overhead, which had been threatening all night, opened up and drenched the crowd. And so too did Jake Mintz. He stormed around the ring like it was Pittsburgh all over again, hollering to the press at ringside. "Dempsey is a thief! Talk about your highway robberies! This is all politics. This is the lousiest decision I ever seen. It stinks to high heaven!"[28]

Mintz was so furious he threatened several times to faint right in the ring. He never did, but conceded later that his "ulsters were in an uproar." Arcel, a relative stoic, observed in the dressing room, "Instead of adding dignity to the fight game, Dempsey has added disgrace."[29] Only Charles, by this time apparently accustomed to being shafted, reacted relatively unemotionally.

"He never hurt me once. He pushed me around and shoved me, but he was the same fighter I beat last October. I thought I won it all the way—especially in the late rounds," he said. "Layne didn't even know the fight was over."[30]

All of this was true. Charles clearly deserved the decision, but there were those again who believed he could have saved himself the trouble of getting robbed if only he'd fought harder. *The Ring* reported: "Charles was his own worst enemy ... because he didn't take advantage of the many openings given him for a concerted attack and his failure to follow through when he stunned his opponent with deep punches to the mid-section."[31]

Also, Dempsey, while refusing to address with the press how he had managed to score seven rounds even in a ten-round fight, said afterward that Charles' lack of activity and aggression had cost him. "I gave the fight to Layne as I saw it," he said. "He was the aggressor. He carried the fight to Ezzard and was always willing to make a battle of it. That's more than I can say of Charles. I awarded the bout to Rex because of his aggressiveness. Charles was too cautious. You cannot give a man a round for failing to fight."[32]

Sure, Charles had won the fight. Sure, Dempsey was full of it. But just as he had in the last Walcott fight, Charles gave them a way to screw him. He gave them a chance. In the fight business that was all it took. You'd have thought he'd have learned that by now. He hadn't.

Rocky Marciano had no such failings. Six weeks after Charles lost to Layne, Marciano went to war with Walcott in Philadelphia for the heavyweight title. As expected, Walcott boxed Marciano silly for most of the fight and even dropped him in the first round, the first knockdown of Marciano's career. But as the battle dragged on, bloody and savage, just the way Marciano liked it, fans at Municipal Stadium could sense the challenger getting closer. After twelve rounds the local judges—including Zach Clayton—had Walcott well ahead. In the thirteenth a right-hand bomb exploded on Walcott's jaw and knocked him unconscious, and the world had a new heavyweight champion. Even better than that, he was white and could punch.

But forget about the writers, ecstatic over a new champion who had the same color skin as they did. Marciano didn't need an honest judge or referee. It didn't matter to him if everything was on the up-and-up because if it wasn't, all he had to do was plant his right fist on the other guy's jaw. He could make it clean. He could make it right. You can't call a fight fixed when the other guy's teeth are in the first row.

And so the fans loved Marciano, especially compared to Charles, and you couldn't blame them. Because where Charles hesitated, Marciano attacked. Where Charles feinted, Marciano punched. Where Charles waited, Marciano took charge. Charles was so wary of Walcott's left hook in their last fight that every time Walcott feinted with it, Charles half jumped across the ring. When Walcott feinted the hook against Marciano, Rocky said to hell with it and punched him in the mouth.

Still, Charles claimed to like what he had seen. "I always thought I could beat Marciano," he told the press. "And now, after watching him against a rough guy [Walcott], I'm convinced that I can."[33]

Mintz and Tannas and the IBC all knew immediately what everyone else did after the title fight in Philadelphia: Marciano was now the cash cow of boxing. The way to make big money was to get in the ring with him—the Walcott fight produced a gate of more than $500,000. When people see a gate like that, their eyes light up. Somewhere down the line (not too far down the line, because Charles was 31 by now, no longer a young kid in the ring), they wanted to get him in there. Even if he couldn't handle Marciano, at least they'd all make a big pile of money for getting him beaten up.

They had to bring him back right, and they had to get him to open up his style more. No more timidity, no more carrying guys for this or that reason, no more being content to box to a decision win. If he wanted Marciano he'd have to fight his way into Marciano's neighborhood.

Charles had to start knocking guys out and had to look good doing it. Toward that end, Mintz arranged a bout with Bernie Reynolds at Cincinnati Gardens in October. In Cincinnati, Mintz figured, Charles would at least be at home. He might even get a few cheers. It would be good for him. Charles needed an easy fight and Reynolds fit the bill. Once a hot prospect who many had thought would someday be heavyweight champion, Reynolds had come up in the same stable as Gus Lesnevich. But that was a lot of years ago and a lot of losses. He went into the Charles fight having lost six of his last nine; Marciano had stopped him in three rounds five months earlier. He was just what the doctor ordered. Ezzard's old friend Sam Becker would co-promote and they'd show it on the regular Wednesday Night Fight Series with Pabst Blue Ribbon sponsoring.

Overestimating how enthusiastic his old fans in Cincinnati still were about Charles, Becker said in the days before the fight that he'd get between 8,000 and 10,000 butts in Cincinnati Gardens. Really, that would have been an insult; capacity was 14,000. Even at that, Becker had been overly optimistic. Just 3,710 fans, generating a gate of $10,395, showed up and booed Charles mercilessly after a left hook–right cross combination put Reynolds down face-first and out at 1:40 of the second round.

It didn't matter that Charles had stopped Reynolds a round sooner than had Marciano, or that Charles, weighing 189 to Reynold's 187, had fought aggressively from the start. He was Ezzard Charles. So they booed—even in his home town. During the television broadcast the television microphones repeatedly picked up cheers and encouragement for Reynolds. "I'd really like to fight Rex Layne again," Charles said afterward, unperturbed, at least outwardly, by the booing. "After that I want to do what everyone else wants to do—fight Rocky Marciano."[34]

Mintz didn't want Layne again yet and neither did the IBC. They wanted to build the rubber match into a big fight and then go after Marciano, so two weeks after Reynolds,

Charles was in Madison Square Garden against tough Argentine Cesar Brion. Brion was tall, awkward and an easy night for no one; if the plan was to get Charles a knockout, he wasn't the guy to go after. He'd never been stopped in his 45-fight career and that included the two fights with Joe Louis. He was two inches taller than Charles, 10 years younger and on fight night weighed 196 pounds to Charles' 186. But this was who they wanted him to fight, so this is who he would fight.

Mintz did his best beforehand to sell the press on the idea they'd be seeing a "new," attacking, aggressive Charles in the ring. It wasn't the first time Mintz had given them that line and it wouldn't be the last. Ezzard pitched in, too. "I'll go in there at the opening bell and just keep throwing punches until he drops—or I do," he said. "I'll let my fists be the ring officials."[35]

Whether or not he truly intended to go after Brion, he knew what everyone else did—winning wouldn't be good enough anymore. He was still better than most of the heavyweights out there. It wasn't a question of who he could beat. On a given night he could beat almost anyone. But he was in the entertainment business and after two consecutive decision losses, he had to be spectacular.

"I know I've got to try for a knockout all the time," he said. "I used to fight that way before I became champion. Then I became too cautious. I'll be in there swinging those combinations all the time now."[36] "You've got to slaughter a guy to convince people," he continued. "When I had the title I froze myself up. I didn't want to lose it. Consequently, I lost it."

Someone asked him what the moral of the story was. "You've got to throw more," he said. "It's not that you should get reckless but you can't lay back and wait for that one good shot. Not when you don't have the title. That's the way I used to fight. When I fought Walcott in Philadelphia last June I was sure I could beat him. I just wanted to keep him missing and then get over that one good shot. But I never got it over and I know now why I didn't," he said. "I'd throw one punch and stop. Then one more and stop. Never combinations. You have to throw a series of punches to get a man. It was all in my mind. That's all there was to it. I've got it all straightened out now. I'm looking for no more decisions."[37]

That last sentence put a smile on the faces of Mintz and Arcel, who were standing nearby. That's what they wanted to hear, and maybe they believed him, but if they did it was because they wanted to. They had been around long enough to know that a fighter who talks like that is doing too much thinking. If he has to remind himself to fight the way he should, it's all wrong. It has to be second nature or it doesn't work. It might for a time or two, but it won't stick.

No one had to tell Dempsey or Louis to throw more punches. Marciano didn't have to talk himself into bashing the other guy. It came naturally. It had come naturally to Charles once, too, when he was a starving middleweight and light heavyweight and he had nothing to lose. When he was in his twenties and had all that anger and desperation that slum kids carry around with them, he never had to remind himself to throw combinations. He didn't have to remind himself of anything in the ring. Once he learned the mechanics, it came naturally, as naturally as it did when he was ten years old fighting in makeshift rings in Lawrenceville or when he was a teenager fighting in bingo halls in Cincinnati.

He never thought of himself as a killer then, but he was. And now, he wasn't. He was a thirty-one-year-old heavyweight who had a wife and two baby daughters at home, a closet full of expensive clothes and a nice house. He'd already been to the top of the mountain. The man who had beaten Sam Baroudi to death was long gone. He had to know that. He also had to convince everyone, including himself, that it wasn't true.

The "new" Charles, a 5–1 favorite, wobbled Brion in the first, second, eighth, ninth and tenth rounds, leaving most of the left half of Brion's face bleeding and swollen, but Charles could not stop him and settled for a unanimous decision in front of a disappointing crowd of 5,726. Those watching him go after Brion could almost see him forcing himself, like a man who hates liver gorging himself on the stuff at gunpoint.

He would rather have outboxed him from a distance, nice and safe and nobody gets hurt. But he needed to give the lie some truth. He had to put in the work. Being someone you're not requires effort. "I wasn't too satisfied," Charles said afterward. "I looked bad because he was bobbing and I couldn't hit with a good right hand. My trouble was that I was waiting for that one good punch. I could have thrown more."[38]

Tannas laid out Charles' short-term schedule. "We've got offers to put Ezzy in next month against [Jimmy] Bivins in St. Louis, Chicago, Detroit, Cincinnati and San Francisco. If not Bivins, we'd like Danny Bucceroni, Rex Layne, Harry Matthews or anyone else that will move Ezzy closer to a title shot. He's going to keep busy."[39]

Tannas wasn't kidding. A month later old rivals Charles and Bivins met in Chicago at the stadium. Bivins, more shot by this time even than he'd been against Louis a year before, but still a tough nut and skilled, opened as a 3–1 underdog. Nine long years had passed since his rousing win over Charles in Cleveland, and Charles had aged better. Bivins was an old thirty-three and though he'd stopped the prospect Coley Wallace a couple of months prior, he was done and he knew it.

So did everyone else. Just 2,799 fans showed up to watch him and Charles clinch and maul over ten dull, nationally televised rounds with a first-round knockdown by Charles being the singular highlight of the evening. If you knew Charles and what kind of man he was, you might have thought he was carrying his old rival, because he and Bivins had both come up the hard way fighting for pennies against all the other hard, black fighters the white fighters wouldn't face, and so they shared a bond. Maybe Charles didn't want to hurt him any more than he'd already been hurt by life and by the game, and so he was even more willing than usual to clinch when Bivins wanted to clinch, and to wait when Bivins needed a rest. Bivins, the same type of fighter inside that Charles was, was happy too not to press things and take it easy and be himself.

Or maybe Charles just wanted to be who he was in the ring again. Either way, you take the wins where you can get them and move on. The main thing was to keep busy. The IBC was appreciative of how frequently Charles had fought when he was champion, and against whom. All he had to do was keep busy and keep winning and he would get his shot at Marciano, Mintz and Tannas had been assured, probably after the Marciano-Walcott rematch.

A month later it was journeyman Frank Buford in Boston. Though Charles scored a kayo this time, he looked terrible. "Fans Boo Charles for Sloppy Fight," one headline read.[40] "Charles Looks Unimpressive in Comeback" another scolded.[41]

Charles agreed. Outweighed 202 to 187 pounds by the woefully chubby Buford, he scored more or less at will but couldn't hurt Buford save for a body-shot knockdown at the end of the fourth and a fight-ending right hand in the seventh.

"I'm better than I looked tonight," he said afterward. "Buford was hard to fight because he was trying for one wild punch. I took a couple of right hands on the head to open him up." It was the first time Charles fought in Boston. The 5,095 in attendance booed throughout. "Wait'll Marciano gets a hold of you!" several hollered from ringside.[42] They'd long ago decided Marciano was their man and not just because they were in Massachusetts.

Mintz was unbowed. "We've got a few opticals to overcome but Charles will meet Marciano some day!" he yelled afterward.[43]

Next it was on to St. Louis, Missouri, where Charles stopped young, rugged Wes Bascom in nine rounds. Bascom had started his career in 1950 with thirteen straight wins. He was coming off consecutive losses to Bivins and Tommy Harrison but had never been stopped. He was stubborn throughout and made Charles work, but he was in over his head. The referee saved him with a round left in the fight. Stay busy, stay busy, they told Charles, and we'll get Marciano, so three weeks after Bascom it was Tommy Harrison in Detroit, but there was a wrinkle—for the first time in a very long while, Charles would not have Mintz in his corner.

At about 6:00 a.m. on January 29, Mintz suffered a heart attack while preparing to fly out to Detroit from his home in Pittsburgh's East End. Mintz being Mintz, he said to hell with it and got on the plane anyway. "I've been in Ezzard's corner in every fight he's had since we teamed up," he said.[44] Shortly after arriving in Pittsburgh, Mintz was stricken again and took the first flight back to Pittsburgh so he could be seen by his personal physician. Tannas went out to Detroit instead.

Harrison was a young kid, just twenty-three years old, and *The Ring*'s sixth-ranked light heavyweight. Three straight wins, upsets each, over Charlie Norkus, Bivins and Bascom got him the fight with Charles. It wasn't often that Charles got to fight light heavies anymore. After so many years with the big boys he knew he could take it to any 175-pounder in the world, and Harrison, of Los Angeles, was in big trouble. Charles was more confident than usual. "If I had any doubt about my ability to beat Harrison maybe I'd be foolish to take the match. But I know I can beat any fighter in the world," he said. "If I can't beat Harrison I don't deserve to fight Marciano."[45]

He was right about that. He beat the hell out of Harrison from the start, fully justifying the 3–1 odds in his favor. He had nothing to fear from Harrison's punch, and he won every round except the fourth, which referee Lou Handler took from him for a low blow. By the eighth poor Harrison's left eye was closed and he bled from the mouth and nose. A big right hand floored him, and after the round Harrison's manager, George Parnassus, along with the ringside doctor, stopped the slaughter. It was widely seen as the best performance by far of Charles' comeback. Even he seemed satisfied. "I'm ready for a title fight any time now. And I think I should be the first one to get a shot at the Marciano-Walcott winner. I plan to keep on fighting at least once a month until the championship fight comes."[46] (Harrison later fought in unsanctioned bouts posing as contender Bob Satterfield. After retiring from boxing he lived on the streets of Los Angeles and continued to pose as Satterfield, leading to the *Los Angeles Times* magazine article and feature film *Resurrecting the Champ*.)

Getting the winner of Marciano-Walcott wouldn't be easy, mainly because they couldn't put the rematch together. Bocchicchio was on the outs with Norris and the IBC and was breaking their chops over Walcott's guarantee. He'd let Walcott's contract with the IBC expire, and his only connection to them after the Marciano fight involved a rematch clause that gave Walcott first shot at the title if he lost it. He and Weill met numerous times with Norris to bang out an agreement but couldn't come to terms. Finally, Carbo broke the stalemate. He stepped in and told Bocchicchio to sign the contract for a flat guarantee for Walcott of $250,000. He dictated the terms. End of story. Carbo was the boss and whether or not Bocchicchio liked it that was the deal.

The fight was finally signed in early February for April 10 in Chicago, almost eight months after the first fight. (It was later rescheduled for May 15 after Marciano injured his nose in training.) The deal infuriated Marciano, who had already earned a reputation for his obsession with finances, and he never trusted the IBC again, if indeed he ever had. He would receive 30 percent of the net and 30 percent of the $300,000 in television money. By the time all was said and done, he made, on paper, just $166,038.60.[47] That Walcott, the challenger, made almost $90,000 more than Marciano was a slight Rocky never got over.

At any rate, Charles' win over Harrison and the way in which it was accomplished convinced the IBC, Mintz and Tannas that Charles was ready to go after Layne again. In late February they put it together for April 1 in San Francisco at Winterland Arena. The IBC sold it as an "elimination bout," with the winner guaranteed to face the Marciano-Walcott II winner. This was wholly a testament to Layne's popularity (owed in the main to his skin color) rather than to any "earning" he had done to get a title shot. Since his highly dubious win over Charles in Utah, he'd beaten club fighter Al Spaulding and lost a split decision to contender Roland LaStarza. Over the same period Charles had won six fights in a row, four by knockout. Even if he looked like hell half the time and was boring, at least he was winning. That he had to beat Layne again to get Marciano was an insult of the highest order.

Mintz, still recovering from his heart attack, would watch the rubber match on TV from his home in Pittsburgh. Arcel also would be absent for the fight. Tannas brought in Chicago-area trainer Izzy Klein to assist Brown in the corner. Klein had been one of the three men in Sam Baroudi's corner five years earlier, on the night Baroudi died. That Klein ended up in Charles' corner was almost certainly not Charles' choice and looked suspiciously like the result of some of Klein's friends in high places wanting to get their man some work.

On the other hand, Klein had been around a long time and worked with some big names—the great welterweight champion Barney Ross, for instance, top-rated welterweight Chuck Davey, heavyweight champion Max Baer, and Max's brother Buddy, who twice challenged Louis. He was anything but a novice. He worked Charles' corner for several fights in place of Arcel, who got a job making matches for a fledgling television boxing series on the ABC network called *Saturday Night Fights*.

There wasn't big money involved but Arcel drew a decent weekly paycheck. Some suggested to him that the powers-that-be—namely, the IBC, which controlled television rights to virtually all worthwhile bouts—wouldn't be happy with him for working against them. In fact, in March, Arcel had received a phone call in the middle of the night during which he was warned to "get out of the TV racket if you know what's good for you!"[48]

Arcel wasn't worried and neither was Charles, who would pocket some decent money again going against Layne, at least on paper. The promoters would get $25,000 in television money with each fighter getting $7,500, plus 30 percent of the net gate. It wasn't the money Charles was pulling in as champion, but it was far better than the peanuts he'd been making fighting the likes of Harrison and Bascom.

Everyone knew how important this fight was. Marv Jensen, Layne's manager, brought in local heavyweight Grant Butcher to help Layne, primarily a right-hand puncher, develop his left hook. Butcher was no great shakes in the ring but was said to have the best left hook of any heavyweight on the West Coast. Layne needed all the help he could get, but Butcher didn't budge the odds in Layne's favor. Charles remained a 4–1 favorite right up to the night of the fight, when, in front of a near sellout of 7,200, which produced a gate of $34,083, he gave Layne the beating of his life, dropping him in the first, sixth, seventh and tenth rounds, though at least two of those knockdowns were not ruled as such by referee Frankie Carter.

Charles, weighing 187 to Layne's 203, started faster than usual, cutting Layne over the eye with the first punch he landed. Layne ended up bleeding and bruised under both eyes and under his lower lip, as Charles, by this time completely confident in his ability to handle Layne's best punches and eager to establish himself as the logical opponent of the Marciano-Walcott winner, threw aside his usual timidity and took Layne apart piece by piece.

"The 31-year-old Cincinnati Negro put on one of the finest battles of his lengthy career when he battered the Lewiston, Utah gamester into a bloody hulk last night," one newspaper writer put it.[49] Layne was as game and ever and brought the highly partisan crowd to its feet when he rose from the tenth-round knockdown and stood toe-to-toe with Charles until the final bell, though to little avail. The decision, this time, was to be rendered by three judges rather than one near-sighted and biased old legend. Referee Carter and judges Toby Irwin and Johnny Lotsy each scored it in Charles' favor.

"I was trying for a good, clean, pretty knockout. I just couldn't make it. He's a game boy with a big heart," Charles said later. "What are you going to do with a guy who comes off his knees slugging? I think another fighter might have knocked him out tonight, but he was just too determined [for] me—and it was determination that held him up."[50] Layne had high praise for Charles as well. "Charles is the greatest fighter I ever met. He gave me more trouble than Marciano or Walcott."[51]

Still campaigning for a shot at Marciano, which somehow or other was not definite after all following the win over Layne, Charles was in the ring again a month later, this time in Toledo, Ohio, against journeyman Bill Gilliam, a 6'2" puncher from East Orange, New Jersey, who had made a name recently by fighting the highly rated Bob Baker four straight times. Though he beat Baker just once in their series, the fights were good and he handled himself well. After a points loss to the excellent Harold Johnson, Gilliam had upset the giant Cuban Nino Valdes at Johnstown, Pennsylvania, to earn the shot at Charles. Valdes was being talked about as an eventual challenger for Marciano.

Gilliam had never been stopped, and Charles couldn't do it either. In fact, he had trouble with Gilliam's style, and over the first five rounds it was anyone's fight. But from the fifth round on, Charles, a 2½-to-1 favorite, blasted Gilliam, clearly displaying the vast difference in their skill and talent levels. Charles was a world-class fighter, if a bit past it by this time, while Gilliam, who weighed 208 to Charles' 188, just was not at the same level. A short right dropped Gilliam in the tenth and final round, sealing the decision for Charles by scores of 53–47, 52–48 and 55–45.

Five days after Charles whipped Gilliam, Marciano and Walcott finally met in their long-delayed rematch. After all the ballyhoo and negotiating, it was hardly worth the wait. Midway through what had been a nondescript first round that featured mostly grappling, a whistling right uppercut caught Walcott on the chin and he flopped onto his back as though he'd been dropped from a third-story window. Referee Frank Sikora picked up the count, and Walcott, kneeling and seemingly clear-eyed, watched him quickly toll off the seconds and then jumped up a half-second after he reached "ten." Walcott claimed he misheard the count. Later he and Bocchicchio screamed bloody murder. They offered to fight Marciano again and donate their share of the purse to charity just to prove Walcott hadn't gone in the tank, at worst, or hadn't decided to just take his $250,000 and go home with all his marbles, at the least.

Though the sentiment among some was that Jersey Joe had received a quick count, this was mainly fan reaction, especially among those watching at home on television. The writers crucified him, with reason: he earned approximately $1,274 per second for his 145 seconds in the ring.

"Looking at it from the press benches I got the impression that the veteran, Walcott, welcomed the quick ending," wrote one. "This fight, if so it could be called, was bad. Bad in itself, bad for boxing, bad for sports," wrote another. Still another observed that the bout was "one of the most farcical heavyweight championship fights in the Queensberry era." In ten seconds Walcott had unwittingly undone all the good will he'd built up beating Charles. "After 23 recorded years as a professional fist fighter," wrote one respected reporter, "the former champion went out in a total disgrace, which no excuses can relieve."[52]

Eleven days later Charles busted up and stopped Omaha light heavyweight journeyman Larry Watson in Milwaukee, dropping him five times before stopping him in the fifth round. Charles, weighing 188¾ to Watson's 175¼, toyed with his opponent and took his time ending it. Marciano scouted his future opponent from ringside. "He sure is a busy, smart, fighting man," Marciano said. "Charles looked very good. Of course, he had a pretty good edge in weight against Watson, who showed plenty of gameness in there."[53] He added, "Ezz also showed he's a good body belter. I would say he is not such a terrific puncher as he is a punisher. Ezz is a good finisher once he has a man in trouble. He does a real workmanlike job in there. He never lets up."[54]

When it was over, many in the crowd of 6,850 booed Charles, in part because it was the law, apparently, and in part because he appeared to have landed a time or two below the belt, particularly in the fourth round. Marciano defended him. "It's too bad the fans boo him. He's not a dirty fighter," Marciano said. "Charles takes his fighting seriously and when a punch strays I'm sure it's not deliberate."[55]

Nine straight wins into the comeback, Charles, Mintz and Tannas were feeling good. Charles was still getting booed, but he was knocking guys out, fighting aggressively, more or less, and staying busy. Sure, most of the guys were light heavyweights and even the ones who weren't were a full level or two below the top contenders, but he was staying busy and winning. That's all he had to do to get Marciano, whose style, Charles felt, was made for him.

All he had to do was keep it up and the IBC would have no choice but to get him a title shot. After the win over Watson, Mintz and Tannas pushed for the fight but found out that at the same time they were pushing, the IBC and Weill were negotiating a deal for Marciano to face Roland LaStarza in New York. So it came down to the two of them. Who would get the title shot? A writer with a good sense for how things worked out took a stab at fortune-telling: "The best heavyweight next to Marciano undoubtedly is Charles, who has been working his way back with a two-bums-a-month campaign. But Ezzard is so cautious when he gets in with a good fighter and is such a dreadful gate attraction that the IBC will probably give Roland LaStarza the shot."[56]

He was right. It became official on July 16: LaStarza, and not Charles, would challenge Marciano for the heavyweight title on September 24 at the Polo Grounds. Weill hadn't wanted Marciano to fight again until the following year, but the rematch with Walcott had been such a farce that he felt pressure to get Rocky in the ring again to atone for it.

It made sense for the IBC to pass on Charles. LaStarza had given Marciano a hell of a fight back in 1950 at the Garden, boxing rings around Rocky early before getting hurt and floored in the fourth. Even after that he fought on even terms, using a great jab to keep Marciano off balance. Marciano had to work hard to get a split decision, and a lot of guys said LaStarza had been robbed.

"I knew how close the fight was—everyone did," LaStarza said. "It just depended on what the judges and the referee saw as important, my jabs and counterpunching or his constant attacks. But overall, I'm sure as income taxes that I outscored him."[57]

Over the next several years, LaStarza was offered fights with Louis, Walcott, Charles, and Bob Murphy. He turned down all of them because he suspected that Weill, working as the matchmaker at the Garden, was trying to get him out of the way. He'd come closer than anyone to beating Marciano—too close for Weill's liking. That's why he'd kept Marciano away from LaStarza for three years. Now, finally, Rocky had improved to the point where Weill felt LaStarza was a safe opponent. He wasn't as sure about Charles.

With Charles out of the running to be Marciano's next opponent, Mintz and Tannas sent Ezzard home for a short vacation. No use fighting him every month anymore with Marciano and LaStarza already signed for September. Charles was so disappointed that he thought about retiring. He hated the waiting around. The boredom killed him. Mintz and Tannas talked him out of quitting. Mintz got busy lining up a pair of fights that were sure to keep Charles on Marciano's short list of challengers. They would be against Nino Valdes, the big, hard-punching but inconsistent Cuban, and Harold Johnson, the highly rated light heavyweight out of Philadelphia.

The fight against Johnson came with some risk; he was fast and highly skilled, and the press respected the hell out of him, even if the fans found him dull. Valdes was the opposite: exciting but low on skill. He would be a tune-up for the Johnson fight. He was just the kind of guy that Charles, on a good night, would outbox without much trouble.

Valdes had gotten the break of a lifetime, even if he didn't know it then, in 1945 when the outstanding featherweight, Phil Terranova, was in Havana to fight Miguel Acevedo. Terranova's manager, Bobby Gleason, had Terranova at a local gym where Valdes was training, and Gleason, who like everyone else always wanted a great heavyweight, saw Valdes, big at 6'3" and 210 pounds, moving around the ring like a lightweight.

He inquired about him and was told Valdes belonged to Pincho Gutierrez, who had taken Kid Chocolate to the top in the 1930s. You don't try to steal one of Gutierrez's guys, so Gleason forgot about it until 1952, when Valdes arrived in the States. When he heard Valdes was looking for a manager he figured what the hell, with the heavyweight division what it was, what did he have to lose?

Gleason signed Valdes and found out some things right away. Valdes spoke almost no English, a failing Gleason remedied with his passable grasp of Spanish. Also, the fighter was lazy and hated training, and relied at least as much on Cuban rituals and superstition to get him though sparring sessions and matches.

Gleason countered this with the type of psychology good fight managers specialize in. The result was a short winning streak that had an effect precisely opposite to the one they'd hoped for: It scared everyone away. After fighting five times in five months, Valdes sat at home for the next five months while Gleason looked for opponents. It didn't help that Gleason ignored overtures from the IBC, who wanted Valdes on their roster. If there was one sure way to get locked out of fights, it was to ignore the IBC.

Finally Gleason got an offer but there was a catch: the opponent would be Johnson, who no one wanted to fight, even the guys no one else wanted to fight. But Gleason was desperate to make some money on his heavyweight, and sure enough, Johnson took Valdes to school in Brooklyn. It didn't help that Valdes hadn't fought in five months.

Then came an offer to face Archie Moore in Saint Louis. Gleason was no more eager to fight Moore than he'd been for Johnson, but the money was pretty good so he took the fight. Moore beat Valdes six ways from Sunday. Next came Billy Gilliam in Johnstown, the New Jersey guy Charles had beaten, and he outpointed Valdes, too.

"That's three in a row," an exasperated Gleason said to Valdes in Spanish. "What's the matter?" Valdes replied, "I don't know, someone's got a curse on me or something."[58]

After that, Bob Baker got into the act, getting a lousy decision over Valdes in West Virginia. Gleason by this time was a couple thousand in the hole on Valdes and was almost relieved when his visa ran out, forcing him back to Cuba. But while he was down there, Gleason got an idea: Why not match Valdes against the other well-known Cuban heavyweight, Omelio Agramonte, the guy Louis had beaten twice during his comeback, and make it for something like the heavyweight championship of Latin America?

That was the great thing about boxing. You could make up a title like that out of nowhere, just pull it out of your ass really, and throw in a couple guys no one cares about otherwise, but attach it to a region, and the locals would go nuts over it. Gleason had no trouble finding a promoter to go along, and in July 1953 in Havana, Valdes stopped Agramonte in the tenth round of a great slugfest.

Before Gleason knew it, his phone was ringing again. One of the callers was Angelo Dundee, the brother of Miami-based promoter Chris Dundee. Angelo wanted to know if Gleason would be interested in putting his heavyweight in with Ezzard Charles in Miami. With all the Cubans down there they'd do a tremendous gate.

"Does Chris want to get [us] killed?" Gleason asked Dundee, but pursued the fight anyway. He had good reason to. Back in 1952 Valdes had sparred with Cesar Brion before Brion's loss to Charles and had said afterward, while watching Charles beat Brion, that he was sure he could whip Charles. Gleason believed him; Valdes didn't say he could beat someone unless he was sure he could.

That was on Gleason's mind later, too, when he negotiated the fight with Mintz, who wanted a return clause in the contract. Gleason said to him, "Jake, I will give anybody a return match contract, but if you can't beat this big bum of mine, why should you want to return anywhere?"[59]

Mintz fell for it, forgetting about the rematch clause and at the same time signing an agreement for Charles to face Johnson—in Johnson's hometown of Philadelphian, no less—a month after the Valdes fight.

Everything was in place for an upset. You couldn't draw it up any better: Charles was a 6-1 favorite, had a more important fight against a much better opponent already signed, and hadn't been in the ring in almost three months. Mintz wasn't even concerned enough to insist on the rematch clause, and if handicappers were looking for more reasons to bet the underdog, the fight would be in Miami—in August. It was the kind of heat Valdes had been born in. He loved the heat. To him it was home. To Ezzard Charles it was just goddam hot.

If all that wasn't enough, Valdes's obstinacy and superstition were unsettling. When the fighters got their physicals and weighed in with the commission, both brought along the trunks they would wear during the fight. Both were white trunks with a black stripe. This wasn't permitted; one of them would have to switch to black trunks. Protocol dictated that Charles, the top-rated contender for the heavyweight title, be permitted the choice. Valdes loudly refused to switch to black trunks. It wasn't going to happen.

"Nino is very deep with this voodoo business," Gleason told the Miami commission. "Black trunks mean death and bad luck and Nino wants no part of them. He wore them against Archie Moore and got beat bad. That was enough for him. He fights according to the stars. It doesn't make sense to me, but if it helps him beat guys like Ezzard Charles, I'm all for it."[60] After a lengthy standoff and much haggling, it was agreed that Valdes would wear his white trunks turned inside out.

On the night of the fight, a sellout crowd of 3,834 crowded into Miami Beach Auditorium, generating a record gate of $15,612.50 for promoter Chris Dundee. Another thousand were turned away at the door. The crowd was overwhelmingly pro–Valdes. Charles weighed in at a career-high 191½, but was nevertheless outweighed by 18 pounds.

Things started well for Charles. He won the first three rounds handily and even came close to ending it in the second when a whistling right cross rattled Valdes against the ropes. A second right just missed; Valdes recovered and even charged into Charles before the round's end.

Starting in the fourth, a change seemed to overtake both fighters. Valdes became fearless, exuberant and impervious to the sting of Charles' punches, no matter how many landed. Charles would bang off a combination of blows of the type that had sent other recent opponents to pieces, and Valdes would take them, bang his gloves together, beat on his chest, or smile at Charles and then charge in and wail away.

Charles, meanwhile, though aggressive in his own right and industrious, couldn't hurt Valdes, couldn't get out of the way of Valdes' clubbing advances, and could not find an effective strategy. No matter what he tried he couldn't keep Valdes off. His sheer strength and awkwardness overwhelmed Charles.

Maybe a couple years ago Charles' speed would have made the difference. Maybe his body punching would have slowed down Valdes. But it wasn't a couple years ago. It was 1953 in Miami and it was hot as hell. Charles was thirty-two years old and had taken this big, crazy Cuban for granted. All those easy fights. They were poison. They had made Charles lazy. But it's too late to do anything about it when you're in the middle of a fight. You just grit your teeth and hope for the best. Charles did that, making it a hard, exciting back-and-forth scrap all the way. At the end of ten rounds it was clear who had won, and it wasn't Ezzard Charles. Two judges and referee Cy Gottfried voted for Valdes, appropriately so, 7-2-1 in rounds.

This wasn't like the last couple of times Charles had lost, against Layne and Walcott. This wasn't a robbery. He'd been beaten by a younger, stronger, more energetic, better-prepared opponent. What was worse, for a guarantee of about $6,000, he'd blown his shot at Marciano. He'd have to start all over again. It was the worst thing that could have happened. He and his team left the ring in shocked silence, heads down, each wondering how it had gone wrong and at the same time knowing exactly how it had gone wrong. They'd taken Valdes lightly. All of them.

They trudged toward the temporary comfort of the dressing room, which, although the loser's dressing room tonight, at least offered some respite from the whooping and hollering of the couple thousand Cubans still in the arena celebrating Valdes' upset. They arrived to find the door locked, and as they stood there, waiting for someone with keys to open it up, indignities piled on top of indignities, Charles cursed—under his breath but loud enough for those huddled round him to hear. He gritted his teeth and in a low, bitter voice cursed himself over and over as he stood sweating in the soaking wet bowels of a tiny arena in Miami. His team stood around him, silent, embarrassed. Finally a guy showed up and unlocked the door. Once inside, Charles got himself together to speak to the press.[61]

"Fighting is just like poker. Some nights the cards just don't fall right and you don't have a chance," he said. "I just wasn't sharp. Much too sluggish. I couldn't get my combinations working right. Valdes is tough—you can't hurt him. A couple times he hit me and I let him step right around me. I wasn't right. Three months is too long to lay off."[62]

Mintz sat in a chair in the corner of the room, looking as though he was melting right away, cell by cell. "It's our fault," he muttered. "We didn't get him ready the right way. We didn't give him time to get used to this heat."[63]

It was Jimmy Brown who gave voice to the bigger picture, saying what everyone else was thinking: the Marciano fight was gone. "This was it. Just what the IBC had been hoping and praying and waiting for. For Ez to get bumped off before he can get at Marciano. We couldn't afford to lose this one," he said.[64] Only Tannas, always the cool head, always business-first and unemotional, kept things in perspective. This was his job. It was what he was good at. He wasn't the guy who fell in love with the fighter and got his heart broken. He wasn't the guy who jumped up and down and hollered when a decision went the wrong way or who made the press laugh or who fainted in the ring. That was Mintz' job to act the fool. Tannas was a businessman. He was the numbers guy, and he knew there just weren't many good challengers out there for Marciano. All Charles had to do was get another couple wins and he'd be back on Marciano's short list. Like everything else, it was a matter of supply and demand. First they'd beat Johnson in Philadelphia, then beat Valdes in a rematch, and everything would be back to the way it was. Charles had only three weeks to get his head together, drop the extra pounds that had slowed him down against Valdes, and change his fighting mindset.

Johnson was the polar opposite of Valdes in terms of fighting style. Where Valdes was a big, emotional, lumbering clubber, Johnson was small, fast, technically sound and a superb counterpuncher. He was usually death at the box office because, as Charles was well aware, the fight crowds liked blood and guts and gory displays of violence. Johnson rarely gave them that. What he gave them was a perfect left jab thrown straight and true, and flawless balance and the cool detachment in the ring of a man who knew exactly what he was doing at every moment, and the one after that and the one after that. The fight press loved him for it, in a way they never loved Charles.

On top of all that, Johnson was just twenty-five years old and had the hunger that twenty-five-year-old fighters have—the natural, desperate hunger that Charles remembered from when he was coming up. It was a different kind from the one he had now. The hunger Charles felt now was to keep from losing ground, to try and make up for all the blown opportunities, and to have some money for later, maybe too to prove he still mattered. Charles' was the hunger of a veteran who had seen everything already, seen the fight game's ugliness up close and knew what it could do for him and what it couldn't. It was a hunger without illusions. It was enough to get him out of bed to run in the morning and to put in all the work at the gym, but it wasn't the same type that drives a young kid to the top. A young fighter believes becoming a champion will make the world perfect. An old fighter knows it makes the world tolerable, but just barely and not for long.

Not that Johnson, for all his skill and for all the hunger his youth gave him, was unbeatable. Despite his gifts he was a little chinny and had the great misfortune of coming up at the same time that Archie Moore, Charles' old dance partner, was still terrorizing the world's light heavyweights. When Charles left the 175-pound class to compete at heavyweight, Moore filled the gap, becoming the best light heavyweight in the world and not by a little. He was exactly that for ten years at least before Kearns finally let him near Maxim for the title. Moore did exactly what everyone knew he would—he outclassed Maxim, about as readily as Charles had the last couple times, and finally won the title in 1952.

But before getting the shot at Maxim, Moore had to go through everyone, and that included Johnson. He beat Johnson three times out of four, but they all were tough fights. There was also that strange night in Philadelphia in February 1950, when Johnson met Walcott, not long before Walcott lost to Rex Layne. The two battled on mostly even terms before Walcott dropped Johnson with a pair of rights just before the bell ending the second round.

Johnson seemed to have recovered, but at 1:05 of the third he dropped to the canvas without having been hit and rolled around in apparent agony while the referee counted him out. Commission Doctor Joseph Levey examined Johnson in the ring for ten minutes, eventually diagnosing injury to a vertebral disc in the small of Johnson's back. It was a strange ending to say the least, but that wasn't all. In June 1936, Walcott stopped one Phil Johnson in three rounds at Shibe Park in Philadelphia. Walcott was twenty-two years old at the time, his opponent about thirty. Phil Johnson was Harold Johnson's father. Thus, when Walcott stopped the younger Johnson in 1950, he became the first and only fighter to have stopped a father and his son—not to mention in the same town and in the same round.

None of this concerned Charles. He knew only that he had to beat Johnson, and beat him good, if he had a chance at undoing the damage of the loss to Valdes. He wasn't thrilled that the fight was taking place in Philadelphia, Johnson's hometown and also where he had been robbed in the last Walcott fight. But it was too late to do anything about that now, so he did what he could: he trained his ass off and ran all the miles. By fight week he was down to 185½ pounds, right where he figured he should be, six pounds lighter than he was for Valdes. (Johnson weighed 177.) He knew how important this fight was. The newspapers wouldn't let him forget it. "There are no ifs, ands or buts surrounding Charles' future if he loses to the ambitious Philadelphian," reported one. "He'll join that long list of former heavyweight kings who failed in campaigns to win back the top boxing prize."[65] Another wrote, "There seems to be no question but that Charles must win this one or go back to his Cincinnati gymnasium."[66] Still another characterized Charles as being "one defeat from the scrap pile."[67]

Charles responded by way of a baseball analogy, saying fans shouldn't read too much into his loss to Valdes. "If the fight fans would regard a defeat by one of their favorites the way baseball fans regard a defeat of one of their pets, they would be wise," he said. "Because the Cubs beat Robin Roberts, say, the fans don't pick him to lose again even if he's pitching against the Dodgers. They know he's a 28-game winner." He argued, "Well, 'cause I take a guy easy and use him for a tune-up and get fooled, like I did with Valdes, why should they think I've gone back? I'm still what you might call a 28-game winner too, just like a regular baseball player. I'll throw my best stuff this time because it means a lot. I wasn't bearing down on Valdes. But I will be bearing down on Johnson. So I'm telling all you," Charles warned, "don't sell little Ez short this time out. You're mighty sure to be fooled."[68]

The betting public believed Charles. Despite the loss to Valdes he opened as a 2–1 favorite, and the odds never wavered. The IBC said the winner would get the winner of Marciano-LaStarza, and certainly this was on the minds of both fighters as they entered the ring in front of 8,462 paying customers who produced a respectable gate of $37,680. It's unlikely any of those fans went home unhappy. The same could not be said of Charles.

Smaller, faster and younger, Johnson let Charles come to him and then countered him silly. In the early rounds it was almost too easy. Johnson would circle around the ring, his darting jabs keeping Charles off balance, until Charles decided to attack, usually with long, snaking right hands thrown from too far away and without very good balance. Johnson, as light on his feet as a ballroom dancer, would take a small step back and then counter with his own right. He couldn't miss. Twice in the first round he landed with enough force to stagger Charles, and it wasn't until the later rounds, when Charles got closer, that Johnson's right-hand counters lost their effect. But for all of the early rounds he tattooed the onrushing Charles, who, as in the past, spent the early rounds trying to wear down his opponent with left uppercuts to the body.

Around the fight's midway point Charles started landing more frequently, and Johnson was less inclined to stand in range. They battled furiously over the last several rounds, more than once bringing the crowd to its feet, and in the tenth Charles scored what looked like a knockdown that referee Buck McTiernan ruled a slip.

Then the decision came in: Lou Tress 7-3 for Johnson; Joe Capristo 5-4-1 for Charles; and McTiernan 6-3-1 for Johnson. Disaster. Mintz put his head in his hands and stomped around the ring crying they'd been robbed again. The crowd went nuts for Johnson. And for the second fight in a row Charles and his team trudged to the loser's dressing room, not embarrassed this time but full of indignation and outrage.

"Santa Claus arrived without snow and before winter," Charles said.[69] He was positive he'd won. Mintz jumped all over reporters who asked, quite understandably, if Charles would retire. This was a routine Charles and his team knew. It was more important now than ever that they make a stink, because they were near the end, and they wanted the shot against Marciano badly.

The problem was this: it wasn't a bad decision. It was a fairly close fight in the other guy's hometown. Even if it had been in New York or Chicago or Detroit there was no guarantee it would have come out differently. This wasn't the fourth Walcott fight or the second Layne fight. For much of the night Charles had just been outfought, and the official judges weren't the only ones who thought so. The AP scored it 5-3-2 for Johnson. The United Press had it a draw. The press, who had in the great majority sided with Charles in the last Walcott bout, mostly shrugged. If they didn't shrug they wrote his fistic obituary.

"Charles was the aggressor but he was outboxed by a confident, hungry fighter who provided ... as pretty an evening of counterpunching as this reporter has seen in years," wrote one.[70] Another writer, a New York guy who had long supported Charles, wrote, "The big touches are over for Charles, who was beaten recently by Nino Valdez in Miami and Wednesday night was beaten up by Harold Johnson, a light heavyweight." This was under a headline that read, "Charles' Heart Never in the Game."[71] Another: "This defeat seemed certain to eliminate the one time champion from any opportunity of becoming the first man to ever regain the heavyweight title."[72]

With two consecutive defeats, Charles seemed farther away than ever from getting a shot at Marciano. You couldn't have blamed him if he said to hell with it and walked away. He'd done all right for himself, all things considered. Had himself a nice home in Cincinnati for Gladys and the girls. Owned an apartment building there in town and another one in Harlem. Plus, he had the athletic club in Cincinnati and he'd invested some in government bonds. He was tempted.

An accountant told him that even with all that, if he retired now, he'd get about $200 a week if he never lifted another finger.[73] That didn't seem possible, that after all these years fighting that was all he could rely on, but that's what it was. So retiring was out of the question. Plus, he still had fighting in him. He knew he wasn't done, even if everyone else thought he was.

12. A Good Race Horse

Eleven days after the Johnson fight, with Charles back home in Cincinnati, Arcel attended Yom Kippur services at a synagogue in Boston. Afterward he ran into the fight manager Willie Ketchum outside the Hotel Manger, next to the Boston Garden. Ketchum's ties to the fight mob were numerous and longstanding, but that didn't bother Arcel. Virtually every manager in the game was dirty to some degree or another. If he associated only with those who weren't, he'd have a hell of a lot of free time on his hands.

As Arcel and Ketchum chatted, a man ran up behind Arcel and struck him on the head with a lead pipe wrapped in a brown paper bag and then sped away. Arcel suffered a concussion and lacerations on his scalp and was hospitalized for nineteen days. The fight press, who loved Arcel, rallied around him, the brave ones anyway, and reported what everyone in the business knew but couldn't, or wouldn't, say: That the assault was almost certainly the work of henchmen associated with the IBC, who didn't take kindly to Arcel working for their competition.

If Arcel had any ideas about who was responsible—and of course he did—he wasn't sharing them with the police. It wasn't worth it. He had been around the fight game all his adult life and knew what its players were capable of. He had a nice family and a good life and he wanted to keep them both. Upon returning to work he kept a decidedly low profile and within a year would retire from training fighters altogether.

13

ROCKY

Two weeks after Charles lost to Johnson in Philadelphia, Marciano squared off against LaStarza in their rematch at the Polo Grounds in New York. Although on the surface it seemed as though little had changed—LaStarza was still the swift, educated counterpuncher, Marciano the clubbing, aggressive brute—Marciano's stature had grown considerably, while LaStarza's had remained static. As a result, Marciano entered the ring as a 6–1 favorite. By the fight's halfway point, he had justified the odds. He swarmed all over LaStarza, and the challenger's offense wasn't nearly as effective as it had been in their first fight. Marciano hadn't just gotten more popular; he'd gotten better.

"The difference in Rocky between the first fight and the second was fantastic; it was much more difficult to land a punch on him [in the rematch]," LaStarza said later.[1] Marciano clubbed the challenger late in the fight and stopped him in eleven rounds. Afterward Weill surprised almost everyone by saying that Charles remained the frontrunner for the next shot at Marciano, provided he beat Johnson in a rematch he didn't know then would never happen. It didn't have to.

There still weren't a lot of heavyweights who could make everyone money against Marciano. Johnson, even with the win over Charles, was still just a light heavyweight. LaStarza had had his chance. Walcott had retired. Don Cockell, Britain's entrant, wasn't ready yet for Marciano, if he ever would be. There was Valdes, if he could put together a couple good wins, and Dan Bucceroni. Mintz and Tannas knew this field was weak and so did Weill and the IBC, who told them to get Charles a couple of wins and the fight would be made. They'd been hearing that for a good long while, but Charles didn't help himself by losing to Valdes and Johnson.

Johnson's managers weren't much interested in giving Charles a rematch. When that became apparent, Mintz and Tannas signed to fight twenty-five-year-old top-ten contender Coley Wallace in San Francisco on December 16. Coley was competent, nothing great. Born in Jacksonville, Florida, he was sent to live with his father in Richmond, Virginia, at thirteen years of age after a white woman tried to seduce him at the hotel at which Wallace worked. This was 1940 in the Deep South; his family was afraid he'd be lynched.

Later Wallace took up boxing in the army and had a solid, if brief, amateur career that included a win over none other than Marciano in the Golden Gloves at the Ridgewood Grove Arena in Brooklyn in March 1948. He started well after turning pro in 1950, winning twelve straight. But as the level of his competition improved, his performances did not, and not even the wide-sweeping influence of his manager, the infamous Blinky Palermo himself, could bestow on him talent he did not have. On the plus side he was big, at 6'2", 200 pounds. That alone would get him some wins, but size alone could take a guy only so far.

Elkins Brothers ended Wallace's winning streak when he stopped him in two rounds in 1951, and thirty-seven-year-old Jimmy Bivins, as shopworn as he was, knocked him out in nine rounds in September 1952 (though to be fair, Wallace was well ahead on points at the time of the stoppage).

Wallace was on a three-fight winning streak and rated number nine in the world going into the Charles fight (Charles was rated third, behind LaStarza and Valdes), but might have been better known as an actor than as a fighter. He'd played the role of a young Joe Louis in the feature film *The Joe Louis Story*, which debuted in theaters in the fall of 1953, just before the Charles fight. That was as far as his resemblance to Louis went, however. He never approached Louis' mastery in the ring, and that was never more evident than it was in San Francisco.

Putting on one of his best performances in years in front of a near sellout crowd that generated a gate of $21,876.75—as well as a national television audience—Charles, favored at 2–1, took Wallace apart little by little, out-jabbing, out-maneuvering, and out-punching him in every round. Wallace's best round was the second, when he landed three hard lefts that slowed Charles for a moment, but otherwise Charles controlled every second.

Weighing 190 to Wallace's 200, Charles did whatever he wanted but took his time, as always. After a long and steady but almost gentle beating, Charles delivered a screaming overhand right that finally dropped Wallace hard in the eighth. A lot of guys would have ended it in that round if not in the next, when all Wallace wanted to do was survive. But that was not Charles' way.

Charles let Wallace flounder around the ring in the ninth, a punch or two away from sweet, sweet surrender. If you didn't know better you'd have thought Charles was keeping him around just to torture him. It was just as likely that Charles was having so much fun being in complete control of a man again in a ring that he didn't want it to end. He wanted to enjoy it. Finally he put Wallace out his misery in the tenth, flooring him with another overhand right. A combination of blows floored Wallace again and referee Frank Brown stopped it without a count at 2:43, which led to some debate afterward when the ring announcer called it a knockout rather than a technical knockout.

The controversy was lost entirely on Wallace, who said, ""Ezzard is the best man I've ever been in the ring with. He has everything."[2] Palermo agreed. "The way Charles fought tonight he can lick any heavyweight living," said one of the most powerful men in all of sport.[3]

Relieved, finally, of the burden of having to make excuses to the press for a Charles loss, Mintz beamed in the dressing room where talk turned, naturally, to a fight with Marciano. "Ezzard will give the Rock a better fight than any man in the world today," he said. "I'm not saying that our boy would win, it would be a whale of a fight. Charles is just like a hometown boy in San Francisco and it would draw a million as an outdoor fight here." He got down on hands and knees and patted the floor. "This is our lucky town. I would like to hold it here."[4]

Mintz was right about that—Charles had beaten Pat Valentino and Rex Layne in good fashion in San Francisco, and now Wallace in a performance that had the newspapers fawning over Charles like he was a young kid on the way up again. "Lean and Mean Charles Back in Title Picture Again," read one typical headline.[5]

That said, Mintz seemed surprisingly at peace with the prospect of having to wait for a shot at Marciano. "Ezzard came up in the boxing world the hard way—waiting and waiting for important breaks. Now, everyone knows he should get a crack at Marciano, but he doesn't mind waiting if it works out to our advantage."[6] Publicly, Charles agreed and added he would do whatever the public wanted him to. "I waited for a long time to get the title in the first place so I guess waiting a little longer won't hurt. Although I have to admit I've been ready for quite a while. If the public thinks I should lick Valdes and LaStarza before boxing Marciano, that's all right with me. I can wait."[7] In private, he fumed and blamed the losses to Valdes and Johnson on getting bored waiting around for a title shot.

Charles wasn't kidding about wanting Valdes again. The day after the Wallace fight Mintz and Pittsburgh promoter Archie Littman met about a rematch with Valdes and then wired Bobby Gleason an offer to face the Cuban again, this time at the Gardens in Pittsburgh. The offer included a $10,000 guarantee for Valdes. Gleason never responded,[8] so Mintz went ahead with Plan B: A Chicago fight on January 13 with Bob Satterfield, the big-punching, wild-swinging, pudding-chinned 180-pounder he'd wanted to get for Charles for years.

Of course, that wasn't the way the Satterfield side told it. It was Satterfield who'd wanted Charles all along and not the other way around, insisted Satterfield's seventy-seven-year-old manager of record, Ike Bernstein. "We've been after a match with Charles ever since Bob stopped Elkins Brothers in New York in 1951," Bernstein said. "However, Jake Mintz saw fit to sidestep the issue, after promising us a chance."[9]

It wasn't as though Satterfield, from Chicago's south side, wasn't dangerous. At this point he'd logged twenty-five knockouts in forty-two wins, was riding a four-bout win streak—all by knockout—and had just upset top-rated Bob Baker with a first-round bludgeoning. He'd also knocked out Lee Oma and somehow managed to outpoint Harold Johnson. (Johnson knocked him out in a rematch two months later.) On the other hand, he'd been stopped nine times in fourteen losses. The book on him was that if you could take his punches, you knocked him out. If you couldn't, he knocked you out. As hard as he hit, that's how fragile his chin was.

Mintz had no worries about Charles being able to take Satterfield's punches. Over his seventeen-some-odd years in the ring, the last dozen or so with Mintz, Charles had really only been badly hurt one time—in Pittsburgh against Walcott. Lloyd Marshall had stopped him that strange night in Cleveland back in 1943, but he was never hurt, never concussed, the way he was against Walcott. He had one of the best chins in the game. Did he have the whiskers to take Satterfield's punches? Come on. Mintz almost felt bad taking 35 percent of the gate to Satterfield's twenty, and when you threw in the $4,000 they got from TV, it wasn't a bad deal.

Satterfield was made for Charles. He always tried so hard for the kayo that he left himself wide open for counters, and if there was a better counterpuncher in the division than Ezzard Charles, even at thirty-two years old and even fifteen pounds over his best fighting weight, no one had ever seen him. If that wasn't enough, Satterfield was inconsistent and didn't always train like he should have. He'd have a couple moments down the road, good moments too, knockout wins over Valdes and a young puncher named Cleveland Williams, but in January 1954 he was no match for Ezzard Charles. Mintz knew it. The bookies did too, and they made Charles a 7–2 favorite.

Mintz set Charles up at the Midwest AC Gymnasium, where he got solid sparring with California light heavyweight Murray Bennett, a local kid named James Chambers, right out of the amateurs, and a big heavyweight from the south side, John Holman. Tannas also brought in a guy he'd managed for a short while before getting involved officially with Charles—a big, fierce-looking ex-con named Charles "Sonny" Liston. Liston's contract was owned outright by St. Louis mobster John Vitale, and later Carbo and Palermo got their hooks in him.

Vitale was a friend of a friend and thought his guy would benefit from some sparring with Charles, so Tannas arranged it. Liston was 6'2" and 215 pounds and could punch like a mule kick, but he was ungainly and top heavy. Several sessions failed to impress Charles. Years later, after Liston had won and lost the world heavyweight title, Charles recalled their sparring sessions and said Liston was "as clumsy as he was tough."[10]

Satterfield, meanwhile, had Toxie Hall and Leo Johnson putting him through his paces at Eddie Nichols' gym, and it looked like he was in shape. You never knew when Satterfield was just going through the motions or working hard. But all reports were that he looked serious and in shape. Mintz still wasn't worried.

"The last time I seen Satterfield, Rex Layne was standing over his prone body," Mintz joked, referring to Satterfield's kayo loss to Layne in 1951 in New York in a wild slugfest. "Don't tell me that bum got off the floor again. All we want to know is, what's par on Satterfield's chin?"[11]

Satterfield, weighing 180 pounds to Charles' 189, nearly made Mintz eat his words in front of a raucous, pro–Satterfield crowd that produced an $18,134.01 gate at Chicago Stadium. In the latter half of the first round he banged home a crackling right hand that briefly stunned Charles, and when Satterfield sensed he had hurt you, there was no turning him off. He opened up and for the balance of the first he battered Charles, wobbling him at least twice and nearly knocking out his mouthpiece. Bernstein, who had predicted an early stoppage win for his fighter, looked like he might be a genius, but this was nothing Charles had never seen before. After all the men he'd beaten and all the fights he'd been in, all the storms he'd weathered and all the punches he'd taken, all the stitches and all the bruises, all the robberies and the boos, this was just another night at work.

This is what being thirty-two years old gave him. This is what all those hard fights gave him. He was a professional as far down as you could go, all the way down to his bones, and so he took some deep breaths and rode it out, rolled with the blows and waited for the bell. In the meantime he forced himself to relax and remembered to jab. In the middle of the chaos he knew he would ride it out and wait for the next round and wait for old Bob to get out of breath and leave himself open. He knew the time would come, as surely as he knew the sun would rise tomorrow. It was Satterfield's nature to do those things. And then in the second round, Charles stepped in with a right cross-left hook combination as pretty as any he had ever thrown, because it was *his* nature to do *that*, and poor Bob Satterfield was unconscious before the back of his head hit the canvas. Charles said later the hook might have been the best punch he'd ever thrown.[12]

Referee Frank Gilmore counted out Satterfield flat on his back at 1:00 exactly of round two. Ol' Bob was free to go out and party that night if he wanted, and he probably did, but Ezzard Charles had no such luxury. He had a date with Rocky Marciano coming up. He knew it, Tannas knew it, Jimmy Brown knew it. Most of all, Mintz knew it. "He was sensationally!" he stammered afterward, as helpless as ever against the wild struggle between his mind and mouth. "He was sensationally!"[13] The IBC's Gibson put it more formally, if less emotionally. "I would say Charles clinched a match with Marciano after his showing against Satterfield," he said in Charles' dressing room. "Marciano and Al Weill would be suckers to sidestep Charles after tonight."[14]

He was right, and it didn't take long for it to come together. Mintz and Tannas panicked a bit when Weill told the IBC he didn't want didn't want Marciano to fight before June, and then maybe against Dan Bucceroni; but Bucceroni was never a serious option. The Marciano-Charles match was formalized on February 4 to take place at Yankee Stadium on June 17.

Marciano, making the third defense of the title, would take home 40 percent of the gate to Charles' 20 percent. Ticket prices ran from $5 for bleacher seats all the way to $40 for ringside. There would be no home television, but the fight would be beamed to sixty-five theaters in forty-five cities outside New York via close circuit. ABC would run the radio broadcast coast to coast, and if it rained on the 17th they'd try again on the 21st. In announcing the details, Norris told the assembled press that if Marciano lost the title he would be given a return bout within ninety days. "That should give us a fine fight for September," he said, grinning. Weill, sitting next to him, nearly swallowed his cigar.[15]

Charles' wins over Wallace and Satterfield had done just what they were intended to do: Recast Charles as a savvy, hard-punching veteran who had at once renounced his old pacifist ways and rediscovered his youth. Gone was the Charles who appeared timid and hesitant against Walcott. Gone was the slow, inept Charles who'd been over-whelmed by Valdes' strength and youth. Gone too was the stale, lead-footed stalker from the Johnson fight, the one who could neither corner Johnson nor get out of the way of his counters. Surely he was a new man.

This was the magic and genius of good matchmaking. Yes, Charles was still a superb fighter and no less than the second or third best heavyweight in the world, all things considered. He was at the same time the Charles who had labored against Valdes and Johnson. He'd been matched against perfect foils in Wallace and Satterfield. Wallace had youth but was wholly inexperienced and never a world-class heavyweight anyway. Satterfield was so full of technical flaws and so entirely fragile that a Charles knockout win was a virtual certainty.

These truths were avoided in the press, because realities like these have no place in the build-up to a big fight. A fan wants to believe that a fighter is changed or re-energized somehow, as evidence that he too can transform and improve himself when it looks like he himself is washed up, and he is more than happy to pay the cost of a ringside ticket if he can share in the fantasy. This is what feeds the fight game, what gives it life, the constant cycle of beginnings, endings, and rebirths—and the hope for miracles.

Not everyone was taken in by the Wallace and Satterfield fights. The odds makers installed Charles as a 4–1 underdog to Marciano. Truth be told, the numbers who wanted or expected him to win were small. Veterans of the boxing beat had heard claims of a "new" Charles many times over the years. In the lead-up to the fight, one writer described him, fairly correctly, as "over the hill physically"[16] due in the main to his seventeen years in the ring and ninety-seven pro fights.

But this was beside the point. It never was really about Charles winning. Marciano needed challengers who could appear, on paper at least, to possess the ability to trouble him, to make him call on the reserves some still suspected that he might not possess. Almost no one wanted Marciano to lose, especially to Ezzard Charles of all people, who had probably the least profitable and least popular reign of all heavyweight champions.

Tannas, for one, believed the wins over Wallace and Satterfield were enormously important—not because they influenced public opinion, but because they were good for Charles' sensitive psyche. "We're happy now that Ezzard was passed up by Marciano last September and that Roland LaStarza got the match instead," he said. "He didn't have confidence then. Those two knockouts have boosted his confidence. He's very determined to get the title back and is in a better frame of mind. All I'm hoping is that he has an 'on' night on June 17. Then we'll get the title again."[17]

Mintz and Tannas set up Charles' training camp at Kutsher's Country Club in the Catskills Mountains in New York. Charles arrived in camp to begin training on May 10, weighing 197 pounds. He planned to come in at about 187. Marciano, who was training at Grossinger's, 14 miles down the road, had been in camp since April 2 and had already sparred 74 rounds. (April 2 was the formal opening of training camp; Rocky had been at Grossinger's off and on since December.) The press asked Charles if he felt like he was behind Marciano in conditioning already. "I've done some sparring myself. I sparred 34 rounds in Cincinnati and I recently gave a six-round exhibition in Denver with two good local boys," Charles said. "Rocky hasn't fought since September, when he licked LaStarza. I had two fights since then—knocked out Coley Wallace and Bob Satterfield."[18]

Marciano's inactivity, which was said to be due to his desire to avoid entering a higher tax bracket, was a concern for some; nine months was an awfully long time to be off, and there was sure to be some ring rust come fight night. It was the job of Marciano's brilliant little trainer, Charlie Goldman, and his sparring partners, Toxie Hall, Willie Wilson and Keene Simmons, to get Rocky sharp in camp and ready for a fighter of Charles' style and abilities.

Wilson, especially, was hired to emulate Charles. He was smooth and fast, and he boxed behind a stiff jab. He bounced left hooks off Marciano's head like no one's business early in camp, but as the fight approached Marciano got better at timing him and clubbing him to the body and with overhand rights.

Charles, meanwhile, just as he did before the Louis fight, surprised onlookers by saying he was going to stand and punch with Marciano rather than trying to outbox him. "I'll carry the fight to him. I'll be more aggressive than ever in training and I'll try to beat Marciano at his own aggressive game in Yankee Stadium," he said.[19]

A writer asked him why in the world he would do that when he had the speed yet and the skills to out-maneuver Marciano from a distance. "Because he's easy to hit," Charles replied. "I can nail him more often than he can hit me if I go after him. Nobody's ever really gone after him. They've let him force the fight. I've got a knockout punch in either fist, and I hit a lot faster than he does. I'll keep him so busy he won't be able to stalk and get set to throw every punch."[20]

This wasn't just talk. From the first day of camp Charles was especially hard on his sparring partners, particularly to the body. A week into training, Jimmy Walker, a heavyweight out of Orange, New Jersey, had to leave camp because Charles either broke or badly bruised his ribs.[21]

Brown and Mintz brought in Bill Gilliam, a stablemate of Walker, Gene Jones of Camden, and Chubby Wright of New York to round out the sparring team. Charles rarely took a backward step against any of them. Joe Louis, the press' favorite on-site expert, was incredulous after watching Charles spar: "You don't get in there and mix with Marciano. The way to beat Marciano should be to stick with the left and then throw the right when he misses. If Charles fights Rocky like he fought against me he could beat Marciano. But he doesn't seem to be training for that kind of fight."[22] He added, certainly for effect, "That man is committing suicide."[23]

It never would have occurred to Louis that other experts had said the same thing about Charles four years earlier, when he was training to face Louis, and that in truth Charles had stood right in Louis' punching range for much of the night. Even after all this

Heavyweight contender Coley Wallace slips inside a Charles left hand in the third round of their bout in San Francisco on December 16, 1953. Charles stopped Wallace in the tenth round, leading to a bout with hard-punching Bob Satterfield the following month (courtesy Craig Hamilton of Jo Sports, Inc.).

time, Louis had to believe Charles had outboxed him, when in reality Charles had *outfought* him. Louis was like all the other heroes: When time stripped him of all his greatness, like it does to all great men, he responded, as they all do, by clinging to a great ego because it was all he had left.

Walcott gave Charles a similar warning. "You don't want to walk into him and trade punches. That was the mistake I made in Chicago the second time I fought him when he knocked me out so quick."[24] Walcott may have been well-intentioned, but like Louis, his advice was self-serving. He had not "walked into" Marciano to trade punches the night Marciano stopped him with a single uppercut in the first round. On the contrary, he backpedaled furiously, threw a few meaningless jabs and clinched whenever Marciano got close.

Charles was polite but unreceptive to the warnings. He believed he could knock Marciano out by doing what no one else had done—walking right to him and blasting away. On one level it made sense. Marciano had made a career of chasing down boxer-types, cutting the ring off, getting inside and knocking them out. What would happen if he became the prey rather than the predator?

That said, Charles' aggression wouldn't be worth much if he couldn't hurt Marciano. That was the key. The press, having seen Marciano go to war with Walcott, a much harder puncher than Charles, doubted Marciano could ever be badly hurt. He had a chin made of steel.

Charles disagreed, saying the fight would not go the distance if he could "get in some of the punches I've been practicing. If I get in some of those punches I don't think it will go to a decision." He repeated something he'd said after knocking out Satterfield in Chicago, when he'd been asked how badly Satterfield had hurt him in the first round. "Nobody has a steel chin. Some seem to absorb more than others, but if you land solid they go. Lots of times you're riding with the punch or turning your head away and they're just glancing blows, even if they look good. But if it lands really solid, nobody can take it."[25]

Moreover, Charles and Brown had noticed while watching film of Marciano's fights that few ever went to his body. Charles had always been a dedicated body puncher, especially with the left uppercut and especially over the first half of a fight. He was willing—some would say too willing—to give up a few rounds early for the benefit a concerted body attack would pay later on. This had cost him a couple times, notably in the second Rex Layne fight and against Johnson. But in Brown's view, a body attack was critical against Marciano.

"The whole camp is very body-conscious—very interested in what will happen when Ez rips into Rocky's breadbasket," Brown said. "Nobody's ever really gone after his stomach before, probably because of his crouching style. But we do know his reactions haven't been good to the few punches landed there. The movies show Rocky can't take it downstairs." A writer asked if he wasn't he concerned he was revealing some secret to the enemy. "Marciano has spies in camp here every day," Brown replied. "They can see what Ez is doing."[26]

Of course, this all was just talk to Marciano, who was as confident and as unflappable as they came—both inside the ring and out. Nothing fazed him, even letters he began receiving in March that ordered him to throw the fight against Charles or suffer dire consequences. The four letters, sent over a three-month span, threatened to kill Rocky and his "ugly, fat family." Marciano's father also received an extortion letter, and Al Weill received at least three phone calls, one threatening to kill both him and Marciano.

The FBI's first suspect was Weill, who they believed might be writing the letters in an attempt to drum up publicity for the fight. It wasn't until June that he was ruled out as a suspect after police compared handwriting samples—and Marciano received another letter.

Each of the letters, which had been mailed in Pennsylvania, carried the same general message—that Charles had no chance against Rocky "without a little cooperation," and that the author's life savings were bet on the challenger. "Listen Cocky Rocky," one of the letters began. "We mean business." Another threatened, "If you think that it is worth the lives of your loved ones to win an old boxing match, go ahead."

The letters were eventually found to have been written by twenty-three-year-old Glenolden, Pennsylvania, resident John Joseph Hannigan, when an official from the Chester, Pennsylvania, post office contacted the FBI about obscene letters several young girls in the area had received. The handwriting matched the handwriting in the letters that had been sent to Marciano. When questioned by police, Hannigan, who lived with his parents, admitted writing the letters simply because he "was for the underdog," and ultimately the extortion charges against him were dismissed.[27]

Meanwhile, Norris, who had predicted the fight would bring in a crowd of at least 40,000 and do a $500,000 gate, grew anxious when the fight approached without the benefit of any of the usual fight-game trappings designed to bring in the fans: good-guy/bad-guy scenarios, "secret" strategies, rumors of injury, etc. Both Marciano and Charles were mature, courteous professionals who held no personal animosity toward one another beyond that which was required to win the boxing match. Above all, they were gentlemen focused on preparing for a difficult and important task. It fell on the publicists, then, to create provocative stories, so they cranked them out.

There was the one that had a thunderstorm arriving in the middle of the night and producing lighting that struck a tree ten feet from the cottage in which Charles slept. Then an improbable midnight fire that broke out two nights later, setting ablaze a cottage one hundred yards down the hill from where Charles slept peacefully, oblivious to the presence and activity of fifty firemen. There were others, notably one that had Marciano mysteriously losing his appetite. Most were aimed at creating doubt over Marciano's superiority, because even if everyone loves an execution, it's more fun when the condemned makes a fight of it.

The fight press, desperate for something, anything, they could use to juice up their columns, jumped at the possibility that Charles was injured when he decided to take a day off from training a week before the fight. What else could it be but an injury? Didn't he know he was fighting to regain the heavyweight title in a week? Charles, to their dismay, gave them nothing. "I just want to hold what I got. Up there in the ring I see everything, I can do everything I want. Anything comes into my mind, I can do it," he said. It wasn't boasting. He had peaked. He was as ready as he could be and didn't want to over-train, as he believed he had in preparing for the third Walcott fight. "I don't have any fatigueness [sic]. I just want to hold what I've got. Couldn't see any use in working today."[28]

Attempts at creating higher expectations for Charles mostly failed, at least among the newspaper boys. In one poll conducted a few days before the fight, twenty-eight out of thirty-three writers picked Marciano.[29] Those who sided with Charles thought his slashing punches would succeed at cutting Marciano around the eyes and might result in a stoppage win. Charles fared better, though just barely, among his boxing brethren, the more scientific boxers, many of whom still resented Marciano's connections and lack of physical grace. The great former champion Barney Ross said Charles would stop Marciano "within four rounds." Walcott predicted Charles would win "easily," and Billy Conn picked Charles to "outbox" Marciano.[30]

The punchers liked Marciano. Louis predicted a Marciano win in ten rounds. Jack Dempsey said, "I like Marciano in 10 but I've got to give Charles a chance because of Marciano's inactivity."[31] LaStarza, who on two distinct nights had built large, early leads against Marciano only to see them crumble under Marciano's will and power, answered the question the only way he could: "Charles is a slashing fighter, a remarkably good fighter. Sure, he can outbox Marciano. But for how long?"[32]

On fight night, Charles weighed 185½, slightly lighter than planned. Marciano was 187½. Asked for about the millionth time how he would handle Marciano's punching power, Charles, clearly tense and with his game face on, snapped, "I know he can hit. I can hit, too."[33] Charles hadn't been so tense before a fight since he beat Louis. It may have been because it all had come so easily to Marciano. He had never had to go through the kind of guys coming up that Charles had. The guys Charles fought on the way up were the guys no one else wanted to fight, and he fought them over and over for peanuts. There was no Charley Burley on Marciano's record. There was no Jimmy Bivins or Archie Moore. Marciano never saw a guy in his life like Kid Tunero or Elmer Ray or Joey Maxim.

Rocky had all the connections he needed at the IBC to make life easy, and the public embraced him like they never had Charles. Marciano was on the *Ed Sullivan Show*. Hollywood stars Debbie Reynolds and Eddie Fischer popped into training camp when they were in the neighborhood. Jerry Lewis and Frank Sinatra were pals. Lewis once said to him, "Do you realize what you are, Rock? You are the boss of the world."[34] Even when he was the heavyweight champion, Ezzard Charles wasn't the boss of anything—not even Cincinnati. So yes, Charles was tense.

Tannas put it plainly for the press: "It's now or never for Ezzard. He knows it's his last chance and he's never been so determined before. He's right on edge. I hope we don't get any rain to spoil it."[35]

It did not rain—not that it would have mattered. Most of the 47,585 fans who showed up on fight night—exceeding even Norris' estimates—would have come out in a blizzard. The type that trudged out to Yankee Stadium on a Thursday night to see Rocky defend the heavyweight title against Charles was there because he sensed he might see something special. He didn't need the fighters to insult one another. He didn't need injury rumors or near-disasters or other fight-game bullshit. He didn't need the fight writers to sell it. This kind of guy knew a good fistfight when he saw one. That's all he needed. He had to get up early the next morning and go to work unless his foreman gave him off, but he was going to see this fight if he had to take six buses and two subways to do it. He was going to get his goddam hotdog and sit in seats that were so far from the ring that if the boys had the same color skin he wouldn't know who was who, but he was going to scream and holler for all he was worth, and it would probably be for Marciano to brain Charles good.

Afterward he'd get a beer with his buddies or with his girl, and before the long ride home a coffee at the diner. The next day at work they'd talk about the big fight. The guys in the suits who sat in the big offices with pretty secretaries would talk about the Senate McCarthy hearings, but him, he'd talk about the big fight, and how he was there and how great it was. This guy, this fight fan, he knew it was going to be special. He could feel it. Real fight fans always can. So they all came out on a Thursday night, all 47,585 of them, to see something special.

No heavyweight champion had ever regained the crown. They all tried to, because the money runs out so fast and the ride is over so quick. Even the really great ones couldn't pull it off. Not John L. Sullivan, not Jim Corbett, not Jim Jeffries. Even Jack Johnson couldn't do it. Dempsey, as great as he was, tried to do it and couldn't. Even Louis, the greatest heavyweight who ever breathed—even Ezzard Charles would admit that—couldn't get the title back once he'd lost it (or, in his case, given it up). Most of them never came close.

Against Marciano at Yankee Stadium, worn-out old Ezzard Charles came closer than any of them. For five rounds he looked like a sure bet to do it. Charles did everything he and Jimmy Brown said he was going to do. He went straight to Marciano. He banged his body with right hands and left hooks. He shot straight right hands to Marciano's head and landed a hell of a lot of them. He had Marciano bleeding from the nose in the very first round and when Marciano tried to rough him up the way he roughed up everyone else, Charles gave it right back to him inside. He even made Marciano do a little two-step. He didn't knock him down the way Walcott had (he wasn't that kind of puncher, he knew that), so he just kept banging away, always a step ahead of the clumsy champion, and quicker, punching and stepping around, punching again, stepping around.

Charles hit Marciano a right hand in the fourth round that he brought all the way from Lawrenceville, as hard as he had ever hit anyone, as hard as he'd hit old Bob Satterfield. It broke open an old wound over Marciano's left eye, the one Johnny Shkor gave him in Rhode Island in 1950. Later it took ten stitches to close. When Marciano walked through it you figured Charles had to be a little discouraged, or panicked. If he was he didn't show it. He kept banging away at Marciano and turning him, sidestepping to get good punching angles and firing.

For five good rounds Charles gave it to Marciano but good, better even than LaStarza had given it to him when Rocky was still fighting ten-rounders. Marciano was such a bloody mess that later a tabloid ran a cover photo of him from mid-fight with a headline that read, "When to Stop a Fight!"[36] Charles knew he was getting good work done when Marciano hit him twice after the bell ending the fourth round. It was out of frustration. The problem was that Charles had to work awfully hard to keep Marciano honest, and five rounds of beating on him, fending him off and ducking his pressure could wear a man down fast, even one as focused and conditioned as Ezzard Charles was on this night. Starting in the sixth, Marciano started to get through a little. He started getting closer. Maybe it was nine months of ring rust falling off, maybe it was Charles tiring, just a little. Being thirty-two years old and near the end of a long, long road will do that to a man. Either way, Marciano began to break through. Where before he took five or six punches to get close and land one, now he took four. Before long it was three to land one and one of Rocky's was worth three of Ezzard's. Physics said that. And Charles' punches were slowing down, just a bit. Every once in a while he slapped with the hook instead of turning it over. He was more willing to clinch on the inside, where earlier he had pushed Marciano back.

Charles and his team out for a stroll on the grounds of Kutsher's Country Club in the Catskills, New York, location of Charles' training camp for his June 17, 1954, challenge of Rocky Marciano for the heavyweight world title. From left to right, Jimmy Brown, Jake Mintz, Charles, and Tom Tannas (courtesy Craig Hamilton of Jo Sports, Inc.).

By the seventh the left side of Charles' face started to show swelling from Marciano's overhand rights, but he kept fighting back, running Marciano into shots and then stepping around, stepping around, but now when he stepped around Marciano was right on top of him, always throwing punches, and the only way to stop him, to get a breath, was to grab him and hold him.

Even that didn't work some of the time because Marciano was so damn strong. He'd shove those meaty forearms in Charles' face and throat and push him back. Charles would get some room then to breathe and then Marciano would be on him again, all fists and elbows and shoulders, and he wouldn't stop. He just wouldn't stop. Poor Charles had to wonder where Marciano got the energy and the hate to throw all those punches, so many of them, one after another after another, all hard, heavy blows. He didn't know that Goldman had prescribed more roadwork than usual for Rocky as a counter to Charles' planned body attack. Marciano already trained with the obsession of a lunatic. The extra roadwork up and down the Catskill Mountains, coupled with Marciano's deepest and most terrible insanities, conspired to make him, late in a grinding, bloody prizefight, something closer to animal than human. Charles was still holding his own in the eighth when Marciano grabbed his head with his left glove and with the right banged him with uppercuts. One of them caught Charles in the throat, on the Adam's apple. You couldn't blame Marciano; when you threw as many bricks as he did you were bound to hit something soft and vital sooner or later. But something went out of Charles then that he never got back. Up to the tenth round it was still a fistfight, if one headed fairly clearly in one man's favor. After the tenth it was a flogging. The question wasn't around who would win, because it was clear by then that Marciano had worn Charles down like he wore everyone down; there was a reason he'd knocked out his last ten opponents. It was about whether Charles would make it to the final bell.

There were moments when Marciano belabored him with three or four clubbing blows in a row, each thudding off Charles' skull with the sickening smack you would expect to hear from a ball bat making contact with a watermelon. Charles looked close to quitting. Later a writer observed, "There were times when Charles, sitting in his corner, looked as though he wanted to cry with discouragement and pain. He always came back for more though, riding with most of Marciano's best blows, countering gamely and accurately."[37]

The crowd, openly rooting for Marciano from the start, found itself, if not rooting for Charles, then cheering his bravery and his heart and his foolishness, when there was a perfectly good canvas at his feet of which he merely had to avail himself to make it all stop.

But as the eleventh turned into the twelfth and the twelfth into the thirteenth, it became clear that not only was Charles not going to surrender, he would try to win right until the last, even as his face swelled to such a degree that you wondered if he ever would look like himself again. This was not the fighter he was supposed to be. He was supposed to go quietly and honestly early on, or run for his life and turn it into a stinker the way he had against Walcott and so many others. He did neither. As the last seconds of the fight ticked away, the crowd, still all for Marciano, of course, had to shake their heads and marvel at old Ezzard Charles, whom many of them had booed over and over throughout his long career for what they saw as cowardice.

Even they had to admit he was no coward on this night. In the last rounds some around ringside were heard hollering, "Stay up, stay up Charles!"[38] It wasn't only the fans who were taken by Charles' mettle.

"No longer can anyone question Ezzard's courage or determination," observed one writer in his column the day after. "He was far greater in defeat than he ever had been in victory."[39] Another wrote glowingly, "Please remember that this was the same Charles who had covered up outrageously and run like a scared rabbit for the last three rounds against Jersey Joe Walcott ... but that rabbit was a lion last night."[40]

By the time it was over a thinking man would deem it an insult to refer to either Marciano or Charles as "prizefighters," because no sane man would put himself through what they had for mere money. The papers said Marciano went home with $200,586 and Charles with $100,293, and sure that was a hell of a lot of money to a working man, but they'd have gotten that if either had quit halfway through.

It wasn't the money that kept Rocky coming through the blood and the hailstorm of right crosses and body shots. It wasn't the thought of new suits that kept Ezzard standing and trying right until the end, when he had to know that landing even the best punch of his life wouldn't be enough to turn things around. Even though everyone knew by the end who had officially won—it was Marciano, of course, by scores of 8–6–1, 8–5–2 and 9–5–1— Charles had won too, especially among the 1,500 or so working press assigned to cover the fight. "If Ezzard had fought all his fights the way he did against the rock-ribbed, rock-jawed and rock-fisted Rocky, he would have been the heavyweight champion of the world for a much longer time," observed one writer, who rarely covered Charles favorably.[41]

"It was agreed by everybody on the boxing beat yesterday that Ezzard Charles was a big winner in his fifteen-round fight with Rocky Marciano at the Yankee Stadium Thursday night," wrote another.[42] "This was one of the great fights for the heavyweight championship. It is no disparagement of the invulnerable champion to say that it was Charles who made it so,"[43] reported one more. The fight itself was praised as well. "Never in modern times had a 15-round fight for the heavyweight championship of the world been more dramatic," gushed one periodical.[44] Charles, for his part, though beaten and battered, was unbowed. Though he kept reporters waiting outside his dressing room for forty minutes, presumably to have his many bruises and swellings tended to, he was defiant and already half-dressed when finally interviewed. "Marciano is not the best fighter I ever fought. In fact, I don't think he beat me; I think I won the fight," he said. "He's strong and throws a lot of punches but he didn't give me as tough a fight as Joe Walcott did. In fact, all of my fights with Walcott were tougher. He didn't hurt me near as much as Walcott did."[45]

Charles didn't say this as much as he croaked it and performed a bit of layman's sign language while Tannas helped to interpret. Marciano's uppercut to the throat had apparently taken the better part of his ability to speak. It also changed the tone of the fight. "I thought I won and there wouldn't have been any doubt about it if it hadn't been for that," he said. "I was ahead when he hit me with it and it slowed me down."[46]

Most gave Charles the benefit of the doubt about the punch to the throat, but he was all alone on the scoring—except for Louis, who claimed he had Charles winning 7–6–2. This probably had more to do with Louis' resentment of a plodder and clubber like Marciano having Louis' old belt than it did with how the fight went. Marciano, who received reporters in his dressing room even before his eye was stitched up, had nothing but praise for Charles. "It was my toughest fight," Rocky said. "He hit me with some good right hands and hurt me in three or four different rounds. But I was never in any real trouble except for the cut. I felt it was a close fight until about the 10th round. After that I was sure I had it. His punches were losing their early steam and I thought I had a good chance to get him."[47]

There was immediate talk of a rematch. Weill had planned to take Rocky to England to face Cockell after the Charles fight, but a rematch made more sense in every way. There was talk of Marciano's defending against the winner of the upcoming Nino Valdes–Tommy Jackson fight, but that could wait too. A rematch made perfect sense, and it was a done deal almost as soon as the two left the ring. "If Rocky's eye is all right by that time, he will fight Ezzard again in September," Weill told reporters.[48] Norris, almost giddy over the receipts from the first match, thought a rematch might "do a million."[49] Everyone was on board. Marciano went off to vacation and heal up in Cape Cod.

Charles went home to Cincinnati feeling better than he had in a while. He'd lost, but he knew he was getting another chance. The best news was that the rematch would happen soon—probably in September. Though many questioned the wisdom of putting him in with Marciano so soon considering the beating he'd taken, as far as he was concerned the sooner it happened, the better. The boredom and waiting was what did him in against Valdes and Johnson. After that, Tannas and Mintz had told him he better start fighting like he knew how or get out. He listened. Charles felt he knew what he'd done wrong against Marciano. For one, he'd stopped going to the body when he opened that cut up over Marciano's eye in the fourth. Rocky was so easy to hit with the right hand he couldn't resist going after that cut. Also, he came in too light. He believed that if he could get more weight behind his punches he could get Marciano out of there. So rather than coming in in the high 180s he'd get up to the low 190s for the rematch. And he wouldn't back off the gas. "You have got to press against a guy like Marciano," he said. "Last time I got into a defensive groove after taking an early lead. I eased off more than I intended and could not get started again. A man can stay 90 rounds if he wants to do that. I want to win and I know you can't win on the defensive."[50]

On July 30 the fight was finalized for September 15 at Yankee Stadium again, with the contracts signed on August 4. Like last time there would be no home television, but 70 theaters in 51 cities would show the fight, and CBS radio would broadcast in America and Canada. Marciano would get the customary 40 percent champion's cut to the challenger's 20 percent. Charles did some light training at his gym in Cincinnati in early August and opened camp at Kutsher's again in Monticello on August 15. Tannas and Mintz brought in regular sparmates Chubby Wright, Al Smith, and Gene Jones and added recent Charles victim Colley Wallace. By the time camp ended a month later, Charles had put in 106 rounds against the three of them, right on target. As promised, he concentrated on heavier punching, but he would never be a mere puncher, which is how he viewed Marciano. All Marciano had was his punch. Charles was better than that.

"He's got to fight hard even in a gym. He doesn't know any other way. He can't lay back and box, study moves like I do," Charles said. "He's got to finish every punch he starts because that's his physical makeup. I am looking for three things in my training—wind, speed and timing. I know I can punch and I don't kid myself that knocking out sparring partners will inspire me. I'm as good a puncher as Marciano, believe me that. I've also been hit a lot harder than Marciano hit me."[51]

Of course, Charles was not the puncher Marciano was; he wasn't close. The knockout wins over Wallace and Satterfield had fooled some of the fans and press, and they had fooled him, too. A fighter is more vulnerable to self-delusion than most and this is for good reason; he must believe he is better than he is, especially when the world sees him as the underdog, which was the case here. It is how he convinces himself to go through with it. Later in camp he told the press, "I'm concentrating on harder hitting this time. Throwing more punches too. I'm getting more power into my left hook following a right cross. It didn't come easy for a while but now it's flowing."[52] He added, "I plan to fight and not box

Charles' mother, Mrs. Alberta Moss, pays a visit to Ezzard's training camp while he prepares to face Rocky Marciano for the heavyweight world title in June 1951 (courtesy Craig Hamilton of Jo Sports, Inc.).

Rocky. This is against the advice of many of my friends and advisors, but I not only think I can beat him, I think I have an excellent chance of stopping him."[53]

Charles' brave talk was welcome in the Marciano camp. The more the challenger wanted to stand and punch the easier it would be for Marciano to catch him with something big. And they already knew from the first fight that although Charles could hurt Rocky, he was not a real threat to stop him unless it was by a cut. Outside that, they couldn't have been happier about Charles' professed strategy. "Charles will take liberties now. He went 15 rounds with Rocky and he wasn't knocked down," Weill said. "Maybe he thinks Rocky can't punch and will take chances. I hope so. It will make it easier for Rocky if Charles opens up."[54] Marciano trained with his customary zeal, logging just under 120 rounds sparring by the time he was done, against the quartet of Bob Golden, Big Gil Newkirk, Joe Gannon and Keene Simmons. If the fight press thought selling the first fight was hard, they hadn't seen anything yet. Every fight for the heavyweight title was big, but Norris wanted this to be an extravaganza and it wasn't heading in that direction in the weeks leading up to the fight. One of the main reasons was that all possible angles had been exhausted in the build-up to the first fight. What could the writers say that hadn't already been said? It wasn't as though Marciano and Charles were busy creating new ideas for them to write about. They were busy getting in shape. So the writers struggled. Finally the Associated Press came up with a novel angle spinning off Charles' temperament, which was always suspect. They sent a psychiatrist, Dr. J.J. Moreno, out to the fighters' training camps to psychoanalyze them, report his findings and then pick the fight's winner.

In the subsequent series, the psychiatrist described Charles as a "dreamer type" who in his dreams was "a mighty invincible fighter who sweeps all before him in a reckless, savage, destructive fashion" but "loses the spontaneity he has in his dreams" because of his myriad "inhibitions." Marciano, on the other hand, had "presence of mind" and "the ability to concentrate immediately on the crisis," and, unlike Charles, had no inhibitions. The good doctor, after noting and then dismissing the possibility that Charles might "knock out Marciano or anyone else if he could wipe out his inhibitions in a frenzy—just for 30 seconds," picked Marciano to win by kayo in eight rounds.[55]

Adding to the press' trouble generating interest in the fight was the unfortunate reality that very few of them gave Charles any chance at all of winning. He was an old thirty-three after all, had fought about the best he possibly could last time out, and had still come in second. How could he improve on that performance, especially after the beating he had taken? Marciano, meanwhile, figured to be better; he wasn't coming off a nine-month layoff this time and there was little chance that he'd be over-trained for this one, as many thought he was for the first match. Plus, he'd proven that even if he couldn't stop Charles, he had what it took to wear him out.

Lastly, three months and endless re-examination had put a sharper focus on the precise nature of what Charles had accomplished in June. Even minor miracles lose most of their magic on close inspection and especially when there's nothing else to talk about. "Ezzard did make a fine fight of it, the best of his life," reminded one scribe, who obviously had never seen Charles at middleweight or light heavy. "But it was a losing fight. It wasn't that he almost won; it was only that he survived when it seemed he must get knocked dead."[56]

Indeed, Marciano opened as a 4–1 favorite, and despite all the tough talk from Charles and his camp, odds never budged an inch in the challenger's direction. In fact, by fight night Marciano was favored 6–1. The odds were 3–1 that he'd knock Charles out. The only expert willing to go on record picking Charles was Louis, still nursing his resentment for the champion.

"I thought Ez won the last time. He will do it officially this trip."[57] Louis' contribution notwithstanding, prospects for a giant gate were reduced further when the fight was postponed on the 15th because of rain in New York, and then again on the 16th. Norris was forced to hand out $60,000 in ticket refunds. When the skies finally cleared on the 17th, the start time was moved to 11:00 p.m. because of a Phillies-Giants game at the Polo Grounds and because Walter Cartier and Willie Troy, a pair of middleweight pugs, were fighting one another on national television in Washington, D.C.

So all things considered, Norris had to be reasonably satisfied with the night's final numbers—a paid attendance of 34,330 (13,200 fewer than the first fight) producing a gross gate of $352,654, plus $160,000 from radio and an estimated $125,000 in theater receipts. On paper at least, it all made Ezzard Charles about $90,000 richer. And it was the hardest $90,000 he ever made.

Charles did well enough in the first round. At 192 pounds, he was bigger, and when he and Marciano wrestled inside he held his own and even managed to rip home a few uppercuts. In the second he was backing away when Marciano landed a thudding right under the heart. That was when everything went to hell.

"I could hear him grunt. I knew I had him then," Marciano said later.[58] You could see the fight go out of Charles. It was over at that moment, even if it went another six rounds. "A different look came into [Charles'] eyes," one of the writers recalled later. "It wasn't fear that front-rowers read there so much as defeat.... He felt: I can't win."[59]

Before the fight a veteran of the boxing beat had predicted this very moment, when Charles would be forced to recall the horror of the first match. "When Ezzard is hit again, he will remember," he wrote. "He won't quit, because he is not a quitter. But he will know."[60] Charles stumbled from the blow, the shock of it. Marciano crashed after him, and three wild, ax-swinging right hands didn't so much concuss Charles as convince him that a brief break would be a good thing, and going to all fours he embraced the temporary safety of the canvas. In his right mind and at his best those punches wouldn't have stood a chance of landing. In truth, none of them landed very flush, but on this night they didn't have to. He rose at two and made eye contact with someone in his corner, and his was not a look that said, "I am okay. I am in control." It was a look that said, "I don't know how this has happened or what's gone on and I don't plan on being here for very long."

For the next five rounds Charles stood right in front of Marciano, teetering, stumbling, clinching whenever he could, and doing just enough to keep from getting knocked out. Marciano's own clumsiness and ineptitude helped here but also prolonged Charles' agony. Rocky was like a novice farmhand struggling through slaughtering a prize hog. He tried and was earnest but just wasn't skilled enough to be merciful, and as a result his victim suffered more than he should have.

Every once in a while he exploded with a clumsy combination. Every punch Rocky landed hurt—especially those he landed after the bell. Referee Al Berl warned Marciano, ever so gently, after the second, fifth and seventh rounds for hitting late, but what difference did it make? Charles couldn't get out of the way of legal punches any better than he could illegal ones. Later people said it was because of his weight. "I gave Ezzard a good chance until I heard what he weighed," Dempsey told the press. "He didn't figure to do much at 192 pounds."[61] Rocky too thought Charles was too big, saying afterward, "He was heavier and it didn't do him any good."[62] But it wasn't the weight. Or, more accurately, it wasn't *only* the weight. It was the weight; Charles had no business weighing that much against anyone, especially not a machine like Marciano. But it was also the memory of the first fight. And it was eighteen years in prize rings. It was Marciano's strength and his will and the knowledge Charles had come upon the hard way in June that even if he beat on Marciano for five or six rounds, beat the hell out of him, Marciano would still be all over him, punching, mauling, butting, pressing, always pressing. And, Marciano was better this time. He was harder to hit and more accurate.

In the sixth Charles almost won in spite of himself. By sheer luck he split open Marciano's nose in such a way that, theoretically, the fight could have been stopped. "He turned to throw a right and hit me with his elbow. It bled like anything. I knew something was wrong because blood was running from it like a faucet," Rocky said afterward.[63]

The newspaper boys and Goldman played it up later like the fight was on the verge of being called and Rocky had to go for the knockout. In truth Berl would have been dumped in the East River if he'd stopped it with Rocky still coming forward throwing punches. You didn't stop a Marciano fight because of a little blood. If Berl had any guilt or anxiety over it, Charles did him a favor in the next round when he crumbled under a surprisingly short left hook followed by several clubbing overhand rights.

For appearances he got up at five, but when he went down again a moment later he took the full count from a squat and then jumped up a second after Berl's count reached ten. The official end came at 2:36. It was the same way Walcott had done it in his own rematch against Marciano, and it made you think there had to be something special about Marciano that he made good, strong, proud fighters like Walcott and Charles essentially quit in rematches.

Marciano was that kind of fighter. It wouldn't have been so bad if his speed and technique were better and he were able to take a guy out with just a punch or two the way Louis did. When Louis stopped a guy he did it early and with a ghastly suddenness so there was little pain involved. It was almost peaceful. Not so with Rocky. He just beat on you until part of your insides died, and the next time you weren't willing to give up that much. It wasn't worth it. So you stayed down and worried about the critics later. Afterward they came after Charles hard.

"[This] was a more familiar Charles, the Charles of the spiritless road shows with that old trouper Jersey Joe, Charles the Ferdinand, who wished they would open the gate because he really didn't want to hurt anybody and he didn't want anybody to hurt him," wrote one.[64] "I believe Charles could have got up before the final count. I think he chose not to get up," wrote another.[65] "Seen from just a few feet away [Charles'] eyes looked clear," reported one more. Another, long a Charles supporter, observed that he appeared "gladdened" by the knockout.[66] "I wouldn't say Ez quit," a fight game veteran said to a writer in Charles' dressing room afterward. "Sure he was hit good and hurt to the body where it don't show. But I will say this, I've seen some fighters get up better."[67]

Charles' demeanor in the dressing room didn't make him any friends either, and if you'd never been in that position, where you thought you had full control of a situation and then it suddenly became more horrible than you'd imagined it could be and you surrendered almost immediately to it in your mind, without remorse, happily almost, then Charles' conduct didn't make much sense. But other prizefighters, especially those who had fought Marciano, or men like him, had to get it.

They knew that the only way to still see yourself as a man and as a fighter after having surrendered so easily in your mind was to create a world in which it had never happened. So whereas after the first fight with Marciano he had croaked, angrily and with great pride to the assembled press and through a swollen, lumpy mask, this time he smiled, casually and without irony, unmarked and unembarrassed. And he seemed to have been in a fight other than the one everyone else had seen.

"I was up [before 10]," he said. "I know I was up. My knees were off the canvas. I was groggy, but sure I could have finished the round. Two more rounds I'd have won the fight."

The writers were incredulous. "How would you have won the fight, Ez?" they asked.

"He'd have been cut up. Two more rounds he'd have been cut up," he answered, while buttoning up a baby-blue dress shirt. They asked him what he did differently than the last time. "I decided I'd knock him out," he said. "I tried to knock him out. I busted his nose with the left jab. I busted his eye with the left jab. Two more rounds I'd have won the fight."

Just then Gladys walked into the dressing room, a silver-blue mink stole around her shoulders. Behind her was Louis.

"Hey!" Charles greeted them, smiling. "No women in the dressing room!"

They all had a laugh. One of the writers asked Charles if he was going to retire. "I'm going to go on fighting," he said. "Knock around a couple weeks and then start training. See who's next on the men-yoo."

Someone asked Mintz what he thought the difference was this time, if it was just that

Marciano was better. He shook his head and sighed. "Ain't nobody gonna lick him for a while. He is more improved now than ever."[68]

As the newspaper guys were filing out Charles turned to Mintz and asked him, "When do I fight again—for the championship, I mean?" Embarrassed, Mintz looked at the floor and said softy, "It may take some time, Ez. It may take some time."[69]

14

How Much Is Enough?

Charles went back to Cincinnati and didn't go near a gym until January. There were no homecoming parades this time, no floats, no near-riot at the train station. More important, there was none of the sense of moral victory he'd had after the first Marciano fight. He'd fought his heart out that night, thought he won it, and even the folks back home who thought he'd lost fair and square looked at him like he was a god. The fight he had showed!

This time there was none of that. A lot of folks had a hard time looking him in the eye—unless they were asking for money. They never had a problem then. But the folks who had told him he'd get Marciano next time looked a little embarrassed for him this time, when he ran into them on the corner or at the club. He stuck to the story he'd told in the dressing room after the fight—that he'd beaten the count and in another round or two he'd have had Rocky bleeding so badly they would have had to stop it. After a while he almost believed it.

Gladys would have been fine with him retiring. The money was nice, but fighting was so dangerous. He had a family to worry about now. What if he got hurt? Mintz and Tannas suggested he retire too. For Ezzard it always came down to the same thing: What would he do if he wasn't fighting? How would he support the family? What could he do that would make him the kind of money he made in boxing? A writer in town pointed out to Charles that on the two Marciano fights alone he had grossed $225,000. Didn't he have enough to retire? "How much is enough?' Ezzard asked in return. "You never know."[1] Retiring was not an option. There was still money to be made, and he still had some gas left in the tank.

Five months off was enough. In February Charles returned against Charlie Norkus at the Garden. Norkus, a twenty-six-year-old ex–Marine, was mostly a clubfighter, but in his last three fights had managed to beat LaStarza, Cesar Brion and highly-touted former football star Charlie Powell. No one knew how he did it, but he did, and that got him the date with Charles, who, despite his thirty-three years and the beatings he had taken from Marciano, was a 3–1 favorite and still was rated the third-best heavyweight in the world. Norkus was rated number nine.

"I can lick all the other heavyweights around. I want to prove that and then try again with Marciano," Charles said as he wound down training.[2] Few thought he would succeed. "For a man who appears to hate fighting, Ezzard Charles is amazingly hard to convince that flattened heavyweight champions never come back," wrote one scribe.[3]

A crowd of 5,304 showed up and paid $17,230 to boo Charles at every turn. Charles went to work anyway. He was rusty and his timing was off, but Charles on the worst day of his life was better than Charlie Norkus on the best day of his. Weighing 191½ to Norkus'

195½, he outboxed Norkus from bell to bell, dropped him in the ninth round with a right, and won an easy decision.

Charles hurt his left hand and suffered a cut over his right eye along the way and pocketed a whopping $4,000 plus 30 percent of the gate. It wasn't $225,000 but it was something, and he needed it—soon, Gladys would give birth to their third child, a boy, whom they would name Ezzard. Now more than ever Charles had to keep the money coming in.

"I'm making no claims on any Marciano bout. I'm ready to take them as they come—Moore, Valdes and the rest," Charles said afterward. "If I should beat them all and get in there with Marciano again, fine. But all I want to say is I'm ready to fight. If I don't catch too many, I'll be around a long time."[4]

The cut and injured left hand kept Ezzard out of the ring for another five weeks. Finally he was scheduled to face South African heavyweight champ Johnny Arthur in Edmonton, Alberta, Canada on April 11. On the 10th Arthur pulled out with a viral infection and Vern Escoe, who was scheduled to face Frankie Williams on the undercard, stepped in. Charles stretched him with a left hook in the third, ending it at 2:15. The bout was insignificant. What happened next was not.

Mintz knew Charles was on his way out. It was no secret. He'd already put the word out he was looking for a white heavyweight he could take to the world title. It was his dream. As soon as he found him he would dump Charles. Legend had it he was so desperate that one night when he was out after dark in a bad neighborhood, a white stickup man put a gun in his back and demanded his wallet. Mintz whirled around and floored him with a right, worked him over and dragged him to the police station down the street. When he got there he got a look at him and thought he might be able to turn him into something. He dropped all charges, refused to testify against the kid and later dragged him to the gym. Alas, he was no better there than he'd been in the street, and Jake gave up on him.

While Mintz was with Charles in Edmonton, he kept hearing about a young amateur middleweight named Wilf Greaves. Fight guys couldn't rave enough about him. He wasn't a heavyweight, but neither was Charles when they'd met. Mintz got in touch with Greaves and they had a meeting. Before anyone knew what was happening Mintz was talking the kid's parents into signing a contract and turning him pro. "He come into my life out of a clear blue cloud!" Mintz telephoned the press back in Pittsburgh. "This kid used to be the amateur champion of the whole British Umpire!"[5]

Mintz spent less and less time with Charles and a few months later sold his interests to Tannas. He started barnstorming for his new guy, just the way he had for Charles. Hey, a guy had to make a living. Two years later he died after having a heart attack at a fight card in Mingo Junction, Ohio. Greaves did okay for himself but never did win the title.

Two weeks after flattening Escoe, Charles was in Miami Beach, the first time he'd been back since Valdes gave him hell that night in '53. He was there to face 6'3", 200-pound Johnny Holman, a so-so heavyweight out of Chicago. A pro since '47, Holman had ten losses already by the time he signed to fight Charles, about twice that many wins, and had established that he could not beat most second-tier heavyweights. Satterfield had beaten him twice. Toxie Hall beat him, and Clarence Henry, and a lot of other guys who weren't awful but would never be in the top ten. For what would be his first fight on television, Holman was a 5–1 underdog. Welcome to the big time.

Charles wasn't worried in the least. If he couldn't beat a guy at this level it was time to get out. And he had no intention of getting out. Not yet. A couple days before the fight he and Tannas met a writer in a coffee shop in Miami on their way to the gym. The writer asked Charles if he still played his bass fiddle. "I've still got the bass but I haven't touched it in a year," Charles said. "Don't have the time. I want to be heavyweight champion again, not a bass player."

"Do you honestly feel you can beat Marciano?" asked the writer. Charles opened up. "I do. I sincerely believe I can. I came close twice. Next time I'll make it. No heavyweight champion has ever won back the title. That's what I want. That's why I keep fighting. I really would.... I sure would like to have that title again," he said.

"You know, in that first fight, about the sixth round, I could hear you guys at ringside talking when I walked back to my corner. 'Boxing history's being made tonight.' Even at the finish I thought I'd done it." He shook his head.

"I almost had him in the second fight. He tricked me. If I'd boxed along and bided my time I'd have had him, sure. But after his nose opened up and I saw the blood I got excited. I got careless and got clipped." Charles had repeated this so many times it had become his truth. He had become an expert liar, like all fighters.

Tannas joined in the lie. "You had him, Snooks. You were saying to yourself, 'Here it is. I'm going to sail high now.' Then..." Tannas smiled and shrugged.

"Ez, aren't you tired of the grind?" the writer asked. Charles was in his sixteenth year as a professional boxer.

"The incentive's the same as it was 10 years ago," Charles said. "I'm still trying to do the same things. To build up to a title shot. Keep fighting to get into position for the championship." He grinned. "Of course, they pay you for boxing."[6]

Except for a flash knockdown he suffered in the first round, Charles, who weighed 193½ to Holman's 202¼, had things all his own way. Even at thirty-three he was faster than Holman and so much smarter that it almost wasn't a fair fight. Sure, Holman could punch a bit, but Charles had been beating punchers for sixteen years, and this one was just like all the rest. He won every round after the first and his body punches had worn Holman down to a nub. A right cross opened a nice cut over Holman's left eye and his right eye was swollen almost shut. The big guy could barely move. The body punches were killing him. Charles could see the Marciano fight down the road. Finish out this fight, maybe one or two more, maybe beat old Archie again and he'd be right in line for another title shot. Just two rounds to go.

Holman all but collapsed on his stool after the eighth. He wouldn't have argued if his trainer, Angelo Dundee, had stopped it. That's how tired and beaten up he was. They told him beforehand that Charles was old and washed up, but this old man could still fight. Two rounds still to go. He hoped he could last.

Dundee could see his boy was all used up. He had to find a way to get him going. He thought if he could just get Johnny riled up he could surprise Charles with something big. Charles had things going his way the whole fight. He was relaxed now, coasting. He didn't fear Holman now. It was a good time to catch him.

Then Dundee remembered that all his life Holman had wanted a house with a yard and a white picket fence around it. He talked about it all the time in the gym. Some days it was all he talked about. Dundee decided to use it. When Holman came back to the corner after the eighth Dundee pointed at Charles in the other corner and said, "You see that guy over there? He's taking away your house with the white picket fence. You're blowing it! You're blowing the fight, you're blowing the money and you're blowing the house! You got six minutes to pull this out. Come on. Let's go!"[7]

Holman walked out to the center of the ring and started launching big right hands.

Charles fought him off, at one point landing five consecutive left hooks, but Holman kept pitching. With about a minute gone one of those rights finally got through and Charles' knees buckled. For the next minute and a half Holman pounded him from one corner to the next, landing over and over with the right.

Charles was out on his feet, but instinct kept him up until finally a left uppercut put him down hard with thirty-five seconds left. Referee Eddie Coachman let him take seven more flush punches before finally stopping it at 2:48. The near-capacity crowd roared its approval.

Afterward a reporter in the locker room asked Charles if he would continue to fight. Ezzard didn't miss a beat. "Sure," he said. "Why not?"

"I had him. He was ready to quit a couple times," Charles said. "I tried to bide my time is all. I figured I'd get him soon enough and there was no need to rush it." He shrugged. "You can't wait in this business."[8] The next day a phalanx of reporters, the type who couldn't give a rat's ass about Charles when he was heavyweight champion, converged on Tannas and demanded to know if he thought, as they did, that Charles was through—and if so, why hadn't he told him yet to retire? It was easy for them to be compassionate now—Charles was no longer a threat to their idealized view of what a heavyweight champion should be. There was no worry he'd turn out to be better than Joe Louis. Now, and only now, was he worthy of their concern. "No, I don't think Ezzard is through. He was ahead, he looked good," Tannas said. "The other guy was ready to die three or four times. Then he found strength somewhere and just surprised Ez. I can't count out Ez on that fight alone. Let's fight Holman back, and if he beats Ezzard again, all right. You know, it's not a case of telling a fighter, 'You're through—quit.' Ez feels if he can do as much in the ring as he did against Holman he'll keep going. It's his livelihood. The last thing I'd do is try to keep him going if he didn't feel that way."[9] A couple weeks after Holman beat Charles, Marciano defended the title against chubby Englishman Don Cockell, a 10–1 underdog. Marciano beat him around the ring until the referee finally stopped it in

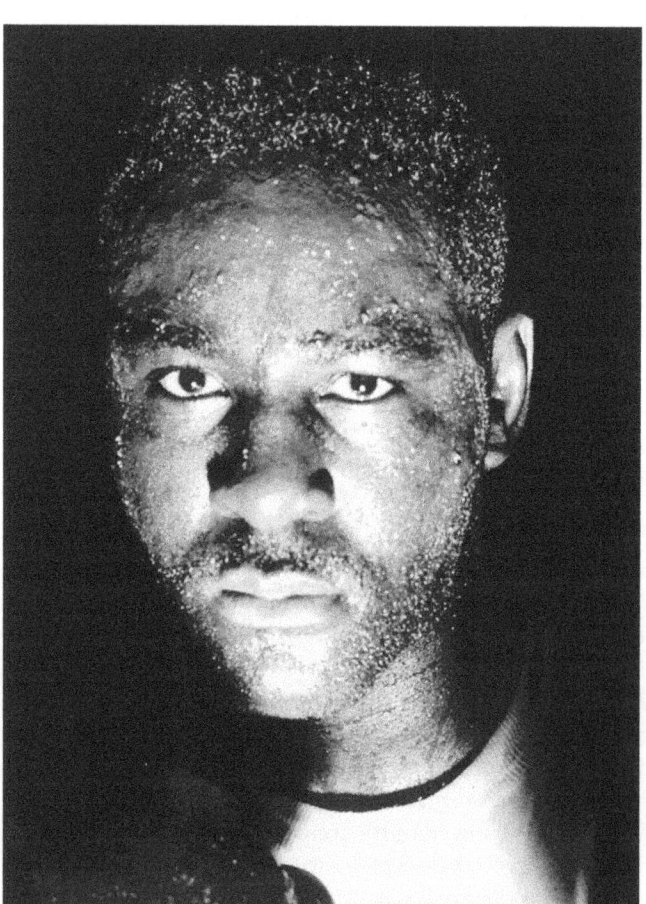

A publicity photograph taken of Charles as he trained for the rematch with Marciano, which was scheduled for September 17, 1954 (courtesy Craig Hamilton of Jo Sports, Inc.).

the ninth round. Meanwhile, Tannas couldn't put together the Holman-Charles rematch fast enough. Bernie Glickman, Holman's manager of record, was reluctant at first, as the rumor mill had him maybe getting a shot at Marciano. Tannas, ever the numbers man, made the benefits of a rematch clear.

"Holman can fight us in Pittsburgh and make $6,000," he said. "That's a lot of dough for a guy who's used to getting $500 and $1,000. Taking a chance? Sure. But what's he going to do, sit around and do nothing for 10 months hoping to fight Marciano? He's got to keep fighting."[10]

Glickman and Holman saw the light and got a good deal: $10,000 guaranteed plus $1,000 for expenses and $4,000 for television. Charles took $5,000 or 35 percent of the net gate and $4,000 for TV. It was the short end, but if Charles was going to make noise ever again in the division, or even if he just wanted to delay the terrible inevitable just a little longer, he had to right things and quick. They made it for five weeks after the first fight and put it not in Pittsburgh, but in Music Hall right in Cincinnati. The bookies made Charles a 9–5 favorite.

Charles was more talkative than usual before the rematch. Maybe he could see his time running down. Maybe he was trying to increase his take-home pay. "I've got my job cut out for me," he said. "I've got to whip Holman if I'm going to get a third shot at Rocky and I feel that's exactly what I'm going to do if Holman is the steppingstone to it.

"I've got a lot of respect for him," he continued. "I've always had respect for an opponent who trained well and Johnny does. He's eager and unafraid, tough and strong—the more reason why I must beat him. I had him in the sixth round in the other fight and I let him get away. Caught me napping, that's what he did. Got me when I was careless for just a fraction. Clipped me over the temple and kept after me. I was stunned, sure enough, but I couldn't do anything about it. I heard the corner shout about what to do, but my legs were paralyzed and I just stood there and took it when I should have gotten away."

He promised it wouldn't happen again. "There'll be no excuses. I look at boxing like this: A pitcher in a ballgame has a bad day and is knocked out of the box. He comes back and has a good season. A boxer is a cinch to get clipped once in a while. Sometimes he gets stopped. But as long as his reflexes are all right and he is mentally sound, I see no reason why he shouldn't come back and win often. That's how I feel about the Holman fight."[11]

Charles was good to his word. Weighing 195½ to Holman's 202, Charles rushed out from his corner at the first bell, put his forehead on Holman's chest and stayed there most of the night. He knew that Holman, ponderous and long-armed, needed punching room to let his bombs go. So he wouldn't give it to him. He fought off Holman's chest the entire night, and with the exception of a moment in the fourth, when Holman got some room and nailed him with a right, Charles was in complete control. He tortured poor Johnny to the body early then switched to the head later.

"I just couldn't get a solid punch," Holman said afterward.[12] It was a hell of a good performance for a washed-up old heavyweight, and a damn shame that just 2,522 of his neighbors bothered to see it.

A month later, July 13, Tannas had Charles in with Paul Andrews, a pasty, white up-and-comer out of Buffalo. Lanky and tall at 6'3" and 190 pounds, Andrews, an ex-paratrooper and just 25 years old, had lost to top guys like Maxim and Harold Johnson, but he beat some decent guys too—Danny Nardico, Yvonne Durell, Oakland Billy Smith. Most of his wins were by knockout, and the New York writers loved his right uppercut.

They put it in Chicago Stadium and on local TV so just 2,123 fans turned out, generating a gate of $5,072. Most of them were there to see the white kid retire Charles, and they booed like all hell when it became clear it wouldn't happen. "I guess they want to see new faces," Charles said later.[13]

Charles outweighed his opponent for the first time in a long time—193 to 189—and he fought the taller Andrews the same way he had Holman in their rematch—on the inside. It served him well. Like Holman, Andrews needed room to punch. Charles didn't give it to him. He stayed inside, pounded Andrews' body and then went upstairs. In the fourth he opened a cut under Andrews' right eye.

Andrews dropped Charles in the second with his vaunted right uppercut, but that was for the most part his only success, and the split decision went Charles' way. One judge gave it to Andrews 95–89; the referee and the other judge had it 94–91 and 96–95 for Charles. Even though he won, the reporters wanted to know when Charles would retire. "Fighting is my business," he said. "I don't have another job. Besides, how can you turn down the money?"[14]

Charles had now twice done pretty well, all things considered, fighting bigger guys inside, a significant change from the stand-up style he'd used most of his career. Against Holman and Williams it worked out, but it wasn't necessarily by design. He couldn't move the way he used to, and not just because his legs were heavier with age. It was that too, but sometimes he just couldn't get his lower body to do what he wanted it to—particularly his left ankle. It was weak or numb all the time and he couldn't rely on it. So staying flat-footed on the inside with these big guys was not just good strategy. It was his only strategy.

Charles' reward for surviving Andrews was a match with temperamental, eccentric, twenty-four-year-old Tommy "Hurricane" Jackson of Far Rockaway, New York, winner of six straight and rising heavyweight contender. Jackson was one of those guys who looked for all the world like he had no idea what he was doing in the ring and maybe actually didn't. His profound ungainliness was a weapon all in itself and confounded one opponent after another. He was trained by the brilliant Whitey Bimstein and Freddie Brown, who knew enough to develop and take advantage of his natural gracelessness rather than try and force it out of him.

One reporter, editorializing on several close decisions Jackson had received, wrote, "Judges in the past have been impressed, perhaps more than they should have been, by Jackson's curious but relentless pawings and slappings, by his stamina and by his ability to confuse prizefighters trained to contend with orthodoxy."[15] Another observed, "Fighting Jackson is akin to fighting a swarm of bees.... The Hurricane leads with his right, swings off balance, tosses double uppercuts (his own invention, by the way) hooks with his right, crosses with his left and outrages every known principle of the manly Art of Self-Defense."[16] Floyd Patterson, who would later fight Jackson twice, summed him up perfectly from the perspective of a prizefighter: "One of the things Jackson does, is to go into a crouch from which he can't throw anything but a left hook. You look for a left hook. What Jackson does is throw everything but a left hook."[17]

This was a thing that Ezzard Charles, thirty-four years old now, hobbled by a mysteriously uncooperative ankle and the effects of 101 prizefights, both easy and otherwise, could not manage. The bookies made him a 4–1 favorite anyway, thinking a fighter as old as Charles had to have seen guys like Jackson before. They were wrong.

Charles started well, blasting away at Jackson and winning the first two rounds, clearly a disappointment to the crowd of 3,636. After that Jackson got his jab going and his legs going, and it was all Charles could do to keep up. By the third he was tattooing Charles with all manner of loopy combinations and double uppercuts and other such nonsense.

The pressure that had worked on Holman and Andrews, as slow-footed as turtles compared to Jackson, did him no good. At the end the decision in Jackson's favor was unanimous. For the first time in his career, Charles was described by a writer the next day as a "plodder."[18]

They put the rematch in Cleveland a month later. A crowd of 4,401 showed up to see if Jackson could repeat, maybe earn a shot at Marciano. Charles did better—he usually did in rematches—but he didn't have the zing or the wind anymore. After a strong start Jackson beat him up down the stretch and nearly stopped him in the tenth.

Jackson was a sensitive kid who had taken up fighting solely to help him survive the mean streets where he grew up. Bullies in his neighborhood used to throw him into sticker bushes. He approached Charles afterward in the dressing room the way a lot of young fighters do after they whip an old fighter they admire. Charles was seated on a stool with a towel around his waist, talking to reporters.

Jackson said to him, "That was one fight I hated to win."

Ezzard looked up at him out of his left eye. The right was swollen shut.

"You've got a lot of ability that most fellows haven't got," Ezzard said. "Put your heart in it."

Tears filled Jackson's eyes. "But I don't want to fight."

"Oh, if you don't want to fight that's a different story. With me it was different. I wanted to fight."

"I fight because there's nothing else I can do."

Jackson turned around and walked away.

Charles continued his conversation with a reporter: "I won't retire. I'll keep on fighting."[19]

Three weeks later Marciano came off the canvas to stop Archie Moore in nine rounds in Yankee Stadium. He was thirty-two years old and just about out of marketable challengers, at least from the current generation. There was a new generation headed primarily by young Floyd Patterson and a couple others, but he was getting tired of the fight business, and especially of making Weill rich. Retirement seemed a real possibility.

Charles took off two months after the second loss to Jackson and went back home to Cincinnati to rest up. By this time he knew better than anybody where he was. A long time before, right after he beat Lee Oma, he had told a writer that he would know when it was time to retire.

"I plan to go right on fighting until I detect that I have slowed up and have little to offer," he said.

"Would you likely be the first to detect this?" he was asked.

"Well, sometimes the athlete finds out about his slipping after spectators have noted it. But I am sure that I will be the first to know if I have begun to slide down the toboggan.

"The champion who outlasts his welcome is a sucker," he said.[20]

He had been referring on the sly to Joe Louis when he let that last line go. Now he was the sucker. Yet it was no disgrace, losing to Jackson. As clownish as Jackson appeared in the ring, he was rated the third best heavyweight in the world. He'd fight for the title soon. So that made Charles feel a little better about things. He called Tannas and told him to get him a fight. He had bills to pay.

Tannas made some calls. It turned out Chris Dundee was looking for an opponent for his heavyweight Julio Mederos, a mediocre puncher from Cuba. Dundee said he and Charles would do a big gate in Miami Beach. Tannas agreed but said he'd have to check with Charles. Charles thought for a minute, remembered that the two times he fought in Miami Beach he'd lost to Valdes, a 6–1 underdog, and Holman, an 8–1 dog. He told Tannas, "It's a no-go. I'm not going to fight in Miami Beach again. That place is jinxed for me."[21]

Tannas got him Toxie Hall in Providence, Rhode Island, for a lot less money than he would have gotten for Mederos in Miami, but Charles was thinking long-term: If he could put together a few wins he might nail down a fight with Patterson and that would be a big-money fight. In fact, there was talk that if he beat Hall impressively he could be in the running for a fight with Patterson on December 21.

Hall was a career sparring-partner for Marciano and allegedly had floored Rocky when Rocky was training for Don Cockell. Being Marciano's sparring partner was how Hall made his living. As a reward he landed well-paying fights on Rocky's undercards, but he was nothing great under the lights. He lost as many fights as he won. Tannas figured he'd give Charles a couple of rounds before going to sleep. He was wrong.

Weighing 197 to Hall's 194½, Charles did well in the middle rounds, outslugging Hall, and even had him hurt in the fifth. But Hall was busier and stronger. He staggered Charles with a right in the first round and again in the eighth and ninth on the way to winning a split decision by scores of 96–94, 96–95 and 95–97. "Charles has plenty left," Hall said afterward. "I plan to keep fighting," Charles said almost before the writers asked.[22]

They held the rematch three weeks later in Rochester. As shot as he was, the old man could still fight on some level. In front of just under 4,000 onlookers at War Memorial Stadium, be beat up Hall from the first round to the last and won a unanimous and lopsided decision.

You could call it his last gasp as a relevant fighter. He knew it. There would be no big-money fight with Patterson, no third shot at Marciano for the title. This was it. From here on it was just chasing a buck and getting as much as he could before he couldn't do it at all anymore.

There were more wins, and then more losses, and then the latter started to outnumber the former. Two weeks after whipping Hall Charles gave up eleven years and twenty-two pounds and still outpointed Bob Albright in San Francisco. Then Young Jack Johnson, a sixteen-fight novice, busted open Charles' lip and stopped him in Los Angeles. Charles came back to stop Don Jasper in Windsor, Ontario, Canada, then lost to another novice, Wayne Bethea, in New York. Bethea had been a pro just twenty-one months, and the crowd booed and stamped their feet at the lack of action. Just like old times for Charles. The bout was notable in that it was Charles' first fight at the famed St. Nick's Arena, one of the oldest and most beloved fight clubs anywhere. "When I was a boy," Charles said in the locker room, "I used to listen to the fights from St. Nick's and wonder if I'd ever make it there on the way up. Well, I didn't, not until now when I'm going down."[23]

A couple months later *The Ring* magazine published its latest rankings. For the first time in fourteen years, the name Ezzard Charles appeared nowhere. Around the same time, fittingly, Marciano got out, announcing on May 1, 1956, that he was retiring as undefeated heavyweight champ. He couldn't stomach making so much money for Weill, that bastard, and besides that, he didn't have the same drive that he used to. It was time. It was true that they all tried to come back sooner or later, but you got the sense that Rocky was different, that when he said he was done he was done.

Charles punched the clock. Another win over Albright, this time in Phoenix, then a points loss to undefeated "Irish" Pat McMurtry in Tacoma. The fans loved McMurtry so much, a big, handsome, hard-punching kid, that they poured $60,000 into the promoter's till. That got the attention of Harry "Kid" Matthews, who had more or less retired the previous year after a couple losses to Cockell. At thirty-four, a year younger than Charles, he got back into the gym, beat a nobody and three weeks later beat Charles at Sicks' Stadium in Seattle, scoring a first-round knockdown and cruising to an easy points win. "When you get as old as we are you're not consistent," Charles said. "You've got to have a good night to win like Harry did. He stunned me in the first round but I wasn't hurt bad. I just couldn't get myself together."[24]

You had to wonder what it would take to get Charles out of the ring, outside of serious injury. Maybe embarrassment? In London in October 1956 against an ordinary, twenty-two-year-old heavyweight named Dick Richardson. Charles, thirty-five years old now, grabbed Richardson in a tight clinch at the opening bell and refused to let go. He did this several more times, prompting referee Frank Wilson to repeatedly warn both him and his corner. When Charles continued clinching, Wilson disqualified him at 2:29 of the second round for "persistent holding."

The crowd of 11,000 exploded in boos and insults. Photos from the fight showed Charles, strangely, laughing and smiling while the verdict was announced. The next day a writer described him as "hazy eyed and flabby at 202 pounds."[25] The British Boxing Board of Control considered withholding his purse but in the end settled for a $200 penalty. Not embarrassing enough, apparently. Charles vowed to fight on.

Charles counters a right hand with a left uppercut to the jaw of Charley Norkus in a bout at Madison Square Garden on February 18, 1955. Moments later Charles dropped Norris for a five-count and went on to win a one-sided decision. This was Charles' first fight after his disappointing loss to Rocky Marciano in their rematch (courtesy Lou Manfra).

In November Ezzard told Gladys he was about to start training for a fight he had lined up against Roy Harris in Texas on December 11. Her reaction was as though he had "hurt her with a pin or a red-hot poker," he said later.[26] She begged him to give it up. She'd been begging him for months. It felt like years. Ezzard's grandmother, too, had been on him to quit the ring, to get out while he still had his health. But he was a stubborn man and a proud one who wanted to make his own decisions. Finally, he relented.

It helped that in November, Moore and Patterson fought for Marciano's vacant heavyweight title. Patterson, fast and powerful, rolled over old Archie, stopping him in the fifth round. If Moore had won, Charles was sure he could have gotten a fight with him. They had all that history. But Patterson? No way. Too young, too good. It made his decision easier.

On December 1 Charles sent Tannas a telegram that read, simply, "I don't want to fight anymore." He cancelled the Harris fight and told the press he had too many irons in the fire, including a restaurant he was planning to open later in the month. Also, there were his kids. "I've got three children. I've got to give them some consideration."[27] And just like that, Ezzard Charles was done. It was over. For now.

15

THE FLOOD

Charles did his best to stay retired. He spent time with his family. He golfed. He tended to his new restaurant when he could make it over there, and to his other business ventures. He bought some real estate in Las Vegas. He did all the things ex-athletes are supposed to do to hold onto their money except be suspicious of "friends" who come around with this or that sure thing or no-risk business deal.

But how was he to know what was good or wasn't? He had been a fighter his whole life, not a business man. He didn't go to college. That's what he had managers for, and promoters. They took care of that stuff. So when he went in on a restaurant or a bar or a nightclub or something he had to trust that the guy who brought it to him wasn't screwing him over, that he would do the right things, pay the taxes on it, not steal from him. All he could do was hope.

After six months of playing golf, running to and from "business meetings" and lazing around the house, Charles was bored stiff. He accepted a job with the city as unit leader at a juvenile detention center. They said they'd pay him $3,200 a year to counsel "impressionable first-timers" and serve as "an example to the boys here of what a person can do to get ahead"[1] while teaching them how to box. It was okay with him. He liked working with the kids, giving something back. He could make $3,200 in a *night* when he was fighting, but he put that out of his mind as best he could. He kept up with the fight game. Patterson was defending Ez's old title every six or eight months. Charles would have starved if he fought so infrequently when he had the belt.

Business bored Charles. Eventually, most things did, even golf. So he sat around a lot. He ate a lot too. All those years at middleweight and light heavy, when he had to watch his diet, stay trim, go to bed a bit hungry, you couldn't blame him now for putting on weight. Even as a puffed-up heavyweight he couldn't go crazy. He had to eat right. Now, who cared? Most fighters put on weight after they retired. It was natural.

By December 1957 Charles had ballooned up to 235 pounds. Gladys was all over him about it. She'd married a slim, athletic man. She hadn't let herself go, and after three kids was as slim and petite as ever. Plus, there was his health to consider. So she nagged him about it.

In January Charles decided he'd start jogging to get the weight down. That was the only reason, he told himself. The first few times he jogged a mile. Then he increased it to two. Soon he was up to three miles and the weight was coming off. He saw the progress, liked how it made him feel and decided to head down to the old gym and work out a bit, get loosened up. That would help, too. There was nothing more to it than that. Just an old retired guy trying to lose some weight. But it sure did feel good, being at the gym. The sounds, the feel, even the smell. Wrapping his hands, loosening up in the ring. It felt like home. The old gang was there. Everyone called him "champ," told him it was good to see him.

Before he knew it he was having fun hitting the bags and shadow boxing. Even as he told himself he was doing it just to lose weight, he knew he was lying. He was training for a comeback. It had taken a year. That was how long it took for Ezzard Charles to forget how bad it had been when he left, and to convince himself that he could do it again. The life of a civilian wasn't for him. He was bored to death. He was a fighter. He'd always be a fighter. It was time to be one again.

Gladys wouldn't be happy about it, he knew that, but if she hadn't been on his case about losing weight he wouldn't have gotten started in the first place. So really, it was her fault. A man could make himself believe anything if he wanted to believe it badly enough. By mid–February Charles was down to 202 pounds and had been checked out by his doctor and the local commission, who both said he was fit to fight if he really wanted to. He was thirty-six years old. A local reported called him up and asked him if it was true that he was planning a comeback.

Ezzard gave him the skinny and then paused and chuckled. He said, "I suppose all this will surprise a lot of people, but gosh, boxing was always my life. It was everything. I really miss all the cheers, and, yes, the jeers of my fighting days. It's a world all of its own. I have a fine job with the juvenile detention home here. But it doesn't fill all my needs, that's all."[2]

Charles said that in the next week he planned on starting serious sparring with some top fighters, and though that might change his mind, he was happy with his reflexes and wind; it was all coming back to him. All he'd really needed was a long rest. It was not, he said, about the money, but it had always been about the money to some degree or another, and besides that, the money was running out fast. But there was more to it than that. Charles had lost his identity, like all once-great fighters do. "I feel lost being out of the fight game and I want to give it another try. I'm real anxious to get at those sparring partners next week to see how well I can do. That will be the acid test."[3]

It didn't hurt that old Archie Moore, at forty-one, was still fighting and doing all right for himself. If he could do it, why not Ezzard?

Lots of comebacks end in the gym, when an old fighter finds out, even with head gear and the big gloves, just how old he is. Charles' did not. He got in touch with Tannas in Pittsburgh and told him to get him a fight. Tannas told Charles he was crazy, to get out while he still had his health and go enjoy his life and his family. Charles insisted, so Tannas got him a fight with a mediocre pug named Johnny Harper from Steubenville, Ohio. They met in Fairmont, West Virginia, on August 28. Charles opened a cut under Harper's left eye and won an easy ten-round decision. Back in Cincinnati, Charles got good news. Before he started training for his comeback, he'd been studying for a job with the state as a safety inspector in the state industrial commission. He passed the test and landed the job in September. It would pay $4,000 a year. It took a back seat.

"The fact that I took this job does not mean I'm ending my comeback," he announced. "I have a fight coming up on September 28 at Juarez, Mexico and I hope to get more after that."[4]

That fight was against left-handed Mexican heavyweight Alfredo Zuany. He was nothing great, and in front of a small crowd in a bullring in Juarez, he beat up Charles six ways from Sunday and sent him back to Cincinnati nursing wounds only old men fighting young men can get. Tannas begged him again to quit and didn't even take a cut from Charles' purse. He knew how it was. Charles insisted again and Tannas got him Donnie Fleeman, the Texas light heavyweight champion, in Dallas for late October.

Charles outweighed Fleeman, a novice, by twenty pounds and couldn't do a thing with him. For five rounds Fleeman battered Charles with a wide-open, slam-bang style while Charles limped around the ring favoring his left ankle. In the sixth he shook Charles with a right hand and then chopped him down with a wild flurry of blows. Charles ambled to his feet again, favoring his left ankle, and the referee stopped it.

He could not have been more wrong or more profoundly deluded when he said afterward, "He never hurt me. This fight doesn't tell the tale for me."[5] It told everything that needed to be told. When the ring doctor asked him about his ankle, Charles said he'd hurt it in training a week before but didn't think it was right to call the bout off at the last minute. It was a lie. It was the ankle that had been giving him trouble for a long while.

A few days later a well-known writer scolded Tannas in a column for enabling Charles' delusions by continuing to get him fights and work his corner.[6] Tannas countered that Charles needed the money. What was he supposed to do—let him starve? He was doing the only thing he could.

The Texas Commission suspended Charles then, initially under the guise that he'd gone into the ring injured and didn't tell anyone, but everyone knew the reason was to protect Charles from himself. The commission hoped the rest of the NBA states would honor the suspension. They didn't have to. At the insistence of Gladys and Tannas he gave retirement another try and sat around Cincinnati again, watching his bank account shrink. It seemed that even trying to make money cost him money.

Back when he still had some cash, he and a couple of old boxing buddies burned through $3,000 in one month just checking out different bars to see if it would make sense for him to open one. He'd drop eight or ten dollars in each joint, and he wasn't even a drinker. He'd arrive home full of ginger ale and cokes and no smarter for it.[7] It got worse. One of his bars, "Round One," went under. So too did the other, "The 19th Hole." He remodeled his home. The money went and went. This business flopped. That one took a dive. This guy took off with the down payment. His last big try was the Ezzard Charles Amusement Coliseum, a place where the kids could come out and dance, roller skate, that kind of thing. Eventually it tanked, like all the others.

In March they fired Charles from his state job. His bosses said it was because he'd taken leave the previous fall to fight in Mexico and Texas. He countered that it was politics. "Everybody knows I'm on the Republican side of the fence," he said, and it was true that that he was hired during a Republican administration and in the most recent elections Democrats had taken control of the Ohio state house and legislature.[8] It didn't matter. Now he had no income and the money was going as fast as ever. He did the only thing he could do. He fought—if you could call it that.

At Lincoln High School, located in a suburb of Cincinnati, Charles met Dave Ashley, a thirty-four-year-old, 250-pound policeman from nearby Lockland, who had lost nine times in twelve pro fights. Charles lost the first two rounds but belabored his tubby opponent's midsection enough to stop him in the seventh and earn a couple hundred bucks. A month later undefeated novice George Logan stopped Charles in eight in Boise. Then on September 1, 1959, Alvin Green beat him over ten rounds in Oklahoma City. Charles, thirty-eight years old now, said afterward he'd keep right on fighting for three or four more years because "it's an easy way to make a living."[9] He was wrong. When he arrived back in Cincinnati,

Gladys laid down the law. Ezzard thought he could do it a while longer, but he was a man who loved his wife and really, he knew she was right. Everybody did. Over the next six months Charles hustled to make a buck any way he knew how. He made personal appearances. He'd show up at a bar or restaurant on their opening night, and he'd shake hands while they showed films of his fights on a movie projector. One night he'd be in Chicago. A few days later he'd be up in Canada. Then he'd be in California. He was hustling, trying to make a living. Just about all the money was gone. The guys he used to run with would see him on the street now and cross to the other side to get away from him, figuring he might ask them for some of the money he'd lent them over the years.

Charles was working as a greeter at a bar in Newport, Kentucky, when in April 1960 a promoter came in and suggested he try professional wrestling. A lot of ex-fighters had done it. Joe Louis had done it after he stopped fighting. "I thought it was just a joke. I started laughing, but when they told me I could make money and how much, I stopped laughing," he said. "It all stems back to being a fighter. You don't want to wait for things to happen. If I want to do something I want to do it. Now I want to wrestle. I like it very well. I'm too old to box yet you have the feeling you still want to stay in athletics. I also like the money that can be made out of it."[10]

Charles started training and then wrestling one-night stands in Canada in the summer of '60. When he wasn't at the gym or at a show he was at home watching the money run out and fending off the bank, which was about to foreclose on his house on Forest Avenue. The electricity was on some of the time. His cars were gone. When he had to get somewhere he took a bus or hitched a ride with a friend. "The friends I hitch-hike with have better cars than I ever had," he told a writer.[11] He seemed stunned at how things had turned out for him.

"I was saving for a rainy day and the rainy day has come. It's more than a rainy day, it's a flood," he said.[12] At thirty-nine years old and a year removed from his last fight, he was flat broke, almost out of his mind with boredom and fifty pounds overweight. Wrestling, all things considered, seemed a good deal. "Here's a guy doing nothing," he said about himself. "I always wondered about people that don't do anything and I've found out. They just don't do anything." He tried to explain how it all went wrong. "The only thing about boxing was you never felt the end of the good days would come. It seemed far off but it was just a few months away." Gladys did her best to keep him busy. She knew he still had to feel like a man, but she couldn't let him laze around the house all day. "When you're a married man," Ezzard said, "your wife constantly is finding little chores for you to do—wash spots off the woodwork, rake leaves, clean up the kitchen. Even with an automobile not in the garage she wants you to clean out that. When you're working alone, your mind isn't there. You're thinking about things that are supposed to happen. But they never happen."[13]

It also was important to Gladys that their dire financial situation never become obvious to the children. They never discussed finances when the kids were around, and she went out of her way to shield them from how desperate things were. One autumn afternoon when Ezzard was off hustling in Canada, she took the kids outside in the yard and had them rake up the leaves. With the leaves all in a pile they set them ablaze and roasted hotdogs, that night's dinner. It wasn't until almost twenty years later that the kids learned they were outside roasting hotdogs because the gas had been turned off.[14]

Charles' financial woes did little to slow his womanizing. He'd been a ladies' man back when he was a fighter and he was a ladies' man now, albeit one who had to work harder. He never brought it home, never brought it to the family, and out of respect did his best to hide all evidence of it from Gladys. Not that she didn't know. She'd always known. It didn't come up unless circumstances left her no choice. That happened once; she'd been going through his pockets and found a note from a woman. She exploded, cussing at Ezzard, slapping, kicking him. Eight-year-old Ezzard II, watching, began to cry. Charles did his best to calm Gladys, went out for a while, and when he came back everything returned to normal. That's how it worked.[15]

It was around this time in 1962 that another opportunity presented itself to Charles. While he was working the door at a bar in Kentucky, an old friend approached him with an offer to do public relations for Gallo wine, makers of a new wine called "Thunderbird." It sold for fifteen cents a pint. The money sounded good and the work easy so Ezzard accepted. There was one catch; he'd have to move to Chicago. He considered it, talked it over with Gladys, and they decided to make the move. Cincinnati had been his home for just about all his life, but it was time for a change. He was desperate.

Around the same time, Gladys took over handling the family finances. Ezzard was just no good at it. For most folks it's a learned skill like anything else, and they didn't teach it in the gym. With Gladys handling the money and Charles working for Gallo, things got slightly better. The family moved into a place on Hyde Park Boulevard on Chicago's South Side and put the kids in the South Shore school system. Gladys took a job as a clerk in a nearby supermarket and started paying down all the old debts as best she could. There was still little money for extras; when Charles' application for a wrestling license was approved it was revealed that he'd gotten all his training gear from a friend who felt so bad he'd given it to him for nothing. "He's broke, that's why he's going to wrestle. I gave him all his equipment. He didn't even have any money to buy shoelaces," said Sammy Frager, who worked as a ring equipment manufacturer.[16]

It didn't take long for Charles to discover that the fight crowds were even less eager to pay to see him as an old, overweight wrestler than they'd been when he was a young, lean, champion boxer. The money was nothing like what he'd been told. Plus, the traveling he had to do for wrestling exhibitions was incompatible with his job at Gallo. He gave it up.

A year later he and Gallo parted ways too, and he was back to hustling. Cashing in again on whatever cachet his name still carried, he landed a job in early 1964 as a car salesman with a Dodge dealership in Chicago Heights. They'd given him a great deal on a Polara, the one with the push-button automatic transmission, and then took him on. That summer he took young Ezzard II out with him every day and let him explore the area, which was mostly wooded. Charles was no great salesman, but between that gig and the hustling he did on the side, things continued to improve financially for the Charles brood, if only incrementally.

In 1965 Charles moved his family into a six-room apartment at 7039 Clyde Avenue in Chicago. The kids were fourteen, thirteen and ten. Charles landed a job in the information bureau at the state motor vehicle facility at 9901 South Park Ave. Like all the others, the job at Dodge didn't work out because you can't take a world champion prizefighter, turn him into a civilian and expect it to stick. Fighters on that level aren't like other people. They can't do banality like everyone else. They're not used to it. It's why wild animals break out of zoos the first chance they get. They can't stand the boredom.

When he wasn't at work examining driver's licenses and answering questions for a steady and soul-crushing $100-a-week, Charles watched TV and smoked his pipe. On the weekends he'd do laundry in the basement or mop the floor or dust some furniture while

Gladys was at work. Thanks to Gladys he had no significant debt anymore, but there also was little money in the bank. And every day, it seemed, someone asked him, "Ezzard: Where did all the money go?" It was all anyone cared about because it made them feel better to think he'd blown it all, that it was his own fault he was broke. If there's anything a working man loves more than a rags-to-riches story it's a riches-to-rags story. Makes him feel better about his own state. They never understood how it could happen, even after he explained it to them. After a while he gave up trying, but if a writer he liked asked him about it he'd tell it all over again.

"One reason I was taken so clean is that I was a guy who believed in people," he told a favored writer. "If a guy said he was my friend I thought he was my friend. There were guys who would come by the house every morning—waking me up. They'd have breakfast, lunch and dinner with me."

"I used to carry what I called an emergency or operating expense fund of $200 or $250 in my pockets every day," he said. "Some guys always seemed to need money. It would cost me at least $30 to go to the corner and talk about events."[17] Because fighters all come from nothing, they know what it means to be poor. So when a man asked Charles for a couple bucks, how could he say no?

Charles still had his bass fiddle from the old days, but he kept it in a closet because it reminded him too much of better times. He didn't want to dwell in the past any more than he had to. "I seldom take it out because it would make me long for the old life again," he told a visiting writer.[18] Same with his old jazz records. Besides that, his daughters were always playing records by the Beatles or the Dave Clark Five, whose music he found "outrageous." Gladys wanted to move from the apartment back into a house, but he wasn't interested. "My wife Gladys is a wonderful girl but she is constantly pushing me to buy a house. I don't want a mortgage. I don't want to cut grass or wash windows and paint and things like that. Some guys are cut out for that but not me," he said.[19] Bigger problems than household chores were coming.

Late in 1965 Gladys started noticing that Ezzard was having trouble walking. "He'd be climbing stairs on his way from the office and there would be this sort of wobble in his walk. A sort of stumbling motion, like he was drunk or something," was how she described it.[20] "He started walking—he began to look like a drunk; not a bad drunk. More like a light drunk. One who has a high."[21]

He had gotten very heavy again—240 pounds. She got on his case about it again, and he lost some and showed some improvement. "He was beginning to look good—he was beginning to get up on his toes as he walked," she told a writer.[22] The improvement was short-lived. In January 1966 Charles' friend Ben Bentley was promoting a fight between Rubin Carter and Willie McClure at the Aragon ballroom in Chicago. He asked Charles to come out to help the gate. Charles obliged and when he arrived, Bentley saw what everyone else did—that Charles was dragging his right foot when he walked, not really lifting it off the ground. He mentioned it, and Charles blew it off, but he knew something was wrong. Some weeks later Charles had his son at the doctor for a routine checkup. He took the opportunity to duck into another room and get a full examination himself.

The doctor diagnosed Charles with high blood pressure and ordered him into the hospital. When he was admitted, the surgical team got him to sign a paper permitting them to operate on his brain. Gladys was outraged. "The first thing they think of a fighter is something is wrong upstairs," she said.[23] They found out soon enough that Charles' problem wasn't high blood pressure, and he wasn't punchy. They didn't know what was causing his symptoms.

Gladys took her husband from doctor to doctor over the next several months. When they had ruled out everything they could rule out, there was only one diagnosis left: what they called lateral sclerosis. Charles had never heard of it; most people hadn't. But they had heard of its more common name—Lou Gehrig's Disease, so-named after the famous Yankee ballplayer who died from it in 1941.

In February 1966 doctors gave Gladys and Ezzard the prognosis, which wasn't especially comforting. Charles' once pristine fighter's body would turn on him. This magnificent body that had given him what he viewed in retrospect, now, in middle age, as a somewhat charmed life, would betray him and break down little by little. He'd gradually lose control of one group of muscles after another. They would cease to obey direction from his brain. As a layman Charles couldn't grasp that intellectually, but he knew it had already started. He didn't have to understand the science to know his leg already disobeyed him.

Each group of muscles would get rigid and then atrophy from disuse. First he would lose his ability to walk. Soon he wouldn't be able to use his arms or shoulders. He would lose bladder and bowel control. Eventually he'd be unable to speak, and after that he wouldn't be able to swallow. Inevitably he would stop breathing too and then he would die by asphyxiation, probably within five years. Most didn't last that long. If it was any consolation, the doctors told him, it was a mostly painless disease.

He didn't have to worry about losing his mind. His brain would remain intact right until the end, even if from looking at him most people would think he'd taken too many punches in his youth and been beaten loopy. The doctors told Charles that the opposite was true; that the physical conditioning he'd undergone over the course of his life had probably delayed the onset of symptoms, and if he engaged a strict regimen of physical therapy and calisthenics, he could slow the disease's progression and maybe even gain back some function. Charles immediately began treatment at the local veterans' hospital in Chicago. It was a lot like boxing training—sit-ups, leg-raises, squats, that type of thing. He didn't see much relief and in early 1967 started seeing a chiropractor.

As occasionally happens, bad news was followed by good—Chicago mayor Richard Daley gave Charles a job in his Department of Human Services with the Commission on Youth Welfare. The press called it a "showcase" job[24] but Charles didn't care. It paid decent money, and all he had to do was make personal appearances, counsel troublemaking kids and teach the interested ones how to box over at the YMCA. He worked in a little office that he shared with three other workers on Chicago's far South Side.

"I go to block parties or show films for people," he told a writer. "Mostly I jive around with the kids, all the kids. But I usually try to pick the worst kid, and jive him. Sometimes it works, sometimes not. We go to parties and eat hot dogs and have soft drinks. And sometimes, if I have a couple dollars in my pocket, I'll send one over to the store for some cookies.

"And there are always two or three who will stick to you, who don't remember or weren't born (when I was champ) but who know what 'champion' means. With the kids it was nothing I planned. You just jive around. You jive them all, but always look for the worst one. You tell him some things, maybe jive him into being a regular guy.

"When I was a champion I had a convertible and I'd load it up with kids," he continued. "And we'd go some place, a park or a drive-in and I'd say, 'Everybody load up, everybody gets what he wants.' And we'd have a good time. That was when I was champion."[25]

The writer, naturally, asked where all the money had gone. "Bad investments, I guess. When you're champion, $2,500 or $3,000 don't mean so much. But that's a tidy sum. I know that now. I tell you something else I learned from boxing. You got to have a will to win, you don't quit until you're finished. I'm not a spiritual bug, but I think I got close to it fighting. I met some wonderful people, and fighting gave me a wonderful life."[26]

The disease progressed, as was its nature. Charles got around with a walker. Sometimes he gave in and switched to a wheelchair. Still, every Monday, Wednesday and Friday he made it to the regional office at the youth commission, which was just a few blocks from his home. On Tuesdays and Thursdays he'd get therapy at the Chicago Rehabilitation Institute. It wasn't cheap. The medical bills threatened to undo the meager gains he and Gladys had made financially over the last couple years. A friend came to his aid.

John McManus was a Chicago cop, a big Ezzard Charles fan and owner of the second-largest collection of fight films of anyone in the world. Every Tuesday and Thursday he'd drive Charles to therapy, hang around and then drive him home. Charles was well past the point of being able to drive a car. One day in 1968 on the drive over to rehab when Charles was lamenting his lost fortune, McManus turned to him and said, "Ezzard, I'm going to get you one last big payday. We're going to have an Ezzard Charles day." Ezzard replied, "You'd do that for me?"[27]

McManus got to work, reserving a hall, printing tickets and readying his fight films. He invited Tony Zale and Walcott and Louis and others but couldn't move any tickets. He rescheduled it for October 27 but again the public showed no interest. If no one bought tickets they couldn't do it. What would be the point? Desperate, he reached out to Charles' old friend Ben Bentley, who had contacts everywhere. Bentley got some writers involved, and then the famous Chicago businessman and philanthropist Joe Kellman got on board and bankrolled it. Together they got it moving again, scheduled it for November 13 at the Sherman House, and hired Chicago Cubs play-by-play sportscaster Jack Brickhouse to play master of ceremonies. Tickets for Ezzard Charles Appreciation Night were $15 at the door.

Gladys, a proud woman, wanted to make it clear beforehand that her family was not destitute. "It started out as a testimonial but now I guess it's going to be a benefit," she said. "We don't need anything now. We're not in debt. All we have are current bills and Ezzard gets paid every week. But maybe for later," she said, and looking at Ezzard, you didn't have to be psychic to know what she meant.[28]

The fighters came out big. Louis showed up. Walcott, too. And Archie Moore. Marciano came straight from Charley Goldman's funeral in New York. A few months earlier he had donated to Charles a bejeweled "title" belt worth about $10,000 that he had won on a radio station's computerized tournament of champions. "I just wanted to do something for a man I tremendously respect," he said at the time. "We boxers don't have any organization to turn to when the medical expenses get too high, and we just have to help each other."[29]

The great Henry Armstrong was there too, and Johnny Coulon, Johnny Bratton, and the deposed world heavyweight champion, Muhammad Ali, who lived near Charles in Chicago and tried to befriend him. Ali was involved with the Nation of Islam; Charles distrusted the group and their message and so kept Ali at a respectful distance. The champ showed up anyway. Charles' mother was there, too, and some of his old cronies from Cincinnati, and some writers. By the time everyone was in and seated about 1,200 fans had shown up, a sellout, and made Charles and his family about $10,000, which was put right into a trust fund for "later." They showed films of Charles when he was young and lithe and one of the greatest fighters that ever breathed. Most of the fighters gave short speeches. Of all of them Marciano said it best.

"I was at ringside the night Ezzard defeated Joe Louis. It was a real good fight. But as

I was leaving all the people seemed to be talking about Joe. How bad he looked and all. In the papers, the very next day, the same thing—everybody seemed to be crying for the loser. Nobody gave any credit to Ezzard. It was if he lost. Well, a little while later, I was booked to fight Ezzard—and he gave me two of the toughest fights of my life. I finally figured it out. People just didn't want to see Louis lose. It wasn't Ezzard's fault—he had simply come along in a time in history when a blood-hungry public couldn't appreciate him."[30]

Marciano turned to Charles and said, "I never met a man like Ez before in my life. Ez, you fought me about the very best of anybody. I couldn't put you down and I don't think anyone can put you down. You've got more spirit than any man I ever knew."[31]

Finally the time came for Charles to speak. He rolled up to the dais in his wheelchair and then Louis and Walcott helped him to his feet and braced themselves at his sides. He leaned forward, using the podium to stay upright. "This is the nicest thing that ever happened to me," he mumbled. They could barely hear him. Those who could had to strain to understand him. "All I can say is thank you. Thank you."[32] And then Louis and Walcott put him back in his chair. He told Bentley, "I never thought I'd hear them cheering for me, but they are."[33]

A few days later Charles told a writer, "I never really expected that. I figured there would just be a few old friends and we'd sit around the table chewing the fat. Then I arrived and saw all those people from every part of the country and all and I realized, for the first time, just how people felt. I tried to give a speech but I couldn't. I just couldn't."[34] A reporter who knew what he was talking about asked Charles if his condition scared him. "I was never scared in the ring," he answered. "Oh, maybe after I'd been fighting a few years maybe I'd think I wasn't in as good shape I ought to be, but I never was scared. I'm not scared now."[35]

The benefit was Charles' last public appearance. He still went to work, wheelchair and all, still did what Mayor Daley paid him to do. He still jived the kids as best he could. Some of them bought it, even if they'd never heard of him and he looked nothing like a prizefighter. "Most of them don't know me. They look at me and see a cripple. But they do understand what a champion is. For many of the kids this means something special," he said.[36]

The weeks passed and the months. Ezzard grew weaker, more dependent on Gladys and eventually on Ezzard II. He remained remarkably upbeat, optimistic even. "Oh, it's tough all right, but I'm going to beat it. It's just the fact of not doing certain things," he told a writer after a round of physical therapy. "On a day like today, I'd be out in the street. Out in the centers, out with the kids. There's also a question of pride involved—not being able to walk like I used to. Or talk so well. It's a feeling you sort of have, of being all by yourself, that no one can help you. That it's up to you."[37]

Life went on. Slowly. In 1970 the editors at *The Ring* magazine voted Charles into the Boxing Hall of Fame. "If he could say the words himself, I'm sure Ezzard would want to thank everybody responsible for this honor," Gladys said on his behalf.[38]

Charles kept on working for the Youth Commission until his condition didn't permit it, and when that time came Mayor Daley kept him on the payroll anyway. By late 1972 he had been in the wheelchair for a full six years, and taking care of him was Gladys' full-time job. Ezzard II would help her carry him to an exercise machine they kept in the house. They had to know it was futile by then, but they kept it up.

She carried him from the bed to the bathroom and back. When he couldn't feed himself anymore, she fed him. For a long while she estimated that she could make out what he was saying about 30 percent of the time.[39] Later, when she couldn't get even that anymore, she devised a system of communication whereby she would recite the alphabet and when she got to the letter he wanted, he would blink. Then she would start over again. In this way he would spell out words to communicate his wishes and thoughts.

In November 1972 Gladys gave Ezzard the news that his old manager, Tom Tannas, had died of a heart attack at his home in New Kensington, Pennsylvania. Mintz was gone. Now Tannas. But they were older than he. Charles was still a relatively young man at fifty-one. There had to be days when he envied them their quick exits, but if he did he didn't let on. The only one who would know either way was Gladys, who took care of him every day without fail. There was a time when they were young when she had avoided the press at all costs. Now she was his voice when they called. "Ezzard is still mentally alert, he knows what you are talking about," she told a visiting writer in October. "He can reply, but it takes him a long while and he'd rather reply by shaking his head yes or no."[40] Soon he wouldn't be able to muster even that.

In 1973 representatives of the Muscular Dystrophy Association of America approached Gladys about allowing Ezzard to appear in a commercial that would run during Jerry Lewis' annual telethon. She consented and the ad, produced by New York–based advertising agency Benton and Bowles, was chilling. It alternated shots of Charles' second win over Walcott with long-range shots of a boxing ring. As the voice-over narrated Charles' career highlights, the camera grew closer and closer until Charles, sitting stiffly in wheelchair with his head bobbing absently to the left, came into view. For fight fans who hadn't seen Charles in years, it was a shocking sight.[41]

It continued like this, the terrible and gradual decline, until March 1974. Finally, Gladys, bone-tired and empty, heeded the advice of the doctors and nurses and her friends and agreed to put Ezzard in the VA hospital—for the last time. Ezzard II tried to dissuade her, saying he would help more if she kept him at home. She told him Ezzard didn't want that, that he wanted his son to go out and live his life.[42]

Ezzard Charles spent the last two years of his life at the VA West Side Hospital on Damen Avenue in room B804. When they admitted him the staff expected to see bed sores and other terrible indignities they saw on folks who had been bedridden as long as he had, many not even as long. Caring for a crippled man is an ugly business. But this wasn't the case with Ezzard. His skin was pristine—a testament to how well and attentively Gladys cared for him.[43]

Her commitment didn't end with Charles' move to the hospital. Her routine merely changed. Every day she got up, took a bath and headed down to the hospital to sit with her husband. She'd find him staring absently at the television on the wall, the sun shining through the window beside him. He'd smile. She'd feed him and massage his throat to get the food down. They'd talk, through blinks and the alphabet and a lot of the time shared a silence that said more than any spoken conversation could.

In late May 1975 the doctors told Gladys it would be soon. On the 26th she and the kids went out to the hospital and saw him alive for the last time, took him outside in the courtyard, took some photos in the sun, then said their goodbyes and drove home. They didn't think it would be the last time, because you never think it will be. Two days later, at around midnight on Wednesday, the 28th, Ezzard Charles died. If you had a heart you had to hope that in his mind, at least, in the very last hours he was young and lithe again, the money was flowing, and he could make his body do whatever he wanted it to. And, just maybe, that they'd forgiven him. You had to hope for that.

Chapter Notes

Chapter 1

1. *Cincinnati Magazine,* October 1977, p. 84.
2. Waymarking.com, "Historic Gwinnett County Courthouse—Lawrenceville, GA," May 9, 2007, http://www.waymarking.com/waymarks/WM1H5Y_Historic_Gwinnett_County_Courthouse_Lawrenceville_GA.
3. *New York Times,* "63 Lynchings in 1921; Tuskegee Institute Gives 4,096 as Total of Mob Victims Since 1885," January 1, 1922, http://query.nytimes.com/gst/abstract.html?res=9F07E6DF1239E133A25752C0A9679C946395D6CF.
4. Robert W. Thurston, *Lynching,* p. 369.
5. ROOTS-L Archives, post by Famtreenow@aol.com, "Shapers of Our Century: Webster Ezzard; Gwinnett Co, GA," http://archiver.rootsweb.ancestry.com/th/read/ROOTS/2000-01/124966.
6. *Cincinnati Magazine,* October 1977, p. 84.
7. W.C. Heinz, *Saturday Evening Post,* June 7, 1952, p. 127.
8. *Ibid.*
9. *Ibid.*
10. Joe Aston, *Cincinnati Post,* via Baltimore *Afro-American,* June 28, 1949.
11. Robert Cromie, *Chicago Daily Tribune,* October 17, 1950, part 3, p. 3.
12. *Ibid.*
13. Joe Aston, *Cincinnati Post,* via Baltimore *Afro-American,* June 28, 1949.
14. *Ibid.*
15. *Ibid.*
16. W.C. Heinz, *Saturday Evening Post,* June 7, 1952, p. 127.

Chapter 2

1. Daniel M. Daniel, *The Ring,* January 1951, p. 5.
2. *Ibid.*
3. *Ebony Magazine,* March 1969, p. 108.
4. Bruce Ingersoll, *Chicago Tribune,* August 22, 1965, p. N2.
5. Nat Loubet and John Ort, eds., *The Ring Boxing Encyclopedia and Record Book* (New York: Ring Magazine, 1978).
6. Joe Aston, *Cincinnati Post,* reprinted in Baltimore *Afro-American,* June 28, 1949, p. 28.
7. Hugh Fullerton, *Calgary Herald,* September 9, 1950, p. 27.
8. Associated Press, *Toledo Blade,* January 13, 1942, p. 15.
9. *Ring,* January 1951, p. 5.
10. Joe Aston, *Cincinnati Post,* via *Baltimore Afro-American,* June 28, 1949, p. 28.
11. *Ibid.*
12. Kevin Grace and Joshua Grace, *Cincinnati Boxing,* p. 53.
13. Jack Cuddy, *Eugene Register-Guard,* June 11, 1942, p. 6.
14. Al Abrams, *Pittsburgh Post-Gazette,* June 19, 1949, p. 22.
15. Al Abrams, *Pittsburgh Post-Gazette,* May 26, 1942, p. 14.
16. John Jarrett, *Champ in the Corner,* p. 180.

Chapter 3

1. Robert Cromie, *Chicago Daily Tribune,* May 29, 1951.
2. W.C. Heinz, *Saturday Evening Post,* June 7, 1952, p. 129.
3. Al Abrams, *Pittsburgh Post-Gazette,* January 10, 1949, p. 16.
4. Hugh S. Fullerton Jr., *Lawrence Journal-World,* February 8, 1943, p. 6.
5. Al Abrams, *Pittsburgh Post-Gazette,* September 11, 1945, p. 12.
6. Al Abrams, *Pittsburgh Post-Gazette,* June 2, 1951, p. 10.
7. Al Abrams, *Pittsburgh Post-Gazette,* May 9, 1947, p. 20.
8. Robert Cromie, *Chicago Daily Tribune,* May 29, 1951.
9. *Ibid.*
10. *Pittsburgh Post-Gazette,* August 14, 1942, p. 18.
11. *Pittsburgh Post-Gazette,* September 10, 1942, p. 17.
12. Chester L. Smith, *Pittsburgh Press,* October 13, 1942, p. 22.
13. Al Abrams, *Pittsburgh Post-Gazette,* September 12, 1942, p. 11.
14. Al Abrams, *Pittsburgh Post-Gazette,* October 27, 1942, p. 20.

15. Al Abrams, *Pittsburgh Post-Gazette,* June 2, 1952, p. 26.

Chapter 4

1. Associated Press, *New York Times,* September 2, 1950.
2. Gayle Talbot, *Schenectady Gazette,* July 29, 1950, p. 20.
3. Army camp conditions from Buffalo Soldiers Research Museum, "Trooper John L. Burden, Sr.: 9th U.S. Horse Cavalry," http://www.buffalosoldiersresearchmuseum.org/research/books/burton.htm.
4. Russell Sullivan, *Rocky Marciano,* p. 216.
5. *New York Times,* December 14, 1944.
6. Peter Heller, *In This Corner,* p. 310.
7. Heller, *In This Corner,* pp. 312–313.
8. *Gettysburg Times,* May 21, 1946, p. 3.
9. *Ibid.*
10. *Pittsburgh Post-Gazette,* June 4, 1942, p. 26.
11. Al Abrams, *Pittsburgh Post-Gazette,* June 27, 1946, p. 14.
12. Bob Drum, *Pittsburgh Post-Gazette,* November 8, 1946, p. 41.
13. Grace and Grace, *Cincinnati Boxing,* p. 61.
14. Harvey J. Boyle, *Pittsburgh Post-Gazette,* November 14, 1946, p. 18.
15. *Ibid.*
16. *Afro-American,* January 11, 1947, p. 18.
17. Associated Press, *Toledo Blade,* March 11, 1947, p. 11.
18. Al Abrams, *Pittsburgh Post-Gazette,* April 15, 1947, p. 18.
19. Joe Aston, *Cincinnati Post,* May 12, 1947, p. 12.
20. *Cincinnati Enquirer,* May 6, 1947, p. 3C.
21. Joe Aston, *Cincinnati Post,* May 12, 1947, p. 12.
22. Al Abrams, *Pittsburgh Post-Gazette,* June 12, 1954, p. 10.
23. Associated Press, *Daily Record,* May 4, 1948, p. 8.
24. Guy Butler, *Miami News,* January 20, 1947, p. 2B.
25. United Press, *Pittsburgh Post-Gazette,* July 22, 1947, p. 45.
26. *Ibid.*
27. Frankie Graham, *Montreal Gazette,* July 29, 1947, p. 14.
28. Oscar Fraley, *St. Petersburg Times,* July 27, 1947, p. 119.
29. *Ring,* October 1947.
30. Frankie Graham, *Montreal Gazette,* July 29, 1947, p. 14.
31. Jersey Jones, *Ring,* July 1949, p. 7.
32. Al Abrams, *Pittsburgh Post-Gazette,* September 13, 1948, p. 20.
33. Oscar Fraley, *St. Petersburg Times,* July 27, 1947, p. 21.
34. *Milwaukee Journal,* August 4, 1947, p. 18.

Chapter 5

1. Jack Hand, *Pittsburgh Post-Gazette,* July 25, 1951, p. 16.
2. United States Department of the Treasury, *Mafia: The Government's Secret File on Organized Crime* (New York: Collins, 2007), p. 715.
3. *Free-Lance Star,* December 3, 1947.
4. Associated Press, *Daytona Beach News Journal,* December 6, 1947, p. 4.
5. *Palm Beach Post–Miami News,* December 24, 1947, p. 29.
6. Mike Fitzgerald, Jake La Motta, Bert Randolph Sugar, and Pete Ehrmann, *The Ageless Warrior: The Life of Boxing Legend Archie Moore* (Champaign, IL: Sports, 2004), p. 72.
7. Al Abrams, *Pittsburgh Post-Gazette,* January 16, 1948, p. 16.
8. *African American,* August 23, 1947, p. 12.
9. Robert Cromie, *Chicago Tribune,* February 15, 1948, p. A4.
10. *Ibid.*
11. *Ibid.*
12. Richard Christmas, interview with author, 2010.
13. Al Abrams, *Pittsburgh Post-Gazette,* February 23, 1948, p. 16.

Chapter 6

1. United Press International, *Reading Eagle,* February 20, 1948, p. 6.
2. Associated Press, *Pittsburgh Post-Gazette,* February 23, 1948, p. 16.
3. Ed Sainsbury, *Montreal Gazette,* February 23, 1948, p. 18.
4. *Ibid.*
5. *Ibid.*
6. Associated Press, *Reading Eagle,* February 22, 1948, p. 29.
7. *Ibid.*
8. *Ibid.*
9. International News Service, *St. Petersburg Times,* March 9, 1948.
10. Associated Press, *Milwaukee Journal,* March 6, 1948, p. 6.
11. Associated Press, *Schenectady Gazette,* February 26, 1948, p. 24.
12. Ray Grody, *Milwaukee Sentinel,* May 2, 1962, p. 9.
13. Associated Press, *Pittsburgh Post-Gazette,* February 23, 1948, p. 16.
14. *Saturday Evening Post,* June 7, 1952, p. 129.
15. Charles Einstein, *St. Petersburg Times,* February 23, 1948, p. 18.
16. Robert Cromie, *Chicago Tribune,* February 24, 1948, p. 31.
17. Ray Grody, *Milwaukee Sentinel,* May 2, 1962, p. 9.
18. *Ring,* January 1951, p. 5.
19. Ed Sainsbury, United Press International, *Afro-American,* November 16, 1968, p. 8.
20. Charles Eisenstein, *Palm Beach Post–Miami Daily News,* May 8, 1948, p. 13.
21. Al Abrams, *Pittsburgh Post-Gazette,* July 16, 1951.
22. Red Smith, *Sarasota Journal,* June 8, 1953.

23. W.C. Heinz, *Saturday Evening Post,* June 7, 1952, p. 128.
24. *Pittsburgh Post-Gazette,* July 10, 1948.
25. Associated Press, *Milwaukee Journal,* February 2, 1949, p. 8.

Chapter 7

1. United Press, *Reading Eagle,* December 7, 1947, p. 21.
2. Associated Press, *Schenectady Gazette,* December 11, 1947, p. 19.
3. Associated Press, *Spokesman Review,* December 17, 1947, p. 34.
4. Associated Press, *Spokane Daily Chronicle,* December 13, 1947, p. 32.
5. Leon Hardwick, *African American,* September 18, 1937, p. 20.
6. International News Service, *Reading Eagle,* October 12, 1942, p. 12.
7. Elaine Khan, *New London, Conn., Evening Day,* August 5, 1947, p. 5.
8. Charles Dunkley, *Milwaukee Journal,* August 6, 1948, p. 38.
9. Conversation between Strauss and Louis recounted in the *Afro American,* May 5, 1956, p. 20.
10. Al Abrams, *Pittsburgh Post-Gazette,* March 4, 1949, p. 23.
11. Ibid.
12. Al Abrams, *Pittsburgh Post-Gazette,* July 27, 1948, p. 21.
13. United Press, *Pittsburgh Post-Gazette,* August 1, 1948, p. 28.
14. Al Abrams, *Pittsburgh Post-Gazette,* August 14, 1948, p. 10.
15. Al Abrams, *Pittsburgh Post-Gazette,* September 11, 1948, p. 10.
16. Al Abrams, *Pittsburgh Post-Gazette,* August 7, 1948, p. 8.
17. Associated Press, *New London, Conn., Evening Day,* September 14, 1948, p. 13.
18. Ibid.
19. Ibid.
20. Associated Press, *Ellensburg Daily Record,* September 17, 1948, p. 6.
21. Al Abrams, *Pittsburgh Post-Gazette,* September 21, 1948, p. 14.
22. Andrew O'Toole, *Sweet William: The Life of Billy Conn,* p. 296.
23. Oscar Fraley, *St. Petersburg Times,* December 9, 1948, p. 22.
24. W.C. Heinz, *Saturday Evening Post,* June 7, 1952, p. 129.
25. *Time,* December 20, 1948, n.p.
26. Jarrett, *Champ in the Corner,* pp. 180–181.
27. Murray Rose, Associated Press, *Reading Eagle,* December 10, 1948, p. 48.
28. Al Abrams, *Pittsburgh Post-Gazette,* December 13, 1948, p. 22.
29. *St. Petersburg Times,* December 21, 1948, p. 24.
30. Carl Hughes, *Pittsburgh Post-Gazette,* December 11, 1948, p. 6.
31. Grantland Rice, *Ottawa Citizen,* December 14, 1948, p. 23.
32. Murray Rose, Associated Press, *Reading Eagle,* December 10, 1948, p. 48.
33. Associated Press, *Daily Record,* December 28, 1948, p. 6.
34. *Spokane Daily Chronicle,* December 11, 1948, p. 8.
35. O'Toole, *Sweet William,* p. 300.
36. Associated Press, *Wilmington, N.C., Morning Star,* February 5, 1949, p. 6.
37. Whitney Martin, *Miami Daily News,* February 13, 1949, p. 3D.
38. Al Abrams, *Pittsburgh Post-Gazette,* March 4, 1949, p. 23.
39. Associated Press, *Ellensburg (Wash.) Daily Record,* March 1, 1949, p. 8.
40. Ibid.
41. *Lodi News Sentinel,* March 1, 1949, p. 6.
42. Associated Press, *Ellensburg (Wash.) Daily Record,* March 1, 1949, p. 8.
43. *Time,* March 14, 1949, n.p.

Chapter 8

1. Martin Kane, *Sports Illustrated,* May 7, 1956, pp. 24–28.
2. United Press *(Dubuque, Iowa) Telegraph Herald,* June 8, 1949, p. 14.
3. Ray Grody, *Milwaukee Sentinel,* Sunday, June 12, 1949, p. 3.
4. Al Abrams, *Pittsburgh Post-Gazette,* August 8, 1949, p. 14.
5. *Baltimore Afro-American,* June 15, 1949, p. 15.
6. Nat Fleischer, *Ring,* August 1949, p. 6.
7. Associated Press, *Pittsburgh Post-Gazette,* June 23, 1949, p. 22.
8. Jeff Moshier, *Independent St. Petersburg, Fl.,* June 24, 1949, p. 12.
9. Associated Press, *Nashua, N.H., Telegraph,* June 23, 1949, p. 19.
10. Red Smith, *Palm Beach Post–Miami News,* June 26, 1949, p. 3D.
11. Associated Press, *Pittsburgh Post-Gazette,* June 23, 1949, p. 14.
12. Ibid.
13. W.C. Heinz, *Saturday Evening Post,* June 7, 1952, p. 127.
14. Mintz speech from Red Smith, *Palm Beach Post–Miami News,* June 26, 1949, p. 3D.
15. Oscar Fraley, United Press, *Wilmington News,* July 11, 1949, p. 8.
16. W.C. Heinz, *Saturday Evening Post,* June 7, 1952, p. 127.
17. Associated Press, *Fredericksburg, Va., Free-lance Star,* July 15, 1948, p. 3.
18. Joe Williams, *Pittsburgh Post-Gazette,* August 10, 1949, p. 31.
19. Carl Hughes, *Pittsburgh Post-Gazette,* August 10, 1949, p. 30.
20. Associated Press, *Milwaukee Journal,* August 12, 1949, p. 10.

21. Al Abrams, *Pittsburgh Post-Gazette,* August 8, 1949, p. 14.
22. Carl Hughes, *Pittsburgh Post-Gazette,* August 10, 1949, p. 30.
23. Interview with Charles from International News Service, *Reading Eagle,* August 6, 1949, p. 6.
24. Al Abrams, *Pittsburgh Post-Gazette,* August 8, 1949, p. 19.
25. *Ring,* October 1949, p. 45.
26. Charles Einstein, *Miami News–Palm Beach Post,* August 11, 1949, p. 2B.
27. Oscar Fraley, *Miami News–Palm Beach Post,* August 11, 1949, p. 2B.
28. Associated Press, *Milwaukee Journal,* August 12, 1949, p. 10.
29. Jack Hand, *Evening Independent,* August 11, 1949, p. 31.
30. Associated Press, *Southeast Missourian,* August 11, 1949, p. 5.
31. Joe Knack, *Toledo Blade,* August 14, 1949, p. 2.
32. Robert Maladinich, *Ring,* September 2001, p. 78.
33. Associated Press, *Milwaukee Journal,* October 15, 1949, p. 2.
34. Associated Press, *Ellensburg (Wash.) Daily Record,* October 15, 1949.
35. Associated Press, *St. Petersburg Times,* October 13, 1950, p. 26.
36. Associated Press, *Pittsburgh Post-Gazette,* November 19, 1949, p. 12.
37. Carl Hughes, *Pittsburgh Post-Gazette,* December 7, 1949, p. 45.
38. Al Abrams, *Pittsburgh Post-Gazette,* November 3, 1972, p. 13.

Chapter 9

1. Robert Cromie, *Chicago Daily Tribune,* May 29, 1951.
2. Associated Press, *New London, Conn., Evening Day,* February 25, 1950, p. 11.
3. Associated Press, *Pittsburgh Post-Gazette,* May 5, 1950, p. 23.
4. *Ibid.*
5. Daniel M. Daniel, *Ring,* July 1950, p. 20.
6. Associated Press, *Pittsburgh Post-Gazette,* May 5, 1950, p. 23.
7. *Washington Afro-American,* April 4, 1950, p. 21.
8. Joe Louis and Art Rust, *Joe Louis: My Life,* p. 214.
9. *Ibid.,* p. 216.
10. *Eugene Register Guard,* January 26, 1949, p. 15.
11. *Miami Daily News,* February 2, 1949, p. 53.
12. Associated Press, *Hartford Courant,* March 29, 1949, p. 15.
13. Al Abrams, *Pittsburgh Post-Gazette,* December 22, 1949, p. 14.
14. Murray Rose, *Spokesman Review,* December 9, 1949, p. 18.
15. Meeting where Ezzard is medically cleared to fight again: Barney Nagler, *Ring,* September 1950, pp. 13 and 43.
16. Al Abrams, *Pittsburgh Post-Gazette,* July 7, 1950, p. 14.
17. Associated Press, *Wilmington, N.C., Star News,* July 7, 1950, p. 11.
18. Conversation between writer, Charles and Mintz while training for Beshore: Al Abrams, *Pittsburgh Post-Gazette,* August 4, 1950, p. 16.
19. United Press, *Pittsburgh Post-Gazette,* July 26, 1950, p. 25.
20. *Milwaukee Journal,* August 18, 1950, p. 2.
21. Associated Press, *Fredericksburg, Va., Free-lance Star,* August 16, 1950, p. 8.
22. *Miami News–Palm Beach Post,* August 16, 1950, p. 3C.
23. Al Abrams, *Pittsburg Post-Gazette,* August 17, 1950, p. 14.
24. Associated Press, *Miami Daily News,* August 15, 1950, p. 3C.
25. Associated Press, *Star-News,* September 4, 1950, p. 7.
26. W.C. Heinz, *Saturday Evening Post,* June 7, 1952, p. 127.
27. Barney Nagler, *Ring,* November 1950, p. 17.
28. *Ibid.,* p. 43.
29. *Ibid.*
30. Associated Press, *New York Times,* September 23, 1950.
31. Sam Lacy, *Afro American,* September 23, 1950, p. 17.
32. Barney Nagler, *Ring,* November 1950, p. 43.
33. Associated Press, *New York Times,* September 2, 1950.
34. Associated Press, *New York Times,* September 25, 1950.
35. Associated Press, *New York Times,* September 11, 1950.
36. Associated Press, *New York Times,* September 20, 1950.
37. Associated Press, *New York Times,* September 25, 1950.
38. Associated Press, *New York Times,* September 26, 1950.
39. Arthur Daley, *New York Times,* September 27, 1950.
40. Associated Press, *Pittsburgh Post-Gazette,* September 12, 1950, p. 14.
41. National Newspaper Publishers Association, *Afro-American,* September 5, 1950, p. 16.
42. Sam Lacy, *Afro American,* September 23, 1950, p. 17.
43. Ed Van Every, *Ring,* December 1950, p. 10.
44. Red Smith, *Ottawa Citizen,* September 23, 1950, p. 20.
45. Associated Press, *Daytona Beach Morning Journal,* September 26, 1950, p. 6.
46. United Press, *Reading Eagle,* September 27, 1950, p. 23.
47. Ronald K. Fried, *Corner Men: The Great Boxing Trainers,* p. 82.
48. Louis and Rust, *Joe Louis,* p. 218.
49. Arthur Daley, *New York Times,* September 29, 1950.
50. Louis and Rust, *Joe Louis,* p. 219.

51. Associated Press, *New York Times*, September 28, 1950.
52. *New York Times*, September 28, 1950.
53. James P. Dawson, *New York Times*, September 28, 1950, p. 1.
54. *New York Times*, September 28, 1950.
55. *Ibid.*
56. *Washington Afro-American*, June 3, 1952, p. 15.
57. Jarrett, *Champ in the Corner*, p. 184.

Chapter 10

1. Ed Van Every, *Ring*, December 1950, p. 48.
2. *Ring*, January 1951, p. 42.
3. Jerry Izenberg, *Chicago Sun-Times*, May 29, 1975.
4. *Ring*, January 1951, p. 4.
5. Jimmy Cannon: *Nobody Asked Me, But: The World of Jimmy Cannon*, p. 117.
6. Associated Press, *Pittsburgh Post-Gazette*, December 2, 1950, p. 10.
7. Associated Press, *Vancouver Sun*, December 14, 1950, p. 17.
8. *Ibid.*
9. Nat Fleischer, *Ring*, February 1951, p. 19.
10. *Ibid.*
11. Al Abrams, *Pittsburgh Post-Gazette*, December 7, 1950, p. 52.
12. Associated Press, *Spokane Daily Chronicle*, January 12, 1951, p. 11.
13. Nat Fleischer, *Ring*, March 1951, p. 48.
14. Carl Hughes, *Pittsburgh Press*, January 13, 1951, p. 6.
15. Associated Press, *Pittsburgh Post-Gazette*, January 13, 1951, p. 10.
16. Associated Press, *Sarasota Herald Tribune*, January 14, 1951, p. 19.
17. Carl Hughes, *Pittsburgh Press*, January 13, 1951, p. 6.
18. Charles' long quote about confusion in the heavyweight division, Daniel M. Daniel, *Ring*, March 1951, p. 8.
19. Associated Press, *Pittsburgh Post-Gazette*, November 25, 1950.
20. United Press, *Deseret News*, March 7, 1951, p. A13.
21. *Ring*, July 1951, p. 31.
22. Daniel M. Daniel, *Ring*, March 1951, p. 8.
23. Russ Newland, *Florence (Ala.) Times Daily*, February 18, 1951, p. 12.
24. Associated Press, *Reading Eagle*, March 11, 1951, p. 38.
25. Associated Press, *Portsmouth Times*, June 6, 1951, p. 14.
26. Associated Press, *Chicago Daily News*, January 9, 1951, p. B3.
27. *Sarasota Herald Tribune*, November 13, 1992, p. 3C.
28. Carl Hughes, *Pittsburgh Post-Gazette*, July 14, 1951, p. 6.
29. *Ibid.*
30. United Press, *Tuscaloosa News*, March 8, 1951, p. 14.
31. Al Abrams, *Pittsburgh Post-Gazette*, March 9, 1951, p. 20.
32. Associated Press, *Daytona Beach Morning Journal*, March 8, 1951, p. 10.
33. Associated Press, *Leader Post*, March 8, 1951, p. 19.
34. Associated Press, *Daytona Beach Morning Journal*, March 8, 1951, p. 10.
35. Murray Rose, *Miami Daily News*, March 8, 1951, p. 2B.
36. *Washington Afro-American*, March 27, 1951, p. 8.
37. W.C. Heinz, *Saturday Evening Post*, June 7, 1952, p. 127.
38. *Ring*, January 1951, p. 39.
39. *Black World/Negro Digest*, June 1962, p. 12.
40. *Ring*, July 1951, p. 4.
41. Associated Press, *Pittsburgh Post-Gazette*, March 9, 1951, p. 20.
42. Associated Press, *Milwaukee Journal*, March 10, 1951, p. 2.
43. United Press, *Greensburg Daily Tribune*, May 1, 1951, p. 20.
44. *Ibid.*
45. Jack Cuddy, *Deseret News*, May 28, 1951, p. 6A.
46. Charles Chamberlain, *Telegraph Herald*, May 27, 1951, p. 13.
47. Frank Mastro, *Chicago Daily Tribune*, May 23, 1951.
48. Associated Press, *Afro American*, June 2, 1951, p. 17.
49. Associated Press, *Southeast Missourian*, June 5, 1951, p. 6.
50. Ray Grody, *Milwaukee Sentinel*, May 31, 1951, p. 4.
51. Lloyd Larson, *Milwaukee Sentinel*, May 31, 1951, p. 3.
52. Ray Grody, *Milwaukee Sentinel*, May 31, 1951, p. 4.
53. Lloyd Larson, *Milwaukee Sentinel*, May 31, 1951, p. 3.
54. Nat Fleischer, *Ring*, August 1951, p. 14.
55. *Ibid.*
56. Red Smith, *Miami News*, June 2, 1951, p. 10B.
57. Jesse Abramson, *Ring*, July 1952, p. 16.
58. Lloyd Larson, *Milwaukee Sentinel*, May 31, 1951, p. 3.
59. *Ibid.*

Chapter 11

1. Gayle Talbot, *Lawrence Journal-World*, February 2, 1952, p. 7.
2. *Washington Afro-American*, June 5, 1951, p. 18.
3. Associated Press, *St. Petersburg Times*, June 13, 1951, p. 18.
4. Associated Press, *Pittsburgh Post-Gazette*, June 14, 1951, p. 14.
5. Murray Rose, *Miami News*, June 16, 1951, p. 3B.
6. *Ibid.*
7. *Ibid.*
8. Al Abrams, *Pittsburgh Post-Gazette*, June 11, 1951, p. 16.

9. Al Abrams, *Pittsburgh Post-Gazette*, July 20, 1951, p. 16.
10. *Ibid.*
11. United Press, *Pittsburgh Post-Gazette*, July 19, 1951, p. 36.
12. W.C. Heinz, *Saturday Evening Post*, June 7, 1952, p. 127.
13. Red Smith, *Youngstown (Ohio) Vindicator*, May 28, 1952, p. 30.
14. *Ibid.*
15. Dan Daniel, *Ring*, February 1952, p. 9.
16. Carl Hughes, *Pittsburgh Post-Gazette*, July 19, 1951, p. 36.
17. Daniel L. Daniel, *Ring*, November 1951, p. 26.
18. Associated Press, *Pittsburgh Post-Gazette*, July 20, 1951, p. 16.
19. Associated Press, *Milwaukee Journal*, July 19, 1951, p. 6.
20. Bob Drum, *Pittsburgh Post-Gazette*, July 19, 1951, p. 37.
21. Associated Press, *Milwaukee Journal*, July 19, 1951, p. 6.
22. Bob Drum, *Pittsburgh Post-Gazette*, July 19, 1951, pp. 36 and 37.
23. Bob Drum, *Pittsburgh Post-Gazette*, July 21, 1951, p. 7.
24. Al Abrams, *Pittsburgh Post-Gazette*, July 20, 1951, p. 16.
25. Nat Fleischer, *Ring*, October 1951, p. 5.
26. Murray Rose, *Milwaukee Journal*, July 19, 1951, p. 2.
27. (Lexington, N.C.) *Dispatch*, July 31, 1951, p. 8.
28. United Press, *Toledo Blade*, January 23, 1952, p. 26.
29. United Press, *Pittsburgh Post-Gazette*, February 5, 1952, p. 28.
30. *Pittsburgh Post-Gazette*, February 5, 1952, p. 28.
31. *Pittsburgh Post-Gazette*, February 5, 1952, p. 28.
32. United Press, *Times-News* (Henderson, N.C.), January 29, 1952, p. 10.
33. *Ibid.*
34. Daniel L. Daniel, *Ring*, October 1951, p. 3.
35. W.C. Heinz, *Saturday Evening Post*, June 7, 1952, p. 127.
36. Steven C. Tracy, *Going to Cincinnati: A History of the Blues in the Queen City*, p. 90.
37. Dorothy Kilgallen, *Toledo Blade*, April 8, 1952, p. 35.
38. Dorothy Kilgallen, *St. Petersburg Times*, July 13, 1955, p. 14.
39. John Erardi, *Cincinnati Enquirer*, February 21, 1999, http://enquirer.com/editions/1999/02/21/spt_the_night_the.html.
40. Associated Press, *Ellensburg* (Wash.) *Daily Record*, n.d., p. 8.
41. *Deseret News*, October 16, 1949, p. C1.
42. *Pittsburgh Post-Gazette*, October 1, 1951, p. 25.
43. Associated Press, *St. Petersburg Times*, October 10, 1951, p. 14.
44. United Press, *Beaver Valley Times*, October 9, 1951, p. 12.
45. Associated Press, *New York Times*, October 12, 1951.
46. Editor, *Ring*, December 1951, p. 14.
47. Associated Press, *Eugene Register-Guard*, October 26, 1951, p. 5.

Chapter 12

1. Associated Press, *Southeast Missourian*, February 18, 1952, p. 5.
2. United Press (Henderson, N.C.) *Time News*, May 23, 1952, p. 8.
3. Murray Rose, *London, Conn., Day*, June 5, 1952, p. 26.
4. Associated Press, *Pittsburgh Post-Gazette*, May 12, 1952, p. 24.
5. Sam Lacy, *Afro American*, June 7, 1952, p. 16.
6. *Baltimore Afro-American*, May 3, 1955, p. 8.
7. Daniel M. Daniel, *Ring*, August 1952, p. 4.
8. Jim Jennings, *Mirror*, quoted by Daniel M. Daniel, *Ring*, August 1952, p. 4.
9. *Pittsburgh Post-Gazette*, June 12, 1952, p. 18.
10. Red Smith, *Sarasota Journal*, June 8, 1953, p. 7.
11. *Ibid.*
12. Arthur Daley, *New York Times*, quoted by Daniel M. Daniel, *Ring*, August 1952, p. 4.
13. Jim Jennings, *Mirror*, quoted by Daniel M. Daniel, *Ring*, August 1952, p. 4.
14. Jimmy Cannon, *New York Post*, June 6, 1952, p. 19.
15. Chester Smith, *Pittsburgh Post-Gazette*, June 6, 1952, p. 33.
16. Lewis Burton, *New York Journal American*, via Dan Daniel, *Ring*, August 1952, p. 4.
17. Red Smith, *Ottawa Citizen*, June 6, 1952, p. 20.
18. Daniel M. Daniel, *Ring*, August 1952, p. 43.
19. Murray Rose, *Windsor Daily Star*, June 6, 1952, p. 27.
20. Al Abrams, *Pittsburgh Post-Gazette*, November 3, 1972, p. 13.
21. Staff Correspondent and Associated Press, *Sydney Morning Herald*, June 7, 1952, p. 10.
22. Whitney Martin, *Ottawa Citizen*, June 6, 1952, p. 20.
23. Oscar Fraley, *Spokane Daily Chronicle*, June 6, 1952, p. 11.
24. *Ibid.*
25. Tommy Holmes, *Brooklyn Eagle*, June 10, 1952, p. 14.
26. A.J. Leibling, *The Sweet Science*, p. 47.
27. Fried, *Corner Men*, pp. 93–97.
28. Clifton E. Wilson, *The New London* (Conn.) *Day*, August 9, 1952, p. 12.
29. United Press, *Pittsburgh Post-Gazette*, August 10, 1952, p. 37.
30. *Ibid.*
31. Nat Fleischer, *Ring*, October 1952, p. 10.
32. *Ibid.*
33. Associated Press, *New York Times*, September 25, 1952.
34. *Miami Daily News*, October 9, 1952, p. 4C.
35. United Press, *Pittsburgh Post-Gazette*, October 24, 1952, p. 42.

36. *New London* (Conn.) *Day,* October 24, 1952, p. 18.
37. Jack Hand, *Meriden-Record,* October 22, 1952, p. 4.
38. Associated Press, *Schenectady Gazette,* October 25, 1952, p. 18.
39. Murray Rose, *Freelance-Star* (Fredericksburg, Va.), October 25, 1952, p. 8.
40. United Press, *Pittsburgh Post-Gazette,* December 6, 1952, p. 27.
41. Associated Press, *Prescott* (Ariz.) *Evening Courier,* December 16, 1952, p. 5.
42. United Press, *Pittsburgh Post-Gazette,* December 6, 1952, p. 27.
43. Al Abrams, *Pittsburgh Post-Gazette,* December 20, 1952, p. 12.
44. *Pittsburgh Post-Gazette,* January 30, 1953, p. 21.
45. United Press, *Pittsburgh Post-Gazette,* February 4, 1953, p. 28.
46. United Press, *Greensburg Daily Tribune,* February 4, 1953, p. 24.
47. Associated Press, *Lewiston* (Maine) *Daily Sun,* December 6, 1960, p. 9.
48. Steven A. Reiss, *Sports and the American Jew,* p. 97.
49. United Press, *Kentucky New Era,* March 30, 1953, p. 17.
50. United Press, *Lodi News Sentinel,* April 2, 1953, p. 7.
51. United Press, *Lewiston* (Idaho) *Morning Tribune,* April 3, 1953, p. 8.
52. All Marciano-Walcott II quotes from *Deseret News,* May 16, 1953, p. 4A.
53. Ray Grody, *Milwaukee Sentinel,* May 28, 1953, part 2, p. 3.
54. *Ibid.*
55. *Ibid.*
56. Stanley Woodward, *Evening Gazette,* January 2, 1953, p. 91.
57. James Dusgate, *Ring,* November 1990, p. 48.
58. Red Smith, *Miami Daily News,* December 27, 1953, p. 2D.
59. *Ibid.*
60. Art Grace, *Miami Daily News,* August 12, 1953, section B.
61. Description of events from Morris McLemore column, *Miami News,* August 12, 1953, p. B1.
62. Art Grace, *Miami Daily News,* August 12, 1953, section B1.
63. *Ibid.*
64. *Ibid.*
65. Associated Press, *St. Petersburg Times,* September 8, 1953, p. 12.
66. Associated Press, *Victoria Advocate,* September 8, 1953, p. 7.
67. United Press, *Beaver Valley Times,* September 8, 1953, p. 10.
68. *Reading Eagle,* August 30, 1953, p. 43.
69. Ezzard Charles, *Ring,* April 1954, p. 12.
70. Ralph Bernstein, *Ellensburg Daily Record,* September 9, 1953, p. 6.
71. Jimmy Cannon, *New York Post,* September 9, 1953, p. 79.
72. Associated Press, *Pittsburgh Post-Gazette,* September 9, 1953, p. 16.
73. Frank Maestro, *Chicago Tribune,* January 1954, p. 17.

Chapter 13

1. James Dusgate, *Ring,* November 1990, p. 49.
2. Associated Press, *Miami News,* December 16, 1953, p. 2B.
3. *Ibid.*
4. *Warsaw Times-Union,* December 17, 1953, p. 5.
5. Associated Press, *Miami News,* December 16, 1953, p. 2B.
6. United Press, *Pittsburgh Post-Gazette,* December 20, 1953, p. 25.
7. *Ibid.*
8. Associated Press, *Pittsburgh Post-Gazette,* December 17, 1953, p. 20.
9. Frank Maestro, *Chicago Tribune,* January 10, 1954, p. 24.
10. Jack Koffman, *Ottawa Citizen,* March 7, 1964, p. 11.
11. Associated Press, *Ludington Daily News,* January 13, 1954, p. 10.
12. *News and Courier,* May 26, 1954.
13. Al Abrams, *Pittsburgh Post-Gazette,* January 18, 1954, p. 18.
14. Frank Mastro, *Chicago Tribune,* January 13, 1954, p. 17.
15. *Chicago Daily Tribune,* February 25, 1954, p. D1.
16. Sullivan, *Rocky Marciano,* p. 219.
17. Associated Press, *New London Connecticut Evening Day,* February 15, 1954, p. 11.
18. United Press, *Times-News* (Hendersonville, N.C.), May 10, 1954, p. 8.
19. *Ibid.*
20. *Ibid.*
21. United Press, *Jeanette News Dispatch,* May 21, 1954, p. 13.
22. Associated Press, *Spence Daily Reporter,* June 14, 1954, p. 5.
23. Red Smith, *Sarasota Journal,* June 17, 1954, p. 11.
24. *Ibid.*
25. Red Smith, *Youngstown Vindicator,* June 10, 1954, p. 36.
26. Jack Cuddy, United Press, *Eugene Register Guard,* June 10, 1954, p. 22.
27. All quotes from extortion letter from Matt Stout, "New FBI Documents Reveal Threat to Boxing Great," Boston.com, May 8, 2011.
28. Red Smith, *Youngstown (Ohio) Vindicator,* June 10, 1954, p. 36.
29. Bob Johnson, *Spokane (Wash.) Daily Chronicle,* June 16, 1954, p. 16.
30. *Ibid.*
31. Murray Rose, Associated Press (*New London, Conn.) Day,* June 17, 1954, p. 31.
32. Associated Press, *Chicago Daily Tribune,* June 8, 1954, p. E6.

33. Murray Rose, Associated Press (*New London, Conn.*) *Day,* June 17, 1954, p. 31.
34. Richard Hoffer, *Sports Illustrated,* July 14, 2003, n.p.
35. Murray Rose, Associated Press (*New London, Conn.*) *Day,* June 17, 1954, p. 31.
36. About the *Police Gazette*: Richard Hoffer, *Sports Illustrated,* July 14, 2003.
37. Red Smith, *Greensburg Daily Tribune,* June 25, 1954, p. 28.
38. Sullivan, *Rocky Marciano*, p. 223.
39. Arthur Daley, *New York Times,* June 20, 1954.
40. Arthur Daley, *New York Times,* June 18, 1954.
41. Arthur Daley, *New York Times,* June 20, 1954, p. S2.
42. Joseph C. Nichols, *New York Times,* June 19, 1954.
43. Red Smith, *Greensburg Daily Tribune,* June 25, 1954, p. 28.
44. *Sports Illustrated,* August 16, 1954, p. n.p.
45. *Chicago Daily Tribune,* June 18, 1954, p. B1.
46. *Ibid.*
47. Joseph M. Sheehan, *New York Times,* June 18, 1954.
48. *Ibid.*
49. *Ibid.*
50. *Age,* September 15, 1954, p. 14.
51. Dink Carroll, *Montreal Gazette,* May 12, 1955, p. 20.
52. Murray Rose, *St. Petersburg Times,* August 31, 1954, p. 9.
53. Associated Press, *Chicago Daily Tribune,* September 5, 1954, p. A6.
54. Associated Press, *Lewiston Evening Journal,* September 8, 1954, p. 7.
55. Leibling, *The Sweet Science,* p. 45.
56. Red Smith, *Sarasota Journal,* September 13, 1954, p. 7.
57. Wilfrid Smith, *Chicago Daily Tribune,* September 13, 1954, p. B2.
58. Murray Rose, *New London Evening Day,* September 18, 1954, p. 14.
59. Budd Schulberg, *Sports Illustrated,* September 27, 1954, n.p.
60. Red Smith, *Sarasota Journal,* September 13, 1954, p. 14.
61. Art Grace, *Miami Daily News,* September 19, 1954, p. 6B.
62. United Press, *Miami Daily News,* September 19, 1954, p. 6B.
63. *Ibid.*
64. Budd Schulberg, *Sports Illustrated,* September 27, 1954, n.p.
65. Milton Gross, *New York Post*, via the *Age*, September 20, 1954, p. 7.
66. "The Age Correspondent" and AAP, *Age*, September 20, 1954, p. 7.
67. Budd Schulberg, *Sports Illustrated,* September 27, 1954, n.p.
68. United Press, *Miami Daily News,* September 19, 1954, p. 6B.
69. Conversation in locker room after Marciano rematch: *Time,* September 27, 1954.

Chapter 14

1. Art Grace, *Palm Beach Post–Miami News,* May 9, 1955, p. 16A.
2. Steve Snider, *Sarasota Herald-Tribune,* February 17, 1955, p. 14.
3. *Ibid.*
4. Jack Hand, *New London, Conn. Evening Day,* February 19, 1955, p. 12.
5. Myron Cope, *Sports Illustrated,* October 19, 1964, n.p.
6. Conversation in Miami diner: Art Grace, *Palm Beach Post,* April 23, 1955, p. 11A.
7. Thomas Hauser, *The Boxing Scene* (Philadelphia, PA: Temple University Press, 2009), p. 174; Art Grace, *Miami News–Palm Beach Post,* April 28, 1955, p. 13A.
8. Art Grace, *Miami News–Palm Beach Post,* April 28, 1955, p. 13A.
9. Art Grace, *Palm Beach Post,* April 23, 1955, p. 11A.
10. Art Grace, *Miami News–Palm Beach Post,* May 9, 1955, p. 16A.
11. Associated Press, *Milwaukee Journal,* May 28, 1955, p. 2.
12. Associated Press, *Kentucky New Era,* June 9, 1955, p. 17.
13. *Chicago Daily Tribune,* July 15, 1955, p. C2.
14. Associated Press, *Ellensburg Daily Record,* July 14, 1955, p. 18.
15. Martin Kane, *Sports Illustrated,* July 29, 1957.
16. Arthur Daley, *New York Times,* June 5, 1956.
17. Martin Kane, *Sports Illustrated,* July 29, 1957, n.p.
18. *Afro-American,* August 13, 1955, p. 17.
19. Locker room conversation between Jackson and Charles: *Gettysburg Times,* September 1, 1955, p. 6.
20. Daniel M. Daniel, *Ring,* March 1951, p. 8.
21. Art Grace, *Miami News–Palm Beach Post,* October 31, 1955, p. 15A.
22. Associated Press, *Toledo Blade,* November 15, 1955, p. 79.
23. Gilbert Rogin, *Sports Illustrated,* July 23, 1956, n.p.
24. *Salt Lake City Deseret News And Telegram,* September 1, 1956, p. A3.
25. Associated Press, *Milwaukee Journal,* October 3, 1956, p. 2.
26. Associated Press, *Ottawa Citizen,* December 3, 1956, p. 14.
27. *Ibid.*

Chapter 15

1. Associated Press, *Kentucky New Era,* May 9, 1957, p. 19.
2. Ray Grody, *Milwaukee Sentinel,* February 18, 1958, p. 3.
3. *Ibid.*
4. Associated Press, *Tuscaloosa News,* September 7, 1958, p. 11.
5. Whitey Sawyer, *Ocala Star Banner,* October 28, 1958, p. 8.

6. Jimmy Cannon, *Miami News–Palm Beach Post*, November 4, 1958, p. 2C.
7. *Black World/Negro Digest*, June 1962, p. 11.
8. Associated Press, *Prescott Evening Courier*, March 31, 1959, p. 5.
9. Earl Morey, *Lawrence Journal World*, September 3, 1959, p. 10.
10. Libby Lackman, *Cincinnati Enquirer*, January 1, 1961.
11. *Ibid.*
12. *Ibid.*
13. *Ibid.*
14. Ezzard Charles II, interview with author, August 2010.
15. *Ibid.*
16. Frank Mastro, *Chicago Daily Tribune*, December 12, 1961, p. C2.
17. *Black Negro/World Digest*, June 1962, n.p.
18. Associated Press, *Miami News–Palm Beach Post*, August 28, 1965, p. 4C.
19. *Ibid.*
20. *Ebony*, March 1969, p. 104.
21. William Barry Furlong, *Washington Post*, May 18, 1974, p. 36.
22. *Ibid.*
23. *Ibid.*
24. Bruce Ingersoll, *Chicago Tribune*, August 22, 1965, p. N2.
25. Dink Carroll, *Montreal Gazette*, October 31, 1968, p. 32.
26. *Ibid.*
27. David Condon, *Chicago Tribune*, November 14, 1968, p. C1.
28. Ed Sainsbury, United Press International, *Afro-American*, November 16, 1968, p. 8.
29. *Sports Illustrated*, September 9, 1968, n.p.
30. *Ebony*, March 1969, p. 104.
31. Associated Press, *Vancouver Sun*, October 30, 1972, p. 25.
32. *Ibid.*
33. Jim Murray, *Spokesman-Review*, December 27, 1968.
34. *Ebony*, March 1969, p. 110.
35. Ed Sainsbury, United Press International, *Afro-American*, November 16, 1968, p. 8.
36. *Ebony*, March 1969, p. 106.
37. *Ibid.*, p. 108.
38. Associated Press, *Daytona Beach Morning Journal*, December 31, 1970, p. 12.
39. Robin Adams Sloan, *Pittsburgh Post-Gazette*, June 13, 1972, p. 4.
40. Associated Press, *Vancouver Sun*, October 30, 1972, p. 25.
41. "1970's Muscular Dystrophy Commercial with Ezzard Charles," https://www.youtube.com/watch?v=ntSVnJr0F1s.
42. Ezzard Charles II, interview with author, August 2010.
43. *Ibid.*

Bibliography

Books

Cannon, Jimmy. *Nobody Asked Me, But: The World of Jimmy Cannon.* New York: Holt, Rinehart and Winston, 1978.
Collins, Nigel. *Boxing Babylon: Behind the Shadowy World of the Prize Ring.* Secaucus, NJ: Carol, 1990.
Curl, James. *Jersey Joe Walcott: A Boxing Biography.* Jefferson, NC: McFarland, 2012.
Fried, Ronald K. *Corner Men: The Great Boxing Trainers.* New York: Four Walls Eight Windows, 1991.
Grace, Kevin, and Joshua Grace. *Cincinnati Boxing.* Mount Pleasant, SC: Arcadia, 2006.
Heller, Peter. *In This Corner...!: Forty-two World Champions Tell Their Stories.* Cambridge, MA: Da Capo, 1994.
Holt, Jerome, ed. *No Cheering in the Press Box.* New York: Holt, Rinehart and Winston, 1974.
Jarrett, John. *Champ in the Corner: The Ray Arcel Story.* Gloucestershire, UK: Tempus, 2008.
Liebling, A.J. *The Sweet Science.* New York: Viking, 1956.
Louis, Joe, and Art Rust. *Joe Louis: My Life.* San Diego, CA: Harcourt Brace Jovanovich, 1978.
Mitchell, Kevin. *Jacobs Beach: The Mob, the Garden and the Golden Age of Boxing.* London: Yellow Jersey, 2011.
O'Toole, Andrew. *Sweet William: The Life of Billy Conn.* Champaign: University of Illinois Press, 2008.
Reiss, Steven A. *Sports and the American Jew.* New York: Syracuse University Press, 1998.
Schulberg, Budd. *Ringside Treasury of Boxing Reportage.* Lanham, MD: Ivan R. Dee, 2006.
Sullivan, Russell. *Rocky Marciano: The Rock of His Times.* Champaign: University of Illinois Press, 2002.
Tosches, Nick. *The Devil and Sonny Liston.* New York: Little, Brown, 2000.
Tracy, Steven C. *Going to Cincinnati: A History of the Blues in the Queen City.* Champaign: University of Illinois Press, 1993.
Thurston, Robert W. *Lynching: American Mob Murder in Global Perspective.* Burlington, VT: Ashgate, 2011.
Weston, Stanley, ed. *Ring: Boxing in the 20th Century.* Illus. by Steven Farhood. New York: BDD Illustrated Books, 1993.

Newspapers

African American
Afro-American
Baltimore Afro-American
Beaver Valley Times
Brooklyn Eagle
Calgary Herald
Chicago Daily Tribune
Chicago Sun-Times
Cincinnati Enquirer
Cincinnati Post
Daily Record
Daytona Beach Morning Journal
Daytona Beach News
Deseret News
Dubuque, Iowa, Telegraph Herald
Ellensburg Daily Record
Eugene Register-Guard
Evening Gazette
Evening Independent
Florence (Ala.) Times
Fredericksburg, Va., Freelance Star
Free-Lance Star
Gettysburg Times
Greensburg Daily Tribune
Hartford Courant
Henderson Times-News
Hendersonville Times-News
Jeanette News dispatch
Kentucky New Era
Lawrence Journal-World
Lawrence Journal World
Leader Post
Lewiston (Idaho) Morning Tribune
Lewiston (Maine) Evening Journal
Lexington Dispatch
Lodi News Sentinel

Lodi News Sentinel
Ludington Daily News
Meriden-Record
Miami Daily News
Milwaukee Journal
Milwaukee Sentinel
Montreal Gazette
Nashua, N.H., Telegraph
New London, Conn., Evening Day
New York Post
New York Times
Ocala Star Banner
Ottawa Citizen
Palm Beach Post–Miami News
Pittsburgh Post-Gazette
Portsmouth Times
Prescott Evening Courier
Reading Eagle
Salt Lake City Deseret News and Telegram
Sarasota Journal
Schenectady Gazette
Southeast Missourian
Spence Daily Reporter
Spokane Daily Chronicle
Spokesman Review
St. Petersburg Times
St. Petersburg Independent
Sydney Morning Herald
Telegraph Herald
The Age
Toledo Blade
Tuscaloosa News
Vancouver Sun
Victoria Advocate
Warsaw Times-Union
Washington Afro-American
Washington Post
Wilmington News
Wilmington Morning Star
Wilmington Star News
Windsor Daily Star
Youngstown Vindicator

Index

Abrams, Georgie 27, 59
Acevedo, Miguel 159
Agnello, Joe 102, 107
Agramonte, Omelio 115, 126–128, 160
Albright, Bob 192
Alexander, Russell 63
Ali, Muhammad 202
Andrade, Jack 87
Andrews, Paul 189
Arcel, Ray 24, 99, 102, 104–108, 117, 126, 134, 138, 143, 145, 147–151, 153, 156, 165
Arthur, Johnny 186
Ashley, Dave 197
Atkins, Larry 40, 51, 52
Atlanta 1, 6, 8, 108

Bachman, Frank 22
Baer, Buddy 99–100, 156
Baer, Max 103, 113, 116, 156
Bainbridge, Georgia 7
Baker, Bob 128, 157, 160, 168
Baksi, Joe 42, 46, 49, 67, 69–74, 85, 108
Ballard, Hank 140
Banks, Charley 79
Barlow, Adolph 36
Barone, Nick 110–111, 113–114, 116
Baroudi, Sam 53–64, 148, 153, 156
Barrow, Lillie Reese 11
Barrow, Munroe 11
Bascom, Wes 155–156
Basie, Count 140
Basora, Jose 27–28, 30
Batche, Fred 13
Battalino, Battling 10
Becker, Sam 18, 21–22, 39, 43, 70, 74, 78, 83, 88, 110, 152
Beckwith, Booker 27
Begun, Jack 54, 59, 61–62
Bell, Shelton 28, 38
Bennett, Murray 168
Bentley, Ben 200
Berg, Jackie "Kid" 10
Berl, Al 182–183
Berle, Milton 128
Bernstein, Ike 168
Berry, Theodore 22
Bertola, Enrico 111

Beshore, Freddie 88, 91–92, 96–98, 111, 113, 115
Bethea, Wayne 192
Bettina, Melio 27–28, 39, 43, 84
Bimstein, Whitey 190
Bivins, Jimmy 29, 31–32, 36–42, 44, 46, 49–50, 52, 67–69, 74, 78, 85, 87, 116, 130, 140, 154–155, 167, 174
Black, Julian 42
Blackburn Jack 42, 48
Bobo, Harry 26–27
Bocchicchio, Felix 49–50, 64–65, 78–79, 118, 126, 128–129, 133–138, 144–145, 155, 157
Bolden, Leroy 17
Bolden, Nate 29, 31, 37–38, 74
Booker, Eddie 37, 68
Bowen, Ray 69
Braddock, Jimmy 16, 30, 79- 80, 84, 112–113, 116
Bradshaw, Tiny 140
Brion, Cesar 115, 131, 140, 142, 153–154, 160, 185
British Boxing Board of Control 77, 135, 193
Brodie, A.L. 58
Brothers, Elkins 103, 167–168
Brothers, George 48
Brouillard. Lou 32
Brown, Freddie 190
Brown, Jimmy 22, 50, 71, 74, 79, 99, 100, 104, 134, 138, 162, 169, 175, 176
Brown, Mose 24, 27, 28, 30, 31, 39
Bucceroni, Danny 154, 166, 170
Buford, Frank 154
Burley, Charlie 23–25, 27, 31–32, 39, 54, 68, 78, 174
Butcher, Grant 156

Camilla, Georgia 8
Canzoneri, Tony 10
Caplan, Leonard 58
Capone, Al 18
Capristo, Joe 164
Carbo, Frankie 19, 51, 67, 144, 155, 169
Carnera, Primo 18, 101, 131
Carter, Ruben 200
Cascino, Dr. Joseph P. 57
Case, Jack 37
Castro, Johnny 17
Catskills Mountains 98, 171, 176–177
Cerdan, Marcel 54, 70
Chambers, James 168

Chard, Howard 44
Charles, Alberta 5-6, 8
Charles, Deborah 114, 118-119, 122, 138
Charles (née Gartrell), Gladys 41, 50, 91, 93, 114, 118-119, 122, 138, 140, 145, 164, 183, 185-186, 194-204
Charles, Leith 138
Charles, William 5-6
Charleston, Oscar 6
Chase, Jack 38, 43, 54, 68
Chicago, Illinois 45, 53-55, 57-59, 61, 67, 71, 73, 78, 82, 89, 93, 95-96, 108, 115- 116, 118-120, 123, 127, 145, 149, 154-156, 164, 168-169, 172-173, 186, 189, 198-202
Chocolate, Kid 10-11, 119, 159
Christenberry, Bob 136, 137, 144
Christmas, Richard 17, 21, 36, 49, 55, 82, 83-84, 91, 99, 138, 149
Christoforidis, Anton 21-23, 27-28, 31, 38
Cincinnati, Ohio 8-13, 16-18, 20-24, 27, 29, 30-36, 38, 40-41, 43-46, 50-51, 67, 70, 72-75, 77-78, 81, 83, 86, 88-89, 91-93, 103-104, 108-111, 113-114, 118-120, 124, 129, 130, 138-140, 142, 145, 149, 150, 152-154, 157, 163-165, 171, 175, 179, 185, 189, 191, 196-197, 199, 202
Cincinnati Cotton Club 119, 139-140, 145
Clanton, Jeff 91
Clark, Dr. Ray 118
Clayton, Zach 146-148, 151
Cleveland, Ohio 10, 29, 31-32, 36-37, 39-41, 47, 51-53, 78, 127, 130, 154, 168, 191
Coachman, Eddie 188
Cockell, Don 166, 178, 188, 192-193
Coco, Ettore 49
Comiskey, Pat 43
Comiskey Park 78-80
Conn, Billy 20-21, 26, 39, 42-43, 66, 71, 73, 99, 102, 116, 128, 131, 174
Conn, Mark 102
Corbett, Jim 175
Costner, George 13
Culbertson, "Baby" Dutch 100-101, 103

Daggert, Charlie 129
DaGrosa, John "Ox" 128-130, 133
Daley, Pat 21
Daley, Richard 201
Davis, Danny 12
Davis, Jackie 32, 51, 52
Decatur, Leroy 61
Dempsey, Jack 8, 11, 19, 40, 67, 70, 74, 79, 101, 103-104, 118, 120-121, 132, 146, 150-151, 153, 174-175, 182
Detroit (Michigan) 11, 48, 53, 77, 94, 100, 106, 108, 111, 114-117, 121, 127, 145, 149, 154-155, 164
Doljack, Frank 32
Dorell, Artie 17
Dougherty, Charles 59
Downey, Jack 88
Drake, Carol 140
Drammis, Dr. J.J. 59
Duncan, Billy 36
Dundee, Angelo 160, 187
Dundee, Chris 20, 24, 27, 160-161, 191

Dunn, Dynamite 7
Duquesne Gardens 26, 29, 40, 43
Durrell, Yvonne 189
Dyer, Charlie 22, 27, 38, 77, 81-85, 88

Eckstein, Billy 140
Egan, "Colonel" Eddie 64
Elkus, Gene 50, 82
Elkus, Max 18, 21-22, 27, 38, 50
Ellington, Duke 140
Engel, George 28
Escoe, Vern 186
Ettore, Al 48
Ezzard, Webster Pierce 5-6

Farr, Johnny 10
Farr, Tommy 84, 116
Felix, Barney 98
Felton, Gene 100-101
Ferguson, Lula Belle 140
Ferlaino, Frank R. Dr. 92
Fischer, Eddie 174
Fitzpatrick, Fitzie 44, 45, 51-52, 87
Fleeman, Donnie 197
Flowers, Tiger 8
Flynn, Johnny 94-95
Forbes, Frank 102
Forbes Field 23-24, 26-28, 36, 38-39, 43, 130-131, 139, 141, 143
Fort Clark, Texas 34, 102
Foster, Maude 8
Foster, Stephen 114
Fox, Billy 37-38, 51, 61, 85
Fox, "Tiger" Jack 48
Franklin, Eddie 57
Fullam, Frank 65
Futch, Eddie 116

Galveston, Texas 7
Gannon, Joe 180
Gans, Joe 7
Gardner, Ava 105
Gehrig, Lou 7, 201
Georgia 1, 5, 8, 31, 32
Gibson, Lloyd 79, 99
Gibson, Truman 67, 74, 98, 104, 144, 169
Gilliam, Bill 157, 160, 171
Gilmer, Frank 123-124
Gleason, Bobby 159-160, 168
Glickman, Bernie 189
Goebel, Bill 22
Goicz, Stanley 36
Gold, Ralph 92
Golden, Bob 180
Goldman, Charlie 171, 177, 182, 202
Goldstein, Ruby 64, 72, 86, 112-113, 143
Greaves, Wilf 186
Greb, Harry 7, 131
Green, Alvin 197
Green, Gov. Dwight 59
Greene, Abe J. 75, 83, 137
Gutierrez, Pincho 159
Gwinnett County Courthouse 1

Hafer, Walter 70
Hall, Toxie 169, 171, 186, 192
Hannigan, John Joseph 173
Hantz, Pete, 17
Harlem, New York 6, 11, 46, 58, 71, 108, 164,
Harlem 'Rens 6, 7
Harper, Johnny 196
Harris, Ossie 37
Harris, Roy 194
Harrison, Monroe 36
Harrison, Tommy 155-156
Haynes, Johnny 73, 74
Hayworth, Rita 26
Henderson, Lulu Belle 83
Henry, Clarence 186
Herrera, Frederico 61
Hickey Park 24, 26-28
Hill, Percy 83
Hintz, Ed 123
Hogue, Shorty 37
Holahan, John 128-130
Holman, John 168, 186-192
Hoosman, Al 89
Horne, Lena 41
Houston, Dr. J.M. 92
Howell, Gene 13
Hubert, Tee 36
Huldock, Fred 99-100
Hurley, Jack 53, 54, 58, 61

International Boxing Club (IBC) 67, 70, 76-77, 78, 80, 82-84, 86, 91, 93, 95, 97-98, 102-103, 105, 110-111, 116, 118-119, 135-138, 140-141, 143-145, 152, 154-156, 158-159, 162-163, 165-166, 169, 174

Jackson, Al 13-14
Jackson, Tommy "Hurricane" 190-191
Jacobs, Mike 23, 27, 38-42, 66-67, 70, 76-77, 79, 95, 135
Jannilli, Fernando 61
Jasper, Don 192
Jenkins, Lew 22-23, 39
Jensen, Marv 156
Jinks, Joe 7
Johnson, Harold 115, 157, 159-160, 162-166, 168, 170, 173, 179, 189
Johnson, Jack 7, 11, 87, 175,
Johnson, Leo 169, 171
Johnson, Lonnie 140
Johnson, Melody 20
Johnson, Young Jack 192
Johnston, Charlie 44, 52
Jones, Clarence 50
Jones, Gene 79, 171, 179
Joseph, Eddie 46

Kahut, Joe 44, 144
Kaiser, Dr. Louis A. 91-92
Kearns, Jack 74, 120, 121, 123, 144, 162
Keene, Julian 145
Kellman, Joe 202
Kenneally, Tom 62
Ketchum, Willie 165

Kid, Cocoa 23, 54
Klein, Izzy 56-58, 156
Krieger, Solly 20
Ku Klux Klan 11

LaMotta, Jake 39, 51, 54, 128
Langford, Sam 7
LaStarza, Roland 156, 158-159, 163, 166-168, 170-171, 174, 176, 185
Lawrenceville, Georgia 1, 5-11, 35, 52, 132, 153, 175
Layne, Rex 114-115, 141-144, 149-152, 154, 156-157, 161, 163-164, 167, 169, 173
Lazer, Roy 48
Lecron, George 46
Leonard, Benny 60
Lesnevich, Gus 24, 31, 36-39, 41, 43-44, 50-55, 61-62, 65, 67-68, 70, 77, 83-86, 88-89, 93, 116, 144, 152
Levey, Joseph 163
Levinsky, Kingfish 103
Levy, Dr. Robert 95-96
Lewis, Bradley 17
Lewis, Jerry 174
Lewis, John Henry 104
Lindsay, Joe 99
Liston, Charles "Sonny" 168-169
Loi, Francesco 61
Lorain, Ohio 7
Lou Gehrig's Disease 201
Louis, Joe 11-13, 16, 19, 23, 30-31, 34-35, 40-42, 47, 53, 60-64, 66, 68-69, 72, 75, 77, 80, 82-83, 85-86, 90, 93, 95-98, 100-101, 103-105, 108-110, 113, 115-116, 119, 125, 127-128, 132, 135, 145, 153, 167, 171, 188, 191, 198, 202
Lutz, Henry 22, 55
lynchings 1
Lyons, Jackie 71

Mackey, Biz 6
Madison Square Garden 23, 30, 34, 38, 40-41, 47, 51, 67, 75, 95, 97, 112, 127, 143, 153, 193
Mamakos, Steve 27
Manager's Guild 19, 39, 59, 144
Manfredo, Frank 88
Mann, Nathan 99
Marciano, Rocky 136-137, 140, 142-144, 150-159, 161-164, 166-189, 191-194, 202-203
Markson, Harry 83, 95, 98, 119
Marshall, Lloyd 32-33, 37-38, 44, 50, 52, 54, 68, 74, 78, 85, 116, 168
Massey, Harvey 37
Matthews, Harry 136-137, 150, 154, 193
Matisi, Joe 50
Maxim, Joey 27-31, 38, 49, 67-68, 73-75, 78, 83-84, 87, 116, 120-126, 144, 147, 162-163, 174, 189
Mayne, Kenny 149-150
McConnell, Mart 1
McCoy, Al 99
McCure, Willie 200
McManus, John 202
McMurtry, "Irish" Pat 192
McTiernan, Buck 128-129, 132, 135, 139, 142, 146-147, 164

Mendel, Harry 67, 75, 78–79
Menendez, Gabe 68
Michaels, Dewey 98
Miles, Marshall 42, 47, 64, 100, 116, 118–119, 131, 134–135, 140
Miller, Davey 81
Miller, Freddie 12
Miller, Johnny 11
Mills, Freddie 42, 50, 68, 77, 84, 120
Mintz, Jake 24–29, 31, 36, 38–41, 43–46, 50–51, 53, 55, 57, 61–63, 65, 67–69, 71–75, 77–79, 81–86, 88–92, 95–99, 106–108, 110–111, 114–116, 118–120, 128–131, 133–137, 142, 145–149, 151–156, 159–160, 162, 164, 166–169, 171, 176, 179, 183–186, 204
Mississippi 1, 6, 36
Modzelle, Joe 90, 97
Monroe, Marty 47
Montgomery, Bob 128
Montgomery, Grover 8
Moore, Archie 36–38, 43–44, 46, 50–54, 68–69, 116, 159–160, 162–163, 174, 186, 191, 194, 196, 202
Moreno, Dr. J.J. 181
Morris, Charlie 17
Motor Square Garden 26
Muriello, Tami 42, 84
Murray, Jim 144
Murray, Lee Q 39
Music Hall (Cincinnati) 10, 20, 23, 39, 41, 70, 74, 189

Nardico, Danny 189
National Boxing Association (NBA) 21, 23, 36, 43, 52–53, 69, 75, 77–78, 92–93, 108, 120, 137–138, 141, 197
Negro League, National 6
Nelson, Pete 145
Nemerson Hotel 98, 99
New York 6–9, 11, 18–23, 30–31, 36 38–39, 41–42, 44–46, 50, 54, 58, 61, 63–64, 68, 71, 73–74, 77, 79, 83–86, 88, 92, 95–96, 98, 102, 104, 108–111, 136, 140, 149, 158, 164, 166, 168–171, 176, 181, 189–190, 192, 202, 204
Newkirk, Gil 180
Newton, Glenn 54
Nicholson, George 79, 97, 99–100, 104
Niederreiter, Andy 70
Nora, Dr. Ernest 92
Norkus, Charlie 155, 185–186, 193
Norris, Jim 67, 69, 75–78, 80, 83–84, 93, 95, 103–104, 110–111, 114, 116, 119, 136–137, 144–145, 155, 170, 173, 175, 179–181
Northside Arena 26
Nova, Lou 99, 104, 112

O'Brien, Jimmy 43
O'Brien, Shamus 100–101
O'Dowd, Mike 71
O'Laughlin, Tommy 24, 47
Oliver, Dixie Lee 94
Oma, Lee 94, 111–114, 137, 142, 168, 191
Overlin, Ken 20–24, 28, 32

Palermo, Frank "Blinky" 19, 37–38, 49, 51, 67, 166–167, 169

Parker, Walter 145
Parks, George 36
Parkway Outdoor Arena 10
Parnassus, George 155
Pastor, Bob 27, 31
Patterson, Floyd 190–192, 194–195
Paycheck, Johnny 97, 99
Payne, Rusty 43
Pep, Willie 103
Philadelphia, Pennsylvania 36–38, 48, 54, 57, 73, 115, 128–129, 145–147, 150–153, 159, 160, 162–163, 166
Pittsburgh, Pennsylvania 28, 30–31, 36–40, 43, 45–46, 53, 67, 71, 73, 77–78, 88–89, 91, 97, 119, 127–131, 133, 135, 137–138, 141–142, 145, 147, 151, 155–156, 168, 186, 189, 196
Pittsburgh Pirates 27
Plumeri, James 49
Powell, Charlie 185
Pryor, Billy 23

Randolph, Teddy 50
Ray, "Violent" Elmer 42–50, 52, 61–62, 68, 84, 93–94, 116, 174
Rebersak, Vic 29
Reddish, Willie 48
Reynolds, Bernie 152
Reynolds, Debbie 174
Rhein, George W. 22, 27, 38, 69, 76, 81, 83–84, 88
Richardson, Dick 193
Rickard, Tex 40
Rindone, Joe 101
Roach, Lavern 92
Robinson, Red 25, 129
Robinson, Sugar Ray 19, 25, 59, 60, 68, 101, 106, 128–129, 135
Rocky Knob, Georgia 1, 6
Rosen, Clarence 117
Rosenbloom, Maxie 22
Ross, Barney 101, 156, 174
Rothstein, Arnold 18
Rousse, Jim 110
Roxborough, John 42
Ruth, Babe 7
Rutledge, Sam 13–14, 16
Ryan, Dan 58, 59
Ryan, Danny 28

Saddler, Sandy 103
St. Nick's Arena 53–54, 92, 192
San Francisco, California 6, 11, 32, 86–88, 94, 121, 131, 144, 154, 156, 166–167, 172, 192
Sarlin, Erv 40, 43, 63, 65
Satterfield, Bob 53–54, 74, 111, 120, 142, 155, 168–173, 175, 179, 186
Savold, Lee 31, 44, 67, 70, 75, 77, 83, 93, 95, 126–128, 131, 135, 140, 150
Saxton, Johnny 146
Schmeling, Max 11, 48, 65, 109, 116, 128
Schoenwald, Irving 54, 61–62
Seamon, Mannie 42, 51, 97, 99–100, 102, 104, 118
Second Cavalry Division 34–35
Segal, Harry 49

Sesto, Ernie 128–129
Sharkey, Jack 103
Sheppard, Curtis 27–29, 37–38, 48, 74, 123
Sheridan, Al 36
Shkor, Johnny 94–95, 175
Simmons, Keene 171, 180
Simon, Abe 34, 49, 99
Sinatra, Frank 105, 174
Small, Georgie 92
Smith, Al 50, 99, 145, 179
Smith, Billy 145
Smith, "Oakland" Billy 37–41, 43, 88, 145, 189
Smith, Wallace "Bud" 12
Solomons, Jack 93, 95
Soose, Billy 20, 23, 31, 102
Spaulding, Al 156
Spinelli, Mike 54, 56–59
Stowe, Harriet Beecher (elementary school) 9, 18
Strauss, Sol 40–42, 46–47, 64–66, 70–71
Stribling, Young 6, 7
Sullivan, John L. 144, 175
Sullivan, Tex 94–95

Tandberg, Ollie 46, 70–71, 74
Tannas, Tom 63, 89–91, 95, 97–99, 106–108, 110–111, 114–116, 118–119, 126, 135, 137, 145, 147–149, 152, 154–156, 158–159, 162, 166, 168–171, 175–176, 178–179, 185–189, 191–192, 194, 196–197, 204
Taylor, Herman 145
Tehan, Dan 83
Terranova, Phil 159
Thomas, Tommy 55, 123
Thompson, "Chicken" Billy 57, 73
Tomasco, Pete 146, 147
Toney, James 17
Tress, Lou 164
Triner, Joseph 81
Tunero, Kid 23, 28, 130, 174
Tunney, Gene 101, 146
Turner, Gil 146
Twentieth Century Sporting Club 23, 40, 65–66, 70–71, 76–77, 79

Uzcudun, Paulino 99

Valdes, Nino 157, 159–163, 166–168, 170, 179, 186, 192
Valentino, Pat 44, 74, 86–88, 93–95, 116, 121
Vela, Joe 51, 61
Villar, Claudio 27

Walcott, "Barbados" Joe 7, 48
Walcott, "Jersey" Joe 39, 43, 45–51, 64–71, 74–75, 77–85, 93, 96, 99, 101–102, 108, 112–121, 123, 125–126, 128–159, 161, 163–164, 166, 168, 170, 172, 174–175, 177–178, 183, 202–204
Walker, Buddy 43
Walker, Jimmy 171
Walker, Mickey 7, 74
Wallace, Coley 154, 166–168, 170–172, 179
Wallace, Eddie 48
Warndorf, Tony 44
Warner, Al 56
Washington, Norma 140
Watson, Larry 158
Weill, Al 98, 136–137, 155, 158–159, 166, 169–170, 173, 178–180, 191–192
Wellinger, Carl 83
West End, Cincinnati 8–13, 17–18, 21, 104, 110, 132, 139
Williams, Bert 13–17, 20–22, 35
Williams, Cleveland 168
Williams, Holman 23, 53, 68
Wills, Harry 7, 100
Wilson, Willie 171
Wirtz, Arthur 67, 69, 75–77, 80, 83, 84
Woodcock, Bruce 42, 77, 83, 93, 127, 135
Woodward High School 18, 109
Wright, Chubby 171, 179

Yankee Stadium 30, 83, 85, 95, 98, 103–104, 150, 170–171, 175, 178, 179, 191
Yarosz, Teddy 20–21, 23, 26, 31–32, 37

Zalc, Tony 27, 31, 60, 70, 202
Zivic, Fritzie 23, 26–27, 39, 128, 131
Zuany, Alfredo 196

www.ingramcontent.com/pod-product-compliance
Ingram Content Group UK Ltd.
Pitfield, Milton Keynes, MK11 3LW, UK
UKHW050530150426
5217IPUK00026B/1869